Natural Process

That Environmental Laws
May Serve the Laws of Nature

by

Mark Edward
Vande Pol

Wildergarten Press • Redwood Estates, CA

Photo 1 – Logging Trestle, *San Vicente Lumber Co. on Little Creek above Swanton Pacific Ranch, circa. 1918. (Little Creek is between Big Creek and Scott Creek on the map on page 52.) Photo courtesy of the Bancroft Library, University of California at Berkeley. This forest was decimated to build San Francisco after the great earthquake. Those people did not pay for environmental protection in the products that they bought. Most of those houses are still in use. Urban owners benefited from the clearcut, in the form of a capital gain on current higher material costs.*

Photo 2 – Cable Yarding *lifts and carries logs over the forest floor. (Photo courtesy Big Creek Lumber Co.) This canyon once looked similar to that in Photo 1. This machine and the loader that goes with it cost $250,000, each. Note the spacing of the trees on the right. It's typical. These forests need thinning or they will be destroyed in a fire. The profit in selling logs supports equipment that does a faster, safer, and cleaner job of keeping a forest from burning to a crisp. Urban residents are killing this business, in part because many people feel bad about Photo 1. Will they make the same mistake twice?*

Natural Process:
That Environmental Laws May Serve the Laws of Nature

First Edition published 2001 by

Wildergarten Press
P.O. Box 98
Redwood Estates, CA 95044-0098
www.wildergarten.com
www.naturalprocess.net

This book is printed on acid-free paper in the United States of America

Typeset in 11pt Times New Roman by

Bud Manzler
Media Innovations
550 Vermont St.
San Jose, CA 95110

Cover Graphics by

LinoGraphics Inc.
San Jose, CA 95112
linotogo@pacbell.net

Library of Congress Control Number: 2001092201

Vande Pol, Mark Edward, 1954–
Natural Process: That Environmental Laws May Serve the Laws of Nature.
Contains: 5 Figures, 8 Photographs, 15 Charts, 2 Tables, Bibliography, and Index.

ISBN: 0-9711793-0-1
Keywords:
Free-market environmentalism, libertarian, political economy, Santa Cruz County, habitat management, insurance, regulation, property law, endangered species, redwood, coho salmon, steelhead, nonpoint pollution, watershed management, Garret Hardin, commons, Constitutional law, Agenda 21, United Nations, takings, preservationist, deep ecology.

iv

Contents

List of Figures, Photos, Charts, and Tables

To Mother Barbara Mitchell, RSCJ,

Without whom

I would not have known.

Author's Preface

It was a '53 Plymouth Suburban, a blue station wagon with a double hatch-back. I'd sort of wake up in Dad's arms, wrapped in a blanket, walking alongside the roses in the morning darkness, loading the car to make the trip. It was Richmond, California, in 1957. It was an awakening.

I fell back asleep. I'd wake up again in a canvas car seat, bombing along Marsh Creek Road out in the late spring flower fields of the Sacramento Valley, on our way to the Big Trees.

It was freedom: a place of joy and solace, a home to visit, with no reservations required. It was just there, as much a part of California as hydroelectric power – something we were told in school was wonderful, clean, and cheap, something far away and conceptual, something I never understood, until it came into being and took my love away. It was the New Melones Dam on the Stanislaus River.

Mom told me about the Sierra Club and how they were fighting the dam, but it didn't mean much. I started to get the idea, though, when I was told that we needed to make that one last trip to my favorite riverbed, to gather those special, smooth skipping-rocks for the last time. I was looking up at the bridge, in shocked disbelief that anybody could ever need that much water, wondering how it was even possible that "my" secret place would be gone forever. Now it meant something.

In 1970, it was mountaineering. Just hitch a ride to University Avenue in Berkeley and seven hours later, arrive in Tuolumne Meadows to disappear for weeks at a time. There was barely a flight plan required; a thing called a "fire permit" upon which I routinely failed to file amendments. I discovered the special things one learns far from trails – things I would try in company versus those I would do alone, often out of necessity.

Summer journeys filtered into weekends spent in off-limits sections of Point Reyes National Seashore or the forgotten marches of various water districts. These were lands that had not graduated to the status of "parks." The challenge was to explore but not to get caught. It was, after all, private property; much of it abandoned ranch land. I learned a lot that I would rather not know about ecosystem health in these forbidden places: damage from cows, rabbits, landslides, overgrown brush, broken fences, impacted forests and other forgotten messes. It slowly dawned upon me that most of it was this way.

My Dad had quit the Sierra Club, muttering things about David Brower and lies, but it wasn't clear to me what it was about. Such things seemed insignificant to me. "We" needed to do whatever it took to save Glen Canyon or Prairie Creek, but it was all in the hands of the lawyers, whoever they were.

So I joined the Sierra Club, started to read about how dire conditions were in various places with which I was now familiar, and noticed that something was wrong: It didn't meet with my experience. I knew better than to believe that forestry was inherently destructive and I knew that government management had its failings too. Their hysterical and antagonistic approach left me with a gnawing concern that such simplistic measures just couldn't work. Chance encounters with Sierra Club "outings" in the mountains were equally disillusioning. The membership lapsed.

I returned to the Bay Area after a mere four years spent in LA learning respectability, only to find The Valley of Heart's Delight gone Silicon. It was favorite bicycling roads in the hills transformed into highways lined with bushes I had never seen. Whole tracts of land were unrecognizably different, buried under miles of identical ranch homes. It was a shock.

My new wife and I undertook the urgent business of saving a little piece of California before it was paved over. Together we scraped together our pennies and promises, bought an infested parcel, and found the condition of the land far worse than imagined. We built a house in the Santa Cruz Mountains and began the process of restoration, only to find the same self-proclaimed environmentalists, whose motives I had already found suspect, were suckling off my cash flow while doing considerable harm to the land.

I paid for my crime as an engineer, devising products, processes, machinery, and design-control systems for the medical device industry. An integral part of the job was obtaining environmental permits. You learn a lot about reality when you have to spend $25,000 cash and $300,000 in product introduction delay to get an air quality permit, to regulate less air pollution than emanates from just one tree. It is even worse when you have to risk your career to do it. We had enough risks going. It was 1992, the business was dying, and there had been 400 competing applicants for my job. Would you bet your livelihood to force a plant manager and a corporate vice president to comply with the law over an untested process (the justifying experiment had been run with a dixie cup and a popsicle stick) when you have a baby on the way, or when you are trying to qualify for the mortgage on the house you had just built? The process worked. The company prospered. It cost me a bonus, a promotion, and a raise. It was worth it.

The final straw was the constant battle being waged by the County of Santa Cruz over timber harvesting rules. I had heard the cries about the "crisis" of rapacious timber harvesting, investigated the claims, and found them lacking. I had expected competence and energy among the activists. Instead I found them flabby, self-satisfied, and arrogant; trading in acculturated opinions as if they were proven facts. What was even more disturbing was how they showed so little interest in controlling the spread of exotic weeds or reducing the risk of catastrophic fire. I earned a bitter introduction to the "consensus" process, drafting the United Nations Local Agenda 21, a process all about power, money, and emotions, not the environment. That did it. I finished my projects, quit my job, and started to write.

You don't wake up in the morning wanting to write something like this. It isn't that it is a lot of work, or two years of your life without pay. It is the concern that you may not have the time and money to get it done or that it might be too late. There is no pleasure to be found articulating the appalling consequences of pervasive injustice, corruption, and ignorance. There is legitimate personal concern for capricious distortion or reprisal against my family. There certainly isn't the expectation of making a lot of money. There is simply a lot at stake here.

That any government cannot directly manage an economy is obvious. Yet this nation has fallen to the notion that government should have a monopoly to manage something as complex as an ecosystem, with policies subordinated to political prejudice instead of technical judgement.

The environmental movement was born out of legitimate goals. There was greed and shortsightedness on the part of resource industries. I have experienced it first-hand. It was appropriate to go to government to get problems addressed. Much of the work that was done was necessary and successful and that is part of the problem with it.

The primary role of government has turned from forcing rapid economic growth to the exclusion of all else, to an obsession with constraining people from anything that can be construed as harmful. It is certainly not encouraging anybody to do "good." It is a politics born out of the paradigm that people are fundamentally incapable of harmonious interaction with each other or the planet. That misanthropic notion has been rolled into a quasi-religious set of beliefs that is being used by those with every intent of motivating the body politic to trade away its most precious freedoms out of unreasoned fear. Now that environmentalists and regulators are in power, we have greed and shortsightedness on their part. It must be stopped before we lose all that is dear.

I don't say this lightly. To these same organizations, I owe many of the pleasures of my youth for having preserved those places that taught me much of my first love for the land, but these are not the same people and they do not share the same purpose. This book is, in part, a response to the sense of having that love betrayed.

As environmental organizations have grown, their common agenda has diverged from its purpose. Their adherents' principle goal has devolved to pursuit of funding to support a political and legal agenda. They have ignored scientific evidence and overridden legitimate discourse over technical differences in the name of preserving entrenched bureaucracies and political power groups feeding off taxes, grants, and lawsuits. It has even led to an odd form of corporate welfare: membership in an oligopoly in return for selling out or buying up smaller competitors. The consequences have compounded. Ruined lives have been rendered into political cannon fodder. In the conduct of battle, the environment has been subordinated to the status of a political hostage. Much like a child in a custody case, the object of the dispute is the one that suffers. The worst of it is, it does not have to be this way.

When one begins a process like this, it starts as a polemic, for much of what starts you writing is a sense of what's wrong. This book takes to task environmental activists, all levels of government, universities, developers, irresponsible loggers, lawyers, rural/suburban residents, bankers, the urban public, politicians, insurance companies, and more! Each of us is a user of the environment and anyone who would buy this book and read it shares such a love of nature and an investment in how we got here. Maybe we have to see the egg on our faces before we can work with those with whom we have struggled for so long. At least we all have something in common.

Perhaps for some it is enough to simply state an injustice, but love of the land won't let you get away with just that and will lead you to wonder what might be done instead. The polemic took nine months. Taking the answers from the abstract, to the concrete, and then to the elegant took far longer. I have done my best to make them simple. I ask your forgiveness for anything less, but this book had to get out. It is time.

One last thing, just to make it clear. This book was written without financial support from any person, corporate or individual. It was paid for with savings and personal debt. I was provided data from numerous sources from all sides of the arguments. There is no motive other than the reward of having helped people do a better job for nature and to find a way out of the injustices they rightly perceive. It is possible to prosper in harmony with the laws of nature once we begin to act in concert with all of them. Best that we start to learn.

No matter how intelligent people are, how much experience they have, or how much they care, we all have major degrees of ignorance when it comes to understanding our interactions with the environment. I have done my best, within my limitations, to make it honest.

Thank you for your time,

Mark Edward Vande Pol
August 8, 2001

Acknowledgements

The People who Made This Possible

First are my dear sweet little girls, who were nearly always so good that I had no right to expect more, though I always do. Every day, when I dropped them off at school, they would offer, "Good luck with your book!" and give thanks at dinner for the progress they assumed was made. My wife let me spend the nest egg, paid the bills, and agreed to additional indebtedness while this was written. To her I have my deepest gratitude, both for her faith in me and her intrinsic understanding of the importance of the work. Worse yet, she had to listen politely in a patient state of exhaustion while I passionately rambled seemingly forever with no clue how to express some arcane idea, and stayed positive over a year after I had promised to be done. Can you imagine?

The People Who Gave Me Data

Don Alley, fisheries biologist; Jeff Almquist, Supervisor, County of Santa Cruz; Terry Beacham, Ph.D., fisheries biologist, Nanaimo, Canada; David Boyd; Robert O. Briggs, PE & Forest Landowner; Steve Butler, Registered Professional Forester; Leroy Brockelman and Bruce Kennedy, Realtors, Lawrence Camp, RPF for the Internal Revenue Service, San Francisco; Barrie Coate, American Society of Certified Arboriculturalists; Jack Du Four; Dr. Ken Gobalet, California State Unuiversity, Bakersfield, Kris Hayward; Roger Haas; Steve Hollett, Forester California Department of Forestry and Fire Protection (CDF); Robert Hrubes, RPF, Scientific Certification Systems; Victor Kaczynski, Ph.D., Fisheries Biologist; Mike Kelly and Bill Ruskin of CDF; Bruce Krumland, Ph.D. RPF, University of California at Berkeley; Henry Lamb, eco-logic; Steve, Howard, and Lester Liebenbergs; Ken Mabie, Registered Environmental Health Specialist (REHS); Bud McCrary, Bob Berlage, and Dale Holderman of Big Creek Lumber Co.; Jennifer Neilsen, Ph.D., fisheries geneticist, U.S. Geological Survey; Alice A. Rich Ph.D., fisheries biologist; Tim Peet, Licensed Timber Operator; John Ricker, REHS, County of Santa Cruz; Bob Rossi and Frank Wilson of the State Board of Equalization, Timber Tax Division; Lisa Rudnick, Central Coast Forest Assn.; Gene Scarborough; David Smelt, Ed Tunheim, RPF; Peter Twight, RPF; Karen Waddell, U.S. Forest Service.

The People Who Read Parts of It and Gave Me Constructive Criticism

Dr. William Allen, Dean Madison School of Government, Michigan State University; Anne Briggs, Forest Landowner; Jim Burling, Pacific Legal Foundation; Dick Burton, Forest Landowner; Steve Butler, RPF, Ed Tunheim Consulting Foresters; Dean Cromwell, California Board of Forestry; my Dad; J. Gordon Edwards, PhD, San Jose State University;

Acknowledgements

Gene Forsburg, Forest Appraiser; Shauna Johnson, People for the USA; Sue Hutchinson, Coalition for Arizona/New Mexico Counties; Victor Kaczynski, PhD, Fisheries Biologist; Henry Lamb, êco•logic magazine; Doug Leisz, Former Assistant Chief, US Forest Service, Floy Lilley, JD, Murchison Chair of Free Enterprise, University of Texas, Austin; Tom McDonnell, Director, Natural Resources and Policy, American Sheep Industry Assn.; Patrick Mauldin, CPA, Mauldin & Assoc.; Dr. Patrick Moore, Greenspirit; Cate Moore, Forest Landowner; Jennifer Neilsen, Ph.D., fisheries geneticist, USGS; Walter Shultz, County Supervisor, El Dorado County, CA; Fred Smith, Competitive Enterprise Institute; Randal O'Toole, Thoreau Institute; and Eileen Wiseman who was the first to get all the way through.

The People Who Gave Me Proof

Diane, Eileen Wiseman, Sue Hutchinson, Dad, Irene Lamb, Joan Manzler, and Dave Fordyce.

The People Who Didn't Read It, But Gave Me Inspiration

Dr. Tad Beckman of Harvey Mudd College, James Madison, Mom, Terry Russell (On the Loose), Jean Sibelius (the Second and Fifth Symphonies, Sir Alexander Gibson Conducting), George Washington Harris, Ayn Rand, Karl Marx, Alexis De Toqueville, and not least Aristotle, Socrates (the Crito), Jesus Christ, Dr. William James Haga, Manfred Eigen and Ruthild Winkler, Douglas Hofstadter (great writer, faulty premise), Rudolph Carnap, Bullwinkle, William Diamond, Ph.D., that Supreme Ascendant Master and Indomitable Stooge, Curly Howard; Neil Wiley, owner, editor, and mouthpiece of The Mountain Network News; and that twinkling old coot, Roger Wicht who got me started at all this madness.

Introduction

This book proposes a free-market environmental management system designed to deliver a product that is superior to government oversight at lower cost. It provides examples illustrating how the system might work and proposes an implementing legal strategy.

Though environmental in origin, the principles this book describes are applicable toward privatizing many forms of government regulation. It does not fall into either of the two polar opposites of the environmental debate. The group with the momentum consists of those inclined toward environmental preservation. Their reaction to this book might be befuddlement:

> 'Why would we need a different way of managing the environment? We just need to make sure it's protected, right?'

Many people hold well-indoctrinated beliefs that the government protects the environment from greedy capitalists at the prodding of selfless activists. They don't think of environmental activists or regulators as destructive to natural habitat. Neither of those beliefs is true any more.

In the other corner are the adversaries of regulatory policy, those who grumble that we aren't really doing that much damage and that environmentalism costs too much for things that we must do to survive. Few people tend to listen to such things unless they are unemployed or feeling threatened.

The other failing of those on the defense is that they rarely come up with a preferable alternative to regulation other than "less." It is easy to complain about regulation, but NO ONE will accept an alternative without checks and balances that value the public demand to protect ecosystem function.

This book challenges the assumption that environmental protection through politics, regulation, and lawsuits can produce anything other than a bureaucracy that derives its funding by deepening environmental problems. This book suggests how we can instead, objectively weigh the value of competing ecological resources and incorporate that value into the conduct of commerce without political price-fixing. The proposed system incorporates rigorous risk assessment, research, and accountability. These principles support responsible expression of individual freedom and protect unalienable property rights to provide ecosystem management as a profitable business.

Activist claims and government plans are rarely subjected to scrutiny. They focus upon continued acquisition instead of demonstrable environmental health. The aggregation of virtually unlimited civic power now renders enormous mistakes inevitable. Even so, anyone should rationally require a clear and objective analysis of the existing system to be convinced that a new approach is justified.

This book imparts new perspectives on existing problems and proposes solutions that at first appear radical, but are in fact, radically basic given those new perspectives. Its principles are extremely simple, but are fully capable of the incredibly complex forms that nature demands. This complexity can be draining when trudging through an antithesis full of hard data without knowing whether it is worth the effort. Most people who are already familiar with the issues and pressed for time are suspicious that such an investment in an antithesis is worth the trouble.

The design of the book therefore presents two paths of study. One is a positive thesis, with examples, and implementation plans that reflect no particular case. Essential chapters and sections on the positive path are marked with an icon ⌨ on the odd page header, and are also noted in the Table of Contents. The thesis path is roughly 225 pages. Those who are pressed for time and familiar with the technical, legal, and economic issues will find the positive path a good first read.

Should one read the full story, there awaits the rewarding tragicomedy in the antithesis regarding the County of Santa Cruz, California, and the bad news of where regulatory government really leads. Agenda 21 may make Catch-22 look pretty, but at least you'll get a chuckle in the deal along with hard data and important insights into the benefits of the thesis and its compelling logic.

The book employs that antithesis/thesis logic as follows:

Part I – A Commons Misconception begins with the principles justifying existing environmental management:

1. People abuse resources for which they don't have to pay, and
2. Regulations prevent harmful behavior.

More important, this chapter redefines a number of principles, by which it exposes several logical fallacies in our existing management system, and opens the opportunity for an alternative (discussed in Parts III & IV).

The book opens its antithesis with an examination of preservation. It shows that protecting altered habitat and expecting it to recover does not work.

As an alternative to preservation, the discussion turns to regulatory government. Environmental problems are so particular to local circumstances as to confuse detailed analyses of regulatory policy. It is local government that has the greatest effect upon people's lives, even when in response to Federal regulations. Therefore, this book focuses its antithesis upon a case study of the rural-suburban forest interface in the County of Santa Cruz, California.

Santa Cruz exemplifies a variety of preconditions well suited for the study of environmental management systems:

Introduction

- The undeveloped portion of the County was logged, burned, and cleared, and now consists of second growth forest or agricultural land, largely abandoned for over 75 years.

- Native ecosystems vary radically, including forests, meadows, rivers, marshes, and oceanfront with widely varied geology and climate.

- It adjoins a highly urbanized and industrialized area: Silicon Valley. The County has exerted various forms of regulatory controls over suburban development over the last 30 years.

- It still has active resource industries and agriculture.

- It has a university with a well-deserved "progressive" reputation.

- It has an activist county government with entrenched political constituencies that has maintained continuous control over the study period.

- It has a large, and politically active, preservationist community.

After a brief contextual discussion of the justifications for civic regulation, the book then opens the exposition of its antithesis:

Part II – The Forest for the Trees documents the case history in the County of Santa Cruz. The case demonstrates that many programs regulating timber management, sold to the public as having environmental purposes, function at variance to their intent. These chapters analyze graphical data detailing the conversion of private, non-industrial timberland to suburban residential development. This discussion instills the technical, political, and economic background with which to understand the alternatives proposed in Part III.

Part III – Globally Thinking, A Motivational Ethos introduces the thesis with a philosophical proof of why and how a free market environmental management system is preferable to political control. The next three chapters develop its several aspects into a structure and explains the rationale for each component, complete with necessary checks and balances. The final chapter integrates the components into a system capable of global operations.

Part IV – Get What You Pay For contrasts existing environmental control systems, with applications of the proposed alternative. It suggests specific pilot programs with which to address complex environmental problems. The chapter topics are: the timber landowner and fire management in the rural suburban forest, exotic species control and pesticide management, coho salmon and the Endangered Species Act, and watershed management and nonpoint pollution control.

Part V – The Moral High Ground examines the reasons that professionals working within the existing system might prefer the free-market proposal. The program can start on a small scale in competition with civic regulation and grow where it proves to be superior. Part V then recounts the mechanics by which regulations propagate using the case of nonpoint water pollution. It provides an example of a landowner who can turn the legal mechanics of the regulatory system against itself, in defense of the health of his family's property. The story traces the lineage of current rule-propagation mechanics to a corrupt alliance among wealthy foundations of international financial manipulators, with only subsidiary interest in ecosystem health. Part V closes the work with a legal counter-strategy.

It might have been easier to gain support for a new perspective through an emotionally appealing work of fiction or allegory than to state a proposal directly. That device unfortunately allows fantastic examples to operate with only internal consistency, and obscures opportunities to evoke constructive criticism. There is also a concern that the reader would only hear and identify with the story wouldn't see the principles at all.

Though this book was never intended to read like a novel, it ends up constructing a story that unfolded out of the process of research. It grew out of analyses of the propagation of the current regulatory system; an ominous warning that appears entrained in the tide of history.

The goal of this book is to introduce the means to develop management processes by which to foster better ecological health without having to rely upon confiscation, compulsion, coercion, lawsuits, legislation, and other wastes of the very wealth and human energy needed to heal the land.

The land is where the money is needed, not for lawyers, paper shufflers, grant administrators, and police. Nature needs people and money both in the laboratory and in the field to do productive work identifying the best means of helping it flourish. It needs just as much a system that rewards people if they succeed.

Enjoy the read.

Part I   A Commons Misconception

The Principles and Evolution of a Socialized Commons

Part I examines the philosophical and economic principles underlying environmental management and serves as an abstract for the rest of the book. The evidentiary case against existing environmental management systems, exemplifying the principles discussed in Part I, will be presented in Part II.

Chapter 1 – Stuff, and What You Do With the Stuff will examine the theoretical basis for public claims on the ownership and use of private property. It will then progress through the "prevent harm" ethic and its effect on the regulatory products of environmental organizations.

Chapter 2 will expose the logical fallacies behind the preservation ethic.

Chapter 3 will define the problem statement of environmental management as practiced with the analytical basis for the case to be developed in Parts II, IV, & V.

📖 Chapter 1 – Stuff and What You Do With the Stuff

The social mechanics inducing political control of property

The Tragedy of the Commons, by Garret Hardin, was a pivotal article published in the journal of the American Association for the Advancement of Science in 1968. In that article, Mr. Hardin argued that increasing global population was converting the entire earth and its supporting ecosystems into a form of "commons," a body of resources that, because they can not be privately owned end up being destructively over-exploited. He argued that, in the interest of preserving a future for the human race, human procreation itself must be restricted, and access to natural resources heavily regulated. Excerpts are as follows:

> "We can make little progress in working toward optimum population size until we explicitly exorcise the spirit of Adam Smith in the field of practical demography... he contributed to a dominant tendency of thought that has ever since interfered with positive action based on rational analysis, namely, the tendency to assume that decisions reached individually will, in fact, be the best decisions for an entire society... If the assumption is not correct, we need to reexamine our individual freedoms to see which ones are defensible."

> "But the air and waters surrounding us cannot readily be fenced, and so the tragedy of the commons as a cesspool must be prevented by different means..."

"Coercion is a dirty word to most liberals now, but it need not forever be so. As with the four-letter words, its dirtiness can be cleansed away by exposure to the light, by saying it over and over without apology or embarrassment. To many, the word coercion implies arbitrary decisions of distant and irresponsible bureaucrats; but this is not a necessary part of its meaning. The only kind of coercion I recommend is mutual coercion, mutually agreed upon by the majority of the people affected."

"The problem for the years ahead is to work out an acceptable theory of weighting. Synergistic effects, nonlinear variation, and difficulties in discounting the future make the intellectual problem difficult, but not (in principle) insoluble."

"It seems to me that… those who are biologically more fit to be the custodians of property and power should legally inherit more. …We must admit that our legal system of private property plus inheritance is unjust -- but we put up with it because we are not convinced, at the moment, that anyone has invented a better system. The alternative of the commons is too horrifying to contemplate. Injustice is preferable to total ruin."

– THE TRAGEDY OF THE COMMONS, by Garrett Hardin

The pathology is evident in this archetypal and hugely popular piece. One might politely call it, "The Elitist's Paradox." Hardin's assumptions are that:

1. Individuals do not act in the collective economic interest.

2. The public will be forced by its failures to cede their individual freedoms ("rights," Mr. Hardin) to really smart and altruistic people, like him

The intellectual elite will conduct the "rational analysis" and then design control systems to "coerce" everybody else into altruistic behavior? Where is the "Trust me, Me, ME!" part in that old story? Given the historical record, who "mutually agrees" to being coerced by government? Since when did acquiescence to the police power of the State constitute mutual agreement? Can the State act in objective disinterest when tempted with the power to control the factors of all economic production? Is a State monopoly inherently competent to manage the environment?

Hardin acknowledged private property as, although imperfect, the best system for environmental protection. He wished that success in ownership was determined in part by Darwinian competition in stewardship, but acknowledged that there were no objective criteria upon which to base such a market. The alternative of allowing government to control the factors of production is a process that inevitably leads to bureaucratic tyranny and environmental harm, as he acknowledged elsewhere in the essay citing the degradation of the National Parks.

Like many critics before him, Mr. Hardin was better at recognizing a problem than constructing a prescription. He tacitly defaulted to regulatory control until "an acceptable theory of weighting" could be derived. Unfortunately, the economic distortions and political and bureaucratic fiefdoms of regulatory control preclude development of such an objective system.

How much capital is wasted operating centralized planning systems that should be invested in the land? Is government bureaucracy the only tool to manage the environment? How would an alternative be implemented?

This book proposes answers to those questions, but first we must begin with an analysis of the assumptions that have locked us into our current dilemma.

It is commonly understood that civic management of the economy doesn't work. Meanwhile, the public believes in political protection of the environment, which ends up equivalent to the same thing. The unconscious barriers to realizing the alternatives are a direct result of all that "saying it over and over." It is a faith, born out of practical habit, which is badly placed.

Properties of the Commons

People abuse resources for which they don't have to pay. Public claims on private land uses transform those assets into socialized commons, because they are acquired at no apparent cost.

Humans are born with a sense of personal space. It is a deeply rooted property, a natural property of being human. Humans compete for individual advantage among ourselves as well as among other species. Were it not for our intelligence and our propensity to socialize, we would not be inherently competitive animals. In order for humans to be competitive as a species, individual competition must operate according to natural law; thus, social contracts must reflect the governing principles of human behavior.

Living beings compete for control of goods that have relative degrees of scarcity. Whether it is space for roots among competing plants, hunting range, or food stored for a winter's meal, control of goods matters to all living beings as the means by which to compete and survive.

Goods of which humans retain control are defined as property. Humans survive by the use of property, whether it is one's body, food, shelter, tools, weapons, or various resources by which to attract a superior mate or rear offspring. Goods cannot be used or exchanged unless possessed as property, whether physically or by social contract. To control the use of property therefore, is functionally equivalent to ownership.

Humans combine constituent goods to form useful composites. Not all goods are uniformly distributed or available for use. Humans exchange control of goods in order to complete composite uses to the competitive advantage of both transactors. Individual respect for tradable rights requires enforcement of a social compact against competing interests.

Mobility or continuity in a resource complicates the definition of ownership. Unlike fixed property, retaining control of mobile or continuous goods (such as air or water) can only be effected via physical containment. Humans combine such factors with other chemicals, with which the biochemical processes of the human body produce tissues and perform work. The only time the air or water is actually controlled is when they were contained within the body.

Are they really contained in the body? Humans can't store the value of air or water any more than they can stop breathing or prevent sweat from evaporating. Humans must constantly exchange air and water with the surroundings to stay alive. How is it, then, that the air or water is "owned" when it is only, in fact, controlled? Perhaps what is owned, is not the air or the water, but the operating series of biochemical processes that use air and water to perform work while they are contained within the body.

We can use this analogy of air and water contained in the body to consider ownership of those mobile and continuous goods contained on property. **Just as the processes within the body combine mobile goods with other inputs to produce the body itself, the natural processes within property boundaries, transform inputs into the physical attributes of the property itself.** Those processes that transform the state of mobile inputs into products for exchange are defined here as **process assets**.

Humans combine factor inputs with process assets to produce goods for economic exchange. The sum of process assets and factor inputs, called the **factors of production**, are either purchased (such as land, raw material, tools, intellectual property, or labor) or merely collected and used, not requiring a price of acquisition (air or rainwater). This book will refer to factor inputs that are collected without payment as **zero-priced goods**.

Zero-priced goods include:

1. Goods sufficiently plentiful that a discrete pricing mechanism is too costly to consider.
2. Goods sufficiently difficult to contain that a pricing mechanism is mechanically impossible.
3. Goods without identified economic worth or use.
4. Goods with positive and negative worth so closely balanced that their net market value does not justify a pricing mechanism.

Ownership of zero-priced goods is typically not defined or enforced by contract. Their economic value is considered equivalent to the cost of collection, containment, and preparation for use. That they are intrinsically valuable is not in dispute; a person certainly needs air to breathe, and a commercial fisherman needs an ocean but, in practice, we pay little to nothing for them.

Few individuals attempt to own them because the cost of control exceeds the benefits of restricting use by private ownership. Among resource biologists and economists, environmentalists and politicians, these zero-priced goods have come to be known as **commons**.

Commons are a superset to zero-priced goods because they include resources that have economic value, but their prices are fixed at or near zero by social compact. Public access parks for example, though they are valuable, are used as if they were free because no price for use can be agreed upon among those with an equal claim and are therefore clearly commons.

The term "commons," then, will be reserved for those goods that, although they might have market value, are used as if the price of acquisition is zero.

Under conditions of decreasing supply or increasing demand, zero-priced goods can rise in scarcity to the point where individual claims are subject to competition. People then do work to define ownership as appropriate to their perception of unit value. A claimant will collect, unitize, measure, rent, mark, describe, and exchange property with increasing precision as its economic value increases. If a good does not have discrete physical boundaries, then the limits of ownership have to be defined in other ways, for example by the manner of containment or measurement. Once the boundaries to these claims are determined, ownership appertains to an economic person whether individual, partnership, corporate, or political. Goods then graduate from the status of commons to that of property. To establish the distinctions of ownership among competing persons, then requires definition of containment boundaries by contract.

When the amount of property under control exceeds physical containment limits, precise definition of property boundaries becomes more problematic, especially for a mobile or continuous good. Even physical boundaries on land are not static. River channels move, ridgelines are subject to erosion, roads are relocated, even continents drift. The claim to ownership of "fixed" property has thus often had much to do with the human perception of permanence within specific boundaries. In a very real sense, **all goods are mobile**. In response to that mobility, humanly delineated boundaries now reflect artificial lines more often than physical landmarks reflecting the competitive need for precision and the cost of measurement or dispute.

This issue of mobility becomes particularly troublesome with continuous goods that move rapidly. Whether they are air, water, oil and gas, schools of fish, or migratory animals, as long as they are not contained it is difficult to define the boundaries of ownership. Some mobile goods move from place to place instantly, such as the emotive benefit derived from light reflected off a form that someone finds pleasing.

The economic value of these seemingly ephemeral goods is real. People know it. They pay to look at reflected light or to listen to vibrating air for entertainment. They notice the loss when a customary use is withdrawn. They get angry when a dam engulfs "their" favorite rafting river. They resist the introduction of a shopping mall onto a childhood playground even if they no longer live in the area. In each of these cases, there is definite sense that one has lost something that one "owns" or upon which one has a claim whether or not they had ever paid for those goods.

These claims are not always fanciful. A person may have purchased property because of the speculative value of the use of mobile goods: the view, the quiet, air quality, or available groundwater. He or she has a definite sense of ownership of those mobile commons, if not defined by contract, then by habitual use. Whether or not these valued commons were in the price of purchase, they are so defended should that use be threatened or withdrawn because they are necessary factor inputs for their customary use of property.

Commons are factor inputs for the production of all economic goods. Their potential uses do not change unless a chemical or physical process alters their attributes. The potential uses of oxygen change when it bonds with hydrogen. The uses of water change when it evaporates, chemically dissociates, or inherits pollutants. The changes wrought by process assets upon factor inputs are the **transformation products** of those processes.

> **Author's Note:** One rationally despises a term like "zero-priced good" or "transformation product." Unfortunately, the easily sub-vocalized (or, as my mother would say, "euphonious") terms such as "priceless resource" or "byproduct" are so loaded that they had to be rejected, regardless of the temptation to the impish punster. The necessary evil of such cumbersome verbiage will be restricted to the few theoretical discussions in the book.

It is difficult for a single person to make a claim against a loss of a use of commons when they can lay no claim of ownership. The economic costs or benefits associated with transformation products, that are not accounted in the price of goods when exchanged, are the economic **externalities** of the use of those processes. Claims against economic externalities focus upon those transformation products that leave property in mobile commons. The complaints contend that those transformation products are damaging to the use intended by those outside the property boundaries.

> **Another Author's Note:** The notion of economic externality is an important economic concept in the rationale for environmental regulation. Assume the manufacture of a product produces pollutants that cross the plant boundary suspended in a mobile, zero-priced good, such as air or water. The cost of the pollution is not born by the producer of the good for sale, nor is it reflected in the purchase price to the consumer. The cost of the pollution is external to the buyer/seller transaction because it is borne by those affected by the pollution, who supposedly derive no benefit from production or sale of the

product. Environmental regulations coerce the producer to incorporate the cost of pollution control into the product, thus supposedly forcing the consumer to evaluate its "true" price compared to other purchase options.

Because the contested use is inside private boundaries, claimants against externalities enlist fellows to coerce surrender of control by its owner. The most powerful fellow available is government because it has a monopoly to enforce social contracts with police power. Unfortunately, any civic agent also has an individual competitive interest in controlling the use of property. This is the single reason that civic agency must never be able to express interest in controlling private property; else it irreversibly accrues to itself control of all factors of production.

In a democracy, legislation regarding transformation products can effectively limit the use of private property to that of the majority preference. Assignment of that control by political or legal means is therefore to take private property in the interest of a democratic majority. Hence is the argument, that extension of a majority claim on the use of natural process assets transforms a natural resource into a **democratized commons**. Its use is restricted to the majority preference and little or no compensation is offered for legal restrictions preventing alternative economic uses.

To democratize a commons may seem like a good way to keep people from doing bad things. In the end however, it is a terribly destructive thing to do. It is to convince a democratic majority that taking public control of private property without just compensation is in the public interest.

To democratize a commons is also destructive to the contested asset because **the maximum number of people extend their claims at a minimum unit price.** Claims then proliferate without limit because their cost is virtually zero. There is then no motive to maintain or improve the condition of the asset, or to invest in controlling the release of undesirable transformation products, because there is no prospect of a return on investment thereby. Private property is thus effectively destroyed because it has no economic use.

The coercive means by which a majority exercises collective claims is the power to control social assets outside private boundaries. The owner must rely upon a social contract to use public assets in order to produce salable transformation products. Public roads transport supplies and goods for sale. Recognition of the value the owner's money and bank account is a social resource upon which the owner has a contractual claim. The police power of the state enforces contracts and maintains respect for private property, as is necessary for commerce. Collective action to control access to any such factor is a threat to the property owner's economic survival and the source of the coercive power of a democratic majority; in other words, democracy is in fact a collectivist system.

The legislative branch of our republic, therefore has Constitutionally limited power to effect direct claims upon the use of property. It is to these mechanics that the Fifth Amendment to the U.S. Constitution addressed uncompensated takings. For without a check on the exercise of democratic power to lay claims against private property, such claims proliferate until private property eventually ceases to exist.

Unfortunately, government has every power to enact laws regarding discharge of transformation products across property lines because the concept of property as ONLY consisting of a social contract for use of bounded processes is poorly understood. Once a civic agent has the power to control transformation products in commons, then that agent has full control of how property can be used.

Once an economic factor has been rendered into a democratized commons, claims against uses producing transformation products can then be effected through the courts. These claims can be brought by anyone and focus exclusively upon controlling negatively valued transformation products without consideration of the total integrated impact of the contested use. (Since when did anybody sue in order to pay for a positive externality?)

As concentrations of transformation products in process outputs approach zero, minute reductions in pollutants can greatly increase the cost of treatment. As the cost of compliance consumes a higher fraction of the sale price of the economic good, the return on the original use approaches zero. Once the return on assets goes negative, investment in improving technology to reduce production of negative externalities becomes negatively valued as well. Few would develop new control technology because few could pay for it. If there is no return on the use of the asset, that use of the property will be abandoned, as it has become a zero-priced good. Negative investment return destroys the market value of the use.

Both claimant and agent are thus motivated to focus upon those transformation products that are most difficult to control, because it is those properties that are most likely to convert the use of the asset to that which they prefer. The fight between landowners, regulators, and activists then degenerates into increasingly trivial arguments regarding specifications, measurements, and enforcement that have increasingly large financial consequences for the owner. Remedial measures thus structurally diverge from an objective assessment of the total impact upon environmental health because that was never the claimants' primary objective.

Rarely does either acquiring interest consider the possible unintended consequences of their actions, among other reasons because they have little experience in actual operations and no accountability for the consequences. The legal process is thus alienated from its purpose to establish justice, just as the regulatory process is directed away from ecological health. There is little civic accountability for maintaining a successful balance among competing interests, indeed, very likely the contrary is true. Problems are sources of civic claims by which to control the entire economy, a motivational structure antithetical to the very purpose of regulation.

As claims proliferate, the legislatures and courts are overwhelmed with cases that are technical and difficult to prove. They rely upon opinions from supposedly disinterested experts regarding the impacts of transformation products. Neither legislators or courts have the power to enforce a judgement; that power lies exclusively with the executive branch of government. The demand for expediency seduces legislatures and the courts to default upon their Constitutional responsibility, to the only civic agency with relevant expertise and police power. Control of use and, thus ownership of that use, is effectively transferred to the executive branch of government.

When taking land out of production profits the financial sponsors of a claim, it is cheaper to control the target use than to compensate the owner or buy the property. All it takes to manipulate a resource market by democratic means is to buy out the competition by manipulating majority perceptions about the risk of ecological harm associated with that target use. The few who can profit by taking competing resources out of production then have reason to sponsor the investment in political or legal action. They focus the first case against a weak target or obvious problem (which is why most such takings appear as local actions).

Established precedent then extends the applicability of cited legislation and lowers the cost successive claims. Property owners gradually lose their ability to finance the cost of compliance or legal resistance. Absent a profitable use, the market value of the target use approaches zero. After repeated exercise of external controls, purchase of the residual asset value concludes any remaining claim by an owner.

When a rival owner produces a competing or substitute good, the financial advantages of such tacit property acquisitions can be enormous. For example, if a developer funded public concerns about the negatively valued transformation products of farming to render the use of farmland non-economic and ripe for development, the land becomes less expensive to purchase.

This politically-sponsored dissolution of the Separation of Powers Principle, combines all three branches of government into one, that can derive power and funding by manufacturing claims on the use of property. The more externalities are regulated, the more power accrues to the agency to control the use of the producing asset to turn its use to corrupt purpose. When agency control is sufficient to alienate the interest of the agent from the democratic majority, the asset has then degenerated into a **socialized commons**.

The claims by which a commons is socialized are ironically often the same precedents as were used to extend the original democratic claim; i.e., by extending claims against the transformation products of the *democratic* use of the resource. With the legal precedents in place that were used to take control of the factors of production on individual property, the civic agent now has the legal tools to take control of ALL related private property. Control of the use of land is now in the hands of an agency that is alienated from accountability to the public claim for healthy ecosystem function. The agency instead serves the limited interests of the politically dominant, who use the power of government to gain *de facto* control of ALL factors of production.

History teaches that this is not a good thing.

A socialized commons is an evil to the environment because the resource is under a controlling agent with no structural motive to prevent or eliminate ecological problems. Quite the contrary, civic management of the environment not only doesn't work, **it has every reason not to work**. As ecological problems worsen and resulting economic crises deepen, the power acceded to government agencies expands!

Commons are factor inputs to all economic goods. **The power to socialize a commons by regulation is the power to transfer control of ALL factors of production to government.**

That includes you. Let's take a break with an example.

From Ranch, to Ranchettes

Consider a ranch. What the rancher owns are the rights to use its assets within defined boundaries. The rancher selects means to employ them as factor inputs for process producing goods for exchange: in this case, beef and logs. Natural process assets (fungi, native grasses, mineral soils, a creek, and soil bacteria) are combined with purchased factor inputs (fertilizer, seed, trees, electricity, and diesel), to convert these inputs into forage and trees. The rancher combines labor, intellectual property, capital investments (breeding stock, fencing, or a dam), and zero-priced goods (sunlight, carbon dioxide, rain, oxygen, and nitrogen) to produce a range of economic transformation products (burgers on the hoof or logs on a truck). Those same processes also induce non-economic transformation products: a pastoral view of the ranch, riparian nitrates, rainwater runoff, carbon dioxide, flies, oxygen, and various unpleasant gases.

Most transformation products of ranching do not produce economic returns but do affect the use of commons by others. The rancher earns nothing for the view or brush control in the forest, and pays no penalty for horse flies or methane. These are economic externalities of ranching.

Suppose that the rancher sells some land to pay taxes. A developer buys it and converts the use to residential housing. The new residents might have paid a higher purchase price for their homes because of proximity to the ranch. They enjoy the light reflected off the ranch as a view. They consider access to the ranch for entertainment an entitlement of their purchase. They don't particularly complain about the quiet of the countryside or the other positive externalities of the ranch, nor consider that its economic viability maintains open space. They like to go hiking there.

The residents consider some transformation products of ranching deleterious to their residential use of commons. They extend claims only against what they consider negative externalities in order to enlist a civic agent to award control of the producing asset to them. They complain about the taste of the water in the creek and its suitability for swimming or fishing. They ask that the rancher stop burning brush so that they can have clean air. Fires scare them and the rancher can't afford the risk posed to houses in a forest.

A civic agent inevitably recognizes that to enforce control of the ranch is equivalent to acquiring ownership. It's a nice job: getting paid to work outside in the forest, without having to buy the land. The focus of action on the part of both civic agent and claimants then becomes controlling the transformation products of ranching because they derive their preferred use thereby.

Control is exercised by regulation of those processes that acquiring interests believe to be the source of the negative transformation products: cows. They draft rules to be enforced by the civic agent who funds the technical experts that justify the rules. Acquiring interests have no accountability for accuracy or profitability in ranching. They have no motive to weigh the total impact of cows because the uncompensated benefits of cows have nothing to do with the interests of their grantors. The rancher loses the ability to compete with industrial feedlots or perhaps foreign suppliers that have no need to meet the regulations. Cows become increasingly unprofitable. Meanwhile, property taxes keep rising because of the demand for the proximate housing.

Suppose our rancher has a stand of timber. The rancher announces a plan to harvest the forest. The residents claim that the rancher's harvest produces transformation products that degrade the economic value of their residential use of those commons that leave the rancher's land. The air could carry dust and the noise from chainsaws and helicopters. The light reflected off the property might carry a potential loss of "view-shed." There is seldom a dollar value to such claims; the residents just want the rancher to stop cutting trees.

The residents broaden and advertise the threat of harm to enlist democratic support from more numerous urban fellows. They demand protection of "priceless" forest resources, claiming that the harvest threatens urban uses of commons. The runoff after the harvest might carry sediment into a reservoir.

Logging trucks may damage roads. A democratic majority can then demand that a civic agent exert coercive force over the rancher's use of public assets, such as an access road or permit. If they lack political or legal power, the residents might enlist an activist organization with sufficient resources and legal expertise to "force" a civic agent by lawsuit into asserting control over the rancher's property. Those who had financial interests in the use of the property would have every reason to make a tax-deductible donation to such an activist group, for instance, a developer.

A civic agent has the power to execute coercion through jurisdiction over public roads, operating licenses, or permits upon which the rancher relies for the conduct of timber operations. The civic agent can block access to the harvest, or place specifications on the transformation products of the harvest such that the control measures are expensive enough to render harvesting the forest unprofitable. An example of the latter would be a "zero discharge" specification for silt from timber harvesting. Although erosion is a necessary natural process, the smaller the amount of dirt allowed in the creek, the more expensive it becomes to verify compliance, until eventually the timber itself has degenerated into a commons.

The residents never once had to contest the property right of the rancher to cut the trees, but instead removed the profit in selling them. The trees are now worthless as timber, and their residual value is reduced to a specific set of uses: scenery, entertainment, and residential capital gain **all accruing to the surrounding residents**. The residents have thus converted the use of process assets that grow trees within the rancher's property lines from out-side the property boundaries. Its only products are democratized commons, because its uses are constrained to the majority preference.

The rancher now has no economic motive to invest in the forest. It costs too much for too little return. The cows no longer browse the brush, he can't burn, and the fuels accumulate. With no trees to harvest, there is no reason to reduce the fuels mechanically. Meanwhile, taxes have kept rising because of the houses, traffic is making it very costly to make and take deliveries, and suppliers are going broke and leaving town. The cost of compliance is such that lumber from overseas is now more competitive. The rancher tries to cash out whatever is left of the land value to a developer who has sufficient clout to overcome the objections of the local residents. The sale is probably at a considerable discount to the total resource and residential value. Everybody loses, except the developer.

If the residents have sufficient political power, they can get the state to buy the property as a public park. The use still accrues to the democratic majority and benefits the property value of local residents. Since the urban population derives no direct benefit, they resist paying for the maintenance. The forest falls into a deeper state of neglect, recreational overuse, lack of maintenance, pest infestations, and eventual catastrophic fire that might take the residents with it. The civic managers then move to protect the forest from the public thus accruing its use to themselves. Everybody else loses, especially a combusted forest, stripped of topsoil, overrun with weeds, and eroding fast.

As long as there is a problem with the forest or a nearby creek, the agent now has the power to control the local residents by the same mechanics used to take it from the rancher. The agency declares overuse a problem, fire protection too hazardous, or cites sediment from development to be a threat to the same creek and forest that the residents had democratically acquired from the rancher. Agency action will focus upon regulating negative transformation products of the residents and perhaps even the urban majority with similarly expensive compliance measures and restrictions upon their use. There will be no accounting of the degradation due to civic management, indeed, the forest is now held hostage by the agent who can demand funding to protect it by any means, regardless how inefficient. A civic agent has every motive to maintain the asset in distressed condition because it generates justification for additional funding to solve the problem. The forest is now a socialized commons serving the interests of a managing agent with police power.

To socialize a commons thus transforms a productive forest into an economic liability and environmental catastrophe.

And Back Again

Hopefully the reason for all this arcane terminology is now a little clearer. **The employment of a civic agent to regulate transformation products in commons establishes legal mechanics that can then be used to control the democratic majority,** if not by rulemaking then by court order and precedent. This example clarifies how the use of political and legal coercion to manage the tragedy of the commons paves the road from a constitutional republic, to democracy, to socialism.

Collective claims upon private assets can be exercised against uses of only those processes that induce transformation products adverse to collective uses of commons. The person who purchased the land loses asset value with each newly defined claim. Claims can be effected simply by manipulating popular opinion, by reinterpreting even natural transformation products as negative externalities. One need only base claims upon subjective accusation of harm evidenced by normal dynamic changes in ecosystem attributes.

As the cost of acquisition drops to the cost of publicizing opinion, the size of acquisition required to provide the same perception of emotive benefit rises accordingly. The claims become ever larger. The greed for acquisitions is insatiable because they are acquired at minimal cost. As claims proliferate, asset value continues to decline in anticipation of additional claims. The land ends up being treated as if it is worthless because none of its assets can provide a predictable return upon investment.

The ambiguity, scope, and number of claims eventually meet declining availability of property to take. The claims eventually overlap. The process has no means to weigh competing claims but political. The battles become vicious because public participation in each particular interest has been acquired by attribution of a survival motive. Political struggles over resources with survival value have historically led to... Do we have to be reminded?

People get frustrated when they don't get what they want, especially when they believe that their combined individual desires justify a collective claim upon the use of private property.

To enforce such a claim by political compulsion is to own without title or payment. It is a tragic outfall of history that those who popularized the exercise of a collective claim on the use of private property were motivated to acquire personal control by means of political dominance. To acquire dominance then requires no more investment than to persuade a critical mass of the population according to the fashion of the moment.

These fashions can grow without limit and can be combined into functional majorities. Once democratic acquisition of the use of property is codified under the power of government, commons are forever subject to political control. Economic goods that originate from the land become desired for the collective perception of individual benefit, because the cost is but a whim.

The asset, the environment, has been thus devalued to little more than that.

First, people want to control a view, then they want it as a place to hike, then add the water in the creek for protection for fish, a wetland for migratory birds, a whole watershed to control all erosion, or to add a buffer zone to reduce encounters with overpopulated bears. Then they want it to be closed to all public entry so that they don't feel guilty, then they want it connected to a corridor to transmit genetic variability, then they want a whole forest region as a carbon sink, then a mountain range as a bio-zone for the expression of spiritual life forces, then…

Given that the ability to gain personal control of commons is based upon the ability to make a political sale, there are several prerequisites:

- A simple justification to maximize the applicability of the claim to individual perceptions and desires.
- A majority perception that acquisition comes at minimal personal cost.
- Collective benefits that are difficult to measure or long deferred.
- Powerful beneficiaries with sufficient personal interest and resources to fund and execute the taking.

Control of communications media to consolidate political forces becomes the means to control the factors of production and key to the control of wealth.

Does the need to maintain a sense of crisis lead to shortsighted decisions? Does it lead to the unconscious realization of self-fulfilling prophecies? Does it create a smokescreen for the exercise of corrupt intent? Does it overtax the ability to generate capital? If we adopt an ill-conceived plan, could such an exercise irreversibly damage the resource? Could the repeated application of mechanics like this lead to the unwitting vengeance of self-destruction?

There are those who have come to regard the exercise of external claims upon private property as a structural evil, a distorted exercise in "ends" just-ification for personal gratification disguised as altruism. It is truly curious that the same people, who warn us that the cause of ecological problems is a lack of individual motivation to care for commons, propose solutions that are in structural antipathy to maximizing the value of the assets. The very act of collectivizing the factors of production has historically destroyed their value. That loss can propagate rapidly. People get desperate because the process of political acquisition of private property is unsustainable.

Is it possible that property rights, as a matter of natural law and as protected by the Fifth Amendment, are really that important? If the price for the control of land resources is but the deflection of the winds of political fashion, the available wealth to support, defend, and nurture the land is minimized. What ends up forgotten in the political acquisition of "commons" is the need to maximize the economic value of these goods to the land. With the declining public perception of marginal benefit is a declining marginal value of the land itself. You can plot the price on a graph, as you will see in Part II.

Ecological issues are seldom simple. They vary considerably with different situations and over time. They often involve enormous costs to a few indiv-iduals and have public benefits that are difficult to measure. The enormous economic value to those individuals who would gain political control of private resources provides motive to invest in making the political sale regardless of the technical or ecological compromises. It thus becomes unlikely that, in the heat of political and legal battle, the solutions offered will adhere to the principles of the scientific method.

Any democratic system is manipulated by the politically dominant. It comes as no surprise that the ownership systems the politically dominant propose are to be "collectivized" among the people, but administered by an agency dedicated to their interests. Under such a system, that frightened mob may well get the environmental crisis that they so greatly fear.

First, Do No Harm

An effective tactic to enlist a majority interest is to offer a common survival motive. The practice raises the perceived value of the acquisition and lowers its apparent cost. To avoid accountability for predictive accuracy, the pitch artist need only assert that there is a hidden possibility of harm that can be averted if preemptive measures are immediately adopted.

It is perhaps a consequence of having satisfied our most basic needs as a society that so many people have become absorbed by fear of loss. Environmentalists have taken advantage of this, denoting the foundation of that security, human economic activity, to be innately harmful. The public at large has been beaten senseless with this unfortunate premise, interpreting nearly every act for its risk potential without regard to possible benefits. We are ironically negating what we actually have to lose, or what we might inadvertently take with us.

People who derive an income by such a democratic process are tempted to inflate the enabling threat. It's easy to do. One can construe virtually anything as having harmful potential, and nearly any mitigating restriction as a necessary precaution. It is a means capable of controlling any property. As long as Fifth Amendment protections can be avoided, democratic acquisitions use potential harm as a valued currency for economic transactions.

A system that so artificially distorts its priorities is not likely to render an objective resolution among competing risks, particularly when there is so powerful an ulterior motive. The more such competing claims proliferate, the more strident are the expressions of concern, the greater becomes the subjectivity of justifications for speculative measures with an increasing likelihood of grossly destructive errors.

One such error is manifested in the Precautionary Principle. This policy starts as a reasonable suggestion: Any proposed action must be proven beneficial before it is adopted. It is analogous to the presumption of innocence in a criminal trial, that winds up as a destructive paradox: One would have to risk harm through taking action to prove the benefit of proposed practices, not allowed under the policy. It presupposes that preventing action in a dynamic system has no adverse consequences, an assumption to which the Precautionary Principle itself has not been subjected. It is a premise that is incapable of objectively weighting relative risks.

To analyze the balance of risks under the variety of circumstances as exist, will take an enormous number of experimental trials. Private capital can provide the necessary financial resources, only if it can regenerate itself. Donated and confiscated public funds cannot do the job. It is just too big.

If we should destroy the wealth-generating basis found in resource lands, we will lack the tools, money, and knowledge to do the work. Without the objective efficiency of market-based capital allocation processes, the distribution of resources will not efficiently differentiate according to need.

A management system that derives power by constraint automatically biases the system toward allowing no human intervention of any kind. If one prevents action and the crisis never materializes one can then claim success, whether or not the threat was real. Attribution of potential harm is thus the preferred means to consolidate the political majority to democratize a commons, without fear of accountability.

Unfortunately, preservation of anything but pristine and unaltered habitat is fully capable of inflicting its own kind of "harm." Given 30,000 years of adaptation to the presence of humans and the naturalization of so many introduced exotic species, there is hardly any truly 'pristine and unaltered habitat.' Even if it were a unanimous goal that we should return much of the continent to its pre-aboriginal condition, one would have to ask how it could be accomplished in practice. Considering the constantly changing boundary conditions, such as climate change since the last Ice Age, such a project would be a huge amount of work that could have disastrous results. Similarly, the assumption that if nature is "preserved" it will somehow evolve to an optimally productive condition is usually erroneous. Nature has no prospective preferences, even for the survival of life itself.

Every dynamic variation in an ecosystem has benefits for some individuals and adverse consequences for others; it is the nature of differentiated and competitive systems. It is not uncommon for species virtually to disappear, only to return years later after a natural disturbance, such as a fire, flood, volcano, or recovery from over-predation. To claim that any change in the distribution of natural populations justifies radical changes in land use could be appropriately regarded as extreme until science had proven otherwise. Even so, mandated neglect is still the preferred means to prevent or repair subjectively defined and admittedly remote risks of ecological harm regardless of the obvious potential for disastrous consequences

It is astounding that so many potential risks associated with action are so seldom weighed against the virtual certainty of errors of inaction. This has been especially true in the case of early infestations of exotic pest species. The confining nature of the "prevent harm" ethic leaves its advocates with the constraint that control measures must be minimally intrusive, even if destructively ineffective. Risk-aversion, as virtue, coupled with human action as innately harmful, shield administrators and activists from accountability for cost-effective and positive results. Under the control of those who derive their mandate by environmental problems, the patient's condition will likely worsen; a victim of a self-fulfilling prophecy, no matter how much money is spent in desperate efforts to manage the resulting crises.

The idea that neglect is always benign presupposes that natural systems can fix any problem unassisted and contradicts the very purpose for regulatory policy. How then, do we devise an efficient and objective system that motivates and extends the state-of-the-art of ecosystem management?

This book is not about pristine, undisturbed lands. If such a thing exists, there are so few left in the continental U.S. that are not already protected, that there is no point in writing yet another book about "preserving nature." This book is about motivating people to profit from the study, restoration, and development of healthy, productive ecosystems on the other 95% of the land.

The "prevent harm" ethic constrains law-abiding practitioners who might make things better, and abets the avaricious and unethical. Activists, not recognizing their complicity, use these examples as reasons for yet more laws that regulate only the ethical operator even further, and confiscate yet more land when they go bankrupt. They dismiss such rampant injustice with the flippant belief that their ends justify the means, and deny accountability for less than desired results. Meanwhile, substitute sources of raw material have their own, often greater environmental impacts.

Trying to prevent all harm is impossible. It is a process that is logically-incapable of meeting its inferred goals.

Chapter 2 – Artificial Preservation

Environmental Preservation as a Type II Error

The limit of preventing harm by action is preservation. Examination of a policy of environmental preservation shows that it is founded upon a logical fallacy, a Type II Error, sometimes called an error of inaction.

Statisticians have developed mathematical analyses of error to reduce the probability of adopting a false hypothesis from experimental data. The purposes of the theory were: first, to determine the minimum sample size necessary for the desired degree of confidence in the conclusions derived from an experiment; and second, to distinguish whether experimental data values fell within a range that could be regarded as worthy of unambiguous conclusion. It's important stuff. One does not want to adopt an alternative hypothesis (a proposed model for how things work) without evaluating the risk that one might be wrong.

The way statisticians defined it, you can be wrong in two ways:

1. Type I error is a false conclusion that the alternative hypothesis is true. It is sometimes called an error of action.

2. Type II error is a false conclusion that the null hypothesis is true. It is sometimes called an error of inaction.

If you make a Type I error of action, you will likely find out that it was a mistake because the result can be clearly assigned to a cause. In the scientific community, the Type II error is considered the more egregious. If you make an error of inaction, you may never learn of it.

In this discussion, the null hypothesis is the contention that Nature is most productive when undisturbed by humans. The alternative hypothesis is that nature can benefit from human intervention and we had better go about learning how best to do it.

Let us examine the underlying assumptions that led to the null hypothesis.

Thinking Deep Thoughts

A Preservation Hypothesis represents a series of logical errors.

The alternative hypothesis proposes that people can coexist with nature and possibly even help. Environmental preservationists consider this a Type I error of action. The more archetypal adherents consider nature functionally incompatible with human habitation and technology, which upon analysis exposes a destructive self-fulfilling prophecy.

The first problem with the preservationist belief system is that of self-contradictory definition. "Natural" is defined as any thing or process undirected or unaltered by humans. Given the observation that all natural processes are interactive and the effects humans have had on the planet, there is hardly any of it that is unaffected. There is nothing that is, can, or will ever function as purely "Natural" as long as there have ever been large numbers of people.

Second is the assumption that to take no action constitutes such; i.e., that passivity in a dynamic environment constitutes preserving anything. In fact, the withdrawal of human interaction would be the biggest environmental change in millennia. This observation contradicts that idea that the null hypothesis could even be performed, and again illustrates the logical fallacy underlying the bias of the Precautionary Principle against human action.

Akin to the negation of dynamism is the supposition of reversibility. It is a common belief that Nature can return to a pre-aboriginal composition of ecosystems by maintaining isolation from humans. The usual extension of that idea under is that, since these are the ecosystems from which people sprang, they are those best suited to support human development. Strangely, the destruction of human development is usually regarded as a necessary step in completing the process.

If one believes the activists, humans significantly affect climate, consume large amounts of water, alter the flows of rivers, and introduce exotic species all over the planet. If one is willing to accept whatever state into which "nature" evolves after humans abandon it, while encumbered with all these alterations, then the logic becomes self-reinforcing. In other words: Whatever "Natural" it becomes will be natural because people did not execute the process, which of course has little to do with either restoration, or ideal conditions for humans. One wouldn't think that this is what most activists want, although there are those who think that this is just fine. However, if that is so, does it really matter how much humans muck with it first?

The fourth contradiction is to assume that human activity can be bounded after withdrawal. The Sierra Club and the UN propose huge, undisturbed, no-entry zones surrounded with "low activity buffer zones" intended to minimize human influence upon Natural systems. The problem is that there is no such thing as a "boundary" at which nature (or human influence) stops. The effects of human activity would propagate into these "no-entry" zones.

To begin to make this idea work, one would have to identify locations within which to isolate humans so that they would have minimal impact. This process is already in progress through Sustainable Development per the United Nations Agenda 21. Various proposals confine existing cities into "Sustainable Communities" surrounded by "greenbelts." Unfortunately, most large cities are along coastal bays or riverine floodplains. These are among nature's most productive habitats. There is no dynamic motive in the UN proposal to reduce the impact of siting habitation through new technology. For example, should transportation or water treatment technology change, urban centers might otherwise slowly relocate.

The most extreme proponents of isolating humans from nature are the so-called "deep ecologists." These people urge that humans adopt a "biocentric" perspective (as opposed to an anthropocentric, or human-centered view-point). The purported goal of biocentricism is to incorporate all of nature into one's perspective, to identify with all ecosystems in nature as one's personal interest. Sadly, deep ecologists seem incapable of expressing that perspective themselves. The first three tenets of Deep Ecology, as articulated by Arne Naess and George Sessions, dialectically separate humans from nature, rendering a biocentric perspective, an impossible paradox:

1. All life has value in itself, independent of its usefulness to humans.

2. Richness and diversity contribute to life's well-being and have value in themselves.

3. Humans have no right to reduce this richness and diversity except to satisfy vital needs in a responsible way.

The principles of Deep Ecology (there are 8) fall afoul of several constraints. First, (as they constantly remind us) humans already are an interconnected part of nature, competing for our individual benefit in our own manner as a species. Second, "Richness and diversity" are perceptions of value, important only to humans (near monoculture is a common phenomena in nature). Third, the idea that humans are responsible for maintaining a status quo among populations of existing species as a matter of "rights" is imposing a human set of values onto the results of mortal competition among species. It is a denial of dynamic equilibrium in natural selection and antithetical to the cyclical ebb and flow of populations of predators and prey.

If humans are so inherently destructive that they must be separated from nature, how could it be possible for humans to have a biocentric view? There would certainly be no hands-on opportunity to learn one. Although that might save having to expend a lot of physical effort, how would it help?

Further, these same people believe that nature is so robust and so rugged that it is fully capable of recovery without intervention, but that it is too fragile to survive our attempts to help. To decide not to take action because of the view that nature will somehow "know better" what to do, is just as much a projec-tion of human impressions onto nature, as is the conclusion that the situation demands the investment of time and money. There is no mechanism in the process of natural selection, that implies volition on the part of nature, much less prospective reversibility.

On the other hand, humans DO exhibit prospective volition. However, if we adhere to this perspective of doing nothing, what good is preventive intervention? How would we learn to exercise it effectively and benevolently? How would we learn to reduce the impact of urban technology if we did not interact? Such a process bias toward inaction precludes even the significant probability of constructive errors.

A biocentric perspective also presumes that humans are capable of anything other than human perception. If one is busily experiencing a totality, from what perspective does one notice that?

If humans cannot assume this pan-perspective, and are operating under the belief that they are inherently destructive, then why would they consider the effort to learn it of any redeeming value? Would that choice not also be corrupted by human desire? Why, then, act to prevent action?

Any humans action in a competitive system results in harm to something. Deep ecologists would feel distraught at the loss and guilty of the failure to prevent it. Thus, to actively seek collective dominance over people they disdain, politically forcing others into mandated inaction in order to protect themselves from risk to their personal feelings, is not only anthropocentric; it is an **egocentric** view.

Perhaps that is why it seems to be so popular!

Finally, the projection of persona, spirit, or rights upon anything other than citizens is little more than a twisted democratic power play. It is a claim of an exclusive franchise to represent an artificial constituency. Maybe those plants do need protection; but who gets to decide by what means, and to what end?

A biocentric perspective projects the spirituality of being into everything. To a deep ecologist, a rock would have a rock's spirit, a rock's consciousness, and thus deserves civil rights equivalent to human beings, which they alone purport to represent.

This is a debilitating thing to do to one's own mind, much less to a republic. To claim to represent the rights of rocks is to project a subjective human impression of a rock's preferences onto rocks. What if they were wrong? Perhaps the rocks might feel more appreciated by a mineral geologist who would want to make aluminum cans out of them? Did anybody ask the rocks? You guess.

When deep ecologists demand rights for rocks and plants, what they are really doing is demanding disproportionate representation of their interests as the self-appointed advocates for the rights of rocks and plants. Unfortunately, to enforce a right requires the police power of government, the only agent so capable. Government acquires this role because it is assumed to be a disinterested arbiter of competing claims.

History suggests quite the opposite.

When government gains the power to confer rights to any constituency, it acquires the means to confer power upon itself as an enforcing agent. There is then no limit to the power to dilute the rights of citizens. Civic respect for unalienable rights of citizens then exists not at all.

It is rather tragic that deep ecologists don't seem to understand their own motives, much less what preserves their freedom to express them. They understand even less of what preserves rights of citizens to protect their property from limitless democratic claims upon the use of ecosystem assets. Indeed, they exhibit direct antipathy to the principle of private property. If they don't understand the consequences of their actions or know where they're coming from, how could they know where they are going?

Which brings us to goals.

Goals

What are we preserving if we don't understand the environment as it is, much less, as it was? How then could we have a goal of how it "should be"?

Deep ecologists and environmental activists have argued for restoration of North American habitat to pre-Columbian or even primeval conditions. Why this is the preferred goal presupposes that such would achievable, much less desirable. There have been so many enormous changes over the last 500 years, whether climate change, introduced species, extinction of native plant and animal species, or physical changes wrought by humans, that to return to anything resembling pre-Columbian conditions could not be done with the commitment of all the technology and wealth known to humanity.

Even if a pre-Columbian park was physically and economically possible, it is still an ephemeral goal. The constitution and operation of pre-Columbian ecosystems can be only estimated. We know even less about pre-aboriginal conditions. Given the continuity of natural selection, one might have to reconstruct entire global environmental histories to know how we arrived where we are, much less to have an understanding of dynamic relationships at any point in the past. Given that we do not understand how it works now, that doesn't seem too likely. Is there any point in adopting a plan if we can't perceive the goal?

Worse, the boundary conditions (such as weather patterns) in which ancient systems operated are not reproducible. Though many are somewhat cyclical, it is unlikely that, by the time an ice age repeats or a major cataclysm erupts, the same genetic preconditions could exist. Even if one could reproduce a starting point, the system would still not recover to the same state because it is continually subject to random events. Mutant individuals can forever alter the parent species. The chemistry by which DNA is constructed in genes is irreversible. Even if that unknown pre-Columbian genetic distribution of plant and animal populations could be recreated, and all the species properly trained in their original behavior without any corruption from the process, they would not all survive and they would not evolve the same way. There is no going back in nature, even without humans. It could be disastrous to try.

Undaunted by reality, some deep ecologists are demanding a pre-aboriginal target condition for all North American ecosystems. There are various proposals including introducing Indian elephants to North America to compensate for the aboriginal extirpation of the woolly mammoth. Now that a frozen mammoth carcass has been found, there is reported interest in reintroducing the original after a mere 15,000 years without it. Is this George Orwell, Stephen Spielberg, or Woody Allen?

Such IS the stuff that dreams are made of, and dreams are powerful things. It is hard not to hear about how forests should return to Old Growth conditions which presupposes that this is even achievable. It may well not be. Nature will just start from where it is and evolve into something else. It might be OK without intervention, then again, the indications are that to do so unaided might not be optimal.

A forest is not a static thing, even with respect to its location. Many forests in California are a dynamic distribution between interdigitated meadows, chaparral, broadleaf forests, conifers, riparian corridors, strip malls, roads, vineyards, and houses. The boundaries of these regions have moved with changes of climate, cycles of fire, exotic species, major soil disturbances, and changes in the Federal Funds Rate.

Even if there was a goal fixed in mind, the problem is that natural systems are not fixed. Thus, this proposal of "preservation" with a goal of producing conditions approximating those 500 years ago, is a passive restoration of an infected body with altered genetic composition to a moving target of poorly understood properties, operating under unprecedented conditions while still subject to human interference. The ignorant hubris required to adopt such an impossible goal on a scale as huge as is currently being mandated nationwide needs a moment of contemplation to be appreciated.

There is no "Goal" even possible! How will they get there?

Methodologies

If we don't know how ecosystems work now, and don't know how they "should be," how could anyone claim that preservation as a *method* is the best means to manage them?

Many preservationists demand that humans go to any length to prevent extinction of specific genetic variants of species (alleles). Though most say they understand evolution, they act as if the differentiation and hybridization of potentially successful new variants must be halted at all costs. Successful alleles are those best suited to the conditions. Each location has a unique history of boundary conditions. Each species has a unique developmental sequence and arrangement of competitors.

That some lose the battle and die off often has less directly to do with human industry than the negligent introduction of exotic species. The golden hills of California (primarily European annual grasses) testify to the scope and permanence of exotic monocultures and the limited ability of a local habitat to adapt (many native California plants and animals are now extinct). The very idea that bio-diverse natives are somehow more suited to local habitat, and will ultimately return to dominance without human redress, is simply false. It is a denial of irreversibility in both biochemistry and natural selection and a lack of accountability for intellectual and physical sloth.

Let's say we have a second growth mixed forest, typical of coastal California. It has redwood and mixed hardwoods on a hillside with a creek at the bottom. The ridge is weak sandstone and shale buttressed with agglomerated landslide deposits. The topsoil has been stripped off the rocky surfaces and there are deep gullies from erosion through the alluvium. The hillside has been structurally undercut by creek bed erosion. The conifer forest is densely populated with thin trees sprouted from stumps. Many forest floor species are missing, buried in tree droppings and deep shade. Let's assume, for the sake of charity, that there are no major infestations of exotic species present.

Now, the environmental preservationists say they want an "old growth" forest and that we have a "fragile" patient. What to do? Take out the roads and let it wallow in sickness in the hope that the stronger will survive? Keep the patient alive whilst allowing landslides and such? Leave the stump suckers until it burns and see what we get? How many fire cycles will that take? How many life cycles of the redwood will it require? What do we do to protect the fish in the meantime? What about those missing species, if their seeds lose viability buried under the duff? How long is it going to take to see if it is working? 100 years? 500 years? 1,000 years?? If all that doesn't work, how far down that road will we be? Could we then change our minds?

If the objective is to mandate that nature be left undisturbed, then could there ever be a method to manage it, much less to coexist? The obvious conclusion is, if you aren't asking the right question, struggle among immiscible goals, and prevent anybody from doing anything, then you can't have a method except for preventing action. The problem is that it is logically impossible to "do" nothing without ecological consequences that are adverse to some species, even if it is just to withdraw human interference entirely.

The philosophy of preservation preserves ignorance of ecological systems by destroying the resources and tools to fund, measure, mitigate, or reverse historic damage. It could also make the situation impossible to fix.

It is not possible to develop a working knowledge of a system without perturbing it in some manner. Conducting varied experiments entails numerous trials to assure repeatability. We have diverse ecosystems with wide variation in physical circumstances, cost of labor, material, and the net extractable value of the resources. Such variation in economic factors and physical circumstances requires the need for development of a range of possible treatments. Preservation not only limits our ability to perturb the system to see how it works, but also the means to conduct LESS intrusive science because it destroys the motive to develop capable tools.

If you were requested to dig a hole in the ground, the first thing you might ask is "Where?" or "How big?" You ask those things because you know a thing or two about digging holes. You need to know where to put the dirt, how much time you will have, or perhaps that it might even be a bad idea to dig that particular hole in the first place. What you know about digging holes tells you a lot about whether you need a shovel, an excavator, or high explosives. You must rely upon other people's experience of digging holes to support the very existence of hole-digging tools. If nobody were making any money digging holes, the tools would be lousy. If nobody is making any money in the habitat management business because the bias of public policy is against action, we will have less opportunity to develop tools to learn how nature works or fix a problem.

Think of the physical scale required to eliminate weeds from a marsh. Think of the size of public works program it would take. Now recall that there is no goal, and no established method and no criteria for success. Now how much money are we talking about? At least in the case of the welfare state, we have an idea what a successful outcome might look like. This is worse.

How will they know if it's working? If action is not allowed, does it matter? Aren't ideologues demonstrably susceptible to self-delusion? Do they plan to measure and evaluate their results?

Output Variables

If the Preservation Hypothesis does not exist, if there is no goal, and if there is no method, then there can be no way to test the efficacy of the system. The preservation policy, therefore, cannot be justified.

Even under the most rigorous and controlled conditions, the conduct of experimental science can encounter difficulty collecting reliable data with a known degree of uncertainty. If the goal has no structured form, if the technical method can't exist or is so passive as to make cause and effect relationships undetectable, if the decision making process is distorted by political whim, then there can't be a set of output variables by which to measure the relative success of the experiment. If a set of interdependent output variables can't be directly measured, is confounded by other inputs, or is perturbed intermittently by external events, this renders the interpretation of the output measurement subjective. Perhaps deep ecologists want it that way.

Under a banner of "subjective science," the interpreter is always free to conclude that the results confirm the hypothesis or that the data are flawed. Deviation from expected results can be assigned to problems to be resolved by a subsequent study and additional funding or by merely affixing blame. Grants for activities based upon subjective criteria have become so prevalent that there is now among deep ecologists a culture of antipathy toward objective measurement! It is derisively called "mechanistic thinking."

Accurate data is expensive and usually does not justify sweeping conclusions. The civic motive to collect it is minimal unless it can be used to lay claim to the need for either more funding or more control. The motive to make data acquisition cost less through better measurement instruments and data processing tools is similarly skewed to ulterior purpose. Continuing problems requiring management are the investment assets of a government entity because continuing the perception of threat maintains justification for an operating cash flow. The entire measurement system is thus distorted by ulterior purposes. If preservationists are so often concerned about oversight, how can they tolerate a system like that?

They wouldn't let anybody else get away with it!

This system is particularly convenient to both government and the activist community. Activists desire the power to control, but not the responsibility for results. Agencies prefer to confine study to problems with economic causes because these increase the scope of their control over the economy. Management system failures create a bigger budget so they don't have to care about the results. There is, thus, no money for maintenance of what they already have under their control.

The activists lobby for either regulatory taking or acquisition by a non-governmental organization (NGO). The government takes over the operation, sometimes through direct purchase from the NGO at a fat profit. The money again becomes available for grants to the activists. As long as the situation can be interpreted as dire, the bureaucrats can continue justification for funding. The worse the situation becomes, the more money becomes available. There is thus structural motive to maintain the object of funding in deteriorating condition. Problems become assets.

If the means to attain control are political and legal, then the focus of data collection will be for the purpose of political and legal advantage, not for ecologically rigorous management. If, however, the output variable is the degree of resource control, then the measurement has nothing to do with improving the health of the environment, other than to use its lack as continuing justification.

The dependencies of the regulators are thus likely to force interpretations of results that, because they are admittedly not objective, are self-reinforcing. Subjective interpretation is extremely perilous with any technical investment. If career status is calibrated by budgetary funding obtained by proving that an ecosystem is under threat, is it not entirely likely that the results of those continuing operations will be at least ambiguous, if not destructive?

So not only is the premise of political control of the environment logically unable to deliver upon its promise, its subjective nature corrupts its motives for the acquisition of objective data. That fact, alone, indicates that the results are unlikely to be very promising. It also portends that the acquiring interests will focus upon only those problems that keep the money flowing. It is probable that confounding factors will interfere in producing promised results and that typically inadequate operating budgets will inhibit the ability to account for efficacy. The money is for acquisition, not maintenance. The one variable preservationists do seem to be able to measure is acreage.

The Deep Ends

Rudolf Carnap (a rather under-appreciated modern logician and philosopher) suggested that if people have been wrangling with a problem for a long time, then they are probably posing a question with no solution. The preservationists may be guilty of a massive error of inaction, but it is worse than that. They didn't even set up the problem correctly.

If the Preservation Hypothesis does not exist, if the guiding assumptions are flawed, if there cannot be a goal, if there is no technical method, if there are no output variables by which to judge the results, how can it work? If the motives of those employed by the decision-making system are toward acquiring power through environmental failure, then the results are likely to be destructive. If the sponsors of an illogical and destructive system seek control of all factors of production, then their motives must be founded upon either faith or greed.

Consider faith. Deep Ecologists deny that their body of practices and beliefs constitutes a religion, although they publicly engage in animist and shamanist rituals and speak reverently of Gaia (the "Earth Mother Goddess") as the source of true scientific knowledge:

> "Gaian perception connects us with the seamless nature of existence, and opens up a new approach to scientific research based on scientific institutions arising from scientists' personal, deeply subjective ecological experience. When the young scientist in training has sat on a mountain top, and has completed her first major assignment to 'think like a mountain', that is, to dwell and deeply identify with a mountain, mechanistic thinking will never take root in her mind. When she eventually goes out to practise her science in the world, she will be fully aware that every interconnected aspect of it has its own intrinsic value, irrespective of its usefulness to the economic activities of human beings."

> – STEPHAN HARDING

Gaia was supposedly a Minoan earth goddess, adopted by a clearly wealthy, and reputedly earth-worshipping and pacifist civilization on Crete. Unfortunately, the popular beliefs about Minoan civilization largely represent the neurotic whimsy of Sir Arthur Evans, the first major excavator at Knossos. Evans was obsessed with proving that Minoan civilization had Aryan origins, and demonstrated a propensity to contort his observations in order to project upon them Druidic beliefs. Current evidence suggests that constantly warring Minoan city-states were overrun by Mycenean Greeks, perhaps after a nearby volcanic eruption. Maybe they had been weakened and their numbers were reduced. They did sometimes eat their children. One thing that we do know: They are no longer with us.

Some Deep Ecologists think that a consequence such as befell the Minoans might not be so bad. Such are adherents to the Voluntary Human Extinction Movement (VHMT, pronounced "vehement") or the Church of Euthanasia (whose central tenets are: Abortion, Sodomy, Cannibalism, and Suicide).

If a belief system has a flawed foundation in logic, a codified structure of beliefs, a hierarchy, icons, a personified supernatural deity, and spiritual rites, then it is equivalent to a religion whether it has a 501(c3) or not. If a religious body of belief starts to direct policy, it is equivalent to an establishment of religion capable of confounding all civic deliberation with its irrational body of belief. Perhaps the only thing that keeps deep ecologists from being sued successfully is that they don't have an office or a bank account.

These folks are on the power curve. Consider greed.

Together, environmental activists and agencies of the United States government have advocated a plan of human withdrawal and ecological inaction over 50% of the continental United States: The Wildlands Project. The plan is to set aside enormous "core reserves" with "connecting corridors" surrounded by "buffer zones." The plan is being enacted over the objections of both landowners and many ecological scientists. The published goal is to institute the plan, as soon as possible, nationwide. They have done so on the mere assumption that to withdraw human action constitutes preservation of natural resources. There has been no fractional experiment with published expectations, established methods, or means of measuring relative success. There certainly has not been an experimental trial. The first indications are by no means promising and, because of the preconditions listed above, are subject to interpretation. The real goal is resource land acquisition.

In order to get the land it sometimes has to be acquired over the pesky objections of its owners, with the temerity to indicate that the preservationists have no idea what they are doing. The key point of leverage is control of the water in the connecting corridors. Given the democratic claim on the use of water as a commons, the key to a public taking becomes the management and interpretation of specific provisions under either the Clean Water Act, or uses of water pursuant to the Endangered Species Act. Determination of the outcome nearly always involves a court of law where the assumptions of a judge and the infinite legal resources of government render the decision nearly a *fait accompli* or a *coup de grâce* (depending upon your perspective). The agencies and activist organizations are armed with experienced lawyers and "experts." The landowner and their legal representatives are usually unschooled in the conduct of dispute or technical argument and are very unlikely to have either deep pockets or sufficient data from expert witnesses.

The experts are, of course, scientists. Technical testimony in environmental cases is often composed of value judgements of the degree of threat to or criticality of an ecological resource. These experts are representing themselves to the courts as objective witnesses of activist organizations, universities, and government resource agencies. If, however, these same scientists have been trained to subject their observations and data to what is, at least functionally a religious belief system, then they make their testimonies before courts of law on the bases of such subjective science.

Under a biocentric ethic, our Gaian scientist believes that everything is ecologically critical and all economic value to the property owner is to be disregarded. Such a "scientist" is fully capable of the delusion that subjective interpretation is equivalent to objective data or that dishonesty 'in the defense of nature' might not be a moral failing.

A judge is no judge of technical integrity and has no experience upon which to evaluate testimony other than by considering university credentials and the quality of the legal presentation. Consider the above quote in that regard as applies to the expert testimony of such a scientist.

The courts are predisposed to make judgements on the behalf of government agencies under the erroneous assumptions that the testimony is objective and that employees of the U.S. Government are representing policies according to laws passed by Congress. Nothing could be further from the truth.

First, most Federal resource agencies are members of international non-governmental organizations (NGOs) that are likely to take positions in the legal conflict, contrary to the agencies' constitutional and organizational mandates. These private NGOs require agencies of the United States Government to adhere to multilateral treaties as a prerequisite to membership, WHETHER RATIFIED OR NOT. Some such treaties have been specifically rejected. The texts of these treaties grant virtually unlimited power governing land use within the United States to those agencies.

These treaties, such as the Convention on Biological Diversity, were designed and drafted by activist NGOs such as the World Wildlife Fund (WWF) and the International Union for the Conservation of Nature and Natural Resources (IUCN). Congress never allotted payment of Federal Agency membership dues to these international organizations. Both these organizations were started with grants from private, tax-exempt, "non-profit" foundations of the major stockholders in oil companies. These treaties, originating at these NGOs, were blessed by United Nations Environmental Programme (UNEP) and routed for "approval" to the respective member governments of the UN.

Would the UN be representing an interest in acquiring global control of all resources? Under the current plan for reorganization, the UN plans a congress of NGOs that subsists entirely off grant money as supposedly representing civil society: The People's Assembly.

What kind of government gets to decide who represents "the people?" One that is sponsored by greed and controls "the people" by fealty to faith.

In addition to the philosophical bias on the part of testifying NGO grantees and agency professionals, are also direct career interests. Agency executives often circulate through a revolving door, at either environmental NGOs or private foundations. There is obvious reason for these political appointees to exert pressures upon technical civil servants with few other career options. The inherent conflict of interests in technical testimony thus deepen, to say nothing of the ethical considerations regarding ecosystem health. Though the human propensity to cower in compliance in return for personal security can be understood, it cannot be morally condoned.

The members of any group, with deeply held beliefs in a cause, will suffer frustration if they don't get what they want. It is natural for them to elevate the consequences of failure to heed their claims. Upon attributing the point of contention to an issue of collective survival, it isn't hard to justify internally any means to achieve their ends. It is predictable then, that they rely upon the courts, executive fiat, or the irreversible slide down the road to command economy. Once they get their paycheck in service to that cause, it makes the case more personal. Desperate activists will accept support from any source, even if that source was the historic cause of the very problems they seek to solve! They do it to get their way, through legal coercion at the pleasure of its direct beneficiaries: a moneyed elite interested in manipulating the commodity value of resources or their substitutes on a global basis (as we shall see in Part V).

To socialize a commons is to control the factors of production. It is a way to power. A financial elite can dominate the political appointees in charge of administrative bureaucracy. That elite will always subordinate ecology to the acquisition and maintenance of power. It is an ultimately corrupting process destructive to its purpose.

Social "scientists," subsisting off of the ill-gotten cash from the scions of the industrial robber barony, are gleefully destroying the very foundations of individual freedom that have the best hope of fulfilling their dreams. They are selling scientific subjectivity and a biocentric ethic to dedicated human beings, confused into believing they are engaged in unselfish acts. They are mucking with the scientific method. They are destroying the technical integrity of young people, who commit their lives to save the environment.

The antithesis of this book is designed to connect the results with the perpetrators, the philosophy with the policy, the motive with the means, and the local with the global. Each of us will see our own piece of this terrible conflict. The message to many environmentalists, here, is this:

You are being used. It doesn't work the way you think it does.

To render observation subjective is to engage in self-deception. A scientist, engaged in such art, is trafficking in opinionated guesswork for the mere benefits of self-aggrandizement and a subsistence paycheck. Without technical integrity, deep ecologists may do irreparable damage to everything they say they love, to their great personal sorrow.

Chapter 3 – What's "The Problem"?

The Underlying Assumptions of Environmental Regulation

If preservation of disturbed habitat is unlikely to work, how do we regulate behavior without creating new forms of harm? If the life-support systems for humans require a viable resource industry, should government enjoy a monopoly to regulate resource use? These questions form the context for Part II.

The idea, that government should hold a monopoly franchise to coerce politically preferred uses of private property, presupposes several errant assumptions:

1. Policy-makers (civic or private) are uniquely capable of environmentally appropriate economic choices in every instance.

2. Administrative government possessing coercive powers is an objectively disinterested arbiter.

3. The unintended adverse environmental consequences to the regulation itself will not outweigh the benefits.

4. There is no preferable alternative with which to motivate extension of the limits of resource management technology.

The historical record addresses the first three assumptions. With regard to an alternative management system, the situation is currently binary; i.e., to regulate by civic authority or not at all. This results in a public choice of whether to use government to coerce more intrusively or less so.

It is human nature to wait for a political system to grossly fail before risking a change. With the scale of environmental systems and the historic propensity for irreversible growth in government power, waiting for failure is enormously perilous. A historic analysis of civic regulation *as a system* is therefore necessary to justify a new direction. This will be done in Part II.

There really isn't an alternative environmental management system that requires no governmental intervention. Part III proposes such a system. Parts IV and V show how it can develop in parallel with the current civic monopoly. The purpose of parallelism is to make it possible for both systems to optimize their capability through competition.

Preceding that, let's look at the some of the hidden assumptions of current environmental management system design, to define a context for the problem statement of how to do better.

What IS "The Environment" Anyway?

The Environment is an expression of concern for how human interaction with natural systems alters their function. It is therefore essential to confine investigation of the effects of policy to a limited scope.

So, if it isn't "Natural," what is it? What is "The Environment"?

People usually talk about the environment in terms of human effects upon Nature. The threats supposedly emanate from an irreconcilable conflict of interest with nature: our auto emissions when we drive to work; our demand for mechanized agriculture (especially meat); or our urban lifestyle that places demands upon the surroundings to support it. The environment is supposedly about our insatiable desire for a house, a lawn, and a hot tub.

When people talk about *protecting* the environment, it is usually about the air they breathe, the emissions exiting the smokestack, the sewage at the end of the pipe, or encroaching development on the edge of a forest. Most political conflict over what we call the environment centers upon the conduct of human economic activities and their influence on the Natural surroundings at the boundaries of that human influence.

Deep ecologists would dismiss this concept, asserting that "everything is connected", and that therefore, everything must be considered as a whole. Few seem to notice just what a destructively nebulous concept that is.

Any system is interactive with its surroundings. One must however, limit study of interactions to yield useful data. Drop a brick on the ground and it's easy to know, within reasonable tolerances, the velocity upon impact and that you should have your feet in a safe place, when that is all that is of interest. However, if everything is connected and interactive, the "equal and oppositely directed" reactions of dropping a brick mathematically extend to the ends of the universe. Planetary orbits are theoretically distorted and relativistic time shells are altered. To measure and characterize them all is of course, a preposterous thing to do. It is therefore, essential to limit the scope of the experiment and analysis such that inputs are controllable and outputs measurable. Engineers and scientists define such a system envelope as a **control boundary**.

A control boundary is analogous to a balloon around the system under test. It is a way of containing a problem to those inputs and outputs that move across that boundary. Make the envelope too big and the effects will be so small or mixed with other events, that the scientist will either fail to observe them, or have to purchase expensive equipment and go through numerous repetitions and calculations to manage minute tolerances. Make the envelope too small and one risks missing effects outside the boundary.

Chapter 3 – What's "The Problem"?

Author's Note: The concept of a control boundary is essential to understanding the thesis of this book. One must set a control boundary for a market to price the manner in which individual properties transform the state of mobile commons. It is paradoxically the ONLY way for a market to integrate global impacts into individual choices. That discussion will be deferred to Part III, Chapter 4.

Thus, in the case of our brick, the control boundary is typically drawn immediately around the brick and its path to the ground. Let go, it hits a barrier assumed to be infinite and rigid (the earth) and stops. Newton's elegant laws of motion can then deliver a solution, telling us how far it will fall and how fast it will be going when it hits the ground. It is now possible to learn about dropping bricks. If the engineer tried to measure the brick from a mile away, he or she would be fired (the scientist, on the other hand, gets a Ph.D.).

Infinite problems are a bummer, unless they guarantee a future paycheck, because **selection of an infinite control boundary is a choice that renders even simple problems practically insoluble.**

In the case of a book examining the results of environmental management, to measure the effects of policy on a global level just isn't very tangible. Such discussions fall to arguments about the validity of the data. (Consider the difficulty scientists have had getting temperature measurements to confirm or refute claims of global warming.) To examine the effects of policy requires that the study area be confined in order to be certain about causes and effects.

Though any local habitat is unique, interactions between regulatory government and the laws of economics adhere to similar principles, regardless of the venue. One would then need to select a representative case. Ranchers aren't interested in urban transportation, city dwellers don't think much of fish (except for availability at the store), and computer manufacturers aren't immediately concerned about forests. Nevertheless, there is a place where many of these interests meet, in one location, under a single jurisdiction, all within a radius of 20 miles.

Santa Cruz County, located on the Central Coast of California, is a particularly interesting place to study environmental policy. It possesses numerous types of human/environmental interfaces that have seen huge changes over a period of but 225 years. (See map on Page 52.) The County has a city with an urban downtown (the City of Santa Cruz) and sprawling suburbs of Capitola, Aptos, Scotts Valley, Soquel, and Watsonville. Industrial activities include farming, high technology industry, a university, timber, and mining.

The weather in the County of Santa Cruz varies radically within a few miles. The summers are almost entirely dry, while the winters can produce anything from 8.5 to 125 inches of rain in five months, depending upon year and location. Temperatures can vary 50°F the same day. A canyon can have a marine climate, while a ridge 100' above has an inland climate 15°F hotter. Summer daytime temperatures can vary 40°F in fifteen miles.

The mountains are largely composed of compressed silt and sand (the word "stone" would be complimentary), clay, and decomposed granite, with enormous slide zones of compacted alluvium. Soils vary from clay to exposed granite, sometimes changing types within a few feet. The deep canyons often have steep walls producing both nearly continuous sun or shade conditions during the day, depending upon orientation.

Habitats include meadows, chaparral, hardwood forest, rivers, and an ocean interface with beaches, sand dunes, rocky tide pools, and estuarine swamps. The local biota reflects every bit of that diversity with unique overlays of species within very short distances.

There are two major watersheds within the County. The San Lorenzo River runs through canyons forested with redwood and, thence, through the City of Santa Cruz. The Pajaro River arises on brush-covered slopes and flows lazily through agricultural lands. The rest of the streams run down the steep western face of the coastal ridges.

There isn't very much of Santa Cruz County that hasn't been ravaged at least once. The rivers were always too polluted with animal waste to drink, so the Spanish relied upon springs for domestic water and used the rivers as sewers. The redwood forest was mercilessly logged and the slash was burned. They dammed the rivers to move the logs and run the sawmills. Oak forests were cleared to the ground to produce grapes, arboreal fruit, potatoes, forage, and vegetables. The original tanbark oak hardwood forests were taken for fuel, charcoal, mine shoring, and leather production. People drilled for oil, mined clay for bricks, and quarried sand and gravel (still do). Rivers were bridged with pilings and lined with levees. Harbors were dredged an guarded with jetties. Estuaries were simply filled. Marine mammals were decimated for oil, meat, and pelts. "Temporary" logging roads have been here for over 100 years and prove it every winter. Erosion problems abound due to roads, agriculture, and natural causes that accelerate when subjected to seasonal torrents of rain or an occasional violent earthquake. Hundreds of thousands of cubic yards of sediment wash down the rivers every year.

The favorable weather conditions in the County support massive infestations of exotic species: annual pasture grasses from Europe, escaped cultivars such as Cape ivy, periwinkle, hypericum, eucalyptus, acacia, gorse, hairy cat's ear, Himalayan blackberries, broom, star thistle and bull thistle, and hemlock.

Much of the mountain region that was converted to agriculture has long been abandoned and has returned to various types of mixed hardwood and softwood forests are now so loaded with fuel that a fire disaster is inevitable. The local faunae are way out of balance. Numerous local species are extinct, most notably the Grizzly bear and an almost mythical form of wild cat for which the town of Los Gatos derives its name. Other native species such as ravens, jays, and sea gulls are predating some of their usual competitors into near extinction because their population is abetted by human habitation.

By the mid 1930s, irrigation and transportation systems had improved to the point that they had rendered the poor soils, steep slopes, and stingy summer water sources, of the Santa Cruz Mountains irrelevant as an agricultural region (except for viticulture). The southern part of the County and the Santa Clara and Salinas Valleys had taken over that economic role. Roads, trucks and railways had dispensed with much of local industry. County officials looked around for what they had to sell and there wasn't much left… except the great weather, the redwoods, the beaches, and proximity to what would later become the industrial Bay Area… TOURISM! The last refuge of those with little else to sell.

People still come here "for Nature"?

You bet! It's pretty. It's hip. It's quaint. There's MONEY to be made! The Environment can be rendered highly profitable by involuting that boundary interface, between humans and nature, over as large an area as is possible.

Developers went bonkers in the San Lorenzo Valley, selling lots for vacation cabins among the redwoods. An amusement park was constructed in Santa Cruz on the sand spit guarding the mouth of the estuarine lagoon of the San Lorenzo River. Postwar '50s tourist hype attractions popped up as Santa's Village (mercifully deceased) and the *Mystery Spot*. Local businesses along Highway 9 still sell redwood burls and sculptures. Santa Cruz remains the only easily accessible place for many miles with a combination of decent surfing, hotels, restaurants, and beaches sheltered from the prevailing winds for sun bathing. Throw in an arts community for color and, Voila! a tourist town. It worked. People (especially young people) started braving Highway 17, driving over the hill on the weekends to play

The University of California system needed to expand and Santa Cruz was attractive. Land and housing were relatively cheap, urban access wasn't difficult, and the County needed the business. They built it in the '60s, and designed the curriculum accordingly.

The number one undergraduate degree is Psychology. Over two thirds of undergraduates are enrolled in humanities and social sciences. Two thirds of the remaining undergraduates are enrolled in biology, environmental studies, and marine biology. One third of the 1999 graduating class was unemployed or working part-time, most of them locally. Given that the bulk of the graduating population is trained in environmental and social sciences, they are largely employed as teachers, employees of general government, resource agencies, and non-profit organizations. It is a powerful voting bloc. The County budget exceeds $400,000,000, and it isn't spent on infrastructure.

Once the State Supreme Court ruled that the students were allowed to vote locally (as opposed to their home districts), the campus and its infrastructure was sufficient have had a significant effect on local politics. The County of Santa Cruz has represented the extreme ideological left for thirty years. It is an archetype of political environmental management.

Silicon Valley is only 25 miles away from Santa Cruz. It is prosperous. It is also full. Housing in the Valley is dear. Santa Cruz County is pretty and not so prosperous. The land is, consequently, cheaper. One need only deal with the commute over the hill on a notoriously dangerous four-lane highway.

The manifestations of suburban sprawl within the County have been varied. The forms have depended greatly upon the politics of the local community. Scotts Valley became a classic spread of strip malls, industry spillover from Silicon Valley, and ranch homes on small plots. The San Lorenzo Valley remained largely comprised of upgraded vacation cabins and middle income residents. The rural mountains gravitated toward 5–20 acre personal baronies for Valley professionals with 2,000–12,000 square foot homes along endless crumbling roads studded with sports cars and SUVs.

There are a lot of these latter people and they are wealthy. They care about the environment, but that issue is about what happens in the forest that surrounds them. They don't really notice (and would hardly admit) that their presence constitutes a serious ecological issue. They are prepared to believe the rant of environmental activists in the local papers. Many join and make contributions to environmental organizations, such as the Sierra Club. The local media are more than happy to be selling advertising for products these people buy, notably the houses in which they live.

Of special interest, therefore, is the rural/suburban forest interface. There are not many things more influential than buying a piece of forested property, blowing out the dirt with heavy equipment, plopping houses on it, hauling in exotic plants, seeding weeds from horses eating imported hay, and paving over the access road that diverts runoff down a deepening trench. Equally interesting are the human interests aiding and abetting its propagation, as well as political attempts at control to benefit specific interests. It is not surprising that it is this battleground under most severe contention among environmentalists, politicians, urban citizens, landowners, and developers.

As residential development continues to consume as much land as it can get, the interests of these new residents combine with regulators, consultants, and activists from the university community, into a majority constituency. The local politicians see more votes from anti-timber environmentalism and more property tax revenue from residential development than from timber harvesting. The appearance of being an anti-timber crusader has been a path of upward mobility in three congressional elections within the region. The

Chapter 3 – What's "The Problem"?

Environment is now a big issue, with residents and the forest landowners each accusing the other of being the greater cause of environmental harm.

Meanwhile, the local timber, agriculture, and mining industries remain in operation. Many of the owners have been here for generations. With but few exceptions, the timber harvest practices they follow are vastly superior to those of years prior and are considered by some to be the best in the world. Activists have found blaming them for both the "crimes" of yesteryear and for the practices of operators from outside the County to be a source of continued political and financial support. These landowners legitimately see new residents as a threat to their ability to retain ownership of their land.

The California Department of Forestry and Fire Protection (CDF) and the California State Board of Forestry (BOF), see things pretty much the same way as the landowners, but not for the reasons the suburban residents might think. To them residential development is more a threat to local ecosystems than is the conduct of timber operations, and they have a point. A house is a permanent reduction in forest cover, along with a host of other impacts: roads, patios, power lines, introduced species, vineyards, orchards, septic systems, pets, and chemicals. Houses preclude the ability to manage vegetation with fire and risks the lives of firefighters. Compared to that, CDF would prefer an occasional timber harvest that grows back in fifteen years and can do a lot to improve a forest, if done correctly. For that conclusion, CDF and the BOF end up as convenient targets of the activist organizations, accused as lackeys of the timber industry.

The Environment is a technical, contentious, and emotional set of issues. One couldn't write a book about it all, even within Santa Cruz County. Although any local ecosystem is unique, the interactions among human economy and regulatory government adhere to similar principles regardless of the venue. This book will therefore define its control boundary for its antithesis around the political and regulatory mechanics affecting the rural/suburban forest interface in Santa Cruz County as representative of similar issues elsewhere.

It might seem therefore, that this book is merely about a local case. **It is not.** One could substitute the encroachment of development, in the rural/suburban forest in Santa Cruz County, for similar demographics in the Sierra Nevada, the Umqua forest in Oregon, "ranchettes" from Montana to Colorado, or the encroachment of suburbia into farmland anywhere in the nation. Although the points of technical discussions differ from place to place, the political and economic principles involved are the same.

If one were to try to generalize across all those cases, the minor differences in local politics, the properties of local ecology, and the price modeling of each industry involved would differ so greatly, the amount of necessary data would be so enormous and difficult to normalize, as to disallow discussion of details supported by sufficient proof of evidence, to betray systemic effects of policy upon economic behavior in a conclusive manner.

The political rationale for "greenbelts" as a barrier to suburban sprawl, is the same in Santa Cruz as it is everywhere else. Political set-asides and eminent domain actions for parks and "view sheds" in Santa Cruz, have been justified upon the same bases as any number of monumental set asides elsewhere.

A discussion of the symptoms of the systemic dysfunction of civic regulation is best confined to a local case with an uninterrupted political and administrative power structure entirely supportive of that system. Such a place is Santa Cruz County, which was the first in the Nation to adopt a United Nations Local Agenda 21, now called Sustainable Development or Smart Growth.

That last fact prompts the final purpose to using a local case for this book: to reveal the local effects of global policy as indicative of global bureaucracy. Local regulatory actions are usually funded by and under the direction of superceding regulatory authority. The policies are invoked one precedent at a time; the takings are accomplished one landowner at a time to be replicated elsewhere. Their technical premises are nearly always based upon how local conditions serve an agenda that is set at a higher level.

Thus, **all environmental politics ARE local.** It is best, then, to examine a local case to betray the plans and consequences of what is, in reality, a nascent Global Governance.

Political Momentum Spawns Bad Ecology

Preservation of pristine habitat has been a historic product of environmental organizations. The method has distorted their aims and habits that evolved to coerce legal preservation of unique and archetypal examples of primeval habitat. These groups now function as large corporations that ran out of raw material. They misapply their preservation product to disturbed habitat for the purpose of corporate survival and acquisition of new market share.

The unrestricted logging of virgin redwood timber during the earlier part of this century engendered resistance by political and legal means. The redwood preservation movement was organized to protect many of these unique and archetypal resource lands. The intent was to preserve what little remained of the primeval forest. There have been many successes, for which we as a society owe much. Unfortunately, the practice of legal tactics toward a goal of preservation has distorted the aim and function of these organizations, much to the detriment of their purpose.

Preservation is a form of conservation that can be understood and supported by urban contributors. It is simple to implement by court order and enforce by administrative government. It is thus an expedient way to extend collective claims. It was out of that demonstrable effectiveness, that preservation organizations derived their public support.

By the late 20th Century, these corporations had been so successful that the amount of unprotected and undisturbed domestic land had dwindled to the point that these groups faced survival concerns. When a corporation depletes its raw material, it considers another source. They needed new objectives in order to justify the donations that supply a continuing cash flow.

The new products were obvious spinoffs of existing organizational capabilities; both designed to prevent harm:

1. "Protection" of other lands both further afield and already disturbed.

2. Sponsoring regulation of industry practice to minimize the harm done.

It was inevitable that these two constituencies would eventually collide, with the latter ceding to the former. In organizations operating under an ethic of preventing harm, it is much easier to assert that preservation prevents harm than to take the position that action is necessary. Over time, preservationists have won out and the regulatory product is now used to reduce the cost of acquisition for preservation purposes.

As preservationists extended "their" holdings, they ran out of primeval domestic habitat to protect. According to the Sierra Club, 96% of more than two million acres of ancient redwood forests are gone. They have been logged. The remaining amount, not already under legal protection, is so small that hyperventilated discussions of preserving ancient forests is in large part no longer applicable to the situation we have. That battle is largely over.

The preservationists had to find other lands to protect. While the prescription of "preservation" had some scientific efficacy in the case of ancient virgin redwood stands, that method does not apply to regions that have been logged.

Most of the redwood trees in a primeval forest sprout from roots those that fell down before them (usually in winter when the ground is soft). When they fall, they rip out the entire root ball in an arc approximately 6 to 15 feet across. On the way down, they also clean off the lower branches of other trees and allow more light to reach the forest floor. The roots remaining in the ground will usually sprout numerous new saplings within a year or two on a similar, or even larger, arc. Sometimes the shoots will start from out of the trunk or from branches impaled into the earth. This is one successful tree. They are awfully hard to kill, even if one wanted to.

A redwood stump from a harvested tree will typically sprout 10–20 new saplings immediately after logging, but within a radius much smaller than is found in nature, particularly if the stump is taller than a few inches. In early logging practice, stumps were usually 4–6 feet tall to reduce the diameter to be hand-sawed. The sprouts often grow right off the side of the rotting stump. Most are not structurally sound trees, nor will they ever be. Others could do well with help, but if not…

Depending upon location, it has been 40–150 years since the initial logging in the Santa Cruz Mountains. If you didn't know any better or were looking off the side of the freeway, you would think it was a healthy forest. If somebody came along with a chainsaw saying he was going to make it better, given the history, you would rationally doubt it. It sure isn't pretty immediately after the loggers get done, no matter how hard they try. So people try to stop it politically, saying they want to "preserve the forest."

It's understandable, but it's horribly wrong.

In many of these areas, after nearly 100 years since their initial logging, these sprouted trees have yet to be thinned. Competition for light has caused many to be thin and unbalanced. The branches of a 100' tree can be an average of two to three feet long, layered down the trunk like shingles. They sway in winds, bash into adjacent clones, and drop massive amounts of dead growth that can pile four feet high in the middle of the stump cluster. Numerous, dead, or stunted sprouts shoot out of the outside of the base of the cluster at severe angles, drooping branches to the duff, providing a fire ladder into the canopy. Lower branches die for lack of light, hanging like a tangled web of matches bare of bark. Some of the smaller trees eventually die and remain standing for years, leaning on their competitors. To the trained eye, it looks much like a funeral pyre. You look, and then you look away. It hurts.

With the additional tannin from the droppings, the lack of nitrogen from all the undecomposed material, and the lack of light that was consumed by an impacted canopy, many of the supporting plant species, normally found on the floor of an undisturbed forest of this type, cannot compete and die out. Such a forest floor is a shadowy desert of brown tree droppings, dead sprouts, naked branches, and blackened stumps.

Frequent fires are not universally deadly to larger trees and can be beneficial. Fire provides nutrients to roots, and removes root suckers, crown sprouts, and understory overgrowth. If too much fuel has accumulated, however, fire can cause significant injury to old growth trees, especially at the base of the trunk on the high side of a hill. It can cause mortality if the fire is too hot.

Second growth trees are much more susceptible to fire mortality than old growth. The fuel density, composition, and acreage of stump-sprouted, second growth forest can engender a fire, such as has not been seen in thousands of years, and certainly hot enough to cause widespread mortality.

Unfortunately, the consequences only begin there.

High fire temperature accelerates erosion. It consumes more organic matter in soils than a cooler fire, reducing the adsorptive capacity to retain and percolate rainwater. Winter raindrops, unimpeded by cover, impinge soil particles, loosening and entraining them into an abrasive slurry. The combustion of branches and leafy organic matter on the ground allows acceleration of the runoff into downstream rills. These transport the soil and cut into the supporting sandstone and shale. The cutting process is especially rapid in alluvia that buttress weak sedimentary ridges. The process cause landslides.

Landslides provide a medium for the transport, germination, and maturation of weeds in full sun. Species such as French Broom, star thistle, Russian bullthistle, German ivy, acacia, eucalyptus, cat's ear, herbaceous hemlock, and various, aggressive pasture grasses are spreading along roadsides and the banks of creeks, poised to establish over wider areas. These plants establish much more rapidly than do most natives, and many produce huge amounts of persistent seed. Broom seed lies viable for up to 70 years. Eucalyptus seed can float a quarter mile on fire drafts. Fire fighting equipment can transport the seed large distances and into new watersheds. Once established, these invaders would likely remain dominant, and extend in scope with each subsequent fire, eventually resulting in a complete destruction of native habitat. The composition of insect populations, herbivores, and predators changes radically. With the continued spread of weeds, many of them toxic, the entire food chain may be permanently altered.

The sad fact is that much of the forest is in no condition to recover from catastrophic fire to anything resembling primeval structure. The fuel levels are too high, the size of area threatened by fire is too large, and the exotic species are too aggressive and well distributed. Massive, hot fires in Santa Cruz will have enormous secondary environmental consequences for native species. (See Endnotes under this section for listed abstracts on fire.)

The response of many environmental groups is to "leave it alone," with the idea that nature will select the stronger trees, while the others will fail, fall, and build soils. Many erroneously believe that native plants are best adapted to this region. There are open suggestions that we have only to wait 200 to 500 years and that we should not judge a preservation policy until then. This presupposes that the forest will successfully compete with exotic species and that we could then reverse course should that theory prove incorrect.

Given the spread of exotic pests, their progress belies the preservationists' "promised" outcome. It leads one to question the ability of preservationist groups to deliver upon their promises, once they have increased the acreage under their control by a factor of hundreds. If they extend such a policy and it proves to be in error, it is also cause for concern about the risks to ecosystem health or our ability to reverse course. This is to say nothing of the effects of conflagration or toxic weeds on animals or, for that matter, people.

Doesn't this seem like an obvious scenario? Why is it that the activists and political appointees seem so unconcerned about fire risk and the resulting damage to watersheds? Is there something intrinsic to the management system that abets denial of such an inevitable result?

You Can't Get There from Here

Political and legal means were used to rape the land. Now we use political and legal means to either "preserve" or regulate it. Are such means capable of delivering ecological health?

The issues of action revolve around means to ends. The operating principles of present environmental management systems are defined and enforced by the same tools that were originally used to create environmental problems. Although the ends appear different, the means haven't changed (when you confront the evidence in Parts II, IV, and V, you'll wonder if the ends have really changed either). The problem is that civic ecosystem management is structurally incapable.

One hundred fifty years ago, economic progress was the consensus goal and the political resource management system made it happen. People wanted cheap materials for houses and supported the public sales of timberland at virtually no cost. People didn't care how many trees were cut, because they were perceived as plentiful and remote. Such popular license was also a serious matter of cultural respect for private property rights.

Over the 19th Century, civic authorities ignored or deferred assigning accountability for environmental damage. Whether it was associated with mining, manufacturing, transportation, or agriculture, government made the final decisions about permits, leases, homesteading, or transportation subsidies. Government also chose to ignore pollution, erosion, or automobile safety until they were serious problems.

The early manifestations of civic management took two forms. The first was dispensation from responsibility (the history of air and water pollution are easily understandable examples). The second form was direct subsidy such as mining claims, agricultural price supports, water projects, and public roads. Individuals and corporations have gained these dispensations and subsidies by political and legal means.

Once people have the spare time to enjoy the benefits of an industrial society, they start to think of relative luxuries, like parks and recreation. They also have the option to feel remorse for the damage done in the past. Rather than buying the resource companies outright and making the desired changes, they make the political contributions, prod the media, and sponsor the appropriate lawsuits to halt access to resources they no longer need and can afford. It is then that the public in general learns to characterize timber industry as robber barons, and advocates passage of measures to preserve "our" forests.

It's cheaper than buying and competing.

When a democratic majority of the voting public took interest in environmental degradation, government forced a change in policy. Although the priorities changed, that transformation employed the same political and legal means as originally used to abet the perpetrators. The intent to improve might seem to be genuine, but are the priorities truly any more ecologically sound?

Trees are politically popular, but we have more forest in Santa Cruz County now than in centuries prior. We are rapidly losing are meadows, coastal parkland, and functional estuaries. Urban development has concentrated in meadows and estuarine landfills because construction and operating costs are lower than in forests. So what do the activists shout about? Forests. Where is the biodiversity and threatened critical habitat? Meadows and estuaries!

Don't these cases sound like the same political and legal decision-making system at work instead of a truly new direction? It is still one group using government to control resources and forcing another group to pay for it.

In that respect, the environmental movement is nothing new. These are blanket prescriptions and extreme solutions because they are political. They are coercive because they are legally mandated. They are inflexible and oversimplified because they are legally enforceable and bureaucratically expedient. In any case, the means are divorced from ecological needs by the narrowly suspect interests of the proponents.

Is it possible that the use of political and legal coercion for the control of resource lands is The Problem? The framers of the Constitution regarded this type of land management as symptomatic of the evils of democracy.

Could we use a free market to identify motives to account for externalities as a self-regulating system, instead of political and legal manipulation? This is not just a matter of which "side" of the environmental debate does a better job of facilitating ecosystem health and human prosperity. It is not a matter of whether we should allow people to do whatever they want, or whether humans must withdraw from ecological intervention to protect or repair The Environment; it is that political and legal processes are the wrong tools

Legal processes are designed as winner-take-all battles decided by the uninvolved and technically incompetent. The assumption is that the technically competent are likely both to be involved and biased. Specialists often lack communications skills with which to make choices understandable to the unschooled, and they are not usually prone to interdisciplinary perspective.

Political processes are no better. Allegiances to voters no more create optimal syntheses of divergent philosophies, than do legal cases. They are still bipolar decisions that mandate compromises among extremes. In cases where one side does not win outright, the warring factions trade whatever they value least. The important factors go one way or the other, depending upon whom is in power, seldom reflecting a harmony of any philosophy.

Within the respective political constituencies, it is extremists who take charge of the group agenda. These are the people who personally benefit enough to expend the energy toward their respective agendas. Extremists are incapable of either compromise or weighted analyses of relative risk because the competing extremists within their group will tolerate them as leaders only as long as the majority perceives that they are succeeding. Political and legal control systems are thus open invitations to manipulation by those with the most to gain. It is deep ecologists, corporate grant-makers, and industry lobbyists who define the agenda for environmental decisions, whether anybody else likes it or not.

The inherent complexity and intensity of democratic struggles over land use is the reason the decision-making process was delegated to appointed panels of experts in State boards. Unfortunately, as the power of both activists and lobbyists has grown, as rules have propagated into thousand-page manuals and the competing interests of numerous federal agencies and court cases has come into play, the pressures on these panels of political appointees have left them with fewer options. Management by appointed boards has consequently devolved to its political and legal origins.

So here we are, with a rural/suburban forest in Santa Cruz County. Between catastrophic fire risk and forest development, the timber industry and the preservationists, crumbling roads and threatened riparian habitat, Sustainable Development and the Agenda 21, nonpoint silt regulations and lagoons filled with dirt, or exotic species and the fear of pesticides, the problems of Santa Cruz County represent a classic (if somewhat exaggerated) case of the pressures and issues to be found affecting The Environment nationwide, and the ability of stringent government control systems to manage them.

How is it working?

Part II   The Forest for the Trees

The Unintended Consequences of Civic Regulation

Part II covers the history of timber regulation and taxation, and their effects on the redwood timber market. Part II is a retrospective examination of the motives, means, and results of civic regulatory systems. The historic record of activism and regulation reveals that when activist coalitions and government gain the power to regulate, that power grows unchecked and is turned to corrupted purposes. The chapters provide an inventory analysis of the timber market, a cash flow analysis of timberland ownership, and covers the encroachment of residential development through manipulation of zoning laws and harvest regulations.

It is upon the distinctions between civic regulation versus the free-market system proposed in Part III that the rest of the book is built. Without them, the proposals would devolve to mere theory. Practical application is what gives simple principles their power and reveals new applications.

Part II is a story of market manipulation by residential developers enacted through politicians, Agency professionals, and environmental activists. The historical cause and effect relationships presented here are relatively new, even to those who are familiar with environmental policy and real estate markets. There is much information that may seem incidental, but is critical to understanding the competitive efficacy of the suggested solutions.

These analyses will be conducted in three chapters:

Chapter 1 – Gamecock Canyon, Proof of Principle is a historical recount of a local logging job and its political role in local rule-making. The events of this story detail the destructive acts of activists and demonstrate the skewed forces operating upon the timber industry.

The remaining chapters are more technical and analytical:

Chapter 2 – For Love or Money? – An Overview of Redwood Timber Markets exposes the historic effects of regulation on the redwood harvesting rates. It details the surprisingly counterproductive effects of political regulation on redwood market behavior.

Chapter 3 – Developing Hostility: Conversion to Residential Use compares the relative profitability of different timber management schema and demonstrates that policies operating on timberland may well have been manipulated to convert its use to residential development.

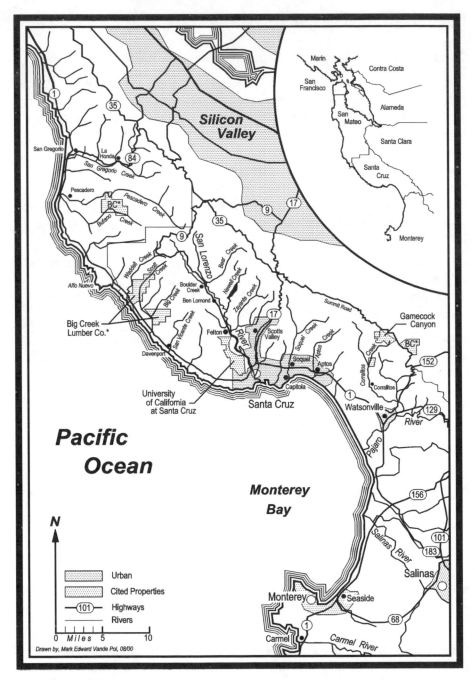

Figure 1 – Map of the County of Santa Cruz, *sources are ICEMaps2, EPA River Reach Files, and property owners. Summit Road (State "Highway" 35, two lanes, if that) follows the central ridge of the Santa Cruz Mountains.*

Chapter 1 – Gamecock Canyon, Proof of Principle

The Ugly Side of Selfish Activism

The following story details the legal and political fight over a real logging job. This case study illustrates a number of symptoms that demonstrate why a change in environmental management systems is needed:

- It demonstrates the principles discussed in Part I.
- It exposes the unintended consequences of civil disobedience and political control systems when they interact with business.
- It provides a technical overview of ecological issues pertinent to timber harvesting in rural/suburban forests and commonly used as justification for civic takings, nationwide.
- It familiarizes the reader with business principles by which applications of the free-market management system are more easily understood.

Gamecock Canyon involved nearly every technical issue used by the activist community to halt timber harvesting: roads, riparian corridors, coho salmon, stream temperature, sedimentation, landslides, old growth, riparian canopy, spotted owls, red legged frogs, canopy insects, and water quality.

The political struggle involved nearly every activist tactic seen in battles over resource land: false technical citations, denial of use of public assets, media posturing, a sacrificial poster child, a fall guy, ineffectual enforcers, physical intimidation, equipment sabotage, permit delay, fines, and pointless lawsuits.

The main element in which Gamecock Canyon was a tragedy had nothing to do with the actual logging job and everything to do with the consequences of how it was used for political purposes. Misleading arguments, attributed by the activist community to the job, were used to justify legal "protections" that eliminated approximately half of softwood timber harvesting in the County. The policy will eventually have enormously destructive consequences. These will be discussed in the remainder of Part II and periodically in Parts IV & V. Meanwhile, **the activists' own behavior made the damage that was done on the job-site worse than it would have been without that struggle.**

Gamecock Canyon did not have to happen as it did, but not for the reasons popularly believed. Everybody could have a timber harvest of which any community should have been proud and done so at a profit. That it transpired as it did is an example of why struggles through character assassination, protests, and lawsuits are so destructive to our ability to nurture both forests and efficient and constructive governance.

Gist in Case

The Santa Cruz Mountains form an ideal bedroom community for the over-stressed working professional. This class of people works at full throttle over the hill in Silicon Valley on the wrong end of an interminable commute. Many Sierra Club posters and calendars adorn the "walls" of their cubicle cellblocks, reminders amid the unrelenting panic, that life exists outside. It is a promise of escape, something permanent, peaceful, and inviolate.

A common dream is to own a bit of that promise of making it big and buying that house, with a hot tub and a horse corral in the quiet of the mountains. Typically, the new owners buy that home "for the view," as far away from the insanity as they dare commit time for commuting. They prefer the edges of large properties of maybe a hundred acres or more: "Timber Preserves." Houses adjacent to timber parcels are advertised as particularly desirable because they are unlikely to be fully developed and offer "free" access to the forest for recreational purposes.

Many such advertisements are found in a free monthly newspaper, the Mountain Network News. The paper rarely covers overcrowded forests, the severity of fire hazards, the spread of weeds, residential drainage problems, or the spread of development in general. Instead, more than sixty percent of the advertising space is for residential real estate. Over the last decade, few topics in the paper has covered more column inches than logging. The owner/publisher/editor networked the local activist groups on his website: Summit Water Protection League, Neighbors for Responsible Logging, Citizens for Responsible Forest Management, and, of course, the Sierra Club. They post their angry letters and exhort each other to greater heights of activism against the "timber industry," all for free. By the time the readers, unfamiliar with the technical issues have spent years intellectually surrounded by interdependent truisms, is it any wonder they end up feeling the need for protection from industrial timber harvests?

Large corporate timber interests have the motive and money to exploit loopholes in the law, stall, and drain the legal resources of such opposition. Once the trees are down there is no issue until they grow back. Large timber operators have a competitive advantage over real victims in the battle: small forest landowners who routinely exceed the standards set by law. These are usually families that have held a between a hundred and a few thousand acres for generations. They need the timber companies to harvest and buy their logs and must pay for legal resistance to additional regulations against an opponent financed by their taxes. The resource value of the land is so distressed and the cost of maintaining it so high, that they face great temptation to sell to developers of residential real estate. These same developers can pay the politicians, buy the media space, and sell to those same suburban residents who think what they are told to think. The developers can then laugh all the way to the bank, along with the County Tax Assessor.

All that is needed to continue the political justification for more laws with which to depress the resource value of land is a few cases, celebrated in the media as "bad timber harvests." Such a case was Gamecock Canyon.

A Cast of Character

Gamecock Canyon is a 900-acre parcel located in southeastern Santa Cruz County on Summit Road, north of State Highway 152 (see Map on page 52). It remains one of the few parcels in the County, large enough for industrial logging. It is a steep-walled valley with the San Andreas Fault running down the middle, currently too remote to be suitable for residential development. It has a redwood forest that had been clearcut in 1893. A redwood can grow to 200 feet in height and from one to five feet in diameter in that time.

The timber industry had significantly declined in Santa Cruz County. The Scarborough Lumber Mill in nearby Scotts Valley had just shut down for lack of steady volume. The only mill left (Big Creek Lumber Co.) was operating at full capacity and could not justify a second shift in such a contentious political climate. Big Creek wasn't paying much for logs because the local supply of logs was more than their mill alone could handle.

Several local buyers had considered purchasing Gamecock Canyon. It is an expensive place to work: large, steep, and located in a politically contentious area. Access was not certain and the stands were somewhat sparse. Loans for large land purchases are usually risky and expensive, with points, high rates, and short-term balloon payments. Few can afford them.

The bid went to a recent player in the local market, Roger Burch. His company, Redwood Empire, has a sawmill in Cloverdale, CA, about 150 miles to the north. Privately held timber was becoming scarce up there, in large part due to regulations protecting the Spotted Owl. Roger had bought excess logs from various forest landowners in Santa Cruz, offering more than Big Creek would pay. Roger saw a competitive advantage in owning more land that could supply a steadier flow of logs to his mill. Like any ambitious person, Roger bought the largest available parcel he could afford that was ready for harvest: Gamecock Canyon.

Mr. Burch was aware of the timber politics of Santa Cruz County, and was confident that he could overcome the politics. In an office setting, he is a tough competitor. On the job site when given a choice, Roger will usually do the right thing. In his mind, the local activists would never be satisfied by anything he could do and remain competitive.

Peter Twight wrote the Timber Harvest Plan (THP) in Gamecock under direction of Zeke Sechrest as the Licensed Registered Professional Forester (RPF) for Redwood Empire. Peter's goal was to gain high growth rates into the future. Growth is pure capital gain and he knows well how to get it: First, thin the forest to reduce the competition for summer water and for light, then plant redwood to replace the tanbark oaks, overcrowded because of the original clearcut-and-burn process. The result would be a healthier forest.

Mr. Twight takes pride in his work. As a consultant to the Sierra Club, he had helped draft the landmark Forest Practice Rules of 1973, the most significant improvement in forest standards in many years. He remains proud of that achievement. He believes that the law he helped originate is adequate for both habitat protection and sustainable forest production. He believes that his practices exceed the requirements of the law. To him, additional concerns are based upon misinformation.

When Roger bought Gamecock Canyon, both he and Peter knew that there might be trouble. Experience told them that it is better to know early and they knew well how to smoke out the opposition. They filed an application with the State for a THP. They didn't have to wait long.

Kathy Dean and Nick Gombos owned a successful gardening business. They had recently moved to a new house overlooking the empty expanse of Gamecock. In Kathy's words:

> "When we purchased land in the Santa Cruz Mountains, we were aware that the land adjacent to ours was "TPZ" I mistakenly thought TPZ (Timber Preserve Zone) meant that the timber was to be PRESERVED, protected and saved."

Kathy and Nick had purchased property next to what is legally termed a Timber Production Zone for access to and enjoyment of somebody else's forest. As far as they were concerned, it was their right and responsibility to save it from logging. She and her husband published their plea to anybody who would listen. She writes:

> "Burch now owns over 5,000 acres in Santa Cruz County. He also has holdings in Santa Clara County and over 2,000 acres in San Mateo County. He recently moved his corporate offices to San Jose. They used to be in Cloverdale, but that's no longer where the action is. Yes, the action has shifted to our area."

Santa Cruz County produces but 2% of redwood production. Redwood Empire has never had headquarters in Mendocino. In fact, RE moved its headquarters into San Jose from Morgan Hill, 25 miles to the south.

Mr. Burch needed a Licensed Timber Operator (LTO) to conduct the harvest. The LTO is responsible for following the THP in accordance with the State Forest Practice Rules. To handle a large and difficult job such as Gamecock requires very expensive and specialized heavy equipment. The local industry was too small to handle a hot potato as big as Gamecock in addition to their existing customers. Expansion would require significant investment in a very risky political climate. RE needed somebody, so they imported an LTO that they felt that they could develop.

Roger contracted Hayward Brothers as the LTO. They were from Mendocino County, further north. Business had been slow up there and Jack and Kris Hayward were looking for work. They placed a narrow margin bid in order to establish the business in a new area with a big customer. Jack Hayward had no idea of the scope of political and technical particulars to timber operations in Santa Cruz.

Tim Peet was managing all RE's jobs in Santa Cruz, not just Gamecock. It was his lot to oversee Jack Hayward and arrange for logging trucks.

Here is where the organization chart gets messy. Roger was the mill owner, the landowner, and both Tim's and Peter's boss' boss. He maintained subordinates between himself, Peter, and Jack, the only player on site not accountable to Roger. In every case, there is a person without final decision-making accountability between the LTO and those financially responsible. Tim is on the job site, but Peter has the authority. Peter's only real power is to shut the job down. With the landowner and company president on both ends of the cash flow, that isn't easy. There would have to be hard justification before Peter did anything that drastic.

CDF inspector, Steve Hollett, had to keep the peace knowing that. His direct contact was first the LTO (Jack), then Peter, the forestry professional. If it is a real problem, he goes to Peter. If he can't get it done there, he has to call for CDF management backup.

The Kitchen Sink

Kathy's first move was to stall the THP, citing technicalities regarding the transformation products of timber production:

> "The County of Santa Cruz appealed the original RE Timber Harvest Plan (THP) because of the potential damage to a $35,000.00 trout restoration project they had just completed directly downstream from the harvest area. They also appealed because GCC contained some of the only significant stands of old growth left in the County. Gamecock Creek was also a designated coho salmon recovery stream."

The County of Santa Cruz has wanted "local control" of timber operations for decades. On behalf of local activists, Fred Keeley, then on the County Board of Supervisors, often filed appeals THPs toward that goal. The State agreed that there was no coho habitat on the parcel, but there were a few pools containing steelhead on the lower reaches of Gamecock Creek.

The story told by Ms. Dean is riddled with such errors, mixed time-lines, and confused subject matter. (It required considerable research to untangle.) For instance, how about a riddle: When is a bridge not a bridge? Answer: When it is a "trout restoration project"! (The money was for bridge construction to replace a large culvert on property downstream.) CDF properly rejected those appeals as technically unjustified.

The curious phrase in the paragraph is, "some of the only significant stands of old growth left in the County." It isn't clear what she means considering the numerous State Parks in the County. Local activists advocate a law to list all trees over 200 years old as "old growth" (an absurd standard given that redwoods live to over 1,000). There were a few old trees left after the original harvest 100 years prior. Some consider it unethical to remove them.

> "The CDF has NOT required a buffer zone for tree removal along the Class 1 river that courses through Gamecock Canyon…. "

Gamecock Creek is a Class 1 watercourse, which means that it contains water and fish (minnows count). It averages about four to ten feet across on Roger's property, hardly a "river." At the time, there were no restrictions prohibiting logging within the area surrounding a Class 1 stream. Such "buffer zones" were a legal objective of the Sierra Club. A logging project along a Class 1 can be beneficial to fish populations if it is done correctly.

It is popular among activists to criticize CDF and the Board of Forestry, as tools of industry, in order to coerce what they want in the way of new rules. It is a useful fundraising tool to assume a stance as a beleaguered band of volunteers taking up the cause of the trees, against a government agency, supposedly collaborating with industry. New residents, such as Kathy, are planting houses in forests all over California. Protecting them from fire constitutes a hazard to CDF personnel. The people within CDF likely consider Kathy Dean's million-dollar estate, with horse corral and outbuildings, to be more of an environmental problem than is a timber harvest by Roger Burch. Would that opinion make them tools of industry or might they be more rigorous environmentalists than is popularly believed?

There were several Pre Harvest Inspections (PHI) involving numerous professionals. These were to review and approve preparations, the trees marked for harvest, and the initial forest canopy measurements in the riparian area. Brad Valentine (CDF biologist), Dave Hope (County Forester), Jack Hayward (LTO), and Peter Twight (Registered Professional Forester (RPF)) met to cover the special preconditions for the job. Ms. Dean complains,

> "According to Redwood Empire's own forester, red legged frogs may be found within the assessment area. Also, according to the forester, the cathedral-like open spaces underneath the canopy of trees could potentially support the reintroduction of the Spotted Owl."

Mr. Twight is required by law to address the possible presence of endangered species in the THP and prudently declared their presence a "possibility." If the harvest even "harmed" such a species, he could face significant fines. The language he chose requests that the State make the final determination about their presence. In the same file as the notices of violation Ms. Dean quotes, is a Pre Harvest Inspection (PHI) report to Mr. Tom Osipowich, Deputy Chief, Forest Practices for CDF. It explains that the CDF biologist had concluded that it was unlikely that the creek was habitat for the California Red Legged Frog. Similarly, Spotted Owls have not been seen in the County. If they had ever inhabited that forest, Roger would have every financial reason to resist such a reintroduction.

As a final precondition of the PHI, the County forester (who was unlicensed at the time) noted his opinion that September was the most important month for forest canopy, and requested that cover be retained for that solar arc. The objective was cooler stream temperature. Peter agreed to the lower sun angle, although it was not required until it was documented in the THP. It is not clear in the file, whether the concession was in trade for, or in addition to the vertical arc. At the time, there was no approved measurement instrument or procedural standard to measure canopy cover. It was a new requirement.

They were ready to go, but how were they going to get there?

The Road from Hell

Roger needed access to the forest to get equipment in and logs out. When Roger first saw Gamecock Canyon, he knew that there was no adjoining public road and no legal way to cut a logging road onto the property.

Summit Road runs above, but does not directly contact the Gamecock parcel. Although Summit Road had been constructed by the State, it was then under the private ownership of the Summit Road Association (SRA). Redwood Empire had used Summit Road in prior years on other jobs. Roger bought an easement for a right-of-way that went up from Gamecock, in Santa Cruz County, onto Summit Road, which passed right in front of Kathy's house on the side opposite Gamecock, in Santa Clara County. She responded:

> "The day we heard of Burch's plan to use our section of road, we had our lawyer write him a letter that told him to stay off."

This neighborly advice was equivalent to a death threat to Roger's business. The easement seller had put a time limit on completion of the road as a condition of sale, supposedly because she wanted it done before she sold the parcel. The time limit was set to expire before the State would have approved the THP. Roger applied to CDF for an Emergency Exemption to cut in the road before approval on grounds of the time limit.

Mr. Twight reports that the way Kathy "heard" of Burch's plan" was that he had advised her husband, Nick of it as vice president of the Summit Road Association (SRA). Still looking to stall the job, Kathy responded through her attorney in writing and appealed the THP on grounds that she had not been "properly" notified. According to Mr. Twight, Ms. Dean was left off the distribution for the notification of the application for a THP by clerical error. The THP was rejected and had to be filed again though CDF granted Roger the Emergency Exemption for the road because the job was proceeding in compliance with State law.

Ms. Dean continued the fight to enlist democratic support to block Roger's access by publicly complaining about the transformation products of roads. An example is the purported threat of sediment, deleterious to a commons: fish in the water of Gamecock Creek.

Many years ago, people cut logging roads alongside creeks. Some of these roads destabilized slopes and caused landslides destructive to spawning beds (the theory is now questioned). Activists use problems with old roads to prevent a logging job that could pay to retire them. Less than 5% of slide-related sediment in creeks is due to modern logging. More sediment is released from poorly maintained private and county roads and residential development. The historic rights of way seldom reflect changes in logging and road construction technologies. Modern cable yarding equipment can haul 15-ton logs up to roads near ridges, in this case 500 yards away from Gamecock Creek.

The Song of the Valkyrie

So Jack Hayward shows up on the job site, and here is this lady who has been working herself up for a year, fighting a series of expensive legal battles over the impending doom awaiting "her park." So far, she has been losing. Her options are limited. The only way for her to stop the job is direct action.

Jack's first task is felling. She's complaining that the access road he is using is illegal, like it's his problem. He is under contract to get the job done before it rains. It's already June. The one thing he doesn't want to do is stop.

It started with his loader. A heel-boom log loader is similar to an excavator with a big gripper on the end; they are big and expensive ($250,000 when new). When they started it, the engine and hydraulic systems crashed due to the thoughtful addition of metal filings into the oil reservoirs. The loader was history. Tim Peet had the presence of mind to order that not another piece of equipment was to be started, and he certainly earned his paycheck that day. Every other piece of machinery had large amounts of dirt in the crankcase. They called in a mechanic, hired a security guard, and had to park the equipment in a defensible place, daily. They had lost a week.

Chapter 1 – Gamecock Canyon, Proof of Principle

What a way to start!

And stop, and start… Remember: **The preferred means of halting the job is to deny use of a collectively held asset:** Summit Road. Nick reportedly planted fence posts along the road to protect a culvert head from truck tires sliding into the ditch. When Hayward and others removed them, Nick later put up numerous 4-inch pipe poles into the road shoulders at tight corners that allowed passage of cars, but restricted large trucks. RE got a court order to have them removed. Kathy then blocked the trucks either by parking her pickup across the road or physically standing in the way to support her claim that the road was private and deny RE access to remove their trees.

While the actual logging was to be done in Santa Cruz County, the near edge of Summit Road forms the boundary with the County of Santa Clara, wherein Ms. Dean resided (her property ran down the middle of the road). Roger filed for a Temporary Restraining Order in Santa Clara County Superior Court to stop Ms. Dean and Mr. Gombos from blocking the road. She claimed that Summit Road was private and that, because she owned half of the land under it, she had the right to limit such access. The judge said she didn't.

It didn't stop the "blocking" or get Roger access. University of California at Santa Cruz (UCSC) students arrived on the scene. There was confrontation and she called the sheriff. When they stopped showing up, she went upstairs.

> "It got so bad, that we eventually had to file charges with Santa Clara County Internal Affairs, asking them to investigate the actions of two of the Sheriff's Deputies. I had a private meeting with our Supervisor, Don Gage, in his office. Charles Gillingham, the Sheriff, and several County officials were in attendance….they threw it out."

> "I really thought we had them… Usually the protesters are on the logger's land, and they are arrested. This time, Redwood Empire would be on our property, our road. We could have them arrested! Ha!"

Kathy was effectively requesting the Santa Clara County Sheriff to intervene in a dispute over access to a road for a logging job under State jurisdiction, in another County, in the face of a court order. When that failed, she attempted to gain superceding legal authority by political means. KEEP THAT IN MIND. It is a key to understanding activists' behavior on a global scale. To them, enlisting any superceding authority to extend their democratic claims against Roger's use of his property supercedes his individual claim for access because his intended use of his property is in conflict with theirs.

Summit Road is one lane. If she can stop the trucks from getting in, they line up in the opposing direction trying to get out. Cueing logging trucks takes room. There isn't a lot of extra room on the job site for heavy equipment to park. (Try to turn around in the middle of a traffic jam with your competitors in line with you.) The landing, where the loader is working, chokes with logs and trucks. The bulldozers skidding logs up to the landing have to stop. They can't turn around either without tearing up the forest floor. The place is impacted with logs and equipment. It turns into a zoo.

Just visualize the scene. There they are, out in the middle of nowhere, amid the trees. Birds are singing. Wispy traces of fog drift overhead in a quiet blue sky, wafting the soft spicy scent of redwood on a crisp summer morning... Diesel engines are crackling at idle, people are yelling at each other, equipment is lined up and down a one-lane road for hundreds of yards, video cameras are running, cell phones are out, and calls are going all over to lawyers, cops, and executives of various sorts... Meanwhile, tree fellers are sawing away down in the valley, wondering what they are supposed to do next and not waiting to find out (funny how they would rather earn a pay-check). They're clambering around in six feet of branches and trunks piled on the ground, cussing (in two languages), cutting trees as fast as they can without getting killed. The landings (a flat loading area for logs) are rapidly becoming clogs of logs… and Kathy, still there, holding her ground in front of the trucks, saving the forest, refusing to move. You have to hand it to her.

Jack had to stop the job. It is awfully hard to keep a good timber crew when the job has a propensity to start and stop like a hotrod with a bad clutch. The workers get paid for the volume of trees dropped and loaded out on trucks. The money they earn over the summer season is all they have for the year. If Tim can't get log trucks, the money stops and the truckers leave.

Log truck drivers are special. It takes an incredibly skilled individual to pilot a top-heavy, short wheelbase, very expensive hunk of iron with a variable and unbalanced load, over a tortuous, steep, perilously narrow track; some-times in the dark. At times, the road disappears under the front of the hood. Just a little slip of mud can turn tires into skis just to add a little thrill.

Good log truck drivers are hard to find and hard to keep. These people take big risks for very little money. They own the trucks they run. They operate under contract and they are paid for each load they deliver to the mill. If the job does not have logs today, they have to go somewhere else. In order to keep them, Tim has to help them find another load somewhere else and pay more to get them to come back. If Roger needs logs he can get three loads per day locally in Sonoma or Mendocino or one load per day (maybe) out of Gamecock. Which do you think he is going to use?

Several of the delays were over a week in duration. To keep equipment and people on a job that size can cost $3,000-5,000 **per day**. On the days that Jack can't get out at least 6 loads he is losing money. In weeks that he loses money, he can't make payroll and the delay to the next paycheck is another two weeks. Any tree feller, choker-setter, log-skidder, or equipment operator worth his paycheck leaves to find work. To keep people from leaving, Jack had to promise to pay them more. The delays of over six weeks, plus the equipment sabotage, were the biggest financial impact on the Hayward Brothers, over $300,000 (not including the loader, which was insured).

Mr. Burch had more than a payroll to meet. Without logs, he would have to lay off people skilled enough to run a sawmill and then try to get them back. He still had to pay property taxes, utilities, medical coverage, social security, unemployment taxes, and severance pay. If he couldn't make deliveries there might also have been penalties or at least lost accounts.

Jack was surrounded. He had CDF on one side, Kathy Dean in front, and Roger forming the rest of the pen. Peter held a security bond of over $50,000 with which to clean up any flaws that Jack might leave behind. If Jack walks off the job, the $50,000 is gone. Jack had come to Santa Cruz with no understanding of the local requirements, intending to cut trees, push dirt, and yard logs in a manner that is customary in Mendocino. The real problem for Jack was that the standards of Mendocino were not acceptable in Santa Cruz.

Jack walked off the job.

Stream of Consciousness

The County of Santa Cruz cited the status of coho salmon as reason to deny Redwood Empire's THP. There is no coho habitat on the property and some experts suggest that Watsonville, may be the nearest coho habitat, eight to nine miles downstream. There are pools containing steelhead on the lower reaches of the property that may benefit from the same provisions used to protect coho.

The California Department of Fish and Game (CDFG) and National Marine Fisheries Service (NMFS) have responded to concerns about the impacts of logging on salmonid habitat. Logging can disturb surface soils that can result in increased sediment in streams. Mud could smother eggs and restrict the escape of salmon hatchlings. Suspended sediment might abrade and clog gills of the fish. Salmonid species prefer cold water. Tree removal can reduce canopy cover, increasing solar exposure that could raise water temperature and reduce the insects falling into the water to feed the fish. (There are other, more significant causes of salmon discussed in Part IV.)

Adoption of CDFG reviews of THPs caused delays in permit approval and strained the CDFG budget. Fish & Game didn't have trained personnel to inspect timber operations. A compromise was struck between CDFG and CDF that, as long as certain "best practice" standards were accepted in the THP, they would forgo additional site review. It was called the 2090 Agreement, published as a Memorandum of Understanding in March 1996, only five months before the Gamecock job started. There were no memoranda explaining how to interpret the law and there were no specified canopy measurement standards by which to comply.

The applicable harvest standard per the 2090 Agreement for Class I and Class II streams is canopy retention (shade) of 85% or greater, only where there are coho and only within 25 feet of the bank. Otherwise, it is 75% or greater canopy up to 150 feet perpendicular to the bank. Because there could be no coho in that section of Gamecock, the 75% specification applied. As stated earlier, the County Forester, Mr. Valentine, and Mr. Twight had agreed to measure canopy as equivalent to shade retention on the September solar arc. The initial data were recorded using a state-of-the-art device called the Solar Pathfinder, capable of 5% canopy measurement repeatability.

The harvest plan was to save the tanbark oaks and maples that overhung the creek, and take out the redwood in such a way that the canopy would remain. It is a tricky job. To an unsupervised feller from Mendocino, maples and tan oaks are large weeds with no value but for padding the fall of a redwood (they don't get paid as much for cracked logs). The fellers dropped the trees directly onto the oaks and maples and crunched them into the creek. Again, it was an issue of supervision, for which there would normally be no excuse.

The job was late in getting started, largely due to the legal resistance from Kathy. Jack was trying to make up for lost time by using a very large crew by local standards. Local fellers were already busy and rightly feared a political mess like Gamecock. Jack could not get good people.

Felling is the first part of the job and the fastest. A lot can go wrong in a big hurry during the process. Most of it was done in only three weeks. For safety reasons, felling usually starts at the bottom of the slope in the riparian zone and work their way up. (Fellers don't really want logs weighing several tons sliding on top of others back down on top of them.)

In this case, for reasons of access and because of the size of the job, felling started on the ridge, and then went to the bottom while they skidded the logs with bulldozers and made room for the yarder on top. RE had allocated people to supervise the fellers, but they were busy managing the job at the top and dealing with Kathy. The destruction of the canopy along the creek was done before they knew how bad it was going. In hindsight, RE was undermanned to supervise a large and inexperienced crew, in two places at once, AND deal with Kathy, for which they are technically accountable.

Does anybody do their best work in the middle of a fight?

CDF officials arrived to measure canopy reduction using a simple, periscope-like device called a "sight-tube." RE had recorded initial measurements using an electronic device, the Solar Pathfinder. Sight tubes usually record 10-25%

lower canopy values than the Solar Pathfinder because it is a point measurement, not an averaging device. The State had agreed to the initial Solar Pathfinder data at the PHI and had no specification for canopy measurements per the 2090 Agreement. The Solar Pathfinder measurements recorded a 4% reduction for the September solar arc, averaging 81–86% shade. Sight tube values averaged 57% coverage, reflecting the damage Jack's people had done to the maples and oaks and the differences in measurement instruments. Officers, called in from the CDF Sacramento office, cited the sight tube data and noted it as a violation of Section 2090, stating that the section would not limit canopy cover to September nor would CDF allow the field officers at the PHI make a concession of the vertical axis in return for September coverage. Ms. Dean's complaints about canopy were, in this instance technically defensible, but exaggerated.

> "Large woody debris was removed from the stream beds. The DFG is requiring a FIVE to ONE mitigation, with redwood logs being cabled into the stream"… "for every ONE log that Redwood Empire illegally pulled from the stream bed (ruining coho habitat) FOUR other redwood logs will be placed in the stream. In addition, FOUR hardwood root wads with as much as the trunk attached as possible, will be anchored into the stream bed."

One log had been removed from a creek that had never been coho habitat. This one really upset Steve Hollet, the CDF inspector (and still does). It was noted as a violation. Mr. Hollet issued the citation and RE paid for compensatory improvements.

Was there really damage to the fishery? In spite of the canopy reduction, water monitoring by the landowner downstream, reports that the 1999 average of late afternoon temperatures was 58°F (standard deviation = 2.8°F) with a peak value during a late summer heat wave of 63.5°F. Morning temperatures were 2-3°F cooler than the afternoon values taken at that time. The 24-hour average summer water temperature is estimated to have been approximately 56°F, well within the desired limit. Field observations from various sources indicate that there was no additional sedimentation after the harvest. The axis of Gamecock Canyon is an active fault line. The natural winter "bed-load" of sediment is many times greater than was released by th harvest. Unless there is a major landslide, the water would likely meet drinking water standards for turbidity most of the year.

Trout populations in Gamecock Creek have increased since the operation. There were **two** steelhead runs in 1998 for the first time in many years.

"Total Ruination"

"Total Ruination" is what Kathy called it. It was no clearcut. There aren't thousands of yards of mud flowing down the canyon walls. It was not even the legal maximum under current rules and certainly was better than is often found along the North Coast. There were violations and some of them were serious. The job was just not up to the standards of Santa Cruz County.

So how bad was it? What was in the CDF file besides three inches of paper?

The most impressive fact is that the file was three inches of paper, almost entirely of letters and memoranda. At least four, and often six professionals, attended most inspections: biologists, foresters, geologists, and management. There were memos from California Fish and Game, the California EPA, The California Water Quality Control Board, the County Counsel of the County of Santa Cruz, and CDF from Sacramento. Each visit yielded about three pages. So the average cost of just one of these visits was, to be conservative, about $2,500. A wildly conservative guess at the total cost of the file to tax-payers alone is about $125,000. Toss in the $100,000 each in legal fees paid by Kathy and Roger in the legal dispute, and the cost of the paper struggle alone totals over $300,000. Now the total cost of strife and resistance is well over $850,000 (including the loader).

Would that money have been better spent on the forest?

Most of the problems in Gamecock Canyon were indicative of hurried and sloppy work that bore all the signs of haste, inexperience, and lack of super-vision, much of it attributable to the chaos induced by Kathy Dean. Manage-ment was trying to make sure than nobody popped a cork and did something really stupid (like deliberately hurt somebody). When tempers get frayed, when the job is running late, when people are losing money, it is easier to make mistakes or justify cutting corners. Tim was begging truckers to "please come back" and the Hayward Brothers screaming about why the lack of them. Peter was bidding other jobs and writing the necessary THPs in his office. (Foresters spend much of their time on paperwork.)

CDF was in a hard spot. Some practices were outside of the letter of the law, but the trees were already down. It was still a better job than was typically practiced on the North Coast. In a noisy political environment, where people were fighting over every minute detail, something had to be done. Most of the violations in the file were minor: fire extinguisher placement, litter, hauling on Sunday, and smoking on the job site. Others would have been serious if they had been left until winter, but could be easily remedied: waterbar placement and a few piles of unsupported dirt that needed to be moved and seeded before winter.

Several more violations were small in scale but more serious in consequence if uncorrected. Trash racks were too close to the culvert openings, they were placed where Jack thought they made sense, the CDF spec said two feet or less to keep branches from clogging the culvert opening. The rock used for a particular stream crossing was smaller than specified (six to eight inches not the 12–18" specified in the THP). It was a management issue.

Kathy made accusations of "overcutting" and that the timber management plan constituted an eventual clearcut. The job was a 50% harvest, which means that 50% of the trees over 12 inches in diameter were to be removed. The legal limit is 60%. The 60:40 rule is defined as sustainable forestry under the California Forest Practice Rules but is thought by some that the minimum reentry frequency on a 60% cut should be extended to 20 years. There was evidence in the file of 12 unmarked trees having been removed.

It certainly was not pretty, even compared to some 60% cuts. Numerous scraggly tanbark oaks had been seriously bashed and abraded during the felling and yarding. Most of these trees suffered from secondary infections of pathogens. In subsequent years, Mr. Twight has had 16,000 redwood trees planted where many of the oaks had been. In the long run, the forest will probably benefit.

There were, however, serious problems with the logging that Kathy never mentioned. People get creative when solving problems with no direction, especially when they feel they are getting chiseled. Fellers are no exception. They get paid for the volume they cut. Many of them had little experience and spoke no English. Did RE really have the time to assure that they took the extra care that costs them time and money?

One of those things that "costs time and money" is cutting stumps close to the ground. A cut redwood sprouts new shoots from dormant buds. For reasons to be explained later, it is essential to force sprouts to start as far down the stump as possible by cutting the stump close to the ground. The practice gets more lumber out of the tree, so this is something that both the forester and landowner want. The downside is that dirt eats a chainsaw. The fellers didn't cut the stumps low and this was probably the worst thing that happened. It is certainly what which most upset Mr. Twight, who got Roger to approve use of Jack's bond money to cut them again.

No complaints about stump height were noted, in the file. A cynical might observe that rules about stump height do not inhibit logging. One would then have to ask about political interests misplacing ecological priorities.

There were numerous and probably justified complaints (in both Kathy's writings and the CDF file) about corridors cut for cable yarding. This is a machine similar to a crane with pulleys on top of a vertical tower. The loggers loop an overhead cable through a big pulley anchored on the opposite side of the valley, usually to a tree. The yarder has a fast winch with multiple spools to pull the logs up and out of the valley. (See Photo 2 on page iii, inside the cover of the book.) A corridor is cut through the trees to allow for passage of the logs. If the LTO is good, you can hardly see the corridors.

Cable yarding can greatly reduce the impact of logging operations compared to bulldozers and skid trails, especially in steep canyons like Gamecock. The overhead cable eliminates plowing the nose of the log up the slope or skidding logs with tractors that tear up the ground. A skyline yarder, as was used in Gamecock, lifts the log off the ground eliminating dragging entirely. One must be careful to keep the log from swinging and bouncing on the cable. (Bashing the log into trees isn't kindly to a $100,000 yarder carriage, either.) The yarding operation in Gamecock had been extremely crude. Corridor width was an issue, as was whacking the branches off what should have been "leave" trees. It was a case of inexperience. Redwoods will sprout new branches and the bark will heal, although it will leave a defect in the tree for which Roger pays later in future lost yield.

This was a situation where the system worked. Earlier corridors in Gamecock started out grossly wide. There is no record in the CDF file of actual width, but there was a notice from CDF that future corridors were to be 25 feet or less. As the job progressed, the corridors narrowed until there was approval of the improvement. The people learned. Good job CDF.

Among the violations, there was a note about too many "extra" skid trails. With the forest jammed with logs, the temptation for the "cat-skidder" is to take another path instead of unhooking, dropping the choker, going back, taking another trail, coming in from the top, and then clearing it out.

Another problem was that some of the skid trails had been scratched clean of cover. It is a common practice elsewhere to drop the blade on a cat when skidding logs. It cleans slash out of the way that can hang up on the nose of the log. It also cuts a groove into the ground that can become a wash the next winter. In Santa Cruz, the preferred practice is to pick up the blade on the bulldozer and crunch the branches into eventual mulch. It either takes time and supervision or a locally experienced LTO.

It could have happened.

Another violation noted in the file was that the "slash" (limbs, log shards, and tops) had not been "lopped down" (chopped up). It was piled too high, constituting a fire hazard. Jack had walked off the job. It was cheaper to forget about the $50,000 than to stay. Peter had the work done later out of Jack's bond money, but at the time the job was closed out, it was still a mess.

These are the kinds of things inexperienced people do under strain to recover lost money. In defense of both the Hayward Brothers and RE, these things happened, in part, because those responsible for supervising and training the labor were so busy dealing with Kathy Dean's acts of logistical sabotage that they could not focus on job supervision.

Direct action in environmental activism, as was exhibited in Gamecock

Canyon, was accountable for much of the damage that was done. Instead of blind resistance, they could have instead spent their time trying to help make it a better job. They could have raised money to buy conservation easements to the spots they thought were so precious. They could have spent their time, considerable resources, and contacts trying to upgrade the skills of the people doing the work or assure that they were excellent in the first place. They could have helped with the remediation by making certain no weed infestations began after the job. It would have cost them less than the legal struggle and all would have a better forest if they had quietly done the work. Instead, they chose to resist from the beginning, distracted everybody from the job, and flushed over three-quarters of a million dollars, much of it to attorneys.

There may have been needless damage, but imagine how many species would be lost after a firestorm. Imagine the sediment in Gamecock Creek after such an event. The fuel reduction Mr. Burch performed could well have saved much of the habitat of Gamecock Canyon. Kathy and her friends will never admit that. They should be ashamed. Instead, she laments:

> "I have been forced to hire lawyers to defend my own property rights. We have spent tens of thousands of dollars on legal fees, plus the past 2 ½ years of our lives, **fighting something that should have never been allowed in the first place.**" (bold emphasis added)

Kathy and Nick eventually lost the trial over the road. The real winners were the hidden antagonists: the activists who got their zoning ordinance, and Roger who got his logs. The losers were Kathy, Jack, and (compared to what could have been accomplished) THE FOREST.

The political claim is that this forest is "priceless." It is a word activists use to inflate the importance of their care and concern. This whole argument is about money. Every plan the activists generate contains restrictions designed to make the job cost more or give them advantages in lawsuits, whether they are ecologically beneficial or not. Virtually every accusation about forestry hisses the word "greed." Considering the more than three quarters of a million dollars **wasted** that could have been spent on making Gamecock Canyon a better forest, and the $2 billion dollars in asset value to be taken by the subsequent County zoning law, they have found a price.

The greed they cannot see is their own:

- The greed for power to control how other people's lands are managed.
- The greed for free-access to the use of other people's land as a park.
- The greed for public accolade as saviors of The Environment.

Will activists be accountable for the ecological destruction due to the severity of fires that will result from adoption of their plans? Will they pay to remove the weeds that will propagate at an accelerated rate after a fire? What would they have done had the land had been sold off to make residential plots because of low return on investment when managed as a low-yield forest?

The Chase

Hopefully, you are wondering where the good part of this story was going to be. Why did this happen, and how could it have been different? Well, you might have got an inkling of the latter. Does it seem unrealistic?

Is it really?

Life is full of small choices that create big distinctions, points of divergence out of which large consequences fall.

OK, here is the reward for your persistence. It could have been a totally different story, **but for a small difference in the profitability of high-quality forest management.** As you might recall from the beginning of our tale, there were other bidders for Gamecock Canyon besides Roger Burch.

Who almost bought that property instead?

Bud McCrary of Big Creek Lumber Company almost bought it. Bud has received awards for some of the best timber practice in the world. He owns timber property near Gamecock Canyon just across Summit Road. He is local, knowledgeable, and a provider of jobs at that mill he wouldn't dare expand because of the risks to his future posed by environmental activists.

Ed Tunheim looked at it to buy for some other local landowners. He also is certified by the Institute for Sustainable Forestry, an adjunct of the Rainforest Alliance. Both Ed and Bud are forest landowners with a proven record of continuous stewardship to the highest standards. Both had considered buying Gamecock Canyon. Both are local. Bud has trucking cost advantages because he has his own mill. Why didn't they buy it?

They were outbid, and not by much.

Why were they outbid?

That is why we have the rest of Part II.

Chapter 2 – For Love or Money?

An Overview of Redwood Timber Markets

So why do these things happen? The following two chapters examine historical and technical effects that politics, law, and economics have created in the rural/suburban forest in Santa Cruz County. To attribute such things to taxes, regulations, and court cases may seem odd, but to the landowner, they are critical factors in decisions determining land use: whether to invest in a forest or to cash out.

All prices in these analyses are in constant 1999 dollars. Source data are referenced in the endnotes. To understand the unintended consequences of civic regulation, it is critical to gain an understanding of what can go wrong with political control systems, and how.

The More Things Change...

The earliest land use policy in the United States was to extract resources as fast as possible. Whether the use was grazing, agriculture, habitation, railroad ties, fuel, or timber, forest conversion was abetted by Federal resource policy. At the end of World War II, the U.S. Government opened the forest floodgates to help generate a peacetime economy. A generation of depression and commitments overseas had accumulated a pent up demand for housing. Abetting the demand were the baby boom, the mortgage interest deduction, property tax deductibility, the Federal Housing Administration, the GI Bill...

Although there had been a timber industry within the Santa Cruz Mountains for over a hundred years, improvements in transportation and general growth in the Bay Area had rendered local forests valuable as residential landscape, weekend entertainment, and a source of tourist dollars. The County of San Mateo in the mid-50s and the County of Santa Cruz in the early 60s were among the first to protect proximate urban interests in the aesthetic use of private forests against the negative externalities of timber harvesting.

Bayside Timber Company challenged the regulatory authority of the County of San Mateo with a lawsuit that was ultimately successful in the California Court of Appeal. The outcry of urban activists from the Bay Area induced the State Legislature to adopt more stringent rules statewide: the Z'berg–Nejedly Forest Practices Act of 1973. From that point forward, every timber harvest had to have the equivalent of its very own environmental impact report, the Timber Harvest Plan (THP). The base price of the resource immediately doubled and stayed there for twenty years (Please see Chart 1).

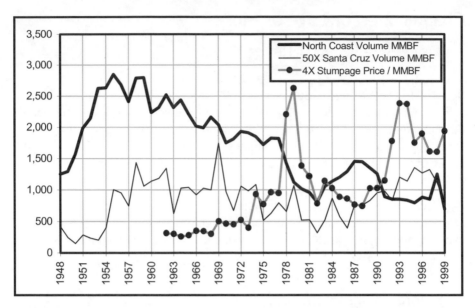

Chart 1 – North Coast and Santa Cruz Harvest Volume/Price Relation–ships for Redwood Stumpage 1948–99. (Santa Cruz Production is multiplied 50X.). Sources: Waddell & Basset, U.S. Forest Service; State Timber Tax data; and others listed in the endnotes under this chapter.

- There was no price response at all to changes in redwood supply until production fell below 2,000 MMBF (2 billion board feet) in 1969. That "small" response was a 60% price increase.

- The first price spike in 1978 ensued when delivered volume from the North Coast fell below 1,500 MMBF. Until then, Douglas Fir commanded a similar or higher stumpage price than redwood.

- There was no production response to price changes in Santa Cruz or any local relationship to total production, until the price increase, induced by protection of the Northern Spotted Owl in the mid-1990s.

- Santa Cruz production is so insignificant to the total market that it had to be multiplied 50X to make it visible on the chart.

Through the 1970s, residential housing demand, as a hedge against inflation and taxation, was rapidly pushing property value upward (See Chart 2, page 74). Annual property tax assessments, often as much as 6%, were forcing out homeowners on fixed incomes. Small farmers were also under pressure to sell, often to the point of choosing between bankruptcy and selling a portion of the property for development. For landowners with marketable timber, there was, however, another option under State law: If the landowner cut more than 70% of the standing volume, the forest was no longer considered a taxable resource for forty years. Like it or not, many timberland owners had to cut old growth trees to pay property taxes.

Between the legal rollbacks of local regulations and property taxes driving people to butcher their land, both environmentalists and landowners were up in arms. The State passed Timber Production Zone and Timber Yield Tax legislation almost unopposed in 1976. Under the new law, if the landowner maintained the land as forest, with but one house per minimum forty acre subdivision, it would be rezoned as a Timber Production Zone (TPZ). The trees would be taken off the tax rolls until a harvest, at which time the owner would pay the Timber Yield Tax. Landowners were giving up property rights to subdivide their land in order not to be forced to choose between cutting trees to pay taxes or selling the land to developers.

Control of the forest asset had been converted to a democratized commons, accruing to the uses desired by urban residents and claimed by taxation for public spending for urban services. Control of the forest was placed under legislative, administrative, and adjudicative powers of the State bureaucracy and has been growing rapidly into a socialized commons, ever since.

The Timber Yield Tax rate was budgeted at the beginning of the year to deliver a fixed level of revenue against the expected harvest. If the size of the harvest fell below expectation, a separate instrument, the Timber Reserve Fund Tax, kicked in at a rate sufficient to meet budgetary expectations. The total revenue requirement was simply divided by the log volume and a bill was sent to each owner at the end of the year.

Now, this was a bizarre system, a truly regressive tax. If the price of timber was low, then fewer logs were cut at lower profit. Lower total revenue then resulted in a higher rate of tax assessments, sometimes as high as 8% on the gross sale! Just imagine: Log prices peak in 1979, landowners, who had resisted cutting, perhaps for a decade while being crucified by an inflated property tax, finally see an opportunity and file for a THP. Then they wait a year to get the permit during which time the price falls by two thirds. Those people were rewarded with a higher tax bill! The State dumped the Timber Reserve Fund Tax in 1984, thus stiffing rural county governments for the promised level of timber revenue and leaving in place a net tax reduction.

The other change in tax policy at the end of the 70s was California State Proposition 13 in 1978. This ballot initiative rolled back annual tax rates from 6% to 1.5% of assessed valuation, and the property assessment levels back to those in 1973. Between Proposition 13, the Timber Yield Tax, and the Timber Production Zone, these changes ended the outrageous demand of harvesting old growth forest to pay taxes driven by inflation.

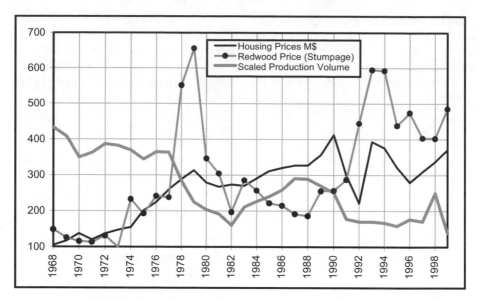

Chart 2 – Inflation-Adjusted Timber & Housing Prices versus Scaled Redwood Production Volume. *The curve of House Prices is a countywide average excluding urban areas such as Santa Cruz, to the extent possible. (See endnotes for source references.)*

- There is an observable relationship between housing prices and timber stumpage price until approximately 1982.
- Redwood stumpage price variation generally corresponds more to constrained supply than increased housing demand.

These drastic changes in tax policy compounded with the sudden and simultaneous end of large-scale, old growth redwood logging through the creation of Redwood National Park (also in 1978). The nation's economy was overheating with inflation. The housing market (then an inflation hedge investment) was nearing historic highs. Redwood production fell by 40% in only two years. Redwood stumpage price shot to an historic high.

The reduction in tax rates and the recession of the early 1980s eased the need for landowners to harvest their trees. Those who had taken the 70% during the prior decade had to wait for the forest to recover. Local harvest rates stayed low throughout the decade. In 1992, however, the Federal government mandated constraints on timber harvesting, pursuant to the endangered status of the Northern Spotted Owl. Delivered volume from the North Coast plummeted below 800 MMBF and stayed there, lower than at any time since World War II. Prices responded exactly as they had before. The pressures to satisfy the market shifted elsewhere, including the Santa Cruz Mountains.

... The More They Stay the Same

From 1950 to 1977, government, through tax policy, was responsible for both expanded housing demand (mortgage interest deduction and inflation) and excess redwood supply (tax-driven cutting). Price increases in both 1978 and 1992 were induced through precipitous civic action at the behest of environmental groups. In no case since end of old growth cutting, has there been a massive price increase attributable to a lack of standing trees.

The current state of redwood forests is thus reflective of the successes of historic management policies as well as their unintended consequences. That history should serve as a cause for precaution: The policies of the last 150 years have much in common with current activist proposals:

- They presupposed democratic control of land.
- They were based upon the political value systems of the day.
- They mandated single methodologies over widely diverse conditions.
- They depressed the profitability of privately held forestland.
- They confiscated the use of the forest for the exclusive benefit of politically dominant urban populations.
- They were enacted through lawsuits.
- There were rapid changes with enormous economic consequences, under a crisis mentality and without accounting for side effects.

Someday, the ecologists of the future may well hold our generation in as much contempt as many now view those of the past; but perhaps not for the reasons many environmentalists might suspect.

Except No Substitutes

As we saw in Chart 1 (page 72), when old growth production drew to an end in the late 1970s, redwood demand had little effect upon price until North Coast production volume fell below 2 billion board feet (BBF). Through the 1990s, the supply volume at which no immediate substitutes existed was less than 800 MMBF, approximately half of the inelastic demand floor of 1978. If that 1990s production level remained constant or fell, one would think that the price for redwood would have remained high. Instead, when the housing market came back in the mid-90s, the price of redwood FELL and remained below peak values, although the supply had not changed (Chart 2, opposite). The term for the adjustment had been four years, exactly the same adjustment period as at the end of the 70s. What happened?

A builder must buy materials as specified by contract. If prices go up, that's too bad, the price is paid. The options are to renegotiate the contract or walk off the job and face a lawsuit. That willingness to pay a higher price in the short term is an example of transient demand inelasticity and an indication of the lack of an immediate and equivalent substitute for redwood.

Rarely is a substitute good immediately available in large volume. Immediate substitutes usually command high prices that supply the motive to be first to market with an alternative. Cedar became the material of choice for outside siding of expensive homes. Pressure treated wood became both more durable and available for earth contact applications. These had been major markets for redwood in terms of total wood volume.

Substitute demand usually takes about two years to develop, long enough for existing construction jobs to be completed. Substitute demand replaces redwood by changing the design of the house. Concrete patios replace redwood decks. Stucco walls replace siding. Decorative concrete and pressure-treated wood replace redwood retaining walls.

Supply substitution takes longer. Manufactured replacements for redwood require development of production processes, supply chains, distribution, sales, and a customer base. By the early 1990s, cemented cellulose, Masonite®, vinyl, steel, strandboard, and aluminum had found their way into the replacement siding market. Composite materials are now gaining popularity as decks and fence boards. Given time, incentive, and alternative raw materials, the market will supply a demand with a substitute product.

Nearly all redwood substitutes require quarrying and/or fossil fuels.

Consider the difference in the relationship between housing prices and redwood prices on Chart 2 before and after 1982. Before 1982, redwood price changes correlated with changes in the price of general housing. After 1982 housing demand was less of a factor in controlling price; the principal price modulator was then relative redwood supply.

The substitution effect is a law of economics, not to be ignored.

Substitute goods limit the price the redwood market will bear for each of its uses. This effect limits the regulatory cost the forest will bear before it effectively becomes a zero-priced good. If the market disappears altogether, will either the forest or humans be better off without the renewable resource?

There are probably some people reading this who will conclude hopefully that, because we can ultimately develop substitute materials for redwood, there is no need for redwood logging. They adopt this view without considering the fact that every substitute good has externalities of its own. Pressure treated wood is a good example: Chromium, mercury, and arsenic are used in approved, water-based, pressure treated wood products. Externalities are worker hazards, waste disposal, energy consumption, and metals in soils.

The problem with classical economics in this case is that the trees don't stop growing. Many second growth forests are grossly overpopulated. Supply is thus, in many respects, more inelastic than is demand. "Some People" please answer: What are we to do to use the excess wood? There are forest uses for some of those logs, but not nearly all of them. How are we going to get the excess trees out of the forest without doing unnecessary damage? How will we pay for it? How do we reduce the threat of catastrophic fire? How will we pay for it? How will we manage the crown sprout from the stumps of those trees? How will we pay for it? How will we manage the woody debris in the creek beds? How will we pay for it? How will we manage the flyways and access to prey for forest birds amid the crown sprouts? How will we pay for it? How will we manage range for large forest predators? How will we pay for it? How will we offset the environmental impact of the substitutes? Who pays for that now?

How do we finance the restoration activities the forest demands? Nothing is free. Take care of the forest or be ready to own the consequences.

As the construction market shifts to other sources of raw material, the economic rent on the land suggests why its use changes to housing so rapidly. **To retain the land in use as a forest requires that we find as many uses as possible for the land as a forest** so that it can economically compete with alternative non-forest uses. That option reduces the pressure on redwood trees to carry the entire opportunity cost of high quality management.

It would also help if we stopped wasting money in needless paperwork. That has its effects on the forest too.

Regulatory Delay and Production Overshoot

One cannot easily just stop a logging job, even if it hasn't officially started. A significant investment will have been made in preparation. An average THP requires well over a year to obtain, costs $15,000, and is good for only three years before it lapses, and five years before it is revoked. For small landowners, similar significant investments are required in preparatory infrastructure and operating capital. These dislocations are less pronounced for large timber concerns that can hold an inventory of allocated THPs.

Consider Chart 3 (on the next page). Until approximately 1984, price and volume changes move in phase. In 1991, however, harvest volume did not respond to the Spotted Owl price spike. In 1992, the lack of an increase in supply drove prices higher into the following year. In subsequent years, although the price dropped, production rates increased and stayed there for the first time. Why?

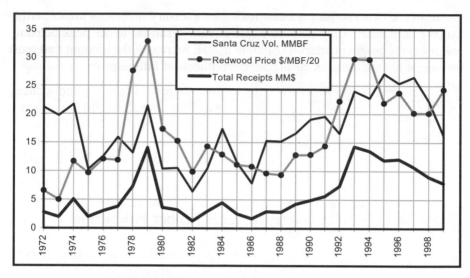

Chart 3 – Timber Harvest Volume and Inflation-Adjusted Gross Receipts and Redwood Stumpage Price. *USFS, State tax, & private data.*

- The transient response time to harvest has increased to over one year. That change occurred around 1984. It is directly attributable to the time required to obtain approval for a THP.

- Regulatory delay can increase the volume of trees cut against conditions of falling prices and declining total gross receipts.

In any supply-chain relationship, slow supply response time induces a larger reaction than would have occurred otherwise. This overshoot of delivered volume appears to follow the initial price increase. Since 1983, increased redwood production rates have lagged price increases by at least a year and, since 1994, by two years.

These response effects are similar to that of a manufacturer and supplier with a poor supply-chain relationship. In the manufacturing sector, Just-In-Time (JIT) inventory control was developed to ease these transitional swings and reduce overall capital costs by releasing production to order against customer forecasts. They reduce the finished goods inventory needed to meet transient demand and lower capital requirements to necessary maintain peak capacity.

JIT systems have the propensity to stabilize supplier prices at a lower level, to the satisfaction of all concerned because they reduce both production costs and purchase prices. Adoption of JIT systems would reduce the total volume of trees cut and sold at discount when prices fall. Until the elapsed time and risk associated with a THP is reduced, these benefits cannot be realized because green lumber has a long lead-time, a short shelf life, and a high inventory cost.

Instability in demand for logs increases the necessary inventory under permit and is a component of the capital required for operations under peak demand conditions. The time required to obtain a THP increases the amount that must be logged to pay for sunk costs under conditions of falling price.

Minimizing work-in-process inventory improves product quality and reduces capital costs. Prices might have risen anyway, but changes could have been more gradual and there would have been much less damage due to frantic harvesting had redwood supply not been managed as a tool of policy. Such response instabilities will remain until government gets out of the redwood production control business.

Taking Stock – Sustainability in Local Timber Production

Activists in the County of Santa Cruz have claimed that recent timber harvest rates have increased to unsustainable levels. This analysis will test that hypothesis as follows: If the rate of harvesting exceeds growth rates at the end of an extended period of steady or increasing removals, a claim of unsustainable removal rates can then be verified.

Forest inventory data were collected over the period from 1984-94 by the U.S. Forest Service (USFS) from the Central Coast Resource Area (which extends from north of San Francisco to Ventura County, 400 miles south). Inventory data were reported in 1987 and again in 1997. The 1997 document reported timber harvest rates for the last 50 years. The data is plotted on Chart 4 (next page), to determine if the harvests were in fact increasing.

Now that we see that recent harvests are not unusual, we will examine rates of growth versus removals. That requires estimates of beginning and ending inventory over the study period. The USFS document reports an estimate of total softwood volume for the County (on page 5) of 812 MMCF (million cubic feet) or 9,744 MMBF with a standard error of ±20%...

Whether ±20% is an acceptable error depends upon the purpose of collecting the data. A redwood tree of marketable size is worth approximately $1,000–$1,500. Imagine that you had acres of thousand-dollar bills lying around every ten feet or so. Wouldn't you want to know how many you had? It depends upon whether those trees really represented $1,000 bills, doesn't it; i.e., if they could potentially be converted into $1,000 cash. When the realizable value is small, compared to the cost of counting, nobody counts and we consequently have only a very vague idea of how many trees there are or how big, much less how they are doing. Because nobody has data, struggles over sustainability get ugly, so we hire the USFS because the measurements are expensive and the results might be contested. Budgetary limits reduce the number of sample plots and increase the standard error.

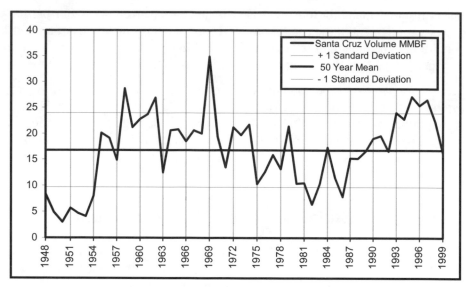

Chart 4 – Santa Cruz County Stumpage Removals 1948–99, USFS data.

- The mean annual redwood harvest rate during the inventory interval is 17 MMBF/year, only 0.5% more than the mean for the period 1948–98.
- There is no long-term trend in harvest rates after 1955.
- The term of the data exceeds the customary reentry time between two successive harvests.

During the writing of this book, NONE of the activists, civic servants, or landowners struggling over redwood sustainability in Santa Cruz County cited this USFS data in public. Thus, this inventory management system yields minimally useful data of which nobody needing the data is aware. It isn't a matter of anybody's fault, it is instead a symptom of a motivational structure, inherent to civic management systems, that produces such results. It is, however, the best data available.

Now that we know about historic production rates and have a source of data, let's consider the inventory balance over the study period.

If the volumetric rate of growth, within the County as a whole, exceeds the rate of removals, that does not mean that the harvest rates on property where harvests are routine are sustainable. Since redwood is, by far, the principal species harvested within the County, the use of the County fraction of total softwood volume for the whole Resource Area was selected to estimate the County fraction of the reported inventory balance. Within the study region, 70% of redwood harvests come from the County of Santa Cruz. The County volumetric fraction was, therefore used to extract an estimate of the average annual growth, mortality, and removals by species and ownership class from

Table 29 of the USFS document. The results for the County are in Table 1.

	Industrial			Private			Total		
	Growth	*Died*	*Cut*	*Growth*	*Died*	*Cut*	*Growth*	*Died*	*Cut*
Fir	4,213	208	0	24,213	2,390	5,642	28,425	2,598	5,642
Rdwd	12,315	446	1,775	71,027	2,523	13,886	**83,341**	2,969	15,661

Actual Annual Redwood Removals	**16,900**
Error, Redwood Removals	7%

Table 1 - Average Growth, Mortality, and Removals by Species and Ownership Class. Estimated Santa Cruz County Fraction of Standing Volume, Table 29 Data.

Even after considering the standard error in the inventory, the data from the USFS are more than adequate to settle the question of sustainability. **The average rate of redwood growth exceeded the rate of removal by over five times.** The inventory error could be huge and this would still pass for "sustainable."

Perhaps it is not enough to know the growth-to-removal balance. What fraction of the total forest is being harvested? What is the total impact?

The production inventory for the resource area is detailed in Table 32 of the USFS document. The County/Resource Area ratio of total softwood volume was applied to Table 32 to represent the beginning and ending inventory in the County of Santa Cruz shown here in Table 2.

	Industrial	**Private**	**Total**
1984 Beginning Inventory	294	3,375	3,669
Gross Growth	136	968	1,103
Mortality	0	(71)	(71)
Removals	(16)	(251)	(268)
Legal Reservations	(111)	(322)	(433)
1994 Ending Inventory	**303**	**3,698**	**4,001**

Table 2 - Estimated Total Inventory by Ownership Class for Santa Cruz Co. extracted from Table 32 data, adjusted to 10 years.

According to the USFS, Table 32 used a more detailed sample plot design than did Table 29 over a longer period than that reported (12 years instead of 10). Even after correcting the 12-year time basis, Table 2 reports that the calculated average removal rate of 27 MMBF exceeds the Table 29 total value of 20 MMBF by nearly 35%.

Whether or not the two tables match removal rates or have large errors from the actual harvest values, the ratio of growth to removal rates is similar for both sampling methods. Over the ten years, of the over 4 Billion board feet of timber in inventory, average annual growth was 110 MMBF while annual removals have averaged only 27 MMBF. Once again, on properties under management, **the growth rate exceeds the admittedly overstated estimate of removals by over four times** with the accumulated harvest over ten years representing less than 7% of the ending inventory of producing forest.

If we consider the actual removals of softwood, against the total softwood volume in the County as a whole (from page 5), including parks, residential, and preserved areas, then **the actual softwood removal rate of 17 MMBF is but 0.17% of the total softwood volume of 9,744 MMBF.**

Compared to the estimated growth, actual removals are so small that one could not possibly conclude that there was some form of hopeful error in the survey. The County must have been aware of it, because the author of the 1997 study did send them a copy. The data had been published and available for over two years prior to the adoption of the 1999 zoning law, and the prior 1987 USFS survey had been referenced on the public record by the County.

From this data, one can conclude that any claims of "unsustainable timber harvesting" were, in fact, more than merely erroneous. The data demonstrate that the publicly unsubstantiated claims of unsustainable harvest rates by environmental activists, as not refuted by County personnel, were so far from the truth as to be considered at least negligent and possibly fraudulent. (The likely motive will be covered in the Chapter 3.)

Unsustainably Sustainable

Please go back to Table 2 and note the degree to which growth exceeded removals, while the usable inventory rose only 11% during the 12-year period. There is a problem here.

One wonders how active timberland in the County could be growing 110 MMBF of softwood annually, cutting 27 MMBF, and end up with a net increase of but 331 MMBF after twelve years.

What happened to the other estimated 433 MMBF of growth?

The USFS reports this once active timber as having been converted to "reserved status," reflecting trees taken out of production by "statute, ordinance, or other legal restriction" (not including the 1999 zoning law in Santa Cruz). It is equivalent to almost seven times the Industrial harvest.

Mean redwood stumpage prices during the period were $500/MBF. Legal reservations in Santa Cruz are equivalent to over $210,000,000 of timber capital. The new zoning law is even worse. What is the total effect on the forest? Regulations severely constrict the amount of land available for production because of the cost of a permit. If we add the cumulative effects of legal reservations and conversions of forestland to residential use, are recent changes in policy asking fewer acres to provide more timber growth?

That hypothesis IS reflected by the data. The USFS Table 32 data for the Central Coast Resource Area reports that total softwood **volume increased** 8% in the ten-year interval between inventories on industrial and private timberland, from 6,697 MMBF to 7,303 MMBF. Meanwhile, privately held softwood timberland **acreage declined** over 6%, from 149 MA (thousand acres) to 140 MA (Table 33).

The land out of production is almost entirely disturbed habitat, much of it in horrible neglect. When one considers the encroachment of development and viticulture resulting from regulatory suppression of timber harvesting, the risk of weed infestations after a catastrophic fire, and the economic pressure on timberland in production, the land use and environmental policies that are advocated by local environmentalists and the County of Santa Cruz are obviously destructive. While forcing consideration of sustainable limits on one type of land, they are growing a forest that is too dense for its own good, and simultaneously destroying the incentive to invest in its restoration.

More offensive is that, while arguments about redwood sustainability have reached levels of near hysteria, almost no consideration is given to hardwood forest. HARDWOOD FOREST ACREAGE DECLINED 18% IN ONLY TEN YEARS, an alarming total (Table 33). Hardwood forests have been victims of primarily residential development and viticulture. Hardwood forests have little to no economic value, while viticulture can generate annual sales of $10,000 per acre. The fact that hardwood forest (with no economic return) declines in area at a rate three times that rate of softwood forest is an indication that **the rate of resource land conversion to an alternative use slows if the resource has economic value.** To save the hardwood forests, therefore might require a way to have them be economically "worth" saving.

The rate of land conversion for purposes of development or viticulture is no surprise. What is a surprise is that the conversion of hardwood forest does not have a higher priority with environmentalists. Quite the contrary, they abet that conversion with the causes, laws, and politicians they support.

That is the problem with errors of inaction: They are hard to see.

The Rumored Mill

The transportation cost in lumber prices is significant in Santa Cruz County.

If the logs originate locally, the cost of trucking is about $25 per thousand board feet. If the logs are exported north, it increases to $75–$100, and again as much to get the lumber back. One would normally think that this extra $150–$200/MBF for the out-of-area operator would give local sawmills a market advantage, but it is not that simple.

There are economies of scale in larger harvests and bigger sawmills, both minimizing inventory and handling costs and maximizing the sale price for each grade and size of lumber. It can take many logs to build a minimum saleable "unit" of lumber of a particular size and grade, because each does not occur uniformly in any particular log. The temporary storage, required to compile a salable unit, induces inventory accumulation and material handling problems in a smaller mill, particularly in high quality grades with large dimensions. These larger pieces come exclusively out of larger logs. If the volume through a mill is high and the average log diameter is large, the operator can accumulate various grades of lumber quickly enough to build a larger number of units of each grade and dimension. This process of value optimization brings a higher total return from each log.

Not only can a larger mill get a higher average price for lumber, economies of scale justify investment to automate the separation, accumulation, storage, and distribution of a larger range of products. Automation has been the biggest cause of job losses in the wood products industry.

Santa Cruz County used to have two sawmills, Big Creek Lumber Co. and Scarborough Lumber Co. These two mills competed for logs, usually originating from small jobs. Both of these mills were small enough that the grade accumulation problem mentioned above applied. Harvest regulations were making a predictable supply of logs difficult to obtain. As a result there are now shiny, new Winnebagos parked where the Scarborough mill used to be.

Big Creek Lumber's mill could handle only so many logs before they had to add a second shift. They would have had to double the mill volume to keep it busy. Any volume in between is losing money. They wouldn't pay much for additional logs until sales and profits justified opening a second shift. The extra margins helped offset the legal and political costs of doing business within the County. Those extra costs and the remote likelihood that they could increase production within the County convinced them that expansion to a second shift was a bad idea.

The low bids from Big Creek were an open invitation for landowners to sell their logs to mill-owners like Roger Burch. Roger started to notice the large logs and growing capacity in Santa Cruz and, quite rationally, decided to cut out the middleman. That is what happened in Gamecock Canyon.

Environmentalists would never attempt to force a landowner to do anything destructive to their forest. They think that they are preserving and protecting it. This explains the denial, dismay, and consternation when confronted with the consequences of their policies. They just blame the industry.

Most people do not recognize the power of economic laws and thus use them foolishly, preferring instead to use political coercion. Simple laws of economics are fully capable of managing complex problems; that is part of their awesome beauty. When activists attempt to overpower economic laws, the results can have all sorts of ways of sweeping around and biting them, aiding the very people they were supposedly trying to fight.

It isn't the ends that are evil; it is the means.

Rules Made to be Broken

The Forest Practice Rules now contain over 1,000 pages, with new amendments adopted every twelve to eighteen months. With each effort to enact new rules, there is a political fight over wording and interpretation that drains everybody involved. Rules beget interpretations, which beget violations, which beget new rules until the system jams with conflicting demands.

From the perspective of system design, rules and enforcement systems are means to deal with system failures. To be fined, one must go beyond the bounds of the law because interpretation of the rules is subjective and a reasonable doubt threshold is difficult to prove. The further a practitioner drifts toward the criminal side of legal timber practice, without facing prosecution, the greater is the competitive advantage in the bidding war for logs. Although a bad actor can lose his or her license, that person can always work under the supervision of another. A punitive system just doesn't work.

One reason for this mess is that many rule changes are written with ulterior motives. Lawyers demand documentation by which to prove a case. Activists seek to magnify the administrative costs and gain power with system failures. Foresters want rules that can be met without ambiguity. The system's attributes end up becoming more important to the transacting participants than is its purpose, which is why we don't have rules for cutting stumps close to the ground.

To provide all that documented expertise, both landowners and foresters must hire State licensed professionals to get the documents necessary for a permit. Every one of these people wants to avoid blame for failure. Each one is, therefore motivated toward recommendations without compromise toward competing considerations, such as minimum total impact.

For instance: To get the logs out of the forest takes a road. To get a permit requires a surveyor to locate it, a geologist to examine the rock for stability and to do a site inspection for fossil potential, an archaeologist to look for artifacts (and often witness the digging), a hydrologist to look at the effects of runoff, geotechnical engineers to design the drainage, grading, compaction of fills, and devise an erosion control plan. That engineer needs to assure that the work is done to specification by having it witnessed and tested at a price that sometimes exceeds that of the tractor work. The owner may need a traffic engineer for the exit path of the logging trucks. Now environmentalists are demanding that the "riparian corridor" be off-limits to the landowner below a boundary, 150' above the "upper full-flow-limit line," as determined by a "professional fluvial geomorphologist." They may need an assessment for endangered species that can require more than one kind of biologist. Now the activists want the roads rocked and oiled, even if they are intended to have bulldozers skid logs on them that make potholes that deflect higher velocity water and... cause erosion.

Those are some mighty expensive roads, especially considering that they are used but once every fifteen years. Maybe the land already has an abandoned logging road that, though not ideal, could be upgraded instead? Not likely, the County wants those "retired."

Well, if you can't do roads, maybe you can use a cable yarder. Cable yarding reduces the need for skid trails or roads. It requires cutting a corridor through the trees across the gulch to the other side of a drainage ditch that's dry nine months per year. Sorry, but that's a riparian corridor now. Back to roads.

When loaded, logging trucks approach 80,000 pounds. County roads often can't take the weight of a logging truck without damage because they are of such substandard construction that the County would never approve them as logging roads! The County inspector gets to decide what caused the damage and how good the repair has to be. No appeals.

The whole prospect of roads is getting somewhat unappealing. One needs to earn money from logs if you are going to thin the forest. The way the County and activists write the rules, you'll need to make a lot of it. That requires more logs, which means more harvest acreage...

Okay, so forget the roads. Maybe you can use helicopters. Great idea! No roads, no silt, no fluvial geomorphologists… Not so fast, you might drop that log on somebody's house, so the flight can't proceed over any part of an adjoining 40-acre property; and besides, the noise is simply deafening!

Isn't the level of sacrifice, that an urban professional and environmentalist is willing to make, truly gratifying? They build a house adjacent to an industrial forest, and while away at work, they don't want the noise a helicopter might make every 10–15 years. That way, landowners can't spend the extra 30% in logging cost so that they won't have to cut the roads those same activists want to be illegal! The homeowners can take solace that the forest landowner wouldn't really save that much money, because they would have needed to cut a landing site approved by the Federal Aviation Administration, complete with an access ROAD. The activists don't want to allow use of an existing landing site on another property with an existing road that is not on the THP.

Whatever happened to "Reduce, reuse, recycle"?

Consider a TPZ parcel with average topography for the County of Santa Cruz. A fifth of it will have slopes over 50% (30°). You can't log that, too much risk of landslides (they say). Assume it has an average frequency of seasonal watercourses of 50–100 yards. The County attempted to forbid entry into any area within 150 feet of one of these "riparian corridors" (they can overlap), so add another 20% to the total area that is off the table. It doesn't rain in California seven months per year, so the bigger trees are usually found where there is shade and water; i.e., along the creeks. That cuts the yield another 20%. Now we get down to the remaining 30% of the board footage, available from the remaining trees. According to the selective cutting rules, you are allowed to take 60% of the trees over 12" dbh by count. OOPS, they want a new rule: "Any tree over 150 years old is now 'ancient' and can't be harvested." A 150-year old tree can be smaller than a 50-year old tree. Without coring and counting them individually, how do we know how old they are? Let's see, redwoods live over 1000 years, and it has been almost 100 years since much of the region was logged. At the time they probably didn't mess with the runts, and perhaps some of them escaped notice. So, those "runts" were, say, 100 years old or less, at that time of the original logging, so a bunch of those might be "ancient" by now... Say, that's a GOOD one!

The fixed and variable cost components of regulatory paperwork consume approximately one half of the Registered Professional Forester's (RPF) charges on an average job of 200-400 MBF. Given the stumpage price during the 90s, the total cost of regulatory compliance amounts to about $35-$40 per thousand board feet, about one-third of the cost of logging the trees.

An RPF firm is paid by a percentage of the harvest. One would assume that their only motive is to increase the size of the harvest. Not so. Many RPF firms instead take the long view that return business reduces the cost of a future harvest and increases profitability. Having the land under management improves the chance to time the next harvest to peak pricing conditions. A long-term landowner will more likely provide that business. That is changing. Anticipation of rules effectively prohibiting harvesting has led some landowners to take what they can lest they be prevented from harvesting in the future. Zoning law in the County of Santa Cruz supports that belief.

For harvests under 35 MBF, the costs of the THP and taxes are such that the job will lose money. The landowner must then pay the forester by the hour, perhaps increasing the cut to more than anyone would prefer. Rule systems provide little reason to reduce the cost of analysis that rightly precedes a timber harvest. Hence is the ubiquity of high fire-danger and poor stand condition on forested parcels with homes.

Most activists believe that preservation is the only safe option. Rather than have their beliefs challenged, activists assail the foresters' data as tainted by conflict of interest. The means by which one earns money then becomes a litmus test by which one can be assailed, negating the fact that a forester needs a forest to have a future. This form of demonization assures that few forest experts whom the activists would respect, would have professional forestry experience. It also negates the fact that many foresters compete by how fast they grow trees, not by how many they cut.

Activists prefer to confer authority to academics, employees of non-governmental organizations, or civil servants, portraying them as impartial experts. If the source of livelihood of these occupations were as obvious as the forest product professional, they would fail the same test of pecuniary taint. The entire structure of academic study and professional activism is now governed by the ephemeral streams or flash floods of grant money. Sources are government, private foundations, or industry, all three of which are motivated by an economic interest in the control of natural resources. The result is that civic professionals and academic experts alike are as likely to be biased by their personal ambitions, as are foresters.

What has been the profit of such an erroneous claim of unsustainable harvest rates to suburban activists? Adjacent private timberland retains open space and a physical exclusivity that the residents have supposedly acquired as "neighbors." They enjoy higher property value and want the convenience of proximity and the benefit of that exclusivity without having paid for them. In order to obtain their aesthetic idea of a view or entertainment, they demand to control the use of private forest by enlisting government to enforce their preference of public parks at the landowners' expense. For example, there have been attempts to enact an ordinance mandating public access hiking trails on private property within the County. Some activists have argued that such rights and privileges were part of an implied contract as part of the purchase price of their house, historically inherited from the original seller of the subdivisions in which they reside. The adjacent forest landowners, however, derived no compensation from the sale of any such rights and made no written promises to the original purchasers of the residential plots.

To acquire control of the use of timberland, these suburban activists have focused upon the transformation products of harvest operations (silt in runoff) as affects a socialized commons ("our" river). Development entails paved roads, patios, and rooftops. These surfaces do not absorb rainfall and concentrate runoff that exits drainage piping at high velocity. Concentrating flow into streams is the primary cause of increased erosion at the base of alluvial slopes. This is to say nothing of the fire risk that they represent. They call themselves environmentalists, but what they really are a is group of spoiled children, using a civic agent to steal the use of someone else's property. It is worse than the pot calling the kettle black.

The activists of Santa Cruz County assert that this fight over the current zoning law is over a small fraction of the land. By their own admission, this is patently false. An outright ban of timber operations on SU zoned land (30% of active timberland) is not a small fraction. The industry estimate is that the reduction in usable land by the new zoning ordinance is 50% of TPZ zoned land, 70% of the remaining area currently managed as timber.

There are 9 billion board feet of softwood timber in the County; 4 billion of which are on actively managed timberland. Between the complete ban of harvesting on SU zoned land and the zoning restrictions on TPZ land, a conservative estimate, of a taking of half of the capital value of actively managed land at 1999 prices, is approximately $2 billion.

How much of that do the County and the environmentalists want to pay? Did they offer their money? There is going to be a lawsuit. Who will pay for it? What would the taxpayers in the County have to pay to buy that timber? A 30-year revenue bond for $2 billion, is very roughly estimated at somewhere between $1,200 to $1,500 per household per year in additional taxes if spread over the entire County. However, why should all those Latino farm-workers in the Pajaro Valley foot the bill for wealthy mountain residents in their personal baronies? If mountain residents feel that it is WORTH taking that land out of timber production, they obviously have some idea how much it is worth. Let's generously say that there are perhaps 25,000 households among the beneficiaries of this largesse. Now our resulting annual household tax bill for those trees comes to over ten-grand a pop. Chump change, right? Did the supervisors tell that to the public before the elections? Did they know? Should they be voted out for greed or stupidity?

What is the cost of the additional fire risk? Will they pay for that too? Will the activists agree to set aside funds to mitigate landslides and additional silt after a fire because they are now accountable for its condition? Will forest landowners be able to sue for mismanagement of their land if it burns to a more destructive degree because of the fuel load, or if fire protection is sacrificed to protect adjacent houses? If there is a problem on the land because of the policy, to whom should they send the bill?

Environmentalists call forests a "priceless" resource. Does it mean they think that trees are worth a lot of money? How much will they pay for this value? Perhaps they call it "priceless" because they don't want to pay anything!

What kind of ecological return are they going to get on that investment? How much will it benefit riparian habitat? There won't be investment in repair or restoration. How much less silt will there be? After the fire, there will be more. How much more water flow will there be? There will be less. What kind of water temperature reduction will there be? It may be warmer. What will the environmental return on that public investment be?

In the short run, however, as a FINANCIAL investment, it's a sure winner. The only remaining use allowed by this zoning law is housing. It is certainly what is what the developers that sponsor the local politicians would prefer and they obviously want to get the land cheaper. Have politicians ever used zoning law to manipulate the use of land in return for support? Have they ever sold that policy in the name of protecting the environment?

We'll see how that works in the next chapter.

Environmental activists in Santa Cruz County are demanding confiscation of the value of the land and control of its use without ANY compensation and without accountability for the consequences. They are taking a productive forest from its owners and converting its use to residential housing. (Some of them even admit it.) By instituting that policy, they are guaranteeing that the forest will be incinerated with all the attendant secondary consequences.

They want it all and they want to pay nothing. It is greed.

Chapter 3 – Developing Hostility

Conversion to Residential Use

Most people assume that "sustained yield forest management," though perhaps not as profitable as a maximum harvest in the short term, is the best way to make money in timber business over the long run. This reasoning implies three assumptions:

1. That sustained yield timber must be sufficiently profitable for operations to remain viable until they reap the eventual reward.

2. That the owner will be allowed to harvest in the future under financially similar conditions (which the State and County have disproved).

3. That the regulatory climate against timber harvesting will not combine with the profit opportunity to convert the forest to residential housing.

This chapter demonstrates that, the way the system is set up now, no one committed to sustainable forestry over the long run could possibly be doing it for a high rate of return. Although there are more benefits to owning forests than just money, considering the cash flow demands, the constant assault on their rights, the public thrashing they get as tree murderers, and the temptation to sell out for development, timber landowners must love forests as much as anybody. Maybe more.

Not for Profit

There are many ways that external factors suppress the investment value of resource land. Examples mentioned so far are: tax policy, zoning law, the threat of eminent domain, the regulatory climate, the competitive climate in industry, and the potential profit of residential development, not to mention natural disasters. The purpose of this analysis is to represent how economic returns motivate an individual landowner to reconsider managing the land as timber and convert it to a more profitable use .

This case study uses financial data from a real forest property: the Newell Creek Watershed in the San Lorenzo Valley, originally clearcut in 1906. The City of Santa Cruz purchased it in the 1960s to protect Loch Lomond Reservoir from the risk of pollution associated with development. Since then, the property has been under the care of Edward Tunheim Consulting Foresters (RPF #79) certified by the Institute of Sustainable Forestry (ISF is part of the Rainforest Alliance, accredited by the Forest Stewardship Council (FSC). FSC members include the Sierra Club, Friends of the Earth, and the Environmental Defense Fund.) From the viewpoint of an environmentalist, Newell

Creek is an example of excellent timber management.

Let us assume we have a landowner of a forest property, identical to Newell Creek, scaled for 40 acres (a size that can not be subdivided under current zoning). Let us also assume that there is no residence and that the property is managed strictly as a forest. We will compare two tax assessment cases related to zoning: TPZ and SU (Special Use) against three timber investment strategies: sustained yield, maximum take, and conversion to residential use.

There are numerous ways to evaluate the return on an investment in a case as complex as this. In one respect, the model selection is immaterial to the conclusion: The degree of profitability between investment strategies is so different, the rational investment choice is so obvious, that any argument over analytical technique is little more than hair splitting.

In this model, a "zero" return represents what the money could have earned had it been invested in a 30-year mortgage bond in any particular year, the **opportunity cost** of funds. A real time basis was selected both because entry, exit, and hold times change investment results so wildly over a period of this duration as to require a multi-dimensional model and because we are interested in what might motivate an owner to convert the use of the property in any particular year.

> **Author's Note:** A description of all criteria that went into the development of the model, the simplifying assumptions, and a glossary of terms are available from the author as an appendix and an Excel file. The model has been reviewed by foresters, an independent forestry appraiser, accountants, tax specialists, and a forest economist. It has 13,000 data cells.

This analysis is constrained to the historic, inflation-adjusted (1999 = 1.0) market value of timber price, acreage prices, property taxes, capital gains taxes, and cost of funds using data from rural Santa Cruz County over 30 years. Return on investment includes income from operations, the impact of interest payments upon personal income taxes, and the capital balance. The return includes the unrealized capital gain, which overstates the cash return while the capital is at risk of civic confiscation or destruction by fire. The capital value of standing stock is not discounted to present value because the harvest date is unknown. Please see Chart 5 (next page).

The high rates of return in the earlier years of the project are due to higher growth rates earlier in the recovery history of the forest. It is a capital gain, but it is unrealized and fluctuates wildly with market price. Meanwhile, the owner is faced with severe cash requirements without an equivalent harvest. Market volatility in stumpage price has an enormous effect on the yearly balance sheet, obscures options, and distorts investment decisions.

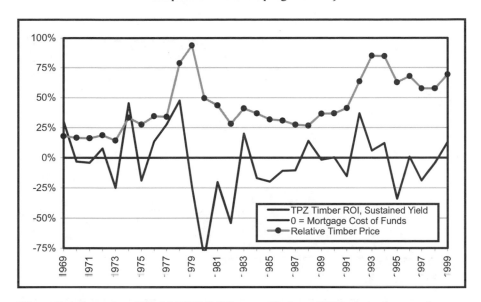

Chart 5 – Sustained Yield TPZ ROI on a 40-Acre TPZ equivalent to the
Newell Creek Parcel (assumes no residential value).

Sustainable forestry, with the objective of enhanced stand condition, doesn't
pay any better than a 30-year, mortgage-backed security. No one would do
this with the rational expectation of making a lot of money. If the level of
harvesting was increased to a rate that matched stand growth after the forest
began to reach a climax state, the model suggests a net gain over the cost of
funds of possibly an average of 1%–3%. This rate assumes that steady-state
growth rates average 3%. This model also assumes that all the capital stock is
eventually recoverable which, because of the changes in regulatory law and
the risk of catastrophic fire, is probably not so.

Just how onerous is the sustained yield case is not apparent until one considers the cumulative capital impact of holding the land invested in standing
trees. While the trees may be growing and look like a return on a balance
sheet, the owner is still making payments and could have put that money to
another purpose. A capital gain on trees is nice, but an accountant might
wonder what the owner was doing, considering that the asset should be
capable of returning the cost of purchase. Please see Chart 6 (next page).

Note that the windfalls of the late 70s were the only return that sustained the
owner through the 80s. In this case, Mr. Tunheim got in a harvest at top dollar at the end of the decade. Had he not done so, the picture would be considerably worse. Once through the 80s, is it any wonder that landowners take
advantage of higher prices in the early 90s? Given that many landowners
have waited 15 years or more to recoup their ownership expenses, does it
constitute a crisis if they respond appropriately to price variation?

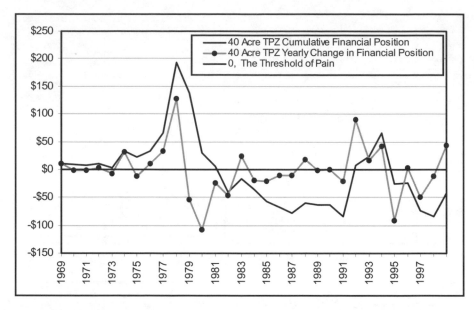

Chart 6 – TPZ Sustained Yield Capital Account *(K$), on a 40 acre Timberland Property equivalent to the Newell Creek Parcel.*

Can you imagine the cash flow? Without a house on the property against which to get at least some utility from the land, how does the owner make the payments without a maximum harvest to reduce the principle? If the owner holds the land outright and is not making payments, this is representative of the deferred value. It looks great if they have owned it for years, but the opportunity cost of the equivalent mortgage rate is safer and less traumatic. This is especially true during the recent years of lost opportunity in equities that are so often followed by lower real estate prices during a downturn. The temptation to cash out is great, especially in the face of new political takings.

The economic hazards are even worse if the parcel is zoned Special Use (SU) or has an identified house site on it. The sacrifices, required to pay property taxes on a parcel with residential potential, are not small considering that, with a sustainable timber harvest plan, the cumulative taxes are seldom fully recovered by the proceeds of timber sales. If the land remains undeveloped, then the full hit for the capital gain on tree growth must be absorbed if it is sold. With inflation, a large fraction of that capital gain is a paper profit that is still taxed when the property is sold because it has not been converted to a principal residence and is, therefore, an investment. Given that the costs of holding property for speculative purposes were originally offset by the ability to harvest timber, the recent zoning restrictions are particularly odious.

Please consult Charts 7 and 8 for the SU ROI and Capital Account.

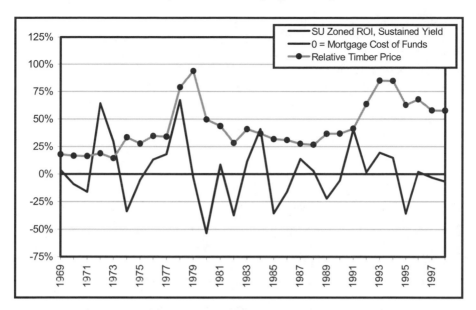

Chart 7 – ROI, SU Zoned Timberland Managed for Sustained Yield *on a 40-acre Timberland Property equivalent to the Newell Creek Parcel. Parcel value for 1972 was interpolated; data were not available.*

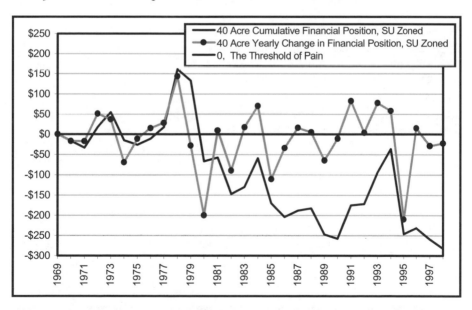

Chart 8 – Capital Account SU Zoned Timberland *(K$), Managed for Sustained Yield on forest, taxes for residential value. Inflation-adjusted cost of funds basis for a 40 acre Timberland Property equivalent to Newell Creek. Parcel value for 1972 was interpolated, as data were not available.*

The model understates the return, in the sense that all taxes in this analysis are marked to market value, not the suppressed rates of appreciation under Proposition 13, because entry/exit times are not established for any yearly trial. The benefit of that lower tax may look good on an operating basis, but remember that a fraction of that benefit is halved by the deductibility of State property taxes on both State and Federal income tax returns. The model also assumes that there is a realizable value to the standing trees, which is an overstatement of the return from the standpoint of cash flow. The standing stock should be discounted for its net present value, based upon an expected harvest date. That could not be done in this analysis because inventory data of trees transitioning to marketable size was not available. Given the degree of market incentive to wait until prices rise, that is risky.

That dive in the 80s is the resting period after the tax induced cutting of the 70s. 1980 and 1995 were awful because a sharp fall in redwood prices combined with a similar drop in residential land value. There was no harvest cash that year at Newell Creek, as had been earned in surrounding years.

When an adversarial overlay of regulatory policy begins to threaten capital value in standing timber, by both confiscating assets and assigning additional liabilities, a capital gain can never be recovered. Thus, an anticipated return on a capital gain is often correctly perceived as illusory.

Taxes and payments remain all too real. How many people have the courage to let $300,000 of cash go out of the bank account in order to wait for the trees to grow back and the land to appreciate while they are making payments? If they were under constant regulatory assault, how many people wouldn't harvest before it was taken? Now, think of how they would feel if, after all that time, risk, and patience, somebody took half that timber value with new zoning regulations? Build a house and sell it, or sue?

Chart 9 (next page) represents the potential to finance the purchase of timberland with a maximum harvest. It computes the ROI, assuming that the land was purchased two years prior (the minimum time required to get a THP and complete the harvest). Again, a return of 0% is equivalent to the 30-year cost of funds pegged to a fixed mortgage interest rate. Typical land-loan costs are significantly higher. The capital value of the standing stock and the cash return are affected by variation in stumpage price and interest rates. The model is thus sensitive to changes in either.

A 60% cut certainly yields a respectable cash return, except in those periods that have sharply falling prices. There is then no potential to make money on the land until the trees grow back, usually in 15 to 20 years. Operating costs are relatively low, as the bulk of the investment has already been financed. This strategy is similar to that used by Roger Burch in Gamecock Canyon.

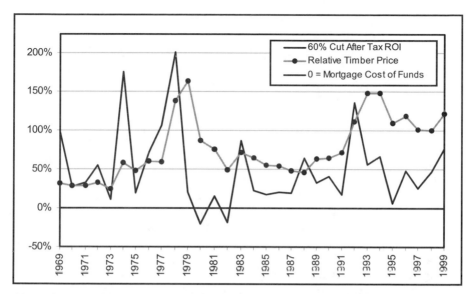

Chart 9 – Maximum Take Potential Return on Investment*, prior to income and capital gains taxes. The property was purchased and logged at the maximum allowable rate of 60% of all trees over 12-inch dbh.*

The point of this section has been this: If a landowner has been letting the forest grow for many years, there has always been a substantial opportunity to cash out. The only reason they would not choose to do so is if they have some other reason for holding it as forest. Perhaps environmentalists should consider what that reason might be... and what might change their minds.

Assessing the Situation

This discussion concerns two specific tax instruments. The first is the Depletion Allowance under the U.S. Internal Revenue Code, and the second is the property tax policy of the County Assessor.

The Depletion Allowance originally was designed for mines, oil wells, and other resources that, once removed, do not return. Because the purchased capital is considered to be the value of the resource when the initial capital outlay is made, the tax law assumes that the capital value is "depleted" when the resource is removed, such as when an oil well is empty or a mine has been exhausted. The timberland purchaser thus has every reason to assign as much of the purchase price of the timberland as possible to trees. The timber appraisers and tax accountants traditionally go along with the idea in order to please their customers.

There is one little difference between a forest and a mine, though; trees grow back. The owner ends up deferring the taxes, to be paid later in capital gains. What results from the use of the depletion gambit is a customary discount of the inherent value of the land, with the purchase price set as if the entire purchase value consisted only of trees. The larger industrial concerns can make a profit on that retained cash as operating capital. This accounting practice is worth a lot to them and represents yet another advantage larger timber companies retain over small landowners.

What the big guys do has to be legal for everybody else; that is, accounting practices must reflect uniform enforcement by the taxing authority. What results is as if the only asset on the land was timber and neither the land nor the ecosystems thereon mattered. Business people tend to notice only assets with financial worth, and can be accused of malfeasance if they don't. This is not to argue that depletion is a bad thing when applied to trees, it only points out that it has perverse effects as a system of valuation.

When the Depletion Allowance is combined with the State system of yield-based valuation, the results compound. If the trees are exempt from property taxes until they are harvested, then the landowner wants the trees appraised as highly as possible to minimize the property taxes on the land itself. Some-how, this asset value of trees ends up being claimed as stumpage, not the gross revenue, net of the cost of operations and yield taxes, because these things are unknown until the trees are harvested. The landowner deducts the timber value from the total market value of the property and pays the taxes on that. As far as the appraisers and the market are concerned, the market value of the land itself is thus, effectively zero. As long as a TPZ parcel is to remain exclusively as timberland, its appraised value is based upon its only source of revenue, the market value of timber.

The net effect of both tax policies is that, if the land is too large for a interest a developer, then the parcel ends up priced at its resource extraction potential alone. That price is usually less than the total value of the standing stock, much less adding its future developable potential. Once over that maximum developable size threshold, the cost per acre drops drastically. The asset value of the land itself ends up being effectively zero.

When the land is considered for its residential value, the trees become worth whatever somebody will pay in excess of its value as a house site, which usually is not much additional money. Once the parcel is a residential site, both the land and the trees end up discounted to an individual residential use.

The State of California and the County of Santa Cruz have historically understood what was good for their income statements. The State directed County Assessors to set the tax base of the land at its highest-value use, instead of its current use. The highest value use of timberland is conversion to residential development. If it is a perfect parcel for building houses and the landowner is growing trees, the assessed valuation and the property tax bill are fixed by the land's worth as a residential plot (as long as one has been identified). Unless the owner is regularly harvesting trees, this is a difficult cash flow to bear. Given the nearly 20% loss of hardwood forest with no economic value, versus the 6% loss of softwood forest acreage in ten years, the policy certainly has had an effect.

Let's use an illustrative example to compare the relative effects of property use on tax revenue (constant valuations for the purposes of simplicity). If the land is 200 acres, it might have a total timber stock value (1998) of $1.7 million or (with a 60% harvest) an extractable value of $1million. The appraised value of the land (without the trees) is only $200,000 (due to the depletion gambit). The annual tax bill on the real property would be about $3,000/yr, coming to a total tax revenue on land of $60,000 after 20 years. If a 60% harvest is conducted once every 20 years, $30,000 in would be paid in timber yield tax, resulting in a hypothetical tax revenue of $90,000 over 20 years.

200 acres is equivalent to five, 40-acre TPZ plots. Assuming a residential lot is worth about $200,000 (a very conservative figure adjacent to Silicon Valley), the residential value totals to a $1 million. Such a property with the trees and the house currently sells for about $1.5 million. If the five parcels are assessed at $1.5 million as residential plots, the tax bill is approximately $22,500 per year or $450,000 in 20 years, 5 TIMES the tax revenue as that derived from a forest. If the residential parcel owner chooses to harvest, the $30,000 Timber Yield Tax still gets paid. Total tax expenses on that $1.5 million dollar investment would be $480,000 over the 20 years against $850,000 in revenue from a timber harvest after paying the Registered Professional Forester and waiting 20 years to harvest. What a deal.

Consider what happens if the new County zoning law prevents access to 50% of the trees. The harvest is now down to $500,000 with $75,000 to the RPF and $15,000 in Yield Taxes. That's $400,000 net revenue against a $450,000 tax bill. We are back to landowners cutting trees to pay taxes, at a $50,000 loss. If zoning laws preclude access to the forest to conduct an economic timber harvest what would be the only investment alternative? Houses. The forest landowners end up paying taxes rates, not determined by what they choose to do, but by what somebody else MIGHT be willing to pay for the alternative "highest use."

What is the incentive for the County there? The average personal barony on a TPZ these days goes for between $800,000 to $1.5 million, resulting in $12,000–$22,000 in annual property tax revenue. Thus, our fabled 200 acres is now kicking in $1.2 to $2.2 million into the coffers every 20 years, versus the $90,000 when assessed as a forest. From the perspective of "greater public good" the land alone can't support the urban democratic demand that its use maximize tax revenue, unless that use includes a residence.

The County wants houses. Baronies are even better.

The landowner pretends that the growing capacity of the land and its support systems have no value. The County agrees that it is worthless unless it can support a house. Once the residential value is "discovered," then it is taxable at that rate.

Does this say anything about how government policy affects how we value natural resources?

Though property taxes and residential housing prices in Santa Cruz are higher than elsewhere, this history indicates of how and why this process repeats itself so often, nationwide, whether the land is in forests, ranches, or farms. So far, we have only discussed half the story: taxation. It gets worse.

De Bait

The remainder of this chapter will explore the history of the conversion of forest land into residential housing. It will show that much of that conversion was due to manipulation of land, timber, and residential value by government policy. It may well have been a case of deliberate political patronage, on behalf of select developers, justified as a defense against "outside interests."

There are only two financially sane uses of timberland in Santa Cruz:

1. Manage it as high yield industrial timberland (which requires expertise, economies of scale, cash reserves, and a thick skin).
2. Convert it to a residential development (connections in government).

It is not currently realistic to manage land as a series of marginal propositions that include sustained yield forestry unless those investments include residential housing.

The cash value of timber on land was once a much higher fraction of the total sale price than it is now, roughly equivalent to the purchase price of the land net of taxes. But was it the residential value of the land that used to be cheap and has since appreciated, or was it that timber was valuable and has degraded, or both? Please see Chart 10 (next page).

What you are witnessing in Chart 10 is conversion of resource land to residential use. During the 1970s, there was good correlation between acreage and timber price. Until 1980, although the price of lots and acreage look similar in the graph, the average acreage was over twice the price of a buildable lot.

After 1980, there was little correlation between acreage and timber price variation. The introduction of zoning laws had discounted the subdivided value of acreage and environmental law had radically reduced access to timber. Lots were now worth more on a per-acre basis than acreage parcels because zoning law unitized the value of both to a single residential unit.

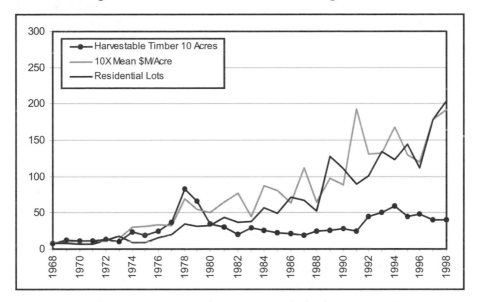

Chart 10 – Net Harvestable Timber Capital per 10 Acres and Mean Price per 10 Acres for 5–80 Acre Plots and Residential Lots*. Timber capital assumes 10 MBF/acre, equivalent to prices of parcels exclusively for timber. (The number of sales identified as industrial timber parcels, was so small that annual could not be derived from sales.) **5–80 Acre Plots** were selected as having single unit housing potential (after 1973 they would be indivisible except as an in-family split).*

What do you get? You get houses spread over a vastly larger area.

Before the late 1980s, landowners in the County of Santa Cruz sold patches of residential plots in the mountains, usually to pay the property taxes. The process established a residential housing market in the County and had a weird way of accelerating the process of conversion. Taxes forced sales, that brought houses, that raised land prices, that raised taxes… Without State Ballot Proposition 13 and the Timber Yield Tax legislation in the late '70s, those parcels would have been sold as residential plots long ago.

If a cash flow can be generated through logging, the cost to set up the land for development is more affordable. The house pads are cut (landings), the driveways are in (skid roads), the surveys are done, and the views will sell. They're profitable (Please see Chart 11). In Santa Cruz County, the process has moved so rapidly that it is almost complete. Look out North Coast.

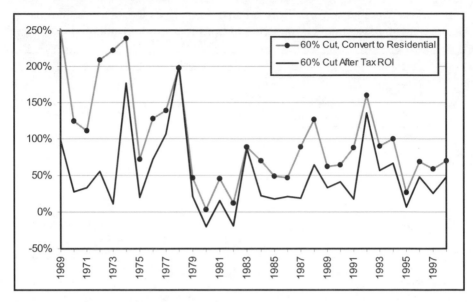

Chart 11 – 60% Cut Return on Investment *on a 40 acre property compared to Logged and Developed ROI when then subsequently sold as residential acreage within two years*

It doesn't matter whether the buyer is a large timber corporation, government park, or a complete conversion in use to a residence or viticulture. The one thing that is certain is that, under these circumstances, the land use is unlikely to remain a forest under the economic pressures of current policy.

This process, of valuing resource land as unit residential value, has progressed rapidly from Santa Barbara to Mendocino, the Sierra Foothills, and elsewhere in the nation, with the rapid development of timber, farm, and ranch lands. The next section will show how zoning law, supposedly intended to resist development, abetted the conversion of resource land to development by depressing its purchase price and raising residential demand.

More Is Less

Trees grow, but dirt doesn't, and in Santa Cruz County, dirt shrinks. When developers run out of dirt to build houses, they have no choice but to go find more lots or go out of business. As the price of land rises along the coast and in Silicon Valley, "more" has historically been resource land: timber or agriculture. It's that big development machine, churning out subdivisions and strip malls, that seems bent upon absorbing the whole State of California.

Most of the people of Santa Cruz County didn't want "more," especially in the mountains and along the coast. All it meant to them was more traffic, more sprawl, more smog, and less space to play. But there was another group that felt differently, and they were in charge. This was a group of special people, who had started out with big chunks of dirt in the '40s and '50s, and made a business of subdividing it, developing residential housing, or leasing commercial property. Each time around the buy-in was higher. The key to profit was to suppress the price of raw material while managing the supply of developable land to keep out the competition. That takes power.

There were bigger players in the development business from out of town, who had seen the opportunity in Santa Cruz and wanted in. To "buy low and sell dear," without bringing in competition that would normally raise prices, requires the power to violate the laws of supply and demand; i.e., the power to control the use of property. The only power government has in that regard is zoning. Some question the Constitutional legitimacy of zoning to alter the value of property without just compensation for that reason alone.

Before the mid-'70s, all that was required to divide a property was to record a split on the title. The development of the microprocessor in Silicon Valley generated sufficient demand for housing to motivate rampant divisions of parcels down to as little as one quarter acre. A parcel that small hardly left room for a driveway and septic system. Various towns within the County were fast converting to sprawling suburbs, characteristic of urban California development. There were complaints relating to the quality of such development, problems with roads, drainage, erosion, and septic systems necessitating more discretion in land use. It was the same over much of California.

In 1972, the State instituted the Subdivision Map Act, placing control of all subdivisions in the State under county jurisdiction. The County of Santa Cruz immediately initiated a 2.5-acre minimum on minor land divisions. The thought was to require the developers to buy more land at higher cost per unit, thus abating the demand for land and forcing less construction of higher value houses. There was no compensation to property owners, whose land had been reduced in value through loss of developable potential. Instead, that value accrued to those who already held houses and whose property value rose due to a constrained supply. Of course, it didn't hurt the people who held already subdivided land either. Please see Chart 12 (next page).

The most significant feature on the graph is the drop in acreage prices immediately after the Subdivision Map Act. (Multiple listings data for 1972 were missing from the file. Data before 1973 were not used because the number of acreage listings was insufficient to infer an average price.) The price of subdivided acreage parcels on the residential market spiked briefly due to demand for plots with existing subdivisions. Once those were gone, the remaining land on the market lost much of its value previously derived from the higher number of units that could be built, thereon. Undivided parcels were suppressed in price by the continuing availability of resource land. At

103

the time, the percentage of available undeveloped land was large compared to that today. At 2.5 acres per new house constructed, that started to change.

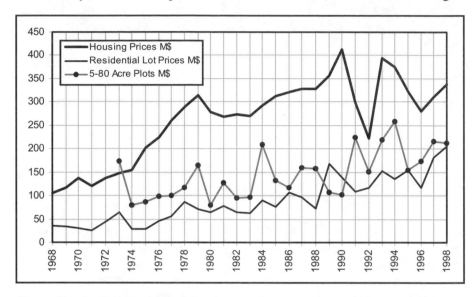

Chart 12 – Inflation-Adjusted Prices for Houses, Lots, & 5–80 Acre Plots.
The plot is of arithmetic averages of listed prices in specific sectors derived from the Multiple Listing Books. The plot of House Prices is a countywide average of rural areas. Residential Lot Price data was averaged among those usable exclusively for residential purposes in timber-bearing sectors of the County. Oceanfront and urban lots were removed from the analysis. 5–80 Acre Plots were selected from the acreage transactions in timber regions as having unit housing potential due zoning laws passed in 1973 and 78.

Notice that first jump in the price of lots from 1971–73 on Chart 12 (the lower solid black line). These were already buildable, smaller, and cheaper than divisible acreage. It doesn't look like as big a leap in price as it really was because of later appreciation, but lot prices more than doubled in less than two years. Houses rose in price about 20% in the same period. Increasing housing prices were thus almost entirely due to increasing land prices.

The tax bill went up with assessed valuation. Annual property tax rates hovered between 6%–8% of assessed valuation; what would be equivalent today to an annual tax bill of over $30,000 on an average mountain home. Though it may have pleased the County, existing residents were not so happy. It was that kind of taxation that brought Proposition 13.

Once the value of land was controlled by a government monopoly, the way to control who made money was to control the way the County drew zoning boundaries. The Board of Supervisors passed the Minor Land Division Ordinance, placing that power under the jurisdiction of the County Planning

Department. It got political. Numerous Planning Directors were fired or quit during the '70s. The newspapers led a public cry for "leadership."

That "leadership" came from a smart politician, whose family had been in real estate in the County for years. He didn't want those big, bad outside developers to take over, any more than his friends did. Were he to take a visible role in defining zoning boundaries, he could wind up in prison. He also knew that voters like to make decisions about the use of other people's land and would believe that the problems of development were a crisis demanding government control. So the Board put it on the ballot and he told the voters what to think. After all, he was "Against Development" and for protection of "The Environment."

It was Measure J, the Growth Management System Ordinance, passed in 1978, designed to "make development more expensive," lower its impact, slow it down, and protect The Environment by requiring larger parcels for single family homes. The acreage minimums were increased to 1 acre in towns, and 3, 5, 10, 20 and 40 acres in the country as determined by boundaries drawn up deep in the County Planning Department.

The Ordinance worked exactly as the previous one had. A "house lot" had suddenly grown substantially in area. If one is callow enough to believe that the only intent of the law was "anti-development," then it backfired. The very people claiming to be against more development had just put the Sprawl Monster on steroids, forcing builders to chew up more land per residence at a rapid rate and forcing development further into the forest.

The first effect of the law was to revalue every existing parcel in the County. The 1-acre minimums in towns made substantial numbers of lots "too small" to be developable. People who owned those "too small" lots before the election got to keep them. Their once valuable property was then "worth-less".

A land rush ensued in those strategically located acreage parcels, with legal subdivisions exceeding the acreage minimums. Which parcels had such subdivisions depended upon where the zoning boundaries limiting a specific minimum parcel size had been drawn. As you can see on Chart 12 (page 107), the spike in acreage prices in 1978-79 was similar to that in 1972. Builders paid anything to stay in business to whoever had the connections or bone-headed luck to have bought them before the boundaries were revealed

A second result of Measure J was to discount the price of moderately sized acreage plots that could no longer be subdivided. If, because of the zoning law, they suddenly became legally constrained to but one residence, that became their worth. This made these larger parcels, outside of town, "dirt-cheap." Note that lot prices at the time were correspondingly unaffected.

The majority of "buildable" lots were on the fringes of the towns. Houses climbed up the hills at an accelerated rate, with all the inherent problems of additional roads and risks of landslides on steeper slopes. Steeper plots had more acreage. Steeper is usually less usable. Before that point, steeper was also cheaper, which meant that now the price of steep was steep too! If it was big enough and had been ignored before, it was now choice property.

Note the convergence in Chart 12 between lots and acreage beginning immediately after the adoption of Measure J, in a manner suspiciously similar to the effects of enacting the 2.5-acre minimums in 1973. This was the first such convergence exclusively due to a relative depression of acreage value alone. That convergence is plotted below in Chart 13. The moment the acreage could no longer be subdivided, the price of acreage went into the tank, while suburban lots held their value against acreage selling pressure.

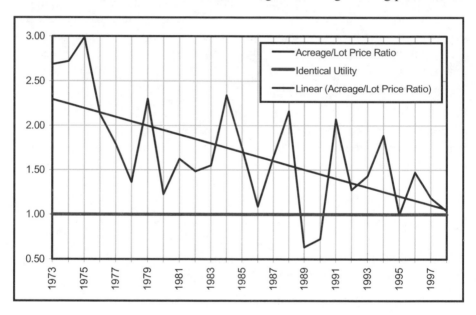

*Chart 13 – **Acreage/Lot Price Ratio** and trend to identical value utilizing Residential Lot and 5–80 Acre Plot data.*

The plot of the convergence of plots and lots, shown in Chart 13 above, is even more striking. As developers run out of lots those acreage properties, that cannot be subdivided or generate resource cash flow, become "lots." This trend is a good an indication of the suppression of the relative value of undeveloped land extrinsic to its worth as a residential lot. The regulatory costs of developing acreage depress the price of rural acreage, as does the inability to recover its resource value via logging. The regulatory removal of assets such as riparian water, timber, and game also depresses rural land prices. Indeed, these assets are now considered, by many, to be financial liabilities, due to the regulatory risks governing endangered species, and now myriad other similar discretionary interpretations of the administrative rules.

If the price convergence shown on Chart 13 between parcels and lots was converting the land to residential use, one would expect the market to confirm the theory. Of particular interest, then would be the years that the prices converged to unity. Notice that in 1989, the price of a parcel fell below the cost of a suburban lot and stayed there for a year. Did the market notice? See Chart 14.

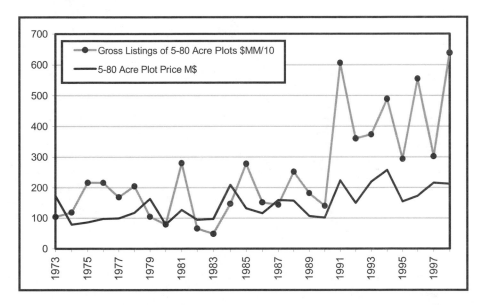

*Chart 14 – **Residential Lot Price** versus scaled **Gross Listings of Acreage Plots**. The latter measure was used to integrate the sales to represent an average purchase price without the occasional larger property distorting the picture within any individual year. The population of sales is too small to yield usable data for a particular segment or location.*

When the price of acreage became equivalent to (or less than) a residential lot, gross listings of acreage properties doubled and stayed there.

Why is this happening?

There is a limit to the size of a development (in number of units) the County will "allow," perhaps based upon the amount of working inventory our developer friends can handle (or the heat the County Supervisors will take). This creates a practical demarcation between what is either a collection of acreage parcels, or a large tract of industrial timberland. Tracts that are "too big" for development, revert to their resource potential alone and are priced (and taxed) very differently from 5-80 acre plots (as discussed in the section: Assessing the Situation).

The timberland owner who holds an amount of acreage beneath that upper bound that is the prime target of speculative takeovers. These people also hold those parcels, most affected by the current changes in zoning laws. What might explain some of the heat on Roger Burch is that he is effectively removing raw material from a tightly controlled, tract-to-acreage conversion market, by maintaining its use as economically productive timberland.

We'll call this little scenario, "The Push":

1. Rezone tracts with future acreage potential to large minimum divisions. The price of those tracts will be depressed by the reduction in their development potential.
2. Big landowners buy timberland, log it to pay for it, and wait.
3. When the time is right, they log it again, develop it, and sell baronies.
4. The County puts up token resistance, justifies new zoning further afield, and environmental laws to prevent "that" from happening again.
5. The new zoning and environmental laws depress the resource value of new tracts and thus the price. The anointed buy the tracts and do it again or force their competitors into selling the property as parkland, thus raising the value of adjacent parcels.

One has to wonder if there were politicians out there clever enough to realize that they could serve the developers, the antidevelopment activists, and the environmentalists, all in one policy swoop. It all seemed so plausible, repetitive, and ubiquitous.

Consider a contemporary example: In 1999, the County banned commercial timber operations on SU zoned land, including large tracts with residential potential not limited to one house per 40 acres, as are TPZ. There is, thus, pressure to sell these tracts because of an unsustainable cash flow (big taxes, no harvest), unless they convert the zoning to TPZ (the next larger designation with but one residence per parcel). Control of that designation is at the sole discretion of the Planning Department. After sufficient delays and harassment to force the requisite number of sales, is the next step the "token resistance to development" part?

The decision, whether the physical attributes of a site could support a cluster of homes, or whether a site is unsuitable for construction at all, depends upon the individual physical circumstances more than property lines or County planner's zoning map, no matter how many "planning overlays" it has. The problem is that a civic management system simply cannot organize itself for an appropriate synthesis of all individual attributes, because of its demotivating structure and criteria subject to political interpretation.

The temptation to play God with other people's property is endemic to democracy because it is a way to acquire the control of wealth without paying for it. It is a personally gratifying thing to do. This disease particularly afflicts those we elect or hire into civic bureaucracy, no matter how well intentioned they are. A planner supposedly has no personal stake in decisions other than personal ideology, continued employment, promotions... unless there is graft involved, or acting under verbal orders of decision-makers... but that would be unheard of, wouldn't it?

Is it any wonder that our noted "anti-development" Supervisor, a man with an unchallenged reputation as a leader in protection of The Environment, came from a family of long-term residents of the County that had made a killing in real estate? Perhaps he really believes that he was protecting the County from those outside interests. Perhaps he and his friends agreed that what he did was the "right" thing, but whom did those measures benefit? Although there are certainly many happy owners of personal baronies, and a few very happy investors, the policy also made entry level housing unaffordable for many of his constituents. Guess what he plans to do about that?

Less Is More

Trees grow, but dirt doesn't, and in Santa Cruz County, dirt shrinks. When developers run out of places to build houses, they have to go find more lots or go out of business. Any lot will do. As the conversion of agricultural land or easily converted timber regions approaches the limit, "more" has been redefined as "in-fill."

It's still that big development machine, only now that it has most of the agricultural land near cities under control, it seems to be set upon making even more outrageous profits by decreasing the supply and increasing the demand for urban residential dirt.

Most local residents didn't want "more" development. All it meant to them was more traffic, more sprawl, more smog, poorer views, and less space to play. There is, however, another faction: wealthy people who like their baronies and the open space around them. They want to be certain to curtail "middle class sprawl" in tract houses and force them out of former vacation homes, "inappropriate" for permanent residences.

Our famed Measure J Supervisor, now retired from the Board, has his very own tax-exempt Non-Governmental Organization, with the professed goal of stopping the same suburban sprawl he helped manufacture 20 years ago. He is advocating "Sustainable Development," "Sustainable Agriculture," "Smart Growth," and "Affordable Housing." The local newspaper is calling our real estate genius "The Environmental Leader of the Century." He is off and running on grant money from supposedly altruistic, Very Rich People. They have all that money and they're giving it to a tax-deductible foundation that exists purely for a good cause of determining where people "should" live and how. It doesn't hurt of course to get a say as to where with the donation.

It is still political patronage but without the spending limits. Our community leaders gained support from the County planners, the local university power structure, and the environmental community to force "in-fill," circumscribing local cities with Greenbelts. After all, people like Green.

They got them. Santa Cruz passed Measure C: the "Decade of the Environment Measure" per their United Nations Local Agenda 21. It was put on the ballot as a zoning law. Measure C will increase rents inside the Greenbelts, much to the delight of those who bought crumbling former vacation houses on the inside as income property prior to the new law. It will do nothing about the continued spread of upper-class development outside the greenbelt.

On the demand side, needlessly draconian environmental regulations are being enforced on low-to-middle income communities in the County hinterland, forcing those residents back into the city. The system Balkanizes the County into zones of rich and poor.

The method can make new rural-suburban lots available for redevelopment using environmental laws in much the same manner as applied to owners of target tracts of acreage properties. As you recall, Measure J had other effects besides chewing up the forest in big chunks. Prior to the election, the people who held small suburban lots in small rural towns owned something that could support a residential structure, worth about the same as any other small urban lot. After the passage of Measure J, a once buildable 3/4-acre lot in town worth $50,000 (in current dollars), a fell to about one-fifth its prior value. Their land was "worth-less."

We'll call this one, "The Squeeze":

1. Rezone suburban lots with urban potential to a larger minimum size.

2. The owners of "worth-less" lots get to hold the bag and pay the taxes.

3. The County recognizes the "urban sprawl" and circumscribes the area by zoning "greenbelts."

4. Prices of residential housing rise due to a lack of available acreage.

5. The big landowners wait for the market to develop and buy the "worth-less" lots for the less that they are "worth."

6. The County recognizes the "housing shortage" and rezones the minimums for "in-fill."

7. The property, now worth a lot, gets developed, and the County rakes in additional taxes.

Now that those "worth-less" lots are worth lots, why didn't the bag-holders keep them?

8. To produce new lots, use environmental and zoning laws to require modifications to building codes that the current class of owners cannot afford. To take the dirt, condemn the property. Sell it to whom?

One has to wonder if there were politicians out there, clever enough to realize that they could serve the developers, the anti-development activists, and the environmentalists, all in one policy swoop. It all seemed so plausible, repetitive, and ubiquitous.

Okay, so "in-fill." Those plots that were "too small" under Measure J, well, the Department of Environmental Health has miraculously thought of a way to make them work so that the Planning Department can help stop suburban sprawl. Of course, it won't hurt the people who just bought those 16 "worth-less" lots for a song from the people who had been holding the bag for 20 years. Those who didn't sell to the right people at the right price, well, the San Lorenzo Valley is now a Significant Natural Area, subject to California Department of Fish and Game jurisdiction and a significant review with a significant price will have to be conducted...

The urban demand side of the picture is a matter of getting people out of the rural houses they currently occupy. These are usually converted vacation cabins, now used on a year-round basis. Some have been remodeled, while others are falling apart. The key to flushing out the owners has been laws governing septic systems. These issues will be discussed in Parts IV and V.

The tradition spans decades and has gone on unabated. Two of our famous Supervisor's compatriots became State Assemblymen and the owner of the local newspaper wants to be lieutenant governor. A predecessor devised a bond measure that was particularly effective to finance the conversion of agricultural land to residential housing. His successor has done more to depress the price of timberland than has any other Assemblyman. In more recent years, the Supervisor who has done the most to push the new zoning law governing timber practice (and is the most "responsive" to the Sierra Club), originally had a practice as … a real estate attorney. He is "next in line" for the move up.

Are politicians and planning bureaucrats really smart enough to set up a system like this, or was this just a misattribution of random events and human nature suffering from the creative scrutiny of some paranoid author? Every lawyer and planner interviewed during the research for this book who was asked that question, stated flatly that the politicians aren't that smart and are ideologically opposed to such things. The subject of one interview how-ever, was (unknown to me at the time) one of the very people who had made oodles of money in the land conversion business. His comment was that there are people who are that smart, and that certain authors should be "careful."

The purpose of this book is not to bust people but to point out the systemic flaws that develop in a system that does not respect private property rights. The flaw is the lack of civic discipline that "limited government" under the Constitution was intended to provide; i.e., the power to satisfy one's urges with other people's money. It is the power to take control of property without compensation. It is the essence of democratic government.

Politicians like tax doling out tax money. Large real estate agents, land speculators, and banks like redevelopment. So do construction contractors, unions, raw material suppliers, home furnishings retailers, and public employees. Activists like controlling individual behavior to serve the ends they think important. Every one of these people did what they did because it was profitable to them under the unconstitutionally distorted system under which we now operate.

The temptation for civic corruption is but one reason why rules have nearly always failed. Economic laws are immutable. Perhaps they can be used to positive effect by incorporating the totality of interests in the consideration of individual transactions.

It's possible.

📖 De-Capitulate

Conclusions to the Antithesis

Part II was a story of activism and political resource management gone awry. Taxation and regulatory schemes caused problems that government blamed upon landowners and used those them to justify taking control of the forest. When they got control, they behaved like any other avaricious landowner and used the environment to maximize revenue, indenture constituencies, and please the appropriate patrons, giving lip service to real ecological problems.

The exercise of power in political systems is just too much temptation to trust its players to manage ecosystems out of altruism.

It is too much power.

Throughout the previous discussion, one has to wonder how a group in control of the financial and political machinery of County government could get away with such an orchestrated operation for so many years.

It isn't hard to do and is not uncommon. People don't have to exercise conspiracy and collusion consciously for it to be such, particularly when governmental institutions are dominated by an entrenched group whose ideas and perceptions are immune to challenge and unconstrained by accountability. A functional conspiracy can be constructed merely out of acculturated personal preferences and social affiliations at the golf course, in civic organizations, at work, or just among friends. These social groups are powerful people: real estate agents, academics, politicians, developers, financiers, planners, and lawyers, who all share a similar focus to implement their preferences by the means at their disposal.

The power of government has become so great that a conspiracy is not necessary to play favorites within the system. It only takes a stated whim or common understanding to exercise that power, to assure either a smooth project or wreck complete havoc. A supervisor could mention to an inspector over the phone: 'Oh, he's a good guy. Come on up and let's talk about what we can do to work this out,' versus, 'We've had complaints about some problems down there. Could you take a look?' Once the mindset of the enforcer is locked in place, that latter practitioner might as well go get an attorney. Such a phone call is a death knell for the project.

Such impressions and preferences are natural to people. Bureaucrats consider the exercise of such preferences to be an entitlement of the assumed expertise associated with a civic mandate. Except for a very few individuals among the development community, research for this book betrayed no evidence of evil intent or conscious conspiracy on the part of civil servants, although there was indication of obvious manipulation, preference, and willing obedience to questionable "requests."

Instead, there is a larger evil. It is an individual sense of entitlement, acculturated through the entire regulatory, activist, media, political, and legal community. It is the subjective propensity to project "what should be done" in service to personal preference and without accountability for the results.

This is, by definition, what it is to covet. It is a self-deception, by which one entitles oneself to take the use of property without buying it first. It takes so long for the results of this kind of thinking to manifest, there is so much struggle involved, and there is so much self-reinforcing subjectivity within a powerful social group, that it really isn't hard to misattribute the results and fail to see the consequences of one's own invisible hand.

This greater evil is inherent to socialized commons. Nobody would think that it is optimal that nature should be managed under a system that knows only coercion. It isn't logical to expect expertise from inexperienced urban youth, blinded by fashionable ideology. One shouldn't expect optimal solutions from bureaucrats with a structural motive to perpetuate problems, nor should ecosystem management algorithms be designed by politicians and lawyers.

To accuse capitalism of environmental damage because of "greed" on the part of individuals belies the fact that the system we are using has been government resource control, all along. It has always served whomever happened to be in power, whether by political payoff or by majority support. Lawyers, foundations, academic grant hustlers, and NGO grandstanders, many of them ignorant of forest practice, are now mucking about with the environment just as destructively as any timber baron ever has, and on a scale of which they could never dream.

The accuser is outdoing the accused.

The sheer scale and intensity of the catastrophic fires, the unabated spread of weeds, and the misery that has befallen so many "reintroduced" species, all have resulted from misguided efforts to force nature to comply with human dreams, coupled with the civic resources capable of making huge mistakes. All are all-too-commonly followed with finger pointing, backtracking, and denial, with the ubiquitous excuse of "insufficient funding."

It is not fixable by "new leadership," more money, or higher standards of professionalism. A regulatory system inherently does not work because its motivational structure can not be designed according to natural law. Nature is dynamic, adaptive, competitive, and integrates individual interests through distributed risk. Free Markets have all of those attributes along with the prospective intelligence and creativity of human beings.

Regulatory government is a tremendously crude system. Compare the speed of decision-making, the number of variables it can handle, and its operating overhead costs against the sophistication and flexibility of a free market. Compare the predictive capacity, adaptive response time, and efficiency of the Chicago Board of Trade, against your county planning department. Compare the complexity of producing a permit review to the manufacture of an automobile or computer. There is no comparison.

The question really is: How would a free market, normally motivated to avoid costs, choose to incorporate the cost of externalities into the conduct of operations? Let's take a look at some clues from our timber analysis.

There IS Room for Improvement

Forests in Santa Cruz County are large and overpopulated. There is great temptation to harvest them hard over large areas. If the "forcign" timber operators have the financial wherewithal to overcome the local regulatory barriers to resource extraction, they will eagerly do so. Hence, Gamecock Canyon (again). The very forces, that were intended to compel "responsible" resource management, have unwittingly abetted timber operators with the exclusive intent of maximizing profit.

The glaring fact remains that timberland has little economic return without a maximum harvest or a residence on the parcel. No one would manage it for large slow-growing trees as an investment, because no one would choose to lose that much money unless they had some other source of income and enjoyed an intangible return. Coastal hardwood forests, having no economic value, suffer even more (there are those developing processes to market tanbark oak and madrone as furniture-grade hardwoods).

Under the current regime, the selection of marketable goods is limited when it comes to leaving the land as a forest. The cost of ownership and careful maintenance can be offset by selling a few logs, and uh… then what? Mushrooms? Natural herb tea? Photographic tours? The valuable goods suffer the price-suppression of socialized commons: flood control, drinking water, grazing, spawning grounds, and outdoor recreation (a popular product that helps government market its political land-acquisition business).

That is precisely the point. Environmental activists are asking for something that no one in their financially right mind would do because they don't understand what they have, in fact, created. When they don't get the results they expect, instead of changing their stripes, they blame the landowner and propose to make the situation worse by fiat. Is the only choice either to convert the forest to residential use or a confiscate it into a socialized commons in a state of mandated neglect?

Spacing trees creates room and light for ground-dwelling species. It fosters biodiversity. It creates flight corridors for birds. It reduces the hazards of a catastrophic firestorm. It creates the opportunity for the kind of prescribed fires to which these forests had become accustomed. Light harvests of slow-growing trees produce forests of straight, fine grained, high value product. This is where excellent forestry practice is of real benefit, the embodiment of the concert among humans and nature.

It takes work. It costs money. How do we pay for the work and minimize the risks without capitulating to the false assumption of natural civic monopoly?

It appears that there is room in the market for both higher timber production levels and higher than historic prices. This is very good news. It means that a 25%–40% harvest over a larger area may be economically possible as long as there is a way for the resulting lumber to remain competitive against substitute goods, and/or there are other products for sale on the property.

In theory, one would optimize the value of a particular parcel by investing the most valued combination of products for which it is especially suited. Unfortunately, government controls the use of many goods and services that land could provide, in such a manner that they do not have an economic return. Thus, no one invests in those intangible uses or seeks to discover their economic value.

Markets can identify the means to find financial benefit in the services that land provides, only if they are free to do so. Under current law, we are illegitimately saddling landowners with regulatory liabilities and declaring private assets to be public property. We are confiscating those uses into democratized commons. It's that tragedy thing again. We all have that compulsive urge to think about what "should be done" with somebody else's land. We want to assume that we have a "right" to dictate the use of private property as a collective good, instead of purchasing a contract for that use. Civic acquisition robs investment value into those very uses we so highly prize. It is a process of enacting what are, in effect, public acquisitions of what are legally constrained to be zero-priced goods. Once the control of those uses succeeds to a civic agent, the means to evaluate and weigh individual cases objectively has been destroyed, devolving into political struggles, as reflect specific interests, not all of which are altruistic.

Even if old growth forests were the "goal" of civic forest management, somebody would have to intervene in the current "recovery" process to foster that transition. Nature has never done it and has no way to know how.

One would think that highly educated stewards of the land, dispersed as appropriate to the topography and resources, willing to invest their own money, and committed to long-term ownership and the improvement of ecosystem function, would be a good thing. Unfortunately, without at least adequate profitability in the investment, it won't happen. Does that mean that these investments have to be wildly profitable to make a free market in environmental management a reality?

There is one, last, crucial factor in this debate, that nobody talks about.

The Heart of the Issue

So, although now you may think you understand why Roger Burch could outbid Bud McCrary for Gamecock Canyon, does that mean you know why Bud didn't buy it?

No. There is one factor missing among all the economics, history, and political manipulation that seems always to be forgotten in this kind of fight.

Bud McCrary was born on Big Creek property, near the town of Davenport, up the Coast. He played there as a child. His kid sister stood for her picture next to a six foot tree that is now over 120 feet tall. Bud has worked in that forest all his life.

Bud is in love with his land, and his lifelong habits just won't let him do what others legally can. No amount of rulemaking can change that.

Isn't that what we want?

Bud wasn't born in Gamecock Canyon. It's 25 miles away from home. To him, Gamecock wasn't a matter of life and death. It was just an investment opportunity to gain some productive timberland in a flaky political climate.

Roger Burch, on the other hand, represents Redwood Empire, a Division of Pacific States Industries, Inc. Roger is not a logger, but a very competitive and successful businessman. To him, Gamecock Canyon is an investment of corporate money. By global standards, his people do excellent work. His vilification has been, in many respects, slander on the part of suburban activists in need of a pariah.

How can an environmental management system treat the Roger Burches of the world and the likes of Big Creek justly, so that they must develop an advancing level of stewardship in order to survive?

How do we motivate the kind of forest management and development that represents the best balance of public need and technical capability? How might a market, trading these products, be structured so that the owner maximizes profit through an objective balance between resource extraction and other productive land uses? How do we do that without the unnecessary cost of civic oversight or possible corruption?

This is why we have Part III.

Where an excess of power prevails,

property of no sort is duly respected.

No man is safe in his opinions, his person,

his faculties, or his possessions,

– James Madison

Part III Globally Thinking, a Motivational Ethos

Part I discussed the principles of civic acquisition of private property. Civic agencies use democratic claims assigning harm to transformation products in commons. Constraints upon economic uses depress their asset value until the enforcing agent acquires full control of the property. It proved that a civic policy of environmental preservation is illogical and that therefore someone needs to do the work of caring for nature. The Environment was defined as the human interaction with Nature at the control boundary of human activity. Part I closed with the observation that politically and legally derived, bureaucratically controlled regulation is the wrong tool to "solve the problem."

Part II showed that once government gets control of the land, those in power will corrupt the democratic purpose to their own ends and deliver a product serving the interests of the politically dominant. The subjective nature of the claims renders a regulatory process, destructive to its ecological justification.

Part III opens the thesis of this book.

Chapter 1 explains why a free market is better adapted to provide superior environmental management. The exposition of market principles reflects two phases common to financial analyses of private enterprise: operations and assets. The chapter distills that discussion into a brief outline of the proposed system architecture.

Chapters 2 and 3 concern risk-management of operational externalities using insured certification to a best-practice process standard. It will proceed from the principles to the historical record of certification and insurance and thence to the mechanics of bootstrapping an objectively priced market in ecosystem assets based upon risk management.

Chapter 4 addresses issues of property boundaries as applicable to mobile zero-priced goods. It observes that many democratic claims on the use of commons are civic acquisitions of land uses. They accrue real capital gains to the claimants. It uses the principle developed in Part I (that all resource assets are neither stabile nor fixed) to define and describe property as a set of mathematical models of bounded processes, capable of modifying the condition of mobile goods. It posits that a fluid market in uses of ecosystem processes would require improved liquidity to reduce the cost of transaction overhead.

Chapter 5 synthesizes these principles and applies them to those goods that move rapidly or have undefined boundaries, such as water, air, migratory animals, or temporary range for predators as applies to the case of the family farm. This analysis posits that caring for these mobile assets is a valuable service: managing uses of natural process assets that have potential to alter the condition of respective mobile goods.

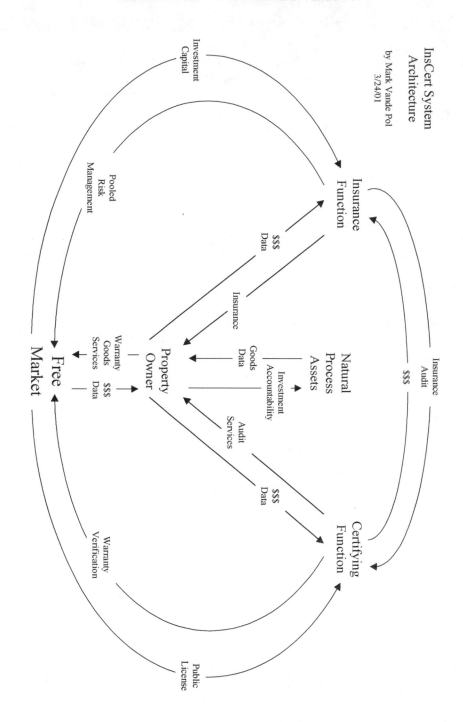

Figure 2 – InsCert[TM] System Architecture

📖 Chapter 1 – The Philosophy of a Civil Alternative

Concerning Natural Law and Ecosystem Management

We are human and we are here. The laws we have created to describe our behavior were as real before we spoke language as they have been since we gave them form. These are laws of competition, scarcity, substitution, and indifference: the laws of supply and demand.

We can't change any of that.

We have altered the planet and we can't change that either, for natural selection is an irreversible process. We can never remake it as if we were not here, nor should we. We have no choice but to operate in concert with our surroundings, the harmony of which will depend upon our behavior.

It is unnatural for us to force upon ourselves static control systems and then expect an evolving organism to flourish. Natural selection is a process antithetical to determinism.

Natural ecosystems are competitive. At any given point, some solutions are going to be more successful than others. The reason biodiversity is so important is that the conditions under which species compete are based upon selection under variable conditions. If the circumstances change, the strong may fail and the weak may suddenly prosper.

Natural selection is driven by chance, mutation, and experiment, with ruthless rejection of inferior trials. Such is a market. Products and services each have their niches, diverse solutions, mergers, dominant species, and bankruptcies. Markets can adapt to changes in technology or events. A free market trading uses of private property is a system better suited to manage the process of natural selection than is bureaucratic regulation.

Free-market solutions to environmental problems are, by nature, competitive. Diverse products and services continuously adapt to serve the needs of individual customers. If the ecological conditions change, a market can have a proven product in production requiring only expansion.

The keys to making markets work is personal integrity in a world of managed ignorance. Irresponsible and impulsive behavior costs us all as externalities to commerce.

Any person: individual, corporate, or political, can fail to be accountable. Irresponsibility is founded upon a failure of self-perception, the belief that anyone really can act alone. It is the failure to measure the costs we cause to others that we ultimately cost ourselves. It is a lack of faith in our ability to fix our mistakes. It is a creature endemic to structured hierarchy managed by punishment. Penance becomes a putting of the total cost upon an individual without escape. It is a way of consolidating and vetting the distributed price of unjustly distributed risk.

The Tragedy of the Commons results from the lack of an individual account of interdependence in free-market associations. Intellectuals such as Mr. Hardin have intoned that there is no market mechanism for managing that collective interest, as if we were all 18th century sheepherders. We gullibly accept the idea out of guilt associated with our propensity to abrogate responsibilities in particular instances. Such guilt clouds our ability to see the means to account for interdependent interests, capable of unitizing personal valuation in a collectively held asset. Though such a means exists, there is no just and efficient way for individual claims to be rationalized politically or legally. The popular belief, that we have no such free-market medium, is sold by the politically dominant, obsessed with the intent to gain greater personal control of resources using the police power of government. That popular story is a lie.

We already have a tradable unit of interdependent ownership: It is stock.

Police power is certainly a way to coerce immediate, visible, and remedial compliance, but it can be an incontinent reaction to "make it stop" without the consideration of how "it" was motivated. Coercion begets resistance, enforcement, and punishment that can be rightly regarded as a destructive waste of energy that all too frequently induces unintended consequences. Such compulsion is an externality to the cost of transactions, a result of com-promises among struggles, more reflective of the respective interests of dominant combatants than the benefit to the object under contention. Boun-dary conditions set by legal settlement consequently become the focus of avoiding constraint. Regulations become webs of intentional ambiguity by which a punishing trap can be sprung. The obsession with power then renders motivational regulatory methods counterproductive to extending individual power through political control.

The key to fitting business solutions to our regulatory pathos is identifying and pricing externalities. The process of mitigating risks and healing existing damage offers the opportunity to measure those costs, and apply that knowl-edge to construct weighted contingencies.

There is a business for that too, capable of valuing risk concerning intangible assets: pooled risk management. Although the insurance industry has done a lousy job of risk management when it comes to natural disasters, this is largely because it is a heavily subsidized, regulated, and, therefore, protected business. It doesn't have to be that way.

Government regulation is structurally at odds with competitive principles, simply because non-uniform law enforcement is an invitation to corruption.

Single solutions are mandated out of the idea that uniformity constitutes "fairness" even though uniform solutions among variable circumstances are not innately fair. When obvious consequences arise, monopoly bureaucracy pursues its own interests; abetting the very corruption that was to be avoided. Government has ignored its service to that paradox in blind infatuation with power. It has resolved to implement the insipid conclusion that justice must be delivered by coercive bureaucratic rulemaking and enforcement as if it was the only option. It isn't.

The Descriptive Nature of Natural Law

Regulatory systems give us complex rules with limited applicability to unique circumstances. Free-market systems start with simple laws and map themselves onto an infinite array options. Rules are not as applicable to the variety and behavior of natural systems as are Laws.

Laws of physics and chemistry operate by descriptive nature. No well-trained scientist thinks that Newton's law of the mutual attraction of bodies describes gravity perfectly. The laws of gravity are only approximations of gravity's behavior with well-defined limits beyond which errors become significant. Exclusive use of Newtonian mechanics to determine the behavior of particles in a nuclear reactor will induce unacceptable errors. In cases such as these, Newton's laws gave way to Einstein's.

Good law is not so much an admonishment or constraint, as it is a description of principle. Economic laws of supply and demand describe human behavior as regards free exchange of private property. When applying economic laws to real transactions, economists recognize that there are situations in which the supply/demand model produces significant errors. These involve costs, inherent to the production of goods that are not reflected in the sale price, defined as economic externalities. Negative externalities lead to excess demand for a good because its price understates the total cost of production.

A clever body politic could govern via systems by which the market has motive to discover and price those goods that mitigate or offset externalities. That process begins with identification of a population, whose documented behavior constitutes a paragon, free to operate within a market-based system of checks and balances. The public can invest in verification businesses that assist individual entities to do their best at accounting the behavior of natural process assets that offset or mitigate human impacts, having a financial stake in that success. It beats paying a technically unqualified District Attorney or unaccountable agency official to investigate a company hiding its worst to avoid punishment for violations of perhaps inappropriate rules.

Instead of a set of standards demanding precise adherence, laws should reflect articulated principles by which people weigh the myriad constituents of individual choices as apply to particular circumstance. A government so constituted would focus upon verifying that contracts are respected, and not so commonly intrude into conflicts over property as an interested party. It would protect validated information as intellectual property and provide a forum to assist economic persons to settle their disputes based upon established facts in the court of civil mediation. Rather than institutionalizing the will of a tyrannical majority, and settling every issue through judicial rulings involving bureaucratic advocacy, the body of individual interests can more effectively settle disputes within the confines of contracts. Legislation, as such, would be more carefully crafted, brief, and rare. They might have time to think about it more carefully.

Such a direction would engender respect for government rather than properly validate its inefficacy. In order to develop the benefits of successful interdependence, we must choose to apply our collective will through reinforcement of individual integrity and respect for unalienable individual rights. We can create a process defined by individual responsibility for the individual share of the whole as a view of the self, enlightened by the price of that share. It is more realistic than to expect an individual to adopt such consideration out of either religious altruism or civic compulsion.

Without structural respect for unalienable property rights, no free market system can function with the integrity, energy, and mutual respect required for successful expression of any interdependent social system. Allocating the benefits of interdependence by rationalizing individual valuation of and contribution to particular assets is the genius of individual stock ownership. It comes vastly closer to the collective ownership of the means of production than that of Marx' misanthropic nightmare.

What's Missing?

Ecosystems are adaptive, diverse, dynamic, and change irreversibly. They are subject to random events of enormous scope. They operate in an interdependently competitive manner. Species undergo random mutation, are capable of near monoculture, and are subject to ruthless extinction. Nature is an entirely objective judge of fitness, not to be underestimated or misused.

The civic environmental control system enjoys what is assumed to be a natural monopoly. Its powers are unchecked, irreversibly acquisitive, maladaptive, unaccountable, and indissoluble. Its motivational structure is to accrue, extend, and perpetuate problems rather than to complete a job and go onto something new. Concentrations of power inherently attract those who would control rather than produce, whether by corruption, nepotism, or manipulation. It has been thus, since the dawn of civilization. It is why the Constitution instituted limited government to guarantee individual rights.

Plants and animals compete for scarce resources in a manner similar to laws of supply, demand, and indifference. Business now applies many of these econometric principles by quantitative computer models in its effort to predict commodity market behavior. Manufacturers must have some idea what the demand for a product might be or they may incorrectly size capacity and lose either the high margins with early market share, or waste capital invested in a turkey. Investors must weigh risks associated with investment choices. They offset that risk by hiring insurers to pool that risk by under-standing how to quantify and efficiently manage the capital to reduce its loss. Much of that investment in analytical tools is available and applicable to manage risk in environmental systems.

Human intelligence is not only adaptive and competitive, it is creatively prospective. The chaos of speculative investment among competing, but interdependent interests can provide the necessary focus and energy to quantify and model competitive ecosystem behavior. The models can rapidly adjust to new information. A free market can integrate the present value of various contingencies into a determined set of adjusted options. These are the real blessings of and mandates to personal responsibility, not achievable under a coercive system, wherein people are habituated to avoid blame based upon retrospective fear. There is no civic authority that has the adaptively prospective ability to manage risk, as does free enterprise.

Political motives have historically been far more corrupting than a managed and audited profit motive under the rule of enforceable contract law. Political corruption is usually harder to detect or redirect because the individual profit to politicians can be indirect, non-pecuniary, or hidden to avoid prosecution. Civil power relies upon third party audit to validate reliable investment data. Civic enterprise has the power and scale to avoid independent verification.

It is harder to attribute individual motives in either a civic or non-profit enterprise than to understand the profit motives of private enterprise (which has been one of the reasons that political environmentalists and non-profit foundations have remained above suspicion for so long). When one looks, however, the political and economic motives of both are easily identified, even if profit via manipulating the power of government is obscured. The problem is: What alternative do we have, once the corrupt motives and acts of the foundation/ agency/NGO cabal are identified and publicized? Which system is inherently more subject to being held accountable?

Can we trust private enterprise to manage the environment? If not, should we give the job to a government monopoly? That is the choice here.

Over the last century, there is a record of over 100 million deaths, citizens killed by their own governments (by deliberate starvation and execution). 'Oh, but that wasn't OUR government,' you'll hear, 'WE have rights under the Constitution.' You hear people say that, even while they are insisting upon violating the Constitutional property rights of others in order to get what THEY want. Constitutional rights don't seem to matter much to them when they pertain to farmers, ranchers, and forest landowners. Now that these precedents have been set, giving eventual control of the use of ALL land to government, why do you think that the bureaucrats won't come after your livelihood, your property, or your children?

It is paradoxical that the very scientists, who advocate biology education based exclusively upon the theory of natural selection, should also advocate the exclusive use of bureaucratic political hierarchy to manage competitive ecosystems. Immersed in a successful Darwinian economy, and in the name of preserving Darwinian ecosystems, it is bizarre that a society founded upon free-market capitalism and private property rights has assumed that civic control of environmental risk constitutes a "natural" monopoly. With an unbroken history of democracy leading to tyranny, it is frightening that a successful society, founded upon republican principles of limited government, should justify an irreversible accrual of power in the hands of a demonstrably incompetent and historically destructive master.

It is high time to break up the civic monopoly in environmental management with the introduction of a viable competitor: the free market itself. The problem with that idea has been identifying checks and balances within the market with which to motivate individuals to freely account for externalities associated with the use of their property. The good news about a free-market management system is that the motives of those in business may be less confounded with religion or political power. Free market behavior is easier to understand and manipulate because the motives and principles are simple.

Who would be accountable for damages in a free-market environmental management system?

Try to find a manufacturer who is not insured or cannot be ultimately held to a guarantee. On the other hand, try to find a government program for which the controlling agency is fully accountable for its product. Neither private industry nor government is perfectly accountable or innately competent. The point is: Which is better suited to the job and which is more likely to extend the limits of competence and be accountable for its mistakes?

Wouldn't one logically want an environmental management system that rewarded the most productive in a competitive market of ideas, observations, and innovations? Can you imagine a fiercely competitive market in eco-system management? Can you imagine an industry producing new tools for ecological measurement, analysis, and restoration activities as competitive as the computer business? Could there be ecosystem management with an insured guarantee? How would it work?

That is the subject of the rest of Part III.

Summary of the Thesis

The proposed civil verification system provides privately certified environmental management with an insured guarantee. Certification companies audit practitioners to validated process specifications. Competitors in the verification business have reason to assure that their customers operate at both minimal risk and cost because they reinsure the practitioners. The program requires continuing research and education toward extending the state-of-the-art of resource management practice. Insured certification, as proposed, must supercede civic permit authority for those under coverage.

The system generates accounting data, necessary to determine the financial worth of insured ecosystem assets, as required of certified operations. This is similar to the way industrial insurers developed their understanding of financial risk via the scope and probability of insured losses. The certified practitioner combines data from compiled from hazard mitigation and habitat restoration projects with required research and continuing education. That data serves valuable purposes within the system.

Identified and accounted risks immediately improve the conduct of operations because they objectively justify and prioritize investments to reduce or offset those risks. Pooled risk also counterbalances less intrusive experiments against those that are more aggressive through purchase of the use of offsetting assets. Uses of parcels and the nature of risk reduction investments then differentiate according to local attributes. Crude pricing schemes begin to take form, by which to market rights to use ecosystem assets capable of offsetting other risks.

Ecosystem assets have financial worth, as long as they can be bundled into valuable units. Recognizing natural process assets as worthy investments will attract capital to successful risk reduction and risk offset enterprises. To reduce the cash flow requirements, one must reduce the transaction overhead.

Many resource assets are mobile or have such low unit value that minimum economies of scale can wildly exceed the bounds of traditional property lines. The solution is to create definitions of property as bounded uses of ecosystem PROCESS assets that transform the state of these mobile goods. Process units could then operate on a noncontiguous, global scale and overlay other economic land uses that may well have their own boundaries.

Stock ownership and the cost of pooled risk engage self-interested consideration of others, holding competing assets as overlays of coincident uses within a particular area or spread among non-contiguous regions. These can extend across the entire planet when connected by an appropriate transmission medium.

This proposal in this book is a synthesis of these components:

- Certified, insured, and guaranteed operations in lieu of civic permit,
- Validated and accounted operational processes and ecosystem data.
- Pricing uses of ecosystem assets through risk analysis.
- Quantitative models describing property as bounded process assets.
- Reduction of transaction costs in contracts for land use, and
- Civic respect for unalienable private property rights.

The system architecture is depicted in Figure 2 on page 120.

The components are applied according this principle:

To improve ecosystem health, invest in shares of private enterprises selling uses of natural processes that are priced by their ability to offset environmental risk.

It seems almost too simple, doesn't it?

📖 Chapter 2 – Getting Off on Good Behavior

The Proposed Free-Market Management System

We return to Garret Hardin's *The Tragedy of the Commons,* by which to recall a popular, though incontinent misconception:

> "Adam Smith… contributed to a dominant tendency of thought that has ever since interfered with positive action based on rational analysis, namely, the tendency to assume that decisions reached individually will, in fact, be the best decisions for an entire society… If the assumption is not correct, we need to reexamine our individual freedoms to see which ones are defensible."

> "Coercion is a dirty word to most liberals now, but it need not forever be so. As with the four-letter words, its dirtiness can be cleansed away by exposure to the light, by saying it over and over without apology or embarrassment. To many, the word coercion implies arbitrary decisions of distant and irresponsible bureaucrats; but this is not a necessary part of its meaning. The only kind of coercion I recommend is mutual coercion, mutually agreed upon by the majority of the people affected."

> – *THE TRAGEDY OF THE COMMONS,* by Garrett Hardin

Few would argue that individual human beings in control the factors of production have ever been guided by "rational analysis." Fewer still would want government to decide which of our freedoms are "defensible." We can do better than the insatiable demands of democratic socialism.

Insured Certification to a Process Standard: InsCert™

What if there was environmental management with an insured guarantee?

This proposal starts with a dual system to manage the externalities of resource industry. It suggests an optional free-market system in competition with civic oversight. It audits practitioners to a best-practice standard of validated processes, by a private, insured, third-party certification enterprise.

Public acceptance of private certification, in lieu of civic permit authority, can be an incentive for a company to adopt practices, so excellent that the civic authority need require no permit or civic review for proposed projects or operations. Permit authority is instead, superceded by the certification process, which manages disputes through civil liability law.

There is no unequal treatment under the law in this proposal. It is within Constitutional bounds to implement quality systems, demonstrably superior to those set by law. Any person, corporate or individual, who could prove the excellence of their operation under a guarantee, insured by a certifying company with financial responsibility for audit to validated process specifications, would qualifies for exemption from civic enforcement. The trick is to determine how to define a best practice standard against the myriad combinations of possible products. A list of the components follows.

The practitioner agrees to operate under:

- Documented, guaranteed, and validated process specifications.
- Insurance to repair, mitigate, or offset externalities of operations.
- Research and education to extend the limits of best practice.

The certifying company:

- Audits validation reports against conditions on the ground.
- Carries reinsurance against insufficient indemnity or bankruptcy.
- Coordinates data and supplies composite data.
- Manages complaints and mediates primary settlements.

A certifying company is financially liable for its verification and auditing practices and would have to carry its own insurance. Pooled risk is a more efficient use of capital than the existing system of putting up bonds for permitted projects. It is also addresses the actual scope or risk of a claim.

The certifying entity can independently verify their customers' practices without requirements for hierarchical traceability to a national or international civic authority because they have a financial stake, both in the success of their clients and in maintaining low insurance costs. Both have every reason to reduce their insurance payments by reducing the scope and frequency of claims. The system is therefore self-correcting. Because the certifying entity would carry reinsurance, the guarantees offered by the system offer multiply redundant coverage.

Can the permit-based system make that claim?

Under InsCert, there is no incentive for a certifying company to burden or extort funds from their customers. This is a competitive market where the certifying agent has a stake in both customer success and minimal risk of a loss. The necessary checks and balances in this system thus have multiple backups. This lowers required capital and pools risk further.

The proposed system also holds practitioners to a standard of continuous research, education, and process development, without requiring civic funding. It will do a better job of allocating research funds toward problems with technically justified returns.

Once freed of the costs of delay in obtaining permit approval, insured forestland owners, foresters, and timber operators, will have the opportunity to take advantage of the spot market. They will have advantages of higher margins, lower operating costs, and efficiencies in inventory management with which to offset the costs invested in best practice management of the forest. Wouldn't it be great to offer the opportunity to react immediately to market gyrations as a reward for continuous, excellence? It would help attenuate the price spikes that tend to motivate rapacity on the part of others by sating transient demand and would reduce the temptation to log more trees to cover costs under falling price conditions.

When asked about certification programs, our local administrative officials respond that they would love to do "differential enforcement." They could focus their efforts on the few "bad" timber operators in the area and leave the "good guys" free to do what is appropriate. Such policy would be unconstitutional under the equal protection clause. The local politicians display an equal lack of comprehension about operations under warranty. To hear a member of the Board of Supervisors call insured certification, "autonomous groups running around" betrays the civic assumption that any system must operate under their control in order to constitute adequate oversight.

It is easy to understand why. Can you imagine what would happen to the Department of Motor Vehicles if insurance companies issued competing Driver's Licenses? Can you imagine what would happen to driver's tests under a "best practice" driving standard? Would insurance rates drop for those drivers? Perhaps they might purchase the option to drive faster at higher prices. Would the insurers expand their markets through training and verification? Might drivers agree to verification (private electronic concurrent validation) for a further discount? Would accident rates fall? Might customers then spend less time in traffic jams and more time improving their skills? There are existing examples of the legality of such a system.

Not all is known about medical science any more than we know all about the environment. Thankfully, we do not yet have a specification-based medical treatment system. Such systems simply cannot work in an environment of constantly evolving technologies and markets. In the medical industry, doctors must work to a "best practice" standard or possibly lose in a lawsuit if there is a problem. Let's try a medical analogy applied to forest practice regulation as it is currently managed by the regulatory system.

Imagine that you are sick. You live in an area politically dominated by a religious group that has managed to get its beliefs reflected in local law. Your doctor has been told what can be treated, how to cut, where to cut, and what CAN'T BE TOUCHED: your circulatory system. All the doctors are wondering how large a blood vessel that means and declaring it the end of medicine. Mean-while, doctors are buying cauterizing lasers like crazy on the claim that if it doesn't bleed then the blood doesn't circulate. Meanwhile, government has, in an effort to avoid lawsuit, determined precisely how to do the work and when it is justified. Everybody's blood vessels are different. Because of a few reported bleeding problems, the authorities want to inspect each job in progress, but they don't have the staff, due to budget cuts, so they hire people off the street. The application will be reviewed by a series of civil servants who have never performed the procedure and whose only motive is avoid approving a mistake. They will get to the application when they can; the group is underfunded. Meanwhile, that religious group has sued to prevent doctors from reinterpreting their intent. You are waiting for approval, and getting sicker. That is how we regulate forestry!

Even if the medical model is not ideal, we are living longer, healthier lives. Improvements in human habitat: sewage and water treatment, safety equipment, shelter, refrigeration, and food packaging, as well as medical science, have delivered upon much of their promise to improve both the quality and safety of human life-support systems. When you go to a doctor, you don't worry whether he or she carries malpractice insurance. The hospital sees to that. You don't usually worry about whether the refrigerator maintains the correct temperature, or the food in the can is free from pathogens (especially if it is Kosher, a private certification system). These things have been dealt with to a remarkable degree with minimal government verification. If that physician or drug manufacturer makes a mistake or if a customer has a unique complication, there is anticipation of the event and a policy to cover the remedy. If things go wrong, funds are allocated to at least compensate for, if not fix the problem.

There are existing certification companies that have no incentive to corrupt their standards for the benefit of any particular industrial concern. The reason is that they have earned their public confidence in diversified markets. The loss of confidence in any one of them would spell total loss for all. In this system, a second level check on their behavior is the financial cost of the reinsurance they carry, based upon their record of misjudgment.

Consider the example of electrical appliances. This industry recognized, long ago, that electrical appliances carry potentially fatal hazards. The products were subject to misuse and damage. Production standards were variable. In order for public confidence to be maintained and to protect manufacturers from either government mandated production standards or capricious lawsuits, Underwriters' Laboratories (UL) was constituted. UL manages tens of thousands of products, without need for civic oversight and few people worry about the safety of their appliances.

UPC validates plumbing products. Independent labs crash-test your car. The ASTM certifies the test methods for materials. The IEEE makes sure that your computer can transmit to your printer and not mess up your cell-phone. Why do we need to have the government run the environment?

The biotech industry saw, in its infancy, that the public would shut them down if they had a significant research accident. They knew that unless they developed their own code of conduct for handling materials in the lab, that the government would do it for them. It was done, and after twenty years, so far no disaster. Would we be safer yet if the industry couldn't hide behind the USDA (U.S. Department of Agriculture) and, instead, had to purchase the cost of risk for genetically modified plants? They might be yet more careful.

Certification of timber practice and forestry is being done in places, but there is no effort to render it accountable to customers or reduce the influence of civic authority. As it is, a certified forester, operator, or landowner has to maintain the overhead to comply with both regulating bodies in the hope that consumer demand for environmentally sound practices will pay the higher price for their products. So far, the consensus is that private, third party certification doesn't work for the certification customer because such pricing premiums are small compared to the associated operating costs.

Under this proposal, civic permit authority would have competition in the verification business and could then focus its energies on maintaining adequate oversight upon a consequently smaller population consisting of those practitioners who can't get someone to sell them a policy. Thus, there is a market incentive for the contractor to be impeccable and a competitive incentive for government agencies to improve their efficiency.

Under InsCert, there is market incentive for the practitioner or landowner to hire the services of those who would do the hard technical work of managing certified processes. Whom might they hire? Perhaps government resource professionals would find such work more interesting? Most of the paperwork in civic agencies exists, not to improve the quality of the work in the field, but to verify that the practitioner is culpable for non-compliance to their rules. Performance "standards" limit the development, implementation, and maintenance of "best practices" to casting politically derived specifications into a set of checkboxes. Positive incentive to improve best practices ends up missing in the controlling legislation. "Underfunded" government oversight programs, overwhelmed by this paperwork, can effectively absolve "marginal operators" of indirect costs and thus, operate as a subsidy. When it is a question of merely getting caught, how do we determine when a practitioner has gone too far?

It is possible to reward trustworthy behavior and assist those who want to do the best that can be done. It is high time that integrity was rewarded in our society. We just might get more of it.

How would government enforce laws governing imported vegetables with pesticide residues? How would they prove beyond a reasonable doubt that a vegetable exporter knew that the pesticide levels were "detectable"? Would a foreign government extradite such a criminal? How much would that cost? How likely is a Federal Prosecutor to press charges under those conditions? How much of a deterrent is a system like that? Is it cheaper for the importer, simply to pay off the inspector? Do you feel safe with a system like that? It is a recipe for acculturating organized crime!

Borders are particularly important insofar as importing biological pollution is concerned. The lack of control of biological pollution constitutes an enormous trade subsidy to numerous enterprises that produce, transport, and sell imported products. The victims of the pests have to pay to rid themselves or suffer their presence. Who is in charge of the borders? If the U.S. Government didn't monitor the introduction of biological pollution, will NAFTA or the WTO do it? You know that answer.

Who oversees the government when it comes to environmental impact? There is a record of corrupted officials the world over looking the other way in such matters. The U.S. Government has already been determined to be liable for over a TRILLION DOLLARS in cleanup costs for its own operations. Who pays for that? NO ONE knows what the bill is going to be for the cleanup of MTBE in California groundwater (MTBE is a mandated fuel-oxygenate, defended by the Sierra Club). Civil liability can invoke increased focus on risk reduction and loss prevention process development because profits are at risk and people lose their jobs if it is not done. Competitive, insured, private certification could assist the incentive to measure and define the limits of liability as well as adhere to and improve preventative practice. Competition in the marketplace assures that it is done at minimal cost.

Insured certification is a way to resolve many trade disputes regarding the assignment of externalities such as safety standards for workers as well as ecological issues. The time is ripe for insurance, priced by behavior, to replace criminal enforcement or waiting for rulings from inexperienced, understaffed, opinionated, and possibly corrupt inspectors. The key to its eventual success will hinge upon how it is implemented.

Let's take a look at the certification market to make these distinctions clear

Principals of Certification, Supply Chains in Chains

A comparative discussion of existing forestry certification systems along with their respective strengths and weaknesses.

Author's Note: When explaining the advantages of something new, sometimes one is reduced to discussing its existing converse to make the reality. That is why the excess inventory, permit delay, and time-to-market issues of regulation were discussed by in Part II. It makes for a book that is more negative than one would like, but it is necessary in order to make the principles more tangible.

There are three existing types of forest practice certification. Each of them has significant structural flaws. So far, forest certification is voluntary. Best to fix the problems before it is not.

Type 1: Voluntary Guidelines of Industry Associations

The largest forest certification program in the world is under the American Forest & Paper Association (AF&PA). This organization is comprised of large, industrial producers of pulp and lumber. The overt purpose of such industry-based organizations are obvious: Weed out bad actors, retain productivity, and get environmentalists off their backs. Recently however, the AF&PA has flirted with the opportunities that abound in vertical oligopoly.

AF&PA certification is a self-policing system. It proposes its own standards and requests self-certification of its membership, a fraction of which resigned when confronted with the requirements. Environmentalists, represented by the Forest Stewardship Council (FSC), have expressed concern that, because the system is designed by an industry association, it might be specified to the advantage of the big players that fund the association budget. It is easy to bias specifications to favor the attributes of property held by specific owners.

No matter what the level of integrity of its membership, the system has a discernable potential for conflict of interest in verification because there is no independent auditing function. This leads to activist concerns about verification (independent third party auditing is under consideration by the AF&PA). That interest in "independent verification" is subject to its own inferred conflict of interest on the part of the environmental NGOs offering consulting certification services. Circumspection on the part of the AF&PA membership is thus quite understandable.

A structure like this will lose a political battle under accusations by environmental NGOs, looking to support their organizations by fees for verification "services," whether or not the inevitable charges can be substantiated. The NGOs' claim to sole legitimate authority for accreditation of third party certification is akin to the acquisition of market share by political extortion. They are not the only game in town.

Setting aside NGO business ethics, there are legitimate questions about their technical competency and there is no reason for them to extend their standard of professionalism. The paper industry, as a competitive business, rightly fears the kind of political leverage that the NGOs represent. Their behavior displays the means and behavioral propensity toward favoritism, in what should not be political decisions. Such process distinctions can be critical in consideration of approval or disapproval of a specific technology; for example a type of hybrid tree or machinery that might have taken years (and millions of dollars) to develop.

There will probably be no way for AF&PA to avoid third party verification. What remains is who should do it, how it should be verified, and who is financially responsible. The AF&PA system does not accomplish these goals.

Type 2:   Third Party Audit to Performance Specification

This type of certification uses independent audit to a performance standard or specification. It has components that are desirable. There are also critically deficient attributes. So far, the way it has been implemented, it has shown many, but not all of the structural problems to be detailed.

There is something intuitively appealing about third party audit systems. It is the reduction of conflicts of interest, a motivational check in the system. The key assumption is the auditor's manifest disinterest, professional expertise, equitable treatment of customers, and financial accountability.

There are two corporations, now operating this type of program: Scientific Certification Systems Inc. and the Institute for Sustainable Forestry (more commonly known as the Rainforest Alliance). Both are accredited by the Forest Stewardship Council (FSC). There are several more companies with relationships that support the FSC program in the marketplace, most notably the Certified Forest Products Council (CFPC). By fat the single largest group under FSC accredited certification hails from the County of Santa Cruz.

The FSC is a NGO incorporated under Mexican law, based in Oaxaca. Its member NGOs include: Greenpeace, the Sierra Club, Friends of the Earth, and the Environmental Defense Fund (to name but a few). The FSC carries a lot more weight behind it than that. It derives much of its funding from the IUCN, the World Wildlife Fund, the Ford Foundation, the MacArthur Foundation, the Rockefeller Foundation, and the Pew Charitable Trust.

If the AF&PA surrenders to activist pressure, it would make the FSC a global forest certification monopoly.

The FSC program is organized as a chain-of-custody system. It regulates forest practices by control of the customer base through "Green Labeling." The idea is that, if the supplier adheres to FSC specifications and operational requirements and subscribes to independent verification services provided by FSC accredited auditors, they can use the FSC logo on their products. The label allows the supplier to claim the endorsement by the FSC for their standards of practice, certified by the accredited auditor. All that remains is to track the product through the entire supply chain so that an impostor cannot sell goods as certified. (There is supposedly a reason for impostors to want to do this.) FSC market research indicates that 80% of customers say that they will pay higher prices for products with green labels. That claim is suspect when it comes to construction materials.

Early applications of the labeling and chain-of-custody principles were applied to the case of "dolphin free" tuna or vegetables marketed as having no detectable pesticide residues. These products require no integration into higher order levels of complexity: The fish stays as fish and the vegetables don't change composition unless they are integrated into prepared foods. There are a limited number of things a fisherman has to do to comply and, other than the difficulty of auditing a boat at sea unobserved, it is pretty easy to determine if they are killing dolphins or not. Once the fish is off the boat, most of it is canned, labeled, and boxed immediately. It is similarly easy to audit vegetables by testing samples taken from a store. It is far more complex to manage chain-of-custody with timber products.

The essential problem using supply chain certification with a raw material like wood is that it is that is integrated into a wide range of processes and products. The number of products and grades that can come out of a lumber mill is staggering. Structural lumber, fencing, pressboard, moldings, 2x4s and 6x10s in various grades such as select, vertical grain, structural select, all-heartwood, clear, or quarter-sawn; siding, blocking, sawdust for pulp or mulch, bender-board, and all in various lengths. The boards do not come off the log in order and some logs can't make many of the products at all. You don't get the mix of log dimensions you necessarily want from the forest. They do not occur in proportions that match demand. It is an expensive inventory problem. With chain-of-custody systems, one must more than double the inventory of both logs and lumber into certified and non-certified categories. You have to find a place within the mill to store a few pieces while you run enough logs to accumulate a saleable unit, particularly of larger sizes or higher grades.

Chain-of-custody of twice the number of products is more than twice the headache. This is a supply management problem of major proportion unless the mill owns sufficient certified forest acreage to supply itself. If a smaller mill operator sells only certified goods, then they must buy logs only from certified forests. These are often further away, with higher trucking costs. If they must mix log sources because either the supply of certified logs or demand for certified wood is insufficient to keep them busy, inventory management becomes extremely complex. If the composition of demand changes, it's a mess.

When the logs come in, certified storage areas must be separate and labeled. It changes the traffic pattern of material through the facility and induces extra requirements for tracking the slabs and boards while they are processed through the mill, routing certified and non-certified product to different accumulation areas pending running it through the same machinery. If a large order for certified wood comes in, one must move all the labels, reroute traffic, and train the people to keep track of it all.

Chain-of-custody greatly reduces the flexibility of production rates, as well. If one cycles either of the two categories through the mill separately, so that internal storage areas need not be replicated, then schedules for deliveries must be altered accordingly. Either way, it is a big material-handling problem for a small mill. The double inventory factor also greatly increases the complications of optimizing the utilization of materials by highest value grade, which decreases the profitability of the lumber. (It also falls afoul of the ecological principle of best use of resources.) It either means that the mill operator must have sufficiently high production volume that these inventory accumulations are not a problem, or compose all inventory of either certified product or not.

When one contemplates how certified-content in residential construction might be verified, or would serve as a market advantage, the benefits of green labeling start to appear increasingly suspect. Once someone sells lumber into a house, does the owner know if it is all certified wood? Is there to be a label on every piece of fire blocking or molding? How much additional inspection would have to be paid for? Not all the lumber produced ends up in the final product at all. Poured concrete foundations use a great deal of wood that ends up unusable or discarded. How would anyone track whether certified wood was used there, by poking through dumpsters?

Certified content may be okay for vegetables because the consumer can choose a different store or even a different bin. It is not so applicable to products with higher levels of integration. Some wood may be in the frame of a house and not in the sub-flooring because such products may not be available. People are much less likely to distinguish among houses by green labels than among cans of tuna or stores selling vegetables. There are too many ancillary considerations in the purchase of a home or book that have much more bearing on buying decisions, such as location or author.

Consumers have not demonstrated the willingness to pay enough for the benefit of certified lumber to offset these lumber production and construction headaches. Landowners and mill operators get stuck for the $40,000 investment and higher operating costs. Few customers will pay a higher price for a house built of certified wood to offset the higher product cost or the difficulty of finding an alternative supplier.

When asked about these problems, the FSC answer is that chain-of-custody is "voluntary," and not a requirement of FSC certification. It is, however, required if the mill wants to put the label on the wood to get that higher price, "promised" by FSC market research. If you do get the higher price, you waste good material getting the product the customer wants at net adverse environmental impact because of waste in obtaining it (that grade and dimension accumulation thing again). If you can't get the higher price for all that was cut then, what good is it?

If the label isn't there, there are consequences that the FSC doesn't mention.

In response to the concern about lack of customer willingness to pay higher prices, it appears that there is a move on the part of the NGO community to use control of market access as an inducement instead. This involves practices that render the programme somewhat less than voluntary. Earth First! and other groups have staged suspiciously timed protests on private property of prominent retailers unless they agree to sell only wood products that are certified by FSC accredited companies. The goal would appear to be constraining market access to only those forest producers approved by those same NGOs. The problem is where the money comes from: The same foundations that fund the NGOs also fund the FSC. One then wonders, who funds Earth First!?

The entire "chain-of-custody" method may well have worked for cans of tuna, from which people can choose among brands on a supermarket shelf. When the product has a sole source the decision of whether the book or house is made of certified paper or wood becomes ridiculous. One can't pick an alternative source of a material and still buy the product.

There are more problems with FSC certified systems than chain-of-custody.

First, the FSC claims to be a legitimate judge of expertise for all forests, worldwide. That claim of expertise is overstated when one considers the degree to which particular types of forests biologically differ around the world and how recently they were entered for the first time. Legitimate disagreement and ignorance still exist about the best way to manage various single types of forest that have been managed carefully for a long time. Thus the FSC claim of expertise, its reason for existence, itself can't be validated.

Why would somebody in the validation business stand for that, unless the primary purpose of the organization was something other than verifying the technical efficacy of forest management? These provisions feel good when you are writing them, if you are a lawyer, activist, or a beleaguered forester seeking relief. They feel really good if you're trying to make a buck in the certification business and get an occasional vacation in Oaxaca on the tab of some large foundation. They don't necessarily reflect or optimize conditions on the ground which is what the FSC is supposedly all about. Isn't it?

Second, the FSC subordinates its ecological management to political and social goals. It starts out with the "accreditation" of the FSC itself by its requirement for adherence to UN treaties:

"In signatory countries, the pro-visions of all binding international agreements such as CITES (Convention on International Trade in Endangered Species of Wild Fauna and Flora), ILO Conventions (International Labor Organisation), ITTA (International Tropical Timber Agreement), and Convention on Biological Diversity, shall be respected."

This hierarchy immediately politicizes the claim of scientific virtuosity on the part of the subject organization. For example: There are unspecified commitments to "maintain community well being" in the FSC bylaws. Who determines what that means? There are requirements to "conserve economic resources" which is equally subjective. There are requirements to "maintain biological diversity" although some forests naturally go through periods of near monoculture. The UN guarantees the "rights of indigenous peoples," and those guarantees are written into the bylaws of the FSC. What happens if a tribe of "Native" Americans makes a property claim against the land? Are the owners required to surrender it?

Given that the FSC is a supporter of the Convention on Biological Diversity, and that the Global Biodiversity Assessment specifically endorses the Wildlands Project, does that mean that the use of the land must eventually conform to the whims of the Global Biodiversity Assessment and therefore, the Wildlands Project? Does this mean that a forest certified under the FSC, no matter how well managed for production, must eventually be surrendered to a status of "no entry"? It is at least a tacit violation of U.S. law to require contractual adherence to the terms of rejected treaties.

Third, there is no regulatory benefit to FSC membership because it subordinates verification to specifications set by local laws. There is no added value if the laws are in error; indeed, it is an overlay of bureaucracy and puts the landowner into the position of serving two masters with differing opinions.

Thus, the FSC operates very much like a protection racket, because it has but one advantage to the landowner: It is the only certification system blessed by environmental NGOs. The landowners and timber operators hope that they might be left alone if they pay for the appropriate blessing. It certainly has advantages for environmentalists as a lever against owners, a potential source of cash through labeling and auditing fees, and a way to require projects to maintain "biodiversity" or "community viability." Whose "community" are they talking about?

These protection benefits have been illusory but for the control of market access by threat of organized protestors. When there have been disputes with local government over what constituted best management practice, the accredited auditors have historically been of no help whatsoever. Reports from those interviewed suggest that the inspectors fall back upon the "adhere to local laws" aspect of their bylaws and defer to the local authority. The most important reason that the timberland owners and foresters have for certification thus ends up producing little real benefit.

Fourth, there is no consideration of offsetting funds or mechanisms for risk management or means to minimize the cost associated with certification to FSC principles, nor is there provision for the certifying company to fix a problem if they are wrong. If the practitioner fails or makes a mistake, there is no backup. Are FSC certifiers accountable for their requirements?

Fifth, there is no motive for the landowner or practitioner to improve the limits of best practice for their unique situation. The FSC is the assumed seat of all forest knowledge, standing in judgement of the certificate holder for their specific combination of circumstances. How is that any better than the expertise of the CDF?

Sixth, the FSC is about forests. Who decides the value of other ecosystems affected by the forest, relative to the local circumstances? What if the forests have overgrown meadows. Do they care about those? There is no structural means to identify the relative contribution of resources and foster the best superposition of countervailing interests specific to an individual property.

Seventh, because this type of certification is audited to performance criteria, the inspections are subject to the interpretations of the inspector. Opinions differ from audit to audit, based upon the interests and goals of individual inspectors. This is a recipe for graft and extortion, not to mention a headache for the forest landowner.

Finally, (and, in the judgement of the author, this is the most egregious failing) once a critical mass of forests are certified by the FSC, what is to keep them from changing their minds as to what constitutes sustainability and/or acceptable performance specifications? These organizations are, after all, beholden to their benefactors. The rules of the group are likely to be defined by the most radical elements of a bipolar power structure. What if the organization dreams up a requirement for "cruelty free" redwood?

If there is an internal coup d'état in one of the governing NGOs, and with it a shift in control of the entire political food chain, what is to keep the social welfare crowd from hijacking the forest from the owner and the environmentalists to make houses for the poor? What if the NGOs at the UN decide that these specifications are to be subject to an overriding global social need? Isn't this a recipe for disaster?

The FSC system, however well meaning it might be, is still unaccountable political control of a resource on multiple levels, and is subject to multiple authorities. While it calls itself "voluntary," its use of leverage borders upon restraint of trade It operates on behalf of "stakeholders," few of whom pay for the claims that they demand, denying both the forest and its owner payment for those services. It thus ends up as is yet another way to lay external claims upon the wealth of the land.

Type 3: Process-Based Systems Audited by Standards Organizations

This third type of certification has favorable environmental properties, in that it is process certification and not a performance standard or conformance certification. There are two organizations offering such products: the International Standards Organization (ISO) and the Canadian Standards Administration (CSA) whose product is traceable to the ISO 14000 environmental process specification. The ISO is accredited by UNESCO (which leads us back to the UN) but, so far, has a fair track record of scientific independence, given its technical origins and composition. The ISO 14000 process specification is currently in the process of developing a chain-of-custody system. Neither of these products enjoys support by environmental NGOs.

The purpose, for any certification system design, is to imbue confidence in its ability to verify the trustworthiness and competence of those under audit. What performance specifications do provide is emotional security attendant to what is supposedly a deterministic outcome. They make people feel good without necessarily knowing why and are thus an easier political sell. Validated compliance to specification does not mean that something will work (much less be optimal), only that the practitioner can prove compliance. That's how the military gave us $200 hammers. It took $200 to prove compliance to specification. Did it make for better hammers?

To attempt to write a specification that describes the form of an outcome of an environmental product is fraught with complications. Performance specification (rule-based) systems may feel good to customers, but they are not dynamic, adaptive, diverse, competitive, or capable of differentiation – quite the contrary. How is the design of the specification itself to be verified?

"Performance Certification" systems are designed to prove that the product is adequate. They more seldom address the distinctions of how the processes are designed and optimized to produce that product. They do a whole lot more for verification to the spec than the improvement of the product design. They do less to integrate quality systems into the mechanics of continuous process improvements. More manufacturers adhere to the ISO 9002 quality system process specification, than the ISO 9001 document that includes design control. Most production and quality problems with manufactured products are design related. So it is with process designs as well.

Yet, it is here that the opportunity and superiority of process certification systems have their greatest opportunity. It is how you do, what you do with stuff, that changes its state. It is here that the bulk of research must be directed, not only to come up with good ideas but to devise systems by which a practitioner identifies and tests the efficacy of the way process improvements are developed and tested. Conformance systems fail because deviation is not allowed.

There is no point in taking the idiotic position that anybody knows what is "best." "Best" should be a verified means by which these things are learned, tested, and subjected to independent review, based upon consideration of the conditions specific to the location in question. It should always remain an elusive target to be pursued with vigor. Our understanding of nature is way too ephemeral for conformance goals to work.

That is what is not being done with either the ISO or CSA products. These certification systems are designed to prove that the systems the operator uses will deliver an output as specified by government. They end up functioning as conformance specifications. That they are a form of process certification is an improvement.

Unfortunately, the process specification systems of the ISO not only rely upon chain-of-custody as a benefit, they do little to push the limits of practice from the design perspective. They offer no regulatory dispensation. They do nothing to manage risk financially, and offer no weighting mechanism for decision-making, nor does the certification company have a financial stake in the successful conduct of experiments. Without these, the ancillary environmental and financial benefits to be discussed in this and proceeding chapters cannot be realized.

We can do better than that.

InsCert™

It is one thing to prove that you did what you were told to do. It is another to prove that your systems produce results that meet civic specifications. Once those two objectives are attained, the only claim to be made is that the work isn't excessively destructive, as determined by the local authorities. Outputs can only be defended by the degree of harm regardless of whether they are, in fact beneficial.

Why not have a certification system design that, instead of obsessing on minimizing harm, focuses on knowing that the work being performed is the best that can be done and continually advances the state of the art? The best practice regimen focuses upon continuing education and the collection and dissemination of data ancillary to forest management for these very reasons. It is intended to build the understanding of externalities such that the risks associated with decisions are accurately considered.

The objective of validated process design and development is to have means to assure that new technologies have a high probability of low risk and high return. To incorporate consideration of externalities by insured guarantee is to assure a rigorous test for an idea, to see if it is worth the risks, and to set aside appropriate funds to cover them. Freedom is scary folks.

This is InsCert. It is a way of using systems to keep us honest and using capital to manage the risk of human error or unforeseen circumstances. Insured certification has no fealty to ideology, it is not NGO-based; it is entirely business-based. There is no politicized governing body other than the stock market to hold this system accountable. If the certifying body does not do a good job, they get to file for bankruptcy and the reinsurance company guaranteeing the certifying entity gets to pick up the tab for the fix. That fact deepens the financial redundancy to three levels. Public confidence in that dispensation is assured by multi-layered financial accountability.

So far, there is not a forest certification program in the world that has any real market benefit for its customers. Insured certification is alleviated from restraint of trade entirely by its civic sanction to a civil account of financial responsibility, similar to UL, and its documented and validated record of best practice. Its customers are deemed insurable by their behavior and subscriptions. There is no requirement for a single definition of what constitutes "best practice" or a single vendor of insurance – quite the contrary, heterogeneous process development approaches are NECESSARY for competition that extends the limits of that technology.

Let's examine the system, applied to forest management, in more detail.

Structural Accountability

This was one of the big problems with Gamecock from a control system perspective. Roger had placed subordinates with minimal decision-making power in position to take the flack. Accountability should be identified and the limits of authority documented for each job. It saves time for everybody.

This is another situation where the certification process has real advantages over the existing system. The RPF, LTO, and landowner would be free to define the structure of responsibilities as reflects the nature of their operation. This reduces unnecessary duplication, minimizes ambiguities in the chain of command, and allows for redesign of the structure appropriate to the specific job or skill sets of the individuals involved.

It is not recommended that any single job function be accountable for collecting data and record keeping, only that accountability be defined and verified by the project participants.

Documented Hazard Reviews

Formal hazard reviews are something with which industrial chemical processors are intimately familiar. If you don't think of everything, trace every pipe, valve, circuit, operation, software command, and possible out-of-bounds chemical reaction, the plant blows up, people die, lawyers come running, TV reporters ask ignorant questions and get unflattering pictures… Nobody likes chemical plants that blow up, especially insurers.

In the case of an exploded chemical plant, we KNOW there is an assignable cause that can usually be determined after the fact. Ecological problems involve a large number of variables; they are easier to attribute and harder to prove. If, after a timber operation there is a landslide, people die, lawyers come running, TV reporters ask ignorant questions, and get unflattering pictures... and we 'KNOW' it is the loggers' fault because the TV crew is so thoroughly indoctrinated. Many "disasters" are, in fact, natural occurrences. What the media don't understand is that sometimes a logger has to do something about a bad situation with a high probability that it may "fail" anyway. So how do we minimize the risk?

Hazard reviews are that moment when we ask: 'Did I forget anything? What is the cost of failure? Do I need any resources?' They are essential to successful low-risk operations. Hazard reviews build the project record that renders risk more predictable and identifies opportunities for improvement. It dovetails with the insurance aspect of the program (to be discussed) by incorporating a financial assessment of risk attributes up front.

Hazard reviews document risk factors before commencing operation. If, for example, a job involves an unstable slope showing signs of imminent failure, the review documents the risks, assesses the scope, and plans a response set. It also assures that precautionary measures are complete (such as notifying people or adapting drainage measures). It may be the best that can be done, if an eventual landslide is unavoidable. If the slope fails, a "post mortem" on the event reviews the file to evaluate if predictions were accurate, whether everybody responded according to plan, and how a better job might be done next time. The review is also a time to incorporate new capabilities into an existing response plan.

Process Design Control

Process Design Control in timber operations? Yes, because it works. It is hard to write things down; the process induces a series of uncomfortable moments when you have to discover how to express what you may not know as clearly as you thought. How are employees to understand what management wants if it isn't communicated clearly?

In the medical and pharmaceutical industries, process design is verified by validation. Whole books are written on the use of validation in quality systems. It is a structured method to measure process inputs and behavior against its outputs to acquire sufficient knowledge to operate the process deterministically. There are three types of validation: retrospective, concurrent, and prospective. Retrospective validation examines system outputs and correlates them with measured system inputs to determine if the output is within expectations. Concurrent validation measures process variables while in operation to assure that each is delivering intermediate results within expectations. Prospective validation operates with the knowledge that, so much is known about the process, its operations are under such control, and results are so predictable, that only monitoring of selected process inputs and settings is necessary to achieve desired outputs. A manufacturer usually starts with retrospective validation, incorporates concurrent, and works toward prospective.

Validated process design is an opportunity to build the knowledge that can prevent problems from developing. It is the foundation for development of an owner's operating manual to a parcel. It is a way to assure competent future ownership should the land transfer by sale or inheritance. It is a basis to communicate land use possibilities among peers and organize data toward forming resource enterprises marketing regional products.

There is a concern with design validation that demands caution: Validation is a word that makes expensive consultants salivate. They can make endless recommendations with futile bureaucratic loops that can break a company financially and do NOTHING for the product if not executed correctly. Any powerful tool, used badly, has the power for great harm to the organization.

The determinant in success or failure using design control systems is the self-discipline required not to promise more than one can deliver. Unattainable specifications can be just as much a problem in design control systems as with rule-based regulatory systems. Design control system-design is beyond the scope of this book, but can be simple and flexible. The key is to confine investigative work to control by very few people and periodically give it a reality check with those more remotely involved. There is less risk in trying a great many things on a small scale and killing them early if they fail than to expend great efforts qualifying an apparently "optimal" approach that is all too often illusory or is superceded by changing conditions. Note that the latter approach is all too common among regulatory agencies. Even a failed approach can be successfully applied to other circumstances, but one must be able to trust the data.

Validated Data

The Timber Harvest Plan in California is a conformance specification document. It details a series of outputs designed to meet public demands on the use of private forests. By contrast, a process document details how operations are to be conducted in order to obtain predictable results. This mechanism manages the experimental process by which to deviate from conformance requirements in order to produce better results. How else could one be certain that instructions produced the expected results?

No one can honestly evaluate and improve the quality of their work without comparing the results of past projects against predictions. That the jobs are often fifteen to twenty years apart almost requires that data be gathered continuously. To do that requires determining who should be accountable for the data, how is it verified, who interprets it, who has access to it, and in what form. Assigning those responsibilities develops from the effort to prove that data are reliable.

Many landowners have been afraid of data and scientists for good reason. It has repeatedly been used against them. Why should they document a unique plant, pathogen, or insect on their land when it represents an opportunity for government to take it? Data are subject to interpretation. Resource agencies often augment operating revenue with fines. Why should we expect people to seek the limits of science unless we have a system by which they are the sole owners of that scientific information?

The other problem with collecting data is that it is expensive. One way of making continuous scientific data collection more affordable is to trade it for dispensation from unnecessary paperwork, delay, and constant political and legal battles, but that is only where InsCert starts. More competition in the habitat monitoring business would improve the development of better and less expensive measurement devices and software products, configured for capturing and processing ecological data. There is a need for map information of plant census and survey data, site geology, insect population distribution, or infestations and pathogens, including external threats. Imagine how useful it might be as a way to identify the progress of an exotic pest vector so that it can be treated early, or at least observed in progress. When the data are related to the proper fix, they can become part of future specifications for a marketable product or service. This is a huge opportunity by which to develop fuel control and fire management processes in rural areas that can be sold as processes to manage fire closer to structures.

Data are expensive and collection never ends. We can put certification systems in place and offer permit dispensations as a carrot, but without a format by which to exchange that information the data don't have practical use beyond the bounds of the property. This is where insured certification has advantages over existing verification services. Validated data calibrate risk. Calibration accounts risk constituents and renders the assets that offset them, tradable (as is discussed in the next chapter). The key is the collection and organization of honest data.

Calibration allows local data to be applied to global analysis. Validated measurements are essential to evaluate and integrate larger risks, and thus the means to weigh competing claims upon ecosystem resources. While a profit can motivate the creative focus to measure the relative importance of ecosystem constituents, you can't sell something that you can't measure, and measurements mean nothing unless the method is reliable. Unless the data are audited they cannot serve as bases for financial transactions in uses of ecosystem assets.

Support for Research and Development

How do we know what to measure?

Every industry has their own R&D, don't they? Nope. If industry operations involve The Environment, government does much of it, "for free," whether it is timber, agriculture, range management, or fishing. Look at that list of industries and consider their prosperity under such technical guidance. The incentive for government employees to expend that research to develop new regulatory markets is so strong that the research product diverges from its mandate in service to job security.

To qualify for a certification to this best practice standard requires private conduct of, or support for, research. The work can be as simple optimizing truck tire pressures to minimize soil disturbance. The work performed by the Monterey Bay Salmon and Trout Project, supported by Big Creek Lumber certainly qualifies as an example. There is no reason that active participation in a trade organization coordinating the work couldn't qualify, as long as the experiments were being coordinated with others in the group and results were being incorporated into validated operational processes.

Meets or Exceeds Existing Practices

This transitional standard sets a starting point for new applications of the system. Once the system starts to operate it slowly transitions to internal standards as superior methods are proven.

Processes start as retrospective validation to produce outputs within existing standards much as with CSA or ISO certification standards. Once that process specification is validated as capable of producing outputs within specification and in control, the specification criteria graduate to adherence to the process standard instead of those defined by the certifying body, state specification, or customary practice. At that time validated data, either developed on site or purchased from others, would provide justification for specific experiments deviating from specified rules for specific purposes.

Once the results were verified and the risk associated therewith calculated, the experimental standard would be incorporated into the process specification for the site. This is how the system differentiates local practice from "one size fits all" uniformity to scientifically supportable site-specific methods development.

Continuing Education, Training, and Publication

The requirement advocated is the maintenance of a documented record of research, development, publication, and adoption of improved methods and practices on all levels of the enterprise.

Everyone acknowledges the value of continuing education; most everyone hates to spend time on it. Most professions seem to benefit from continuing education, why not forestry, timber operations, and land ownership? The problem has been that, if one company institutes an expensive technical training program, other companies hire those people away. Landowners are usually not professional foresters and hire that expertise. Up until now, the biggest benefit of continuing education and training has been problems that were prevented because of smarter people on the job. To this can be added the benefit of permit dispensation resulting in steadier employment and a safer place to work.

Without training, there is no way to validate proprietary process procedures because one can't be sure that the people knew what to do. The lack also complicates disciplinary procedures. Training eases data collection within the usual conduct of operations, and can in fact, save a great deal of money.

Would it be useful if toppers and fellers understood tree pathology and insect identification? Dumbing down has its consequences, doesn't it? Could we train cat operators in a smattering of geology, hydrology, and tree root pathology so that they can perform data entry and identify potential problems before they rip into them further? Would it be worth the money? Validation is a check step that identifies opportunities to optimize training productivity.

Transparency of Operations

Private forestry seldom publishes process data and experimental results because it is proprietary information. The nature of the industry makes it very difficult to protect intellectual property. Perhaps an open standard, interdependent ownership of ancillary assets (to be discussed), and patent protection with a financial motive for licensing processes, will produce motives for disseminating proprietary information with practical application.

The single biggest cause of public resistance to timber harvesting is public ignorance. A common and independent source of composite validated data will help prevent disputes. If one holds a meeting with movies, charts, and learning aids, it is cheaper than a week of delay on the job, or one day spent in a courtroom. It would be worth it. Notify the public of the impact, gather the concerns, write them down, and respond. If there is a dispute, documentation of notification is in place. Notify them also of their liability for slander.

In Santa Cruz, there are RPFs who came to regret it when they made an effort to educate a neighborhood about timber harvesting prior to a job. The pitfall to such openness was that the education organized the opposition. Activists got wind of the notification, enlisted the homeowners with usually exaggerated claims, and provoked a legal battle.

The certification system proposed manages that concern as follows:

1. There is no permit appeal.

The certified practitioner would have a process for addressing complaints, none of which would be related to lack of notification. If the activists are not satisfied with the explanation, they would take the case to the certifying body. They would have the independent expertise with which to evaluate the case because they keep the audited record. If there had been an unusual risk, the cost of job insurance would have been negotiated and the certifying body would already be aware of it. They can testify to records demonstrating that the likelihood of a problem is so small that a written claim would have to be filed before taking action. Upon acceptance, they would have civil recourse to false claims. Sometimes a risk exists whether anything is done or not. The best one can do is to define a system by which to reduce the sum thereof.

1. Process validation provides the certified practitioner with the historical record of practice with which to refute false claims.

This is a long-term process requiring patience and documentation. The speed with which the job can be done and the reduction in unnecessary bureaucracy will offset some of the costs of additional data collection.

2. Process validation provides a format to collect and compare data.

This provides the site-specific record necessary to evaluate risk associated with future proposals and meet the verification standards of certified audit. It also forms the basis for discourse among landowners and a future market in ecosystem assets.

3. Transparency to audit assures that intellectual property is respected.

It preserves property rights to data that drive technical innovation.

Transparency also creates a venue to verify whether intellectual property has been infringed and possibly mediate a settlement. The level of disclosure advocated here does not mean that all data (particularly raw data) belonging to the practitioner or landowner are available free to anyone. It does mean that the composite audit to validated practices, complaint and resolution records, and experimental results are verified by the certifying entity and that the verification record is available for inspection. Perhaps composite data of various owners and practitioners for purposes of furthering general research might be available for sale from the certifying body. The rest is at the option of the insured because it is private property.

Adequate Capital and Insurance

There is ample risk of capital loss associated with civic environmental management with which to interest the participation of insurers. (The residential buffer and flood control proposals in Part IV are examples.)

150

Introductory products and markets will create the opportunity to learn how to price and finance risk reduction, as part of best practice management. These products can then differentiate into new markets. That is the beauty of incremental implementation plan suggested in Part V.

The insured, best-practice management system proposed here can succeed regulatory management as new products and processes are proposed, tested, and improved. The system design extracts the cost of ecological risk from the accounted cost of mitigation projects and designed experiments as part of the insured certification process. This method of bootstrapping the value of ecosystem resources, as will be discussed in Chapter 3.

The objective of the program is to verify that design of the management system by the landowner and practitioners under contract will extend the state of the art to minimize overall risk. The certification process therefore does not focus upon not only whether practitioners do work according to plan. It verifies how they go about experiments to determine what is best to do and assesses the quality of risk analyses therewith.

What is missing, is a way to price the risk.

Figure 3 – Certification, Insurance, and Bonded Guarantees. Standards Groups are everywhere. You trust your life to such people every day. They compete for that trust by providing testing, research, education, certification, audit, and verification services. (These logos are for illustration purposes only. Their presence does not constitute an endorsement of this work.)

📖 Chapter 3 – What's It Worth To You?

The Value of Risk in the Cost of Goods Sold

This section applies the historical development of industrial risk-pricing as a model toward a market pricing of environmental risk.

OK, so Mr. Hardin is still repeating himself without apology...

> "Only a criterion of judgment and a system of weighting are needed. In nature the criterion is survival. Is it better for a species to be small and hideable, or large and powerful? Natural selection commensurates the incommensurables. The compromise achieved depends on a natural weighting of the values of the variables."

A pricing scheme set by an oligarchy and managed by an unaccountable bureaucracy is obviously not equivalent to natural commensuration. So?

> "The problem for the years ahead is to work out an acceptable theory of weighting. Synergistic effects, nonlinear variation, and difficulties in discounting the future make the intellectual problem difficult, but not (in principle) insoluble."

Indeed, not insoluble. Given that academics and bureaucrats have been conducting "rational analysis" for 35 years without an end in sight, perhaps there is someone who already understands the nature of managed risk.

Insurance Pricing Mechanics

Insured certification does far more than to assure mere accountability. Beside the obvious benefits of motivational oversight, the InsCert system design induces investment in ecosystem management enterprises with products priced by their capability to offset measured risk. Though it may be decades before these benefits are realized at full scale, there is every reason to start small and work toward larger and more complex manifestations.

This discussion will start at the level of the individual resource enterprise and demonstrate that, at even this simple level, a free market in risk management of resource enterprise has immediate benefits. After a discussion of fluid property markets in Chapter 4, the theory will extend toward the broader case in Chapter 5. Examples of simple trial programs will follow in Part IV.

Insurance performs many economic functions in a market economy, beyond its primary objective of paying the bill in cases where there is a loss. The cost of capital used to offset risk in the production of a product incorporates consideration of that risk on the part of the buyer. The buyers of a product don't need to know how safe is the factory, or if tornadoes or droughts are a high probability. They automatically weigh that risk, both against competitors within the industry and against the relative benefit of substitute goods. They don't need a green label on the package, because the cost of risk-management is in the price of the product.

Our knowledge of industrial insurance pricing has evolved over centuries. The insurance industry has derived its historic estimates of the risk of capital loss, by factoring the present value of the asset-at-risk against the estimated probability of a loss. Early insurance markets for cargo shipments in ancient China used the knowledge of the construction cost of ships, the purchased price of cargo, the history of losses, and news of current risks in-transit to a particular destination to estimate bids for insurance contracts. That data also directs efforts to reduce the cost of mitigation and lower the probability of loss, thus lowering the total cost of risk.

The process has involved a huge number of iterations constantly reevaluating historic risks against those associated with new information. The result has been improved reliability, safety, and reduced cost of industrial products, while simultaneously managing the pool of risk capital more efficiently.

Let's examine both these principles of asset value and loss probability, against the historical industrial example, to see how they might be applied to environmental management. First is determination of asset value:

The value of assets at risk is estimated from the cost accounts of acquisition combined with the settlement records of related losses.

Actuaries must have an accurate measure of the replacement cost and market value of the insured asset and the probability of its loss in order to price their product. The financial arms of insurance companies are not, however, experts in auto mechanics, medicine, construction, or law, much less the specific process practices of the insured. They don't understand the cost of nails, the price of bandages, or the cost of downtime in a chemical plant; instead they have access to the audited accounts of the insured and similar records of operations of other enterprises. If they require outside information, they can either permanently hire or consult as required in order to render technical information into both accurate estimates of asset value, and probability of objectively defined, accounted, and attributed harm.

Raw data for the calculation of financial risk are derived prospectively, retro-spectively, or experimentally. Prospective asset cost information is acquired through analysis of the proposed design and construction costs of physical plant, and estimation of the extent of damage due to types of possible inci-dents as part of a hazard review. Often, an analysis requires independent verification of experimental or design data. These values are adjusted with other prospective expectations such as interest rate and inflationary expecta-tions, and estimates of functional life versus product life cycle. Retrospective analyses include historical construction costs of similar assets, profit and loss on continuing operations for the analysis of business interruption insurance, and histories of and precedents for legal settlements.

Risk assessments must consider the costs of loss-mitigation. These include repairs to physical assets, or human resource assets in medical care, training, and rehabilitation. Accounted mitigation costs are particularly important where the loss is a significant fraction of the operational asset value or where it has subjective market value, as in the case of human pain and suffering. In any of these cases, audited accounting data provided by the insured or usual and customary settlement costs are critical to deriving insurance pricing.

The second aspect f pricing risk is loss probability:

Loss probability is projected from real-time inputs and historical records appropriate to the attributes of the asset under coverage.

To complete the total pricing of risk requires not only assessing the capital constituents under coverage, but also computation of the probability and extent of a loss. Whether it is frequency of floods, tornadoes, or trucking accidents, pricing the risk of loss is related to how often, how severe, and under what circumstances, losses occur.

Loss probability of is calculated from the historical frequency and severity of claims attributed to accidents or natural disasters in either identical or related industries. Estimates of both probability and severity are also derived from laboratory experiments conducted by service enterprises. (Underwriters Laboratories has developed valuable technologies investigating causes of failure, and means of risk reduction.)

There are many ways to reduce the cost of risk. One could build better houses to reduce the damage due to earthquakes or choose to build them elsewhere because the cost of earthquake insurance is just too high. Once these costs are measured and the loss probability is calculated, a relationship develops between the cost of reducing the size of the loss, inherent to the product, or the cost of avoiding the sources of loss. One might choose to build houses that can resist a magnitude of 7.0 on the Richter Scale without damage, but to do so for an 8.0 or greater, that appears only every 100 years or so, may not be worth it. The decision will be between the capital cost of building houses engineered for 7.0 quakes plus the cost of insuring them against 8.0 disasters, versus the price of houses elsewhere where the risks are different. The market will seek to minimize the total cost of houses in earthquake zones to be competitive with houses elsewhere. The key to the decision is to understand the costs associated with repairing or preventing losses due to earthquakes. Whether it is a Northridge Earthquake, Love Canal, or Oakland Fire, the estimates of the frequency and severity of insured losses derive from historical data. Without data, we cannot calculate the cost of risk.

There isn't much of a financial difference between an investment risk and the risk associated with an insured loss; in fact the latter can be more predictable when the risk is spread among many customers. Historic analyses of pooled risk have had limitations providing accurate assessments of large financial risks to the individual owner of an investment asset. This is particularly true in the case of losses due to causes for which there is no historical basis. Although this makes selecting the appropriate risk instrument difficult, the market has striven to provide a mechanism to manage such events.

Current research, to price financial risk accurately, is focusing upon integrating the total population of actual transactions for both asset value and loss probability, such that specific knowledge can be correctly applied to particular cases. Such risks include research and development investments with long lead times, with a high probability of obsolescence rendered by competing technologies. It takes enormous computing power to integrate millions of individual transactions and extract their appropriate analytical constituents. Pooled risk can do much to protect this invested capital.

Because of the demand for fluid capital, it is now more common for large corporations to purchase insurance against an unexpected financial loss or even earnings below projections. It is a way of dispersing the risk to a long-term investment in a new technology that may be rapidly superceded by a competitive entrant. This is particularly the case in a market where, though the rewards may be enormous, the term of development is long, and risk of failure is high as in the development of prescription drugs.

As financial instruments have matured, they have extended beyond the mere probability of a loss, into a set of purchased financial outcomes. The market price of these options constantly readjusts as new information changes the probability of a particular outcome. In this way, pooled ownership of risk and opportunity integrates specialized knowledge of the causes and effects of potential losses.

Even if resource assets are not high risk compared to insuring profit expectations in the prescription drug business, there is no reason that similar instruments cannot move down-market. In the case of the environment, the theoretical need is to develop cost accounts of mitigation and loss history data. The models and computational tools exist or are developable; what we really need is infinitesimal data, the nails, bandages, and labor hours, of pricing environmental assets. Without motive to reduce acquisitions cost for environmental data, that data will be lacking.

Compare the sophistication of free-market risk management to the political valuations of civic risk management. It is no contest. Free markets are so complex that no one really understands how they work. Somehow, that does not keep us from using them to manage risk.

Assessing ecological risks has been difficult because we don't understand them very well. One reason that they have been subjected to political valuation is that we have had no account of the risk constituents. The publicly purported threats are nearly always drastic, subjective, and almost always leveled by immediately interested parties. Although we have nifty analytical tools, we don't have a decent knowledge of the economic attributes of, and risks to, ecological assets. We don't have the data.

Landowners own the source of that information. They just haven't measured, evaluated, and compiled it. InsCert uses a combination of asset analysis, loss history, and experimentation to compile the cost of environmental risk, as did the development of classical insurance pricing. It starts with tangible risks and motivates development of financial instruments applied to environmental risks. That the risks can be weighted and reduced by the behavior of the insured renders the system a just means of incorporating the cost of externalities into the cost of goods sold. There is a way to get the owners to want to generate the necessary source data, even before it is consolidated into higher-order information.

Loop the Loop

The InsCert process standard operates as a positive "feedback loop" that lowers the cost and risk of hazard management. It simultaneously generates the data that accounts the cost of risk and identifies risk-offset opportunities.

There are five aspects to insured certification as proposed, that bootstrap the proposed environmental risk valuation mechanism:

1. The best practice standard includes data collection, research, and continuing education. It directs the data-acquisition of environmental knowledge toward methods and applications. The data thus have leverage, both toward the immediate reduction of risk and the eventual characterization of its cost.

The companies in the certification business will want to charge competitive rates and have no motive for needless bureaucracy. The entities responsible for verifying the conduct of operations thus have a stake in customer success for two reasons. First, they don't want to pay the cost of insurance claims that end up as higher customer premiums. Second, they need to minimize the cost of verification to be competitive in the price of certification services.

There is another set of counterbalancing considerations on the part of the insured. When the insurance customers are purchasing coverage, they have reason to reduce the probability of loss just as much as the insurer has reason to request proof of a good risk. There is thus a reduced motive to overstate a loss because of the risk of a higher price of coverage. The system is bi-directionally self-regulating, similar to other industries.

2. Process validation produces reliable data that motivate investigation to improve the limits of practice to reduce the cost of risk.

The dual verification systems of certified financial accounting and process standards validated by audit, assures that insured certification processes are capable of delivering reliable data. There is no reason for the insured not to market mature process designs as long as the reliability of the system assures low risk and addresses concerns that intellectual property is respected.

3. Risk management, based upon multilevel insurance, places a cost on risk that a prudent investor in process knowledge will seek to minimize.

This predisposition leads to investment in activities designed to reduce the probability of loss and improve the productivity of the asset. In the case of forestry, process assets support and depend upon the growth of healthy trees.

4. Verify risk reduction history to justify lowering the price of insurance.

That takes data. The logic here is thus a program loop, with a decision point:

Once risks associated with continuing operations are reduced to the point of diminishing returns, what is the practitioner to do with this "stupid" requirement to keep studying and collecting data?

5. Apply the research and continuing education toward an ancillary ecological problem or new opportunities on the property in terms of how it interacts with its surroundings.

Here is where the results of continuing education and research come into play. We may have been learning about the cost of weeds based upon the labor expended for control. Are there better ways to reduce seed transport? Should we use a pre-emergent to wash the seeds off heavy equipment? How should that be done?

Once these questions are asked, concerns about the manner in which the surroundings affect the operation are considered as part of total cost. With that realization comes the opportunity to consider the ecological interactions of the property with the rest of the planet.

This is where the insured certification regimen, as proposed, begins to gain power toward motivating solutions to larger ecological problems and discovery of environmental business opportunities. The program gives both the practitioner and the owner reasons to learn and experiment while maintaining consideration of the risks associated with deviation. It gives the certifying entity a reason to assure continuing reductions in the cost of risk. This takes scientific experimentation and accurate data.

Are we concerned with the nature of the practitioner's perception, skewing the objectivity of the data? Perhaps. Objectivity is a challenge for anyone. It is common to ask a forester a question about forest health and get an answer back in terms of increased timber production. That is, after all, how they get paid. If however, they rewarded for a more-integrated perspective of total forest health, because there was a cost of risk in continuing operations without that consideration, the answer would reflect that broader perspective.

If We Knew What We Were Doing, We Wouldn't Call It Research

Author's Note: This aphorism from an unknown source was the war cry of our product development team when I was working in the Medical Device Industry.

Sometimes you just have to have been an inventor to understand how valuable mucking around in data from kluged-up experiments can really be, or how much fun it is. Unfortunately, even well designed experiments lead to a higher than usual probability of confined mistakes. That is just the way it is with science. The experimenter occasionally gets to feel stupid, take a deep breath, and be thankful it was only a test. Then comes the humiliation of writing it all down for posterity to read and learn about how and why that great idea didn't work. Somebody might see the pitfall in the execution of what was, perhaps, a good idea with a botched experimental trial. As with any error in a learning process, the earlier in the development and the smaller is the scope of the error, the easier it is to repair the damage. Good experimenters anticipate uncertain outcomes and allocate resources to deal with failures in advance.

The goal of experimental design is to confine the scope of damage a mistake might do while capturing the data and communicating it to others to render the trial useful. Multivariate designed experiments performed in nature have too many possibilities to be comprehensive. These circumstances engender the need for screening trials wherein one must push a control variable to the point where the process doesn't work order to observe a process attribute. Conformance specifications, particularly those that are risk averse, do not allow deviation. They are simply too rigid to perform good science.

An example is the clearcut. There are credible data suggesting that, in some types of forest, a clearcut with an extended reentry time is ecologically preferable to selective harvesting. In other types of forest, this would be an outrage. If the governing body specifies group selection harvesting methods and uneven-aged stands as an output for all forests, one may never know which system is better under local circumstances. If instead, landowners, out of a verifiable effort to learn how best to manage each location on their property, conduct an array of methods with careful, scientific monitoring and data collection, why should they not find out? What remains is to minimize

159

the pooled risks involved. Analyzing the distribution of risk and mitigating it appropriately is where the hazard review becomes essential.

How do we best manage local processes of succession after 100 years of fire suppression? How long are meadow seed banks of specific species viable in situ? How would we find out? Whom do we trust to find out? So far, this has been the almost exclusive province of government, operating with motives that can no more be trusted than those of any timber corporation.

Meadow species in Santa Cruz County are truly threatened, far more so than redwood forest. Meadows are principal stores of biodiversity reserves for species that repopulate a forest after a fire. Meadows are threatened by development, fire suppression, and by exotic species that rapidly convert them to a foreign form of chaparral and thence to forest. Meadows are cheaper to develop for housing than forests so they were first under the bulldozer. Given the history, we may need to create a few artificial meadows. Would landings do under some circumstances? It could be that, under some circumstances, concerns about "fragmentation" are more figment than fragment. We just don't know. What is the risk if a "rolling wave of succession" experiment were proposed. What would it cost to mitigate?

This is how risk management offsets the desire to invent pseudo-experiments designed to maximize the take from the land and lower costs for those who would do otherwise. Such an experiment as a clearcut might come at higher risk and, therefore, cost more to insure.

"The best thing to do" may well change over time, in fact, it must. Climate change, natural disasters, and changes in technology will force continuous development. Would it be preferable for us to have process systems, in place, for adaptation to changes in external conditions? Would it not be preferable to have a competitive motive for developing such knowledge? What if somebody invented a machine, which could harvest a redwood by merely ripping it out of the ground like a large garden vegetable, and thus simulate the fall of a mature tree in nature? Should we grind some of the stumps? Should we replace caterpillar tracks with walking machines? Why would anybody develop that equipment without a market? How would we best use these tools and what problems are we trying to solve? Continuous research is the way to generate both answers and, more importantly, new questions.

None of these problems can be solved unless we allow the questions to be asked and tested. The measurements will be meaningless and the answers will have no correlation with the actual conduct of operations unless they are motivated toward economic purposes. Productive purposes are essential to discovering the wealth of knowledge unforeseen, in part because experiments are investments in profits that fund more tests. What fun!

What if the experiments don't work?

Measure for Measure

The practice of mitigating environmental risk accounts the value of offsetting or preventing errors and disasters. This improves the accuracy of estimates of the price of environmental risk

Let's say we continue with our grossly oversimplified example clearcut. The plan is to add a converted patch of forest to a landing to create a native meadow as a natural firebreak, seed reservoir, and access area. The idea is that we can work a minor clearcut across the forest front leaving a functioning succession process behind like a waveform over hundreds of years.

We did the logging, rooted out the stumps, and hired a botanist to plant grasses, locally collected wildflowers, bushes, and broadleaf trees. What we got was an infestation of star thistle from a dirty tractor that dried out most of the natives and killed them in three years. As an experiment, it was a failure. We have choices now: sterilize and replant meadow, or replant a forest.

Let's say we doggedly do the former. Now we find that we have a nifty firebreak, a great tractor washing process, and know a great deal about the process of meadow species propagation and succession, and even more about how often to weed, based upon the type of infestation. There are other problems, however, when it comes to weeds (especially annual pasture grasses); the birds and deer bring them in anyway. It's a two-acre flop.

Forest. We can do that! It is going to take over a hundred years before we get back to where we were and with significantly reduced productivity during the interim. We plant the trees, protect them from browsing, get them growing, and do the requisite stand improvements for 50 years. We also have to devise some other way to confine the prescribed burns. The whole time, we kept track of the cost under a project authorization. OK, what was the bill? There was lost income and increased insurance, the prescribed fire experiment had to be written off, the botanist, the weed abatement, the stump grinding, and planting and tending the new forest. Boy, were we stupid!

At least we can sell the experimental results to an insurer or forest landowner who wants to know what the risks are in trying such a thing. Perhaps others have ideas how to prevent the problems we had. Their insurers might pay to know what the cost of risk might be or how precious are their meadows as biological reserves. Should they fail to guard them jealously, they could no longer market their value to offset the lack on the part of others, serve as a genetic source, or a dynamic model for study.

Learning the cost of repair is key to learning the cost of risk. Under InsCert, actuarial cost data will be derived from compiled financial records of just such mitigation projects, pest eradication efforts, propagation and reintroduction exercises, as well as insurance loss history. Giving people a reason to measure and lower those costs is far better than simply passive measurement. The data is an asset that can lower the market price of risk.

As the landowner accumulates data, not only on products that now have tangible resource value (such as timber), but also on the other physical and biotic attributes of the property that someday might have such value, the processes particular to that location, by which its attributes transform the state of commons, become apparent. That leads to a process of discourse in higher level functions with other participants with commonly held assets. It identifies individuals whose behavior is a threat to their economic value. It also serves as a venue to share the prospect of more remote potential threats (such as a distant infestation) and organizes a contingency response. Such processes of communication lead to negotiations by which to weigh the value of relative risks.

How do we keep it honest?

Insurance, Warranties, and Other Instruments of Bondage

Competitive pricing of risk in ecosystem management is environmentalism with an insured guarantee. Government offers no warranties for its control systems. This proposal allocates managed funds to redress possible mistakes and regulates behavior with the price of risk.

Some people are bound by their promises. We get really upset whenever we pay for a product that doesn't work and rightly demand a warranty before we buy it, which we usually get. We expect the makers of a product that causes subsequent or collateral damage, to pay to redress the loss.

Insurers have to deal with uncertain outcomes among unique circumstances. They are masters of the actuarial mathematics of probability, game theory, statistical uncertainty, and hedged outcomes. Again, the market has modalities to deal with the risks associated with managed ignorance.

Insured certification can do things that government never could. It can guarantee a degree of efficacy. It motivates all involved to minimize the damage due to a disaster. It can offer protection associated with damages. It can efficiently manage risk capital to rectify a problem.

By contrast, government assumes no liability associated with its monopoly to verify conformance to its own specifications. They'll give you FEMA after there is a disaster; fixing problems with your borrowed money, after the source of cash flow has been destroyed.

Many major insurance companies are short of both new markets and better margins. What is lacking in insuring ecological risk is the data that indicate what the limits of liability are likely to be. The insurance industry rightly fears the possible magnitude of liability for economic externalities related to the environment. This is partly because we are operating under conditions of ambiguous political valuation and subject to the greed of trial lawyers. We have thus reverted to government regulation, out of the need for "protection." In that respect, civic financial accountability (through FEMA for example) could be a net subsidy. Civic regulation lowers total overhead expended for measuring and pricing individual ecological risks because it doesn't get it done. Why should the public subsidize that kind of mismanagement?

No single insurance product covers every need. There will be a motive for a much more intimate relationship among landowners, practitioners, and insurers in order for any of this to work (a real job market for graduates of environmental studies programs). A similar approach can be utilized on an individual or neighborhood basis toward drainage control and landslide risk management, road evacuation efficacy, or earthquake hazard reduction and emergency preparedness. All it takes is the will on the part of people to get the insurers out of their debilitating shell of regulated pricing and into the businesses of risk reduction and financing. Society would be richer for it and so would the health of natural habitat. Part IV has examples.

Insurers currently risk catastrophic financial loss due to an underbid market. The problem is that every time there is such a loss the State raises the rate-base and everybody goes back to what they were doing without account-ability to shareholders. Why should the public subsidize that mismanagement of competition? Government misallocates resources because it won't allow insurance companies to measure and price risk based solely upon behavior.

Besides the obvious political interest groups, whom would we be protecting? The very people who funded the tax-exempt foundations that supply grant money to the NGOs. It makes an interesting test of industry claims that bank and insurance regulation is so often unjustified. What unfortunately happens, is that we collectively lose wealth and cause environmental damage because we fail to correctly apportion the cost of risk. The banks and insurance companies don't need to manage the range and extent of environmental risk because you pay for it with FEMA, the FDIC, and "too big to fail."

Wouldn't it help our society to have individual reasons to work together to reduce the cost of problems rather than simply operating out of denial?

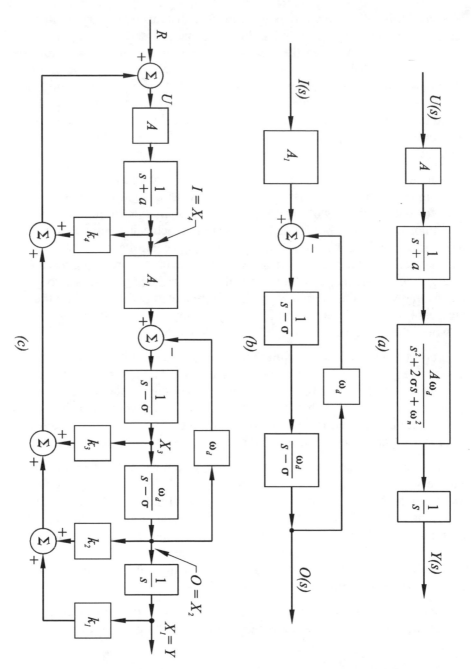

Figure 4 – A Block Diagram of Transfer Functions *models the behavior of a multivariate system. Control System Engineers use these mathematical tools to optimize performance, and improve stabilty of chemical, electrical, mechanical, and biological systems. All we need is the data.*

Redrawn by Mark Edward Vande Pol. See endnotes on this Chapter for source reference.

📖 Chapter 4 – Property Transfer Functions

Ecosystem Assets Offset Economic Risk

We return to Garrett Hardin:

> "But the air and waters surrounding us cannot readily be fenced, and so the tragedy of the commons as a cesspool must be prevented by different means..."

> "...the alternative we have chosen is the institution of private property coupled with legal inheritance... we put up with it because we are not convinced, at the moment, that anyone has invented a better system. The alternative of the commons is too horrifying to contemplate."

This observation suggests that valuing uses of ecosystem assets that affect how air and water are *processed* would be a way to manage the condition of air and water. The political induction of external claims, regulatory takings, and punitive fines works against that principle. The system has affixed much of the cost of compensating for the ecological externalities of urban majorities upon rural landowners, and devalued rural ecosystem assets.

Rendering ecosystem assets fungible and tradable across property lines, as a means to offset ecological risks attendant to economic activity, maximizes their total value. Tradable value would motivate investment in their benefit. There are consequent ecological, social, and financial benefits to a workable system for rendering ecosystem assets easily tradable.

Terms and Conditions Apply

This chapter will, at last start to USE the interminable terms defined at the beginning of the book. **Process assets** transform the state of commons to produce **transformation products**. Examples of transformation products are: smoke, carbon dioxide, oxygen, lumber, silt, nitrates, food, and views. Some transformation products are sold and others constitute positive or negative **externalities**; i.e., costs or benefits not accounted within any transaction. There is nothing inherently positive or negative in an externality or asset in this discussion. One person's asset might well have a positive or negative value depending upon the intended use of another.

Ecosystem assets refers to those natural processes and extractable resources that are indigenous to the property, such as weather, soils, mineral wealth, and composition of habitat for various species. A **process** is composed of that which produces an asset in usable form. Soil constituents, water, solar exposure, and atmospheric conditions support the growth of trees, while plate tectonics, crustal subduction, volcanism, and erosion support the presence of mineral deposits. The term, **boundaries** is used generically to denote the edge of anything: a parcel, a forest, or an aquifer; while **lines** refers to a legal description of the limits of ownership.

Changing the Deal

This discussion centers upon rural residential development. The selection of this subject does not represent advocacy of additional development. It is a set of familiar issues, to which existing law applies.

Determining ownership of many products of ecosystem processes is difficult. Many do not respect traditional property lines because they are mobile, chaotically distributed, or have overlapping boundaries. They are not tradable or valued when the parcel is considered as a single use. Some operate on a minimum scale, too large for a single owner.

The land people purchase is not pristine habitat; it is the buyer's investment. When the previous owner chose to vacate, it was a choice to discontinue that operation. The potential buyer considers the property with the intent either to continue operations or to convert its use toward a more attractive return.

Public claims on the use of private property have induced owners to sell. The public often extends its claims by citing historic "damage" for which they hold the owner accountable. The historical record of the original transaction that induced the damage, therefore demands close examination.

1. The transfer price of a parcel represents the investment value of its assets employed toward the use anticipated by the buyer.

To recall from Part II, Chapter 3 (Section: Assessing the Situation), the price and assessed value of any parcel reflects its intended use. A farm or tract of timber does not typically include appraisal for residential value and residential buyers do not include appraisal of the value of soil fertility or standing timber. Neither of these uses includes an accounting of endangered species, range for large carnivores, rain percolation, or the contribution to the health of downstream flood control and fish habitat in the appraised value. These are unvalued (or in some cases negatively valued) assets that, in this discussion, will be referred to as **external land assets** – so-called because somebody besides the owner derives a cost or benefit from how those processes are managed. The buyer is typically not notified of externalities at the time of purchase, nor are they considered in the purchase price of the land. Unless the property is encumbered by specific legal or regulatory action, the land is only worth the investment value of those assets applicable to the anticipated use. The rest of its assets are not recognized in the purchase price unless they radically effect the intended use.

2. Land purchases are legally equivalent to the purchase of the entire balance sheet of land assets including unaccounted externalities not related to the current use.

The law assumes that, when a person buys title to a property, they have purchased all the assets and liabilities of that enterprise unless contractually stated otherwise. If a buyer finds gold nuggets or rare antique liquor bottles on the parcel, they belong to the titleholder unless mineral rights have been deeded away or recovery of artifacts is prohibited by law. If there is a hidden toxic dump on the site, or a problem with a road, those belong to the new owner as well. It is up to the owner to settle with sellers regarding non-disclosure should the problem pre-date the transfer of title.

Suppose that there is a road on a property constructed for removing logs in the 1920s. If the current owner bought the property in 1970, the road was likely to be considered an asset. The buyer may have paid more for that land based upon the economic benefit of roads. It was access for fire control. It was a way to get equipment to the more remote reaches of the property. It was a way to get to a potential home site, should the owner wish to subdivide the property later. It also had value as a hiking trail for scenic access or for hunting and fishing. It retains every one of those potential uses to this day. The road can acquire liabilities after the time of sale because,

3. Democratic claims, against the historic uses of the asset and its potential transformation products, change its market value after transfer of title.

Suppose a downstream city, that consumes water out of the river, has grown in population. The urban water users assert that all such roads are potential drainage or erosion problems or threats of additional development and that they must be upgraded or removed even if no demonstrable impact exists. That threat of sediment is regarded as a liability belonging to the road owner, placed upon water consumers who supposedly have a legitimate expectation of a pristine forest draining into a democratized commons: "our river."

Now, these adverse impacts may all be somewhat true. One would think, however, that access for fire control was still important. One would think that a conflagration would cause more landslides, sediments, and other problems for spawning fish than a few cubic yards of erosion every ten to twenty years. A road certainly makes habitat restoration efforts (such as removing weeds and managing controlled burns) much more efficient and less risky. On the other hand, roads are a transmission medium for weeds. Does this mean that we get rid of all such roads? Who decides upon which roads to keep, or how they are to be maintained?

These claims are often subjective interpretations of "ecological damage" supposedly visited in the past projected as a liability against a parcel. It is assumed that the only transactional beneficiary and sole perpetrator to this misdeed was the original landowner. Thus, all future costs to remediate the problem are somehow to be born solely by subsequent landowners when they purchase that resource enterprise. There is no means or opportunity for a transaction to weigh these externalities objectively because,

4.   External assets cost or benefit someone other than the owner.

Other people, besides the owners of the road, have personal opinions that determine the negative economic worth of the risk of sediment from rural roads, versus pristine water quality at high extractable volume. These people have no immediate use for it as a road, but do have a collective interest in water quality. Because they don't want to pay to buy and mitigate the road, that mitigation requires a coercing agent. The only effecting agent at the claimants' disposal is government. Government rule systems are particularly bad at weighing individual cases, especially when designed in service to the interests of either the politically dominant or its own.

The urban party to the external claim upon the road has historically chosen to impose regulatory restrictions upon all private roads without consideration of their individual benefits. The legal and political effort to force mitigation of one road is not much less than to do so for all roads. Failure to comply then constitutes a crime, whether or not an actual problem with any particular road is proven to exist. Accountability to mitigate roads is coerced out of the owners because the state has the power to do so and the democratic majority doesn't want to pay for it because,

5.   Retroactive claims on the use of land disregard the participation of the beneficiaries of the original transaction.

Besides the original owners, there are other transaction participants that benefit from the original tree removal and conversion into lumber provided by the road. They did not pay for the externalities of that production. These people are also the sole beneficiaries of the subsequent retroactive political imposition of "remedy."

Consider the original transaction upon which this conclusion is based. The parcel owner, at the time the forest was originally logged, priced the logs in a competitive market that would not pay anything for prevention of sediment in water. The consumer of that product did not pay for habitat mitigation as part of that product. Much of that material, sold long ago, is in use to this day. Those houses, located primarily in cities built of older materials, bring no less a benefit to their current owners, than those in new houses. Higher current construction costs are in part due to more expensive materials that reflect recent timber harvesting standards. The capital gain on existing homes reflects the replacement cost of the original lumber, induced by the current cost of mitigating those original externalities. **That capital gain accrues entirely to the urban homeowners of old houses.** None of that capital gain accrues to the original producer of the lumber or the current owner of the enterprise, indeed the opposite. The owner incurs a liability and a significant operating cost.

The sole parties benefiting from democratized commons are the majority, who demand it by political means derived by superior numbers, and government bureaucracies who demand control using the police power of the state.

The tragically stupid thing about political valuation is that SO MANY things are wrong with it. The public pays too much for grudgingly executed forced mitigation in the products that it buys because of needless civic overhead for expensive administrative and legal conflict. It causes needless damage to ecosystems elsewhere via the substitution effect. It can be counterproductive to the protected resource because of either corruption or the law of unintended consequences. If because of subjective valuation the best of landowners are driven out of business, then their land is either converted, sold to inferior competitors, or is abandoned to civic control.

How does one balance the benefits and liabilities of the road? The answer should depend upon its unique characteristics. One has to go through the steps of evaluating the risks and benefits of any road to arrive upon the balance of its total asset and liability accounts, including externalities. Who is going to find that best balance of uses and claims and then make the investment to make the most of that use? How will it be financed?

How do we create price mechanisms that manage these tradeoffs in such a way that externalities are apportioned justly? How do we include those asset values that are applicable to transient assets such as rest stops for migratory birds or corridors for large carnivores? These things are real and there is a way to make them transactable.

Wanna Trade?

The total value of ecosystem assets is seldom reflected in the market price for land nor are the assets usually severally tradable. When these assets extend across property lines, are fragmented, or are mobile, the situation is more complex. Without appropriate boundary definitions we are left without bases for transaction contracts. In a very real sense, without property boundaries there is no property. Let's see if there are principles that assist defining the problem in such a way that total solutions become simpler.

To recall one of the principles from Part I Chapter 1 (Properties of the Commons): As competition for uses of property becomes more acute, the demand for precise property boundaries becomes more important. The attributes of resource assets that confound boundary definition include:

- Mobility across ownership boundaries,
- Combinatorial factors among resources and processes,
- Changes in technologies employed in the use of land resources, and
- Discrete versus continuous physical properties of particular assets.

Going Mobile

Constructing a definition for a claim of ownership has had as much to do with the perception of permanence, or "residence time" of an asset within specific boundaries, as does its scarcity. Mobile commons, such as air, are sufficiently inexpensive that no one has bothered to define "air rights." In many locations throughout the West, water is relatively a scarce resource. Boundaries and contracts governing water rights are more difficult to define than for dirt because water is a continuous fluid capable of mobility across property lines. Other mobile goods can be regarded similarly. An aesthetically pleasing view of a landscape is an asset that crosses property lines instantly by reflected light. Economic value is acquired by enforcing restrictions upon their use (photographic rights to the Monterey Cypress or the Golden Gate Bridge are examples).

Even things we commonly regard as fixed are mobile as long as one opens the span of time for the movement to be significant. Changes can happen more rapidly than is commonly supposed as has been demonstrated in more than one dispute over property lines defined by rivers, where the channel can be very suddenly relocated by an earthquake or flood. No resource is permanently fixed. Even continents move.

Perhaps this problem with mobile assets is more about how we define ownership than about how we define boundaries. When highly mobile resources become scarce, the definition of ownership boundaries gravitates toward control of the means by which the asset is transported and distributed and the manner in which its state is transformed.

A typical such example is the definition of water rights, both riparian and underground. It is not as important to own the water itself as it is to control its motion. It is nearly impossible to stop water from leaving the property entirely; it evaporates, it leaks into the ground, it leaves in animals, or runs downhill. The owner of the water has the right to use an asset for which ownership is defined, such as the earth within a bounded region with which to make a reservoir. Assets collect, store, or transport the water in usable condition. What one can control, and what does have value are the physical process assets that change the state of the water. The water thus acquires potential value once it is contained in part because a claim of ownership is no longer ambiguous.

There is no actual value in the water until it is used, even if that use is to support ecosystem assets. People may have various opinions about its value, depending upon what it solvated, suspended, or cultured in it before acquisition. Condensed water falls onto the property as snow, melts, and collects a few ions on its way into a creek. It may be ingested by animals, and then expelled onto the ground along with a few amines and salts, undesirable to people, but very desirable to plants. After soaking into the ground to be consumed by bacteria and roots, it might be thrown up a pump, or cross the property line underground, as vegetables for sale, or as vapor.

No one cares as much about the water itself as its condition and availability for a specific use and the cost to acquire control of it. Thus, the issue of ownership of a mobile asset is about HOW it is contained and used. How an asset is used is all about the process assets used to control it.

It is the physical properties of an asset that determine the simplest manner by which to define a control boundary. Water is easier to control as ice than as a liquid, and even more so than as atmospheric vapor. It is well contained within a cow, but not for long. That all physical materials are dynamic, and that they are transformed in state by process assets, is at least something all resources have in common. If one can then define ownership of a process asset, in terms of how it changes the state of a good as it crosses a control boundary, one then has a powerful definition for private property that can be applied to a number of vexing problems.

Could we use that commonality of motion among all resources to simplify the philosophical, and perhaps legal characterization of what appear to be fixed assets that modify the state of commons as they cross a control boundary? Would that quantify the marketable characteristics of the asset?

It should come as no surprise that if control of the use of process assets really is the issue in ecosystem management, that control system mathematics might be useful to characterize their behavior. Control Systems Engineers use a range of capable mathematical tools to describe how signals propagate through a series of devices. These are called transfer functions. The idea is that, if you provide a series of known inputs to a "black box," and measure the outputs, you can eventually learn how that system will respond to any known input within defined tolerances. The model of how the box modifies that unit input is the transfer function of the system. One then uses the math to describe all inputs as scaled and time-delayed multiples of a basic, unit input. It is not necessary to know everything about the internal workings of the box to have a useful model.

Chemical engineers use an analogous beast to describe a process called a characteristic equation, derived by statistically designed experiment (usually a polynomial approximation). Control engineers hate characteristic equations and statistically designed experiments because one can predict system behavior without knowing much about why. It feels like cheating.

Regardless of the approximation tool, it is paradoxically true that the only way to analyze how an ecosystem asset interacts with its seemingly limitless surroundings is to limit analysis of its inputs and outputs to that which transpires across a control boundary. One might then define real property as a right to control and manipulate processes within control boundaries through which resources are transported and modified. There are important practical benefits to this philosophy:

- Legal descriptions of boundaries match the dynamic physical attributes of the assets. This directs the legal and financial descriptions of those attributes toward manipulation of characteristics pertinent to their value.

- There can be no ambiguity about whether civic constraint of a use is a regulatory taking of private property, because all real property is quantitatively characterized as a right to control a use.

- Consideration of the public concern over a manner of use of private process assets can be addressed through a free market and a civil risk management system such as InsCert.

What if one finds a new use for which there is no previous definition? Patent and license the business method! It really makes proprietary process development of means to improve the use of resource assets worth the trouble.

There are minimum economies of scale, necessary for intangible process assets to operate economically, that have no interaction with or impact upon other valued uses (orthogonal to their respective transfer functions). How does one deal with process assets that are themselves, continuous? If the asset control boundary, held by a single property owner, is too small to be worth an investment, might there be an interest in buying or leasing rights to the totality of uses in the area? Is there such a thing as fractional ownership of a land use, or a contract for rent on a use, that can be exercised upon a regional basis? Is there a way to unitize such a product without property owners ceding away all their rights to the use of their land? Is there a way to market these uses while protecting the interests of other users on a parcel?

Combination Lock

Every property has attributes that do not possess market value until they are combined with other goods to complete an economic use. The total account of resource assets, as applied to these combinations, are unique to each parcel and each prospective use. For example: groundwater has different value for irrigation versus mining. The highest value is found in the most profitable combination of uses and resources particular to the parcel.

Each use of property requires a combination of physical, technical, and market factors. It is intuitively obvious that some parcels are particularly suited for at least one purpose, lacking only investment to develop or compensate for its lesser attributes to complete a profitable composite use. Each use has unique account of asset composites and investment needs. Every combination of uses compromises the possibility of others.

To combine attributes of a parcel into a functional composite, often requires modification of one or more of its attributes. We do needless damage to both habitat and capital when legal boundaries or the cost of paperwork render these alterations necessary, or when they force beneficial uses to be foregone. The degree of compromise can be reduced if we make land assets more tradable such that their attributes can be optimally combined into functional units. To make a particular combination of assets a functional entity requires the ability to assign the control boundaries of the necessary assets such that they conform to the requirements of the process.

To maximize total value would then entail that those attributes, unnecessary for the conduct of a particular use, be combined or employed toward their highest valued combination of uses. The obvious answer is to move the control boundaries of constituent assets in order to combine them into their respective composites through purchase of suitable contracts. Conversely, when unemployed constituents overlap, or lie across traditional property lines, they can bring a return by selling a similar contract to complete a composite use. As each of these uses is completed, total land value increases toward its maximum potential. Even if that potential use is for the parcel to remain undisturbed, under this regimen it would be that particular parcel's most valued economic use.

Completing a composite use therefore involves several prerequisites:

1. It must be possible to complete the entire set of constituents.

A site for a residence, having no adequate route for an access road, would not be considered for residential use. Attributes or uses of other parcels can be purchased in order to complete a composite use. Roger Burch's purchase of an access easement completed a composite use of Gamecock Canyon.

Assets to be combined need not be adjacent in order to be functional, as long as they are connected through an appropriate transmission medium. Were one to invest in a chain of wetlands to support a migratory bird a useful proximity through air might be the distance of a safe day's flight.

2. The scale of operation should be appropriate to the attributes.

A plot of land must be at least a minimum size to be a successful farm or National Park. Scale can be offset by a concentration of value. Somebody would definitely go to the trouble to stake a claim on a one-cubic-meter gold mine if it were comprised of a solid nugget.

3. The technology to take advantage of the use must exist.

Soft rock or level soils were once preferred for cutting roads and digging residential footings. Modern equipment has reversed that desire so that houses on ridges or slopes can be more secure in an area subject to earthquakes or landslides.

The original design of property lines reflected land uses as valued by the original settlers, appropriate to the markets and technologies of the time. It is insanity to spend hundreds of thousands of dollars shoring up an unstable slope so that a driveway can get to hard rock, simply because of setback requirements from property lines that reflect design considerations based upon the use of picks, shovels, and horses. One should simply move the lines on the paper to reflect changes in the relative value or the uses of the land given new technology.

4. The cost of boundaries must be appropriate to the use.

Improvements in land surveying technology created a demand for accurate inertial boundary lines instead of physical landmarks. As the demand for consideration of particular physical features becomes more acute, these nice straight, precise lines begin to have their own unintended consequences. They sometimes break up usable resource regions into unusable sub-units, or cut off access to a critical asset.

The precision and tolerance of a property line should be appropriate to the intended use. The greater the demand for a resource, the more important it is to define the boundaries of ownership with great precision. People care about every fraction of an inch of downtown Manhattan, but might not worry too much about a property boundary tolerance of a hundred yards in Southern Utah (unless there is water involved).

The cost of unnecessary precision is a barrier to investment in resources with low returns, particularly those with enormous minimum scale and few interactions with other uses. There is no need to know the boundary of a timber harvest to the nearest hundredth of an inch, much less that of a desert ecosystem. To motivate a market, capable of weighing minute distinctions in the management of resources, demands that we reduce such costs.

Over Our Overhead

Chapters 2 and 3 explored identifying and pricing the value of ecosystem resources to offset economic activity elsewhere. This chapter has discussed the principles by which these assets are definable as tradable units. Now it will address the ecological consequences of institutional barriers to trade.

Complications to property transactions encumber its optimal combination of uses. The means to broker and insure transactions in ecosystem assets are few because it is preposterous to invest in a complex, expensive contract for a use of something that returns next to nothing. Landowners will not go the effort of adjusting boundaries or selling shares in bounded ecosystem assets until it becomes easy to execute such transactions.

Consideration of the value of ecosystem assets is now a cost within contracts and permits controlling other uses with significant economic worth. It might not be so unlikely for an owner to consider each component of land value for its distinct profit potential, once transaction costs are minimal.

As complex interactions among ecosystem processes are better understood, it will be simpler to construct standard agreements by which to trade in their use. The cost of redefining boundaries would fall because of economies of the volume of transactions and analysis. Once such uses are characterized by mathematical model, the agreements governing their use can be constructed with software as easily as we do stock market trades. Control of a constituent asset could be marketed through an easement, rent, contract, partnership, or formation of corporate entity. This could be a whole new business by which the skill sets of title officers and insurers might market their products by the degree of risk specific to the type of use. The market can exist only if an objective accounting of the economic value of the risk exists. Government has instituted policies diametrically opposed to fluid markets in ecosystem assets by virtue of its monopoly to administer land use.

Turf Battle

Few people recognize the cost of preferential regulations restraining trade at the behest of organized groups of State licensees. Consider the case of real estate transactions and title transfers.

Current regulatory law, in the County of Santa Cruz, demands that each residential lot meet all the functional requirements to support a residence before allocating a permit. This is called the "bio-dome" principle. It was proffered as another of those famous ways to "resist development" by attempting to render fewer parcels as appropriate for construction.

This "unit-compliance" policy has forced landowners into far more elaborate adaptations to the less ideal circumstances specific to each parcel. These are consequences of zoning laws, building codes, and fixed property boundaries, but... they made it far easier for real estate agents to unitize each parcel for sale entirely in terms of its residential potential.

It backfired, too. Now every one of these compromises has to have its own technical analysis and disclosure at the time of title transfer (when it is really too late to be telling the buyer and they are being overwhelmed with paper). The net impact is to have massive legal title documentation of a non-optimal situation that does little to prevent a problem. The technical points end up lost in a blizzard of details, that are patched up to close the deal and then forgotten... until huge amounts of money have been spent to file for a permit. Then the problem rears its ugly head and hangs up the whole project, often after significant physical disturbance. People get sued.

The people who pushed the bio-dome law probably had little idea how inventive homeowners and their contractors would be in devising ways to force their will upon the land; or maybe they did? It was certainly a good deal for contractors, civil engineers, consultants, and trade unions. Sometimes the requirement for a license ends up as an extortionate scam. (It is not exactly a good use of capital to pay $65/hour for a $10/hour person to "witness" a grading and compacting operation, in order to make certain that there are no roots in a fill.) Professional license requirements make numerous, easy jobs inaccessible to professionals with cross-functional training, in the name of restraint of trade, professional liability, and barriers to entry. The lack of risk assessment in their employment leads to every one of those professionals covering their personal interests to the exclusion of all else.

The bio-dome is a significant barrier to trade in a fluid market of land uses. Use contracts could be traded and combined across property lines instead.

When but a single professional interest is involved in a decision, ecological tradeoffs are seldom given the consideration they deserve. If the barriers to trade drop, the total volume of analytical work, to determine which among the available technical options is best, will rise. There is little recognition of the potential to be found in a larger total volume of analysis at lower overall liability, but at least we would end up with better development. If the contractors operate under the umbrella of insured and certified best practice general contractor who knows when to hire a licensed professional and when it is a waste of money, isn't the concern about professionalism covered?

Everything Into Account

Turnover and instability of ownership have hidden ecological consequences that are difficult to quantify, but easy to understand and observe. It takes time and dedication to learn about the unique characteristics of any piece of land. People who are more experienced with local ecology are less likely to make mistakes in their choice and manner of uses but, if they are at risk of losing the land, the incentive for long term investment is lost.

Instead of selling land outright, use contracts could transfer at higher velocity without such drastic impacts as sales. Tradable assets foster interdependence and socialize people. They bind neighbors together with motives to cooperate to solve local ecological problems. They reduce the need for redundant capital, site visits by heavy equipment, or government surveillance. They make people more cautious about the character of their neighbors, thus making impeccable integrity as a neighbor, a personal and group asset.

Economic interdependence, generated through free enterprise in economic land uses, stabilizes communities (much to the benefit of children). It slows the spread of development and reduces environmental impact because collective interests bear upon individual transactions. Interdependence complicates the sale of entire bundles of these overlapping investments as real estate transactions, but need not do so when the sales are in but a single use. A market in freely exchangeable use-boundaries would facilitate suburban in-fill redevelopment, by unlocking sites theretofore unsuitable. Isn't that what the government planners say that they want?

Redrawing boundaries for land uses can eliminate many causes of water pollution such as roads, septic drain fields, and overdrawn water rights. By trading in uses, small or marginal sites could be more easily unlocked from existing constraints. Property lines might be redrawn to take advantage of changes in technology. A property owner could buy an unstable alluvial parcel as nothing more than a commercial drain field to accommodate a rather smelly mobile asset with negative value once an acceptable hose was available. Siting would then best suit the land and reduce the propensity to sprawl. A site with particularly hard rock could have asset value as a location to dissipate the energy from winter runoff. A site with available fill dirt (or for that matter a site that could accept it to mitigate an old road) eliminates mining and transporting it. One could then correct a problem before catastrophic failure. Whether it is visual impact, or runoff from a horse corral, trading such uses among landowners employs each property in a manner best suited to its specific attributes with lower total impact. A market can instantly balance all the considerations, but only if all such they have a market price.

Not all boundaries defining such uses need the kind of precision tolerances required for urban boundaries. If a walk with a wireless Global Positioning System (GPS) transceiver was sufficiently accurate for the anticipated use, redrawing boundaries and transferring uses would be less expensive. Software could generate the necessary descriptive maps and translate the coordinates into a legal description. Necessary negotiations could be completed onsite via the Internet. This would allow consideration of details that would eliminate the impacts of accommodating historic boundaries.

The key to all of this flexibility is the recognition of real property as a bounded right to control process assets that transform the state of commons. Once one recognizes that it doesn't matter if one owns the dirt itself, but only what can be done with processes within control boundaries, what one then learns is to define workable boundaries for newly identified uses and conclude the appropriate contracts. In the case of a marketed drain field right, one uses a land process asset to remove and process nutrients that are considered water contaminants elsewhere, and simultaneously invests in harmonious uses that improve the function at a larger profit. Land use contracts might then be a more competitive market. Those most qualified to maximize the profit of such uses as justify a reduced cost of risk at a competitive price, would attract the capital to commit more funds to resource investment operations, much as they do in other markets.

Without a way to trust the motives of the owner, these markets are unlikely; meanwhile, owners won't trade or invest in a use over which they have little control. A civil accountability and risk management system, such as InsCert, has the competitive incentive to address that balance directly and efficiently. The system collects the data, necessary to initiate the mechanics to account the value of ecosystem resources that are the foundation of such markets.

If the public continues to demand a specific use of private property such as preservation, then they should contract for the necessary management services from the landowner at full market value. Anything less is a taking. Why should they go looking to government when a proven resource manager is available with incentive to provide the best possible product at minimal cost? Doesn't the public WANT to pay for a healthy environment?

If the public doesn't pay for such services, where will the money come from to care for the land? Taxes? Who will do the work? Wouldn't it be more expensive if operated by a government agency? What if the work isn't done and the land degrades. Who pays for that? What would be the lost opportunity of taxes on profitable operations? Does bureaucracy have any motive to deliver a self-sustaining system? Can we afford that?

Insured certification and transactable processes assure diversity in property management strategies to minimize pooled risk and improve the limits of quality. Private contractors, insured ecosystem assets, and pricing risk into every product, directs people toward the blessings of self-government and weighs ecological risks scientifically and objectively on an interactive basis.

📖 Chapter 5 – What You Can Do With the Stuff

A Synthesis of the Principles in Part III

This chapter integrates insured certification, risk-based pricing, and trade in bounded rights of use and applies the synthesis to the Tragedy of the Commons.

And now, a next to last blast from Mr. Garret Hardin, Ph.D.

"The tragedy of the commons …is averted by private property, or something formally like it."

"But the air and waters surrounding us cannot readily be fenced, and so the tragedy of the commons as a cesspool must be prevented by different means..."

"Only a criterion of judgment and a system of weighting are needed. In nature the criterion is survival. Is it better for a species to be small and hideable, or large and powerful? Natural selection commensurates the incommensurables. The compromise achieved depends on a natural weighting of the values of the variables.

"The problem for the years ahead is to work out an acceptable theory of weighting. Synergistic effects, nonlinear variation, and difficulties in discounting the future make the intellectual problem difficult, but not (in principle) insoluble."

Correct in principle, but what was his plan to implement this "natural weighting" based upon natural selection? Who gets to it? He grudgingly advocates civic tyranny and feudal estates directed by an academic and financial elite! Undeterred, he continues:

"An alternative to the commons need not be perfectly just to be preferable. With real estate and other material goods, the alternative we have chosen is the institution of private property coupled with legal inheritance. Is this system perfectly just? As a genetically trained biologist I deny that it is. It seems to me that, if there are to be differences in individual inheritance, legal possession should be perfectly correlated with biological inheritance-that those who are biologically more fit to be the custodians of property and power should legally inherit more. But genetic recombination continually makes a mockery of the doctrine of "like father, like son" implicit in our laws of legal inheritance. An idiot can inherit millions, and a trust fund can keep his estate intact. We must admit that our legal system of private property plus inheritance is unjust -- but we put up with it because we are not convinced, at the moment, that anyone has invented a better system. The alternative of the commons is too horrifying to contemplate. Injustice is preferable to total ruin."

Do ends justify means? Systematic injustice leads to total ruin, every time. Our power to ruin is greater than ever. How does this proposition address the

Tragedy of the Commons, other than to resist resource extraction as if all human land uses were harmful? Can't we do better than that?

Risk management as a business, operates as a form of natural selection. Rights to control those process assets that lower the cost of ecological risk, are assets. This motivates investment into the health of process assets to improve their return. Pricing use contracts can be determined by extensions of classical risk analysis against the cost of restoration, mitigation, resource offset, or loss of use. Rights of use can be publicly traded as risk reduction service enterprises. Under InsCert, such a system requires only civic enforcement of private contracts.

As Mr. Hardin obliquely observed elsewhere, the population evidence is clear: People who have interesting work to do decline in population, while people who suffer in poverty have more children to help defray life's misery. Wealth generates the capital to invest in resource enhancement. When people own a defined and tradable stake in each other upon which they hope to earn a capital gain, they make rational choices out of enlightened self-interest. It beats wars, famines, diseases, and pestilence, which is surely what transforming the planet into a socialized commons will inevitably deliver.

Perhaps it is better to be fruitful and multiply than it is to divide and conquer!

An Opportunity for the Commoners

Under current law, no landowner can freely market all the products of the land. As things are now, one does not own its oxygen-producing and water collection potential; one does not own the value a pond has as a stopover for migratory birds. Now, government wants to charge the landowner penalties for deleterious effects to these assets, even when largely caused by others who are immune for political reasons or converted their land before anybody cared. Under current environmental law, these ecosystem assets have become liabilities. No wonder they are undervalued.

The landowners are told that those butterflies that just moved in are rare because somebody else converted their land. If they harm the weeds, preferred by those butterflies, the fine is twenty-five grand, or maybe a jail sentence. The remaining landowners, still paying taxes on the property, just wish the weeds would die so that the butterflies would leave. If they do leave, that landowner will pave it before something like that happens again.

It IS a tragedy.

This type of taking is an evil because it removes value from ecosystems and eliminates the incentive to invest in their health. What the "takers" argue is that the right to control the assets found on a parcel do not rightfully belong to the owner because a particular use is valued beyond the bounds of the property. Curiously, they find little difficulty in claiming that the owners are responsible for all the liabilities, under the same logic. Such political claims are about stuff, who controls it, and at what cost.

These claims were extended because too many people ignored their transformation products and forced their costs upon others. There has been at least a short-term market advantage in doing so, among other reasons, because those who first cleared the land of its natural resources have had less need to worry about such things as endangered species or riparian resources.

InsCert can return some of that market advantage back to the resource landowner. Rendering asset ownership across property lines more tradable has been shown to have the potential to reduce environmental impact. By themselves, these two policies would be better than what we are doing now. When they are combined, however, they can be applied to ecosystem assets that transform the state of commons, extending beyond or moving across property lines. Over the years, wonderful things can begin to happen.

Where the concept of fungible land assets really gains power toward solving major environmental problems, is when it is applied to the Tragedy of the Commons. It is a simple idea, really. It's about stuff, and what you do with the stuff, in reverse order:

1. The best-practice system design sets people free from dealing with needless bureaucracy. They are motivated by that dispensation, its research requirement, and the potential for profit opportunity to use their time and money to study the land and accumulate the knowledge of how its components work as elements of larger systems.

The landowner accumulates data, not only on those products that now have tangible resource value (such as timber), but also on the other physical and biotic attributes of the property. As these are measured over time, other processes particular to that location become apparent. That recognition leads to a process of discourse among landowners with similar assets. Discussion economizes the language of resource function into higher order models. It identifies those processes or behaviors that are causes of expensive risk. Such communications lead to negotiations that weigh the relative value of these processes, and how they might be combined into functional economic units that offset ecological risks.

2. The owners can then combine their data to identify and consolidate operations of contiguous regional systems or non-contiguous systems.

In a search for scientific truth, the motive for collecting and analyzing data is what transforms their application to technology. Rarely are the properties under study fully understood, unless free exchange is conducted in an environment that supports a profit opportunity. People, motivated by common interests, articulate those opportunities. A language of discourse appears. Ideas are realized, their potential excites, and articulations are clarified. Wishful thinking is challenged. Justifications for investments are sold and investment requirements are calculated and allocated. Results are measured and, if successful, there is reinvestment and replication on a larger scale. Successful investors then look to successful inventors for new opportunities. Motivation is what transforms empty compliance into research.

It is a natural process of being human.

The only thing in the way is the all-too-human desire to control the use and take that value, without paying for it.

Civic agency exercises power through collective assent, for which civil approval is not a requirement. A civic agent is the only person armed with the police power of the state, the power to violate private property rights. Civic agency can discount the cost of land acquisition, in the interest of enlisting democratic support, by which to acquire control of the use. Once the value of that good is discounted, there is no longer any investment value in its development, nor is the process readily reversible. Once control of the factors of production is enforced by sufficient police power, there is no longer any value to the collective claim.

Stated more elegantly:

You can't trade what you don't own. You don't own what you can't use. Then what is the use in taking care of it? So nobody pays attention and there isn't any money to do anything about it, anyway.

Such is the devolution to a socialized commons.

Alienation of the individual from the collective interest, with the freedom to control an asset as property, demands the consideration of free trade in order to alter a choice of how to employ that asset. Without identified and accounted alternative investments, with predictable returns and controllable risks, there are no bases for an investor to weigh options of land use.

It matters not whether property rights originate by divine endowment or universal public agreement on inviolable Constitutional law. The mechanics of free trade in ecosystem assets demand unyielding civic respect for individual property rights as unalienable.

The question remains, how do we rekindle such public understanding and render individual choices reflective of interdependent considerations?

Diffusing to Cooperate

Communication within a structured context of risk management opportunity is what selects and organizes products for free exchange.

Recognition of the economic value of ecosystem resources starts a process of individual outreach. Perhaps there are marketable contracts in understory fuel management or absorbing concentrated drainage flows near a residence on an adjoining property (discussed in some detail in Part IV.) Data-sharing and contract negotiation is an ongoing process that leads to the combination of data from one property with others similarly affected. This process helps define how we communicate about ecosystem processes functions.

Discussion of such exchanges builds that common language into higher-level understandings of more macroscopic functions. Their heterogeneous origins demand concatenations that themselves induce redefinition and refinement of the data collection and discussion format. It is a positive feedback loop that simplifies means of understanding interactive processes with multilevel variables and combinatorial effects.

Data, integrated from heterogeneous sources, facilitate discovery of systemic operations on a scale and with a depth, unachievable when managed from the top down, no matter how sophisticated the analytical model. It is far easier to identify systemic function from base data and randomized trials, than it is to posit oversimplified cases for a theoretical computer model, and then query reality for corrections to the lack of fit. Landowners have the benefit of local knowledge with which to identify a spurious or locally inappropriate theory. Trust, as earned by a validated record of excellence, reduces transaction overhead sufficiently to allow the flexibility to experiment with new models of interactivity. Social verification among individuals with interdependent interests can both prevent and limit the scope of needless errors.

Sometimes data bring bad news. An outwardly directed process, with structural provision to profit by risk reduction, will seek to correct them early and share information derived from corrective action. The process necessarily leads to assessment of how plans or problems affect others or how assistance might be enlisted. That motive is founded upon the knowledge that in problems are found opportunities, particularly when the actors are co-invested. There is then reason to trade in economic goods that mitigate the effects.

Does forming a dedicated corporation sound like too much of a hassle for what appears to be a small asset such as a migratory butterfly landing? That reaction you had to the implausibility of the concept is precisely why the system needs to be more competitive. It seems ridiculous only because we have little idea how much the existing system really costs or how big the scope of butterfly management might be. It is a hassle to do only because of current costs of transaction and data processing, in large part imposed by the legal system and government. (Title insurance companies, contract attorneys, Security and Exchange Commission, Internal Revenue Service, County Recorders, State Board of Equalization...) Many transactional externalities exist merely to document evidence for potential lawsuit or to enrich the gate-keepers. The paperwork in resource enterprise incorporation and operations could be completely automated. The corporations currently processing and insuring these transactions could instead be competing to develop efficient ways to assure low-cost transactions in such management contracts, and marketing management tools to reduce those costs. With the higher trans-action volume in use contracts resulting in lower transaction overhead, an investment in butterflies might be justified.

A corporate entity requires cash flow. Historic sources include timber sales and grazing leases. Other uses were combined under those operations to render the total revenue adequate against the cost of management. These simpler forms differentiate as the mechanics of their operation are clarified, the sophistication of targeted marketing develops, and the cost of overhead falls. Early and more traditional products have included recreational access from private roads and trails, hunting, bird watching, fishing, or tuition from educational programs. These exist in scattered locations, but we are still not talking about much money, in many cases because of price suppression by the public park monopoly. Economies of scale will reduce transaction cost but the main reduction in overhead will be that of regulatory cost.

Individual sellers would naturally differentiate their unique products with respect to local conditions. Some locations might be more appropriate to high volume timber production, selling open space access, or offering contracts for forest and fuels management according to the preferences of nearby homeowners or watershed management companies.

The cash flow from many of these goods might be small. Some uses might not be marketable at all unless multiple owners participate, such as chemical management in a watershed or a range for large predators. Other products might not exist until a network can form over huge distances such as migra-tion stops on a flyway. Such enterprises could extend across whole regions, eventually encompassing global markets. Consider that a network of wet-lands on a flyway could well be considered to be such a multinational product, where the birds constitute a mobile asset. A wetland in a developed area might then be quite valuable because, without it, the whole network is badly degraded.

New products will emerge as the legal instruments to trade in use contracts are automated. These can be leases for undeveloped space and unbroken views; charges for rainwater percolation, collection, and transport; mainten-ance of habitat for pest predator insects for development of Integrated Pest

Management techniques; safe retention of minimal populations of pests for test culling of resistive populations and operation of interactive trials... The market can operate under extremely complex requirements, especially when these enterprises are combined and overlaid across multiple regions.

In some cases, the value of these enterprises would rise with their proximity to developed land. People value open space more highly in an urban setting, than they do in a rural setting. (Think of the loss in property value to San Francisco if they paved over Golden Gate Park.) This represents an economic force to counterbalance sprawl. Farms could market some of these "open space" products as an additional source of income to remain closer to urban centers. The purchase of shares in these rights is cheaper than buying the land outright and it retains a source of truly fresh food nearer to the customer. (The value of that product might rise once freshness is recognized as possibly having far more health benefit than does reducing pesticide content. This will be discussed in the section on pesticides and natural plant toxins in Part IV.) The same lands can also be used for hands-on education, or rental space for vegetable gardening, as is seen in much of Holland.

Wetlands manage transitions to estuaries where many of our ocean species breed. Are they important? What valued assets would we have to defer were we not capable of preserving the counts of wetlands species by investing in more detailed management on those that remain? What are they worth? How much would they pay? OK, so we're making progress.

A market can integrate the risks and benefits of competing approaches in order to expand the range of potential trials without forcing them toward extremes. Sharing in pooled risk among different approaches balances the temptation to get too heavy-handed. Where a highly extractive approach might yield a great deal more money from operations, the mitigation and insurance costs might tend to offset that approach. A more gradual extraction method might yield less directly, but could alternatively provide a return by offsetting the more aggressive experiments of others. The market, in that respect, is self-correcting, as long as the costs of risk can be assessed against the conduct of operations. Without a way to trust that these costs and benefits are honestly measured and assessed, none of it can happen.

Discounted futures can disperse the harvests according to a time-managed plan by location and according to initial conditions, relative productivity, and superposition of other considerations by site. A civic authority simply can't do that without being subject to the temptations of corruption through the legal power to apply non-uniform treatment.

Without financial consideration of what land assets provide, we are back to political fights with the resulting mandated neglect, sclerotic information processing and decision-making, and confiscation of the wealth in support of paperwork that the land needs for its own. Every time someone crosses a property line for the purpose of a walk, it is in a very real sense a theft of uncompensated pleasure absconded from the land they came to see.

What has been happening is that the urban public has been taking many of these things for granted and for free. If such uses are truly "valuable," then the fact that they are rendered more tradable through defense of property rights resolves the conflict of competing claims by setting an equitable price for the use. Perhaps the greatest profit opportunities for landowners lie in the discovery of that mechanism.

One could own stock in that collectively-held asset. One could sell shares in land use enterprises and make claims or derive benefit as shareholders or customers. Stock ownership is a mechanism for integrating an external public claim with internal private ownership that is truly voluntary and has a basis in cooperation and common interest. This is a compelling argument for the divestiture of civic holdings into the private sector and going through the effort to learn how to weigh the value of ecosystem resources objectively.

To review what we have covered so far, each property owner would study the land and analyze its individual potential in light of its interaction with the surroundings, as part of the certification process. One can then recognize the net worth of its constituents. Not all the assets and liabilities to be found on a single parcel are entirely contained within its boundaries when considered as an operational enterprise. There are many ecological processes that can only be considered as such, when they are combined with other proximate parcels, for a regional process asset to exist. The capital value might not be much for these factors individually, but they could be quite important when considered in total. Pricing is derived from both the lost opportunities associated with extortive preservation and the cost of habitat restoration and investments offsetting impacts elsewhere.

In any assessment of market potential, the problems and threats to the health of the land become more obvious and weigh against its total capital value. Market systems have the capability, for example, to determine the capital impact of infestations of exotic species. (It doesn't do much good to clear your land of thistles if the wind blows the seed back over the fence.) At least under insured certification, there would be a measure of the economic loss associated with controlling pest plants on wild lands that should properly affect the purchase price and known operating costs. In fact, there is a very good case that mismanagement of what have been historic responsibilities of government, to protect the nation from imported infestations, should be considered grounds for legal remedy for inverse condemnation.

Recording the cost of exotic species control is a way to price the risk of pest introduction. Such information should be worth money to those responsible for pest transport and introduction and might best be derived in cooperation among landowners at both the point of origin and the site of infestation. The cost of insuring transportation companies at risk of introducing pest vectors (such as truckers, grading contractors, and shippers) could be thereby derived and focused upon vector transmission mechanics. Buyers would then be paying the true price of imported goods. Shipping companies or construction contractors could then justify development of control processes by which to pass appropriate boundaries without the extensive inspection and/or quarantine we should otherwise be demanding from governments. If we are going to have a global transportation economy, we must learn how to account costs of infestation objectively and assure that they are correctly borne by transaction participants. If we do not, the consequences can be horrifying, irreversible, and either tremendously expensive to manage or no big deal, depending upon dose, speed, and species. Think of what has been expended on fire ants, or kudzu and the environmental consequences if we fail to stop them.

Which is cheaper, prevention or negligence and to what degree of either?

Sometimes, although the problems can be overwhelming and something that rightly should alter net worth, the net discount on a parcel could serve as an opening to those with the skills and perspective to see those problems as opportunities. What is wrong with that? Wouldn't it be a wonderful change for our society to be thinking about new ways to improve ecosystem health and make a buck solving problems, rather than for young people to be so absorbed with failings that they are talking suicide? As it is, the only existing alternative is to a fight with a foe possessing virtually unlimited resources and wait until they remember that they own it. Once they do, you will have a long wait before you see a carefully tailored and fully funded plan for the property, with no guarantees.

What has it cost us to save the California Condor? This is a case where a hugely expensive, multi-decade preservation program had failed completely before a controversial captive-breeding program was begun. How many dollars were lost in resource and land use value during the preservation? How much was spent in breeding studies, behavior analyses, incubation, training, release monitoring, and then... what are the fines going to be for the homeowners who have the insensitivity to allow the condors to steal the nachos off the back deck? All that preservation with nearly total failure and the birds apparently enjoy the shelter of suburban housing developments. Would it have been cheaper and more successful to have a few houses funding a heterogeneous approach to increasing condor populations? Did we really have to preserve their habitat or would suburban condor overpopulation have driven young birds with better genetic diversity back into the wild? Is there a benefit to having semi-domesticated transitional, suburban condor population reservoirs? Would there be people on the margins of the wild areas prepared to make a buck assuring their success? Do we really know? Is the information, of how much time and effort that went into that restoration and reintroduction, valuable as an estimate of the risk associated with the loss of other species?

None of these countervailing questions would come into play with a risk-based pricing system. Jealous landowners would have already invested in a critical range junction at Gorman Pass (in Southern California) for its value as ideal condor habitat. They would demand too high a price for the land for Enron to buy, compared to other locations with steady winds. Under the current system (sorry), Enron had to find out the hard way after years of site exploration and negotiations. A lawsuit stated that their tax-subsidized wind generators threatened to chew more condors into little bits. Under InsCert, there would have been no lawsuit, no bad PR, no political hassle, and no wasted energy on the part of Enron.

The benefits of a good management system are found, not in how they solve problems, but in how effortlessly they are prevented.

Once the attributes of a parcel are identified and the individual degree of contributions to total utility evaluated, local assets can be rendered tradable, in larger-scale systems. Does that beat Sustainable Development, where the powers-that-be demand all that in-fill that would drive up urban pricing to the point where an economically viable wetland or farm was impossible? Is there a way for a central planning agency to weigh those decisions or does it just get political? Wouldn't you rather have seen a way to economically value the marshland of San Francisco Bay so highly that it would have been too expensive to develop?

Ask yourself: Who are the real forces behind the rural takings? Greenbelts and other constraints upon "urban sprawl" are advocated by investors who wish to inflate the asset value of their portfolios. Manipulating supply, by location, inflates the market price of select assets.

Why is it that large timber corporations do most of the damage, but each successive generation of regulations advanced by those same NGOs do more harm to small landowners who supposedly weren't the problem? The big guys and the activists even admit it in public hearings! It is the same story. To the dominant corporation, environmental rules are an opportunity to flex the muscle of economies of scale.

It is high time for landowners to assume the moral high ground. It is justified. The temptation to corruption makes government a lousy steward of the land.

Still too Ethereal?

What corporations do well is take advantage of economies of scale to make one thing incredibly efficiently. What we need out of resource land management is more than one thing on a frighteningly detailed, site-specific basis.

Who is best suited to do that work?

What we feel, in our loss of family farms and ranches when they go out of business, is the disappearance of all the implicit goods they provide. The tragic thing is that those are the very goods for which we never pay! The more intangibles we need from them, the more we regulate their lives, the more likely they are to go out of business when we punish them for not having satisfied our desires. The answer is not price supports or subsidies; the answer is to return to farmers all the assets that come of their land, and allow them to market the range of goods their land is best suited to provide.

Cities use groundwater and farms collect it. How they manage pests affects the water, but we just tell them to take a yield hit to protect it for drinking purposes by banning pesticides rather than truly minimizing the balance of risks. Birds need watering holes and a network of farms can provide food, and shelter. Major river valleys require flood plains that farms can manage, while improving their soils, managing flows of nutrients, soil minerals, and silt transport for estuarine deposition. Riverine fisheries require nutrients and insects; farms could allot the riverfront to manage that, but what do you pay them for a healthy river? Do we get one by stopping everybody from using their land, taking a poorly compensated fraction of it out of production and calling in the Corps of Engineers to first do the flood control and then do the restoration project to undo it? When faced with managing all these details among the thousands of products the land provides, we need the attention to detail and multigenerational experience that the family farm is in a unique position to provide. They might have a competitive advantage in a diverse array of resource-based risk management markets.

Let's get more detailed with our example. Let's imagine Monsanto is under fire for their genetically modified corn borer-resistant Bt Corn product that is supposedly threatening Monarch butterflies (there is good evidence that it does not, but for the purposes of illustration, it is useful to so suppose). Let's say that this special Genetically Modified (GM) corn is also resistant to RoundUp® (a broad-spectrum herbicide). Nobody wants the GM DNA to escape and cross-pollinate the RoundUp resistance with weeds. Monsanto responded with a gene that prevents the seed from ever cross breeding with anything, because it is sterile. There is concern that, because of its productivity advantages, all feed corn would be sole-sourced, sterile seed from Monsanto factories. People are legitimately afraid of corporate extortion or a failure of a year's worth of corn production resulting in a modest public concern called "famine." Monsanto fears the political resistance.

Let's say that through the research process of best practice, you (a clever family farmer) discover that you can plant cornfields with some viable, non-Bt, seed corn and a fraction of milkweed. These crops could serve as a double risk offset for those who use the improved productivity that genetically altered seed provides. First, the standard corn serves as a store of viable seed. It adsorbs the multigenerational effects of sterile pollen and might even be worked into a crop rotation. Second, the milkweed is a haven for butterflies that might otherwise be killed by the drift of Bt corn pollen. You, a clever investor, quick like a bunny find some co-conspirators to form a corporation to serve as a migratory chain of rotating milkweed fields for butterflies. Then call Monsanto, and sell them the potential for a regulatory dispensation. They can then sell a product that grows more corn on fewer acres of poorer land using less water and the users would pay for an offset on an established migratory path for those, otherwise-would-be-endangered Monarchs, with perhaps some restored prairie in with the deal.

A Personal Author's Note: There were but two 125-acre plots of original prairie left in Iowa when my Grandpa Jake drove me 90 miles to see one over 30 years ago. Are they still there? I dearly hope so. I can still hear the sound of the breeze hissing through the tall grass. Are they financially valuable as a source of genetic material and an operational model for future restoration projects? What would they cost to replace? Should the government take them away?

Would it work? How big must these offset buffers be? How many would be necessary for a migratory habitat? Do they need to be contiguous? Is Bt, RoundUp Ready, Terminator Corn worth it?

Perhaps Monsanto would like to know. What would they pay to know?

The Environment IS about the interface between natural systems and human economy. Best that we understand them both. Maybe more people should be learning how to make the best of both.

Do you want another example of economic value in a family farm? Farms provide for civil defense. In the event of a disaster, they can provide food, shelter, and social services, should a city become uninhabitable. What do city people pay for that now? What if there were a convulsive environmental disaster such as a large volcano, hurricane, earthquake, or (God forbid) a war? Where do people in cities think they will go in such an event? Who would have the tools and knowledge to care for and organize the survival activities of urban dwellers?

In the past, we have viscerally relied upon farmers, ranchers, and resource landowners for all of these services. If we don't act soon, they may themselves go extinct, to the great detriment of us all. Would that assessment be

190

worth investment in the actuarial and financial calculations?

How these markets would generate a cash flow is not always clear, but it is not too hard to come up with scenarios of how they might evolve. Cities and their suburbs occupy critical lands near riverfronts for historic reasons that are now less important. We don't want to move them because of the cost. The practice of concentrating humans has both risks and benefits of its own. Farms might find it profitable to offset some productive area for flood adsorption and wetland capabilities that reduce the risk of floods in cities and towns. Then, surely these benefits should be compensated upon the basis of the ability of a particular to offset urban risks.

To restate the current system: NGOs accept grants from foundations to foist regulations on the landowner reducing asset value and adding both liabilities and overhead. They and the colluding bureaucrats of the acquiring agency harass the owner with fines for failure to comply with ambiguous and conflicting requirements until they sell or die. The inheritors (who wisely chose another source of income) have to choose between an ongoing fight or estate taxes. Sellers of conservation easements (financed by foundations) circle overhead with briefcases offering a way out.

So it goes. Private landowners fall under increasing stress and sell out for a song, and a song is all the property will ever see in the way of an investment in net productivity in the long run. The money will be spent on a bureaucracy with every reason to fail while operating on a smaller tax base. With the land out of production, the alternative resources bring an ever-higher price, while the nation becomes increasingly dependent upon foreign sources and subject to extortion. We are already as a nation, a net importer of food. Four fifths of agricultural investment is to take land out of production. Is that sustainable?

The NGO plan would work, if one could assume that nature will take care of itself, but of course, nature cares not a whit. Nature takes money, knowledge, and individual incentive to flourish.

Where is this money going to come from? Taxes? Then government does all the work and here we go. Has it worked? Given how bad Federal lands are looking, should we give them more? It will likely remain a corruptible political control system that merely benefits those who are in charge.

Resource land could instead become so valuable that it just might stay that way. These assets will only develop with the knowledge of how to render them so. Does that sound like an opportunity? Then buy stock, invest in that enterprise, and earn a return. Really, just a chapter or two ago, were you wondering if anybody would ever find a nickel wanting to do such a thing?

📖 Still Dubious?

Is the system too complex for an average person to understand?

Unlike rules, which are simpler in concept than application (you should see the California Forest Practice Rules), one does not need to fully understand laws in order to use them. Everybody viscerally understands the laws of supply and demand with every product we buy or sell. Nobody understands gravity, but everybody knows how to use it to meet their needs. Laws of gravity were derived by application and observation of its behavior. Few people understand the laws of physics, chemistry, and economics, but that does not keep a market from producing inexpensive computers.

The development of free markets in risk offsets will be no different. Standard units of account will develop through trading. Brokers will offer the services as package deals. Products will differentiate as the cost of overhead drops and knowledge increases.

A management system, based upon natural law, is ultimately easier to use.

People don't think about natural laws, because they are immutable descriptions of seemingly obvious truths. That doesn't mean that all the manifestations will be simple; far from it. The combinations of applications will be as complex as the ecosystem under management demands, to the degree that the cost of overhead will allow. Best that we have reason to reduce that cost.

The circumstances demand it.

Part IV Get What You Pay For

Alternating Examples of Civic Management and the Free Market

Consider the regulatory system as if it were an industry whose product is environmental protection. The boards of directors are charitable foundations, the executives are the NGOs, management is staffed by political appointees of resource agencies, environmental activists and media are the sales and marketing, while the R&D is done at the universities. The investors and customers are taxpayers and future generations, but sometimes they get to be raw material or a way to pay the freight, a role of which some are not enamoured. Investors are usually oblivious unless something goes wrong.

What's wrong with the regulatory industry is this: it is a monopoly. Worse yet it is a monopoly, with no oversight and empowered by force of arms.

What do you get from a monopoly? According to the laws of economics, you get a lousy product that costs a lot. What do you get from a civic monopoly? The historical product has been tyranny.

Given that this book is about an alternative to that approach, Part IV starts by imparting the perspective of the landowner and taxpayer, and then contrasts the existing regulatory system against the proposed free-market management alternative. Each chapter will discuss a specific topic, how it works now and how to do it better.

Chapter 1 – Landowner, On the Loose!!! Timber and fire management at the suburban interface.

Chapter 2 – Dangerous Species Act Exotic species control and pesticide management.

Chapter 3 – Danger: Specious Acts Habitat management for endangered species.

Chapter 4 – A Watershed, Eventually? Watershed management, nonpoint pollution, and flood control.

These topics weave the local case into a larger picture. The stories are representative of the means and ends of the current regulatory system as discussed in Part V.

These examples are brief. It is not the intent to tell everybody how to do these things (even if it would make a dandy consulting business). Rather, the purpose is to interest readers in various fields to apply their knowledge and perspective through the principles laid out in Part III, enough to get started. The whole purpose of this book is for the reader to expand and develop a working knowledge of the principles underlying the system, and to apply those principles successfully to new opportunities. It will take time for this market to grow in scope and sophistication, but then Henry Ford did not know how to make a Lexus.

When the cases to come are taken together, one perceives a totality that communicates in itself. Just imagine what it is like to be a landowner under such circumstances. Think of what we are asking them to do while we beat them over the head with a stick. Many are simply in shock under such a rapid and wildly vacillating regulatory assault, executed on numerous fronts, festooned with conflicting requirements, and gross civic incompetence.

The purpose of environmental law is lost in the struggle, to the great detriment of both the land and your freedom.

We can do better.

Chapter 1 – Landowner On the Loose!!!

This chapter concerns fire and timber management at the rural/ suburban forest interface.

> **Author's Note:** The first three sections of this chapter are about my experience and philosophy of forest management in the Santa Cruz Mountains. If you are familiar with these issues or pressed for time, you may wish to skip to the 📖 Section: Timber and Fuel Management: The Residential Buffer.

In a simpler time, over thirty years ago, David Brower, then Executive Director of the Sierra Club, published an anthem of young discovery in the wilderness of the West; On the Loose, by Terry and Renny Russell. Mom bought me a copy. It had beautiful photographs, it was full of poetry. It sang the song of Triumph, a love discovered among the peaks of the High Sierra. It lamented a Tragedy, a love lost in Glen Canyon, submerged beneath Lake Powell. I spent endless hours, poring through the pictures, recognizing some of the very perspectives I had enjoyed on many a solo trek through Point Reyes National Seashore. It had a forward entailing the risks and travails to be found in the process. The inference was that nobody would do anything that hard unless it was love. This is a personal response:

Have you ever pulled poison oak out of trees to stop it from killing them only to make trips to the hospital until you had an immunity?

Have you ever managed 10 acres of French Broom for 10 years, even though 3 of those acres are not yours?

Have you ever taken the risk of submitting your carefully developed, but hastily written, weed control program to a hostile ecological group for peer review, only to find out that good scientists have to speak in whispers over lunch, because they are so afraid to lose grant money that their agreement with the truth of the data can't be published?

Have you ever had your life threatened for pulling thistles along a road?

Have you ever given away 75 cords of cut firewood so that it wouldn't rot?

Have you ever lugged and hand set 200 tons of rock and mortar to reverse preexisting drainage problems, only to find that you have 20% bone loss from the sweating?

Have you ever tried to set erosion control tarps on a 40° slope, 100 feet above rocks, in the rain?

Have you ever swung around on a 90-foot tree that was less than a foot in diameter at the bottom that you topped just because you didn't want to hit anything with it? How did you feel when you dropped the rest of it and found out that it was rotten half way up the middle? What did your spouse's face look like when you tried to explain to her why it was necessary?

Have you ever found yourself 125 feet up a tree for the second time on the same day to bend it out of the way so that it wouldn't get hurt?

Have you ever dropped a dead 60-foot tall tree on a 60° slope just to keep it from tearing out a chunk of dirt and had to jump down a small cliff so that you wouldn't be sucked into the branches as it slid down the hill?

Have you ever had to run down said 60° slope for a hundred yards at full tilt through a slash of trunks and branches without your glasses because there were yellow jackets in your face and stinging you in the buttocks?

Have you ever dug out a five-foot diameter stump by hand, chopping out the roots with an ax, when the top of it was two feet under an old slide?

Have you ever had to cut up a slash, bridging across a 30-foot deep gully?

Have you ever worked bent over in a ravine with a cliff at the bottom and a mountain lion 30 feet above and behind you, seemingly oblivious to the chainsaw noise? Did you feel like food?

Have you ever watched thousands of dollars worth of timber rot because it was illegal to sell? Did you pay to mill it and then just give it away so that it wouldn't go to waste?

Have you ever taught a six-year old to do a three variable, extreme vertex designed experiment to propagate a native wildflower?

Have you ever inhaled toxic smoke fumes for days on end while you cleared a critical fire hazard?

Have you ever worked 90-hour weeks in a smoky, oily, disgusting, corporate hell to pay for it all?

Have you ever put your job and your children's livelihood at risk, to force a corporate vice president to get an environmental permit, in the middle of a recession with a new house under construction and a baby on the way; when that chemical plant had previously received 43 Notices of Violation?

After you got the job, with 400 applicants competing for your position?

Have you ever bet your life's fortune to commit yourself, full-time, to your dream of saving the habitat you had loved as a child, by fostering an ethic of active harmony among people and the land, in such a way that both might prosper, with the full expectation that you will become a target for having the temerity to tell the truth?

Have you ever had people who said they care about nature, publicly inculcate lies about you, and speak them to your face as intimidation by slander?

Thank you, Mr. Russell, but this isn't about being *On the Loose* in the wilderness. It is one thing to fall in love, it is another to get married. This isn't The Wilderness. This is either an Intensive Care Unit or a Psych Ward.

It is about identifying that latest weed before it gets loose. It's about dealing with acres of broom, acacia, bullthistle, eucalyptus, pampas grass, barnyard grass, joint grass, medusa head, hemlock, hairy cat's ear, and annual rye grasses, and star thistle. It's about identifying the botanical names of ground-covers so that the propagation experiments have validity. It's about researching which cultivars of natives are OK on the fringes of the wild and which are not and then teaching the public authorities the information because the stuff they publish to homeowners is wrong. It's about rousing the government into realizing that while they are busy restricting things, they are doing nothing to help. Worse, they are spreading the weeds and penalizing citizens who do the ecological work that they say that they want.

It's about thinning a forest, planning three cuts in advance, not only to reduce a fuel load but to reduce blight diseases, establish an uneven age distribution of healthier trees, and remove certain natives because they represent an artifact of fire suppression. It has to be done carefully. It costs a lot, even if you do it yourself. Most of the time, there are no authorities to ask how best to do it and serious reason not to trust those who claim to know.

It's about doing your best to get it done, knowing that the one entity, irresponsibly charged with the job of taking care of it, is dead set against you: your government, acting in violation of property rights, supposedly guaranteed under the Constitution. It's knowing that one day, after all that work, sweat, risk, and money, that your love may be taken from you by a civil servant who will leave it to fester.

How do we make the best of what "it's about"?

Clear Thinking

It's impenetrable. To the trained eye, it feels like being in the throat of a working carburetor with wood for fuel. The Santa Cruz Mountains are a typical case of what happens when timberland is cleared to the ground and abandoned. The forest is choking in its attempt at recovery. It is an enormous firebomb just waiting to explode. You look around and it's everywhere: Fuel.

On the ground is a six-inch layer of dead leaves and twigs gathered by their victims, the crumbling trunks of trees, fallen by various fungi. Over there is the home of the nesting wood rat, a meter-tall bale of haphazard twigs, usually supplied by an overhanging, half dead bush, fondly known as "buck brush." It's a nice shrub really, if you can find one alive. They grow to about fifteen feet tall. As their roots rot out in the shade from a tangle of impacted, twisted scrub oaks, or if they get flattened by a falling tree, they spend the second half of their existence as an 8-foot tall mound of tinder with but the occasional living branch. The poison oak takes up residence there; happily chugging the diluted droppings the rat doesn't care to forget. It meanders up and out of the nest, a cargo net of vines clambering through the dead buck brush. It weaves up into the canopy, seeking the tallest tree it can conquer with the weight of its oily, toxic leaves glistening in the sun that it robs from the tree, draping a rotting lacework of discarded efforts left behind. In the corner of your eye is a skeletal manzanita, a black, gracefully contorted candelabra, lamenting the sun that once shown on silver-gray leaves and tiny white paper-shade flowers. Tarzan vines of honeysuckle spiral around the oak trunks constricting the growth into a corkscrew in a struggle to the death. The leaves are up there, somewhere. There are seemingly endless, scrawny, and stunted oaks, many with rotted tops. Half-dead madrone trees reach their blight-blackened fingers to an uncaring sky, their fallen parents or their parts lay busted up and dead on the ground at their feet.

Look up and you see a ceiling composed of perilously thin, thirtyish interior live oaks, packed in like commuters on a subway train, leaning out from the slope as far from each other as they can get. The place was an apple orchard sixty years ago, and these trees germinated simultaneously in what was an open chaparral. They may not belong where they are, on a north-facing slope. They are so packed that you can't tell which branch belongs to which tree. Maybe they hold each other up? Because of their structure, even if they are thinned and pruned, few will ever be structurally sound healthy trees. Most of them have included-bark crotches, or are merely top-heavy. The lack of light and air, along with the extra moisture of the El Niño a few years back, allowed a bad case of twig blight to set in, killing many lower branches.

Charging through the understory is a wave of French Broom forming an impenetrable wall six to ten feet tall, of waxy leaves supported by yet more denuded twigs. After two or three generations, they thin a little bit as the stand clogs with the dead. Here and there are 30 to 60-foot long mounds of decaying broom, piled by bulldozers each time they cleared the land for sale.

The bay trees seem uniquely capable of entrapping twilight beneath them. They poke their heads above the oaks and kill them with shade. That lovely smell is a high vapor pressure solvent. You can burn one to complete ash the same day you cut it, in the dead of winter. In summer, a bay tree can be immolated in as little as thirty seconds. If they don't burn, after the firs and redwoods set in, they can fall over dead of ganoderma rot themselves.

The Douglas firs blast out of the forest floor with their no-longer-needed branches draping onto the ground, forming spokes spiraling up what starts as a trunk but ends up with so many kinks and leaders that it hardly resembles an overgrown Christmas tree. They drip with sap running out of a rotting crotch to a full, resinous climax, often forked and shattered by the winds over the ridge-top, ready to shed one or both subsequent leaders. We had two such trees on the property adjacent to power lines within 100 yards of each other. Either of them would have made dandy igniters. Often those twisted firs ARE Christmas trees, or were. There is an abandoned tree-farm above that eucalyptus grove just outside the north end of our place: a stand of 70 to 125 foot trees that were spaced for harvest when they reached seven to ten feet in height up on the ridge like a Mohawk haircut.

The occasional hefty column of an oily eucalyptus lurks nearby, trashing anything underneath by dropping their branches. Beneath their rags of bark on the ground, the roots release a brew of aromatic oils, toxic to the plants that would challenge them. Eucalyptus is a dominant competitor. In a canyon adjoining one end of the property is five-acre stand, some overhanging power lines, waiting for the day that they get to burn, and spread their seed in the fire draft for a quarter mile. Nothing else grows there. There were two-acre thatches of acacia next to the eucalyptus. Nothing else grew in there, either.

In other canyons and valleys, you find the redwood stands. Unfortunately, the idea that redwoods don't burn is a belief commonly held by the fire-retarded, applicable to primeval forests but seldom to second growth, particularly farther south and east. In a second growth redwood stand a hot fire can kill, especially on slopes where the trunk collects a pile of branches and trimmings on the high side and forms a bonfire at the base of the tree.

In a second growth forest, the cut stumps sprouted so many trees so close together, that it is common to have single stumps that support over 15 trees within a 5-foot radius. They bash into each other in the wind, dropping piles of branches the base of the tree. Many of the crown sprouts don't succeed as full trees, and form a twiggy ladder up into the of lower branches of their bigger brethren. There was nothing growing on the ground in there either.

It was impressive. It was an impending disaster. It was for sale.

When we saw it, we were in love.

It was either love or total insanity. It had to be. To do something that required that much work and risk could be explained by nothing else. This was it. It was a piece of land to cherish, to save, and to raise the children yet to come, to love the land. There wasn't any reason, there wasn't deliberation; this wasn't an investment. This was home.

When we bought the place friends told us to take lots of "before" pictures. We kept telling them that it was fruitless, but nobody seemed to get the idea: "Go crawl inside a bush and try to take a picture. What would it look like?" Blank stare. They must not do much crawling inside of bushes at home. I tried video once, but the auto-focus kept seeing the twigs, while crawling along trying to shove the branches out of the way, so that I could force my body through. Increasing the depth-of-field only made it seem like the inside of a bush again, and it was a mighty jiggly shot, so video wasn't much use.

Heck, if anybody wants to get a feel for "before" around here they only have to go across the road and try forcing their body through over there. There is so blasted much "before" around here, it'll make you sick to your stomach. It can take about 20 minutes to force your body only about 100 yards. (I once found myself lost within 50 feet of the County road until I heard a car on it, so that I knew where I was.) You have to crawl, and leave survey tape tied to bushes at regular intervals just to find your way around. When you've found an area which you can fantasize as both accessible and big enough for a house site, you get the hard choice to put down the earnest money and, with permission, start to clear.

Most people don't know much about such things and neither did we, but with a sort-of-trusty Homelite® 240 in hand we set about cutting our way in, dragging the brush into piles and wondering if we were crazy.

You have to be. The first sort of life-and-death issue to get out of the way is a little matter of poison oak. It's an amazingly adaptable plant. You can find it tangled in brush, wrapped around "widow makers" in the trees, climbing up a redwood over 100 feet (we left that one as a monument), free-standing trees (left a few of those too), crawling along as just another ground cover, or in huge, matted piles. I wasn't trying to get rid of the stuff, it was a matter of getting most of it back onto the ground and out of the trees before it killed them. There is only one problem with dealing with it of course, it can be toxic as hell to people. The stuff is sneaky. When you're pulling it out of a tree, it has this uncanny ability to brush the freshest little fronds right across your sweating face. It's hard not to imagine the sound of hissing laughter.

A case of poison oak can be nasty, especially when it goes systemic on you, covering your entire body. I remembered getting a case of it as a kid, but didn't quite know what was going to happen as an adult. There were all sorts of lore stories from my friends about Indians drinking tea from the stuff (how long did they live?) and other dubious ways to acquire immunity. So, after a couple of trips to the emergency room for prednisone prescriptions, and the associated weirdness that came with that, I got lucky and developed an immunity, and none too soon. It got to the point where I could tolerate the sap spraying off the chainsaw all over my arms, or dripping off the cut stubs as I pulled it out of trees. When it burns, it volatilizes into a noxious cloud. I maintain my hard-won immunity and get an inoculation by working with a little more at least yearly. There is no telling what the long-range effects are on your body. Urushiol, the active in poison oak, can cause internal damage to your organs. I know I shouldn't fool with those *TOXIC CHEMICALS*, but when it's a matter of the health of your forest, what else can you do?

Poison oak is a great topsoil builder, makes a nice groundcover, or a dandy privacy fence when you weave the tendrils into the bushes along the road. It gives them more color in the fall, too. Gophers don't seem to mess with it, so it may well provide a way to help control erosion on the out-fill banks of roads. The root systems are like a mesh of underground cables. Until I develop an efficient propagation technique, I chop it into mulch or burn it.

Maybe you organic gardeners out there wonder about burning, 'Doesn't that cause air pollution? Why didn't you haul it to the dump, or compost it?' Well folks, among other things, there is this little matter of sheer scale.

Within the area immediately around our present house, about six acres, during the first few months of thinning we gave away a mere 35 cords of firewood (about twenty dump trucks full, of oak, acacia, eucalyptus, and junky fir). We generated some 1,100 cubic yards of chopped cuttings. (I had to recalculate the number four times; I didn't believe it either.) It still looks like an oak parkland forest except where the eucalyptus and acacia were (where there was nothing else). One alternative is just to chop the stuff where you are into mulch, but this is subject to total volume. Sometimes it is just too much. Trying to drag the stuff out to a chipper is a bit cumbersome when the closest you could park it is a hundred yards away, you have a foot thick bed of cuttings to tangle with both your feet and that treetop you are dragging on a 30° slope. So you burn.

A lot of the time you don't have too many choices about where you are going to burn. Especially when it is the first one.

Imagine that your job is to reduce an enormous fuel load. Brush and trees are everywhere. Your goal is to have somewhat less of it, so you cut a bunch of it down and build "burn piles." Now, some clever person down at the CDF figured out that the way for the public to do "safe" burning is to have a 4' x 4' x 4' pile with a thirty-foot (30') non-combustible radius around it to start.

One problem: Where in the hell are you going to get thirty feet? You could make more than a 4' x 4' x 4' pile from a 4' x 4' area of brush and scrubby trees! You would end up with so many piles you couldn't walk between them! Besides, how much good was burning one pile going to do with all the rest of the stuff still up in the air above it?

We had chosen the prospective house site in what one might psychologically call a clearing. "Clearing" meant that, by the time we had "cleared," we could SEE thirty feet; the gap between the treetops was maybe ten. Water? A fire hose? Yeah, right, maybe a quarter mile away. The 4' x 4' x 4' piles end up, well, 5' x 5' x 4'?, uh, 8' x 5' x 4'? They were about six feet from the starter pile and about two feet apart. All were oriented to roll into the first pile. It wasn't too hard to visualize. The sparks fly out of the first pile, into the second, a chain reaction starts and forty-foot flames leap into the forest. A conflagration ensues and the only good thing that happens is we don't get sued, 'cause we be charred to a dental record! The emergency plan was to shove the piles into each other to concentrate the fuel and keep it away from the forest. Remember that monk in Saigon?

They won't let you burn until January, because the Central Coast Air Quality Management District wants to wait until the inversion layers have broken down and the CDF has decided that there is NO chance of the place being too dry. To decide by measured fuel moisture content and climatic conditions must not be practical, although we do pay them tax money to measure both. The only problem is that the weather doesn't know about the calendar. The winter of 1989-90 was a drought year. The burn piles kept drying and drying. December kept crawling and crawling. We kept piling and piling. I kept replacing chainsaw parts: bars, chains, and clutches, until finally my dad took pity on me and "loaned" me his Echo 302S (indestructible chainsaw).

Finally it came: January 1. We were on a twelve-month term, 13% renewable land loan (with four points for each six-month extension), with a beneficent lender we called Louie-the-Loan-Shark, one of those "How-to-buy-a-half-million-dollar-house-with-no-money-down" situations. (When the guy laughed, it was scary. Couldn't he just show a little less enthusiasm for his work in the presence of his customers?) "Did you borrow any part of the down payment?" "Oh no, of course not!" We had to burn because we had to get out of this and into something "less dangerous": a construction loan?

Oh yeah, dangerous, January 1. So there we stood, rake and shovel at the ready, looking at the first burn pile. It was almost all broom, a compressed mass of twigs, three feet high and five long. I cut it in half. It was cool and clear, one of those California winter mornings to die for. It was still a little too dry. Well, at least whatever was going to happen was going to happen fast. It was easy to visualize the embers flying out of the top. Maybe they would cool enough before they came back down? Grab the Ace Hardware, homeowner-grade propane torch, strike, light, deep breath, and it goes straight up in a thin column between the trees.

I can still hear it. Thank you God, thank you.

Roll the second pile into the first, then the third. They rolled a lot more easily than expected, but the body gets a mite abraded and the spiders that had taken up residence in the piles, weren't too happy with me. After a day of this, after drinking about three quarts of water, and after a whole lot of worry about the pounding heart from probable carbon monoxide poisoning, it was done. We had a clearing. Now we could start thinning trees, now we could have some REAL burn piles. Some were sixty feet long. The area under control grew to about four acres. We could breathe, and see, and build.

After some ten years of this process, we have almost achieved a degree of mitigation of the fire risk sufficient to begin undergrowth control by less aggressive means. Another way to say this is: Reduce the dominance of the pest, then let the trees, bushes, and groundcovers recover. Thin and prune the trees to the point that they can recover from blight diseases and survive a relatively cool fire, and then have one. The current plan is to conduct a partial factorial array of controlled burn experiments in conjunction with CDF. The purpose is to monitor the sprout rate of broom versus native bushes, and determine in places if this sort of program works to help germinate some natives without their being overwhelmed by sprouting broom. Hopefully, it works to reduce the broom seed bank.

Oops! One problem, the permit will require a "Vegetation Management Plan" stamped by a Registered Professional Forester: $2,500 (and a LOT more for a fire contractor). If CDF won't do the backup, imagine what the insurance for a private fire contractor would be, all because of fuel that is NOT on our property. Then there's the setup and… gosh sounds sort of like timber harvesting where you have to do a minimum amount to justify doing it. Then we have bigger fires that are harder to control with higher risks. So nobody does it. (Help me sell books and I'll give it a shot.)

Then you get weed infestations, then a pest die-off, then conflagrations, then landslides, then weeds, then…

After dealing with the brush and scraggly runts of half-living trees, it was time to deal with the monster weeds. Many of these were exotics such as eucalyptus and acacia, but others were merely out of their normal place, such as the firs up on the ridge. The latter, I came to judge as an artifice of fire suppression. As mentioned earlier, several overhung power lines, but, because there was more than 10 feet of clearance, the power company wouldn't touch them. Public Utilities Commission specifications, you know. None were healthy. (One was "S" shaped, had five tops with a dead spike up the middle, and termites thirty feet up from the bottom.) All were less than 40 years old. $800 later, down they came. Luckily a friend of mine hauled off the logs to make something of them or it would have cost a lot more time.

Try dealing with a 4' diameter eucalyptus tree over 150' tall without heavy equipment. We had a half dozen such trees and scads of smaller ones. The branches can be 12-18" in diameter. If they are growing among trees you want to keep, you have to climb them and perhaps even lower the branches on a cable block… When you climb them to take them apart from the top, it takes a lot of cutting… which takes a bigger saw and LOTS of trips down for gas, oil, food and water and then its back up again. It takes a while. Two-foot long rounds can weigh a couple of hundred pounds and branches half a ton.

One of these monsters, a four-footer, was arching way over a public road, loaded up on its own weight like a giant catapult. Under a load like that, it can split and run a crack down the trunk that kills the climber cabled to the tree. We pulled it back over center with a D-6 cat and a BIG winch. It crunched a nice madrone on the way down, but the euc is gone. The madrone resprouted from its roots. It was worth the trade.

After you have gone through the considerable project of getting one of these monsters down without killing anybody, crushing any structures, blocking a public road, taking down power lines, or destroying bunches of trees, there is still the problem of getting rid of all that mass. That takes heavy equipment too, unless you want to leave four-foot diameter rounds scattered about.

Who wants to split 50 cords and figure out how to sell it? It was a high school dropout with a splitter and a dump truck. How did he get them out?

That takes a road. One of the reasons we bought the place was that it had lots of roads to get to the trees, do the work, and get them out. Though eucalyptus makes dandy pellets, nobody wanted them enough to cut them down for me. At least they paid for hauling them away and didn't go to waste.

Then there were the acacias. They look innocuous. They aren't terribly big. There were hundreds of them. The problem is that they fall over, regularly, and lay on top of each other in a 30' thick tangle. The darned things load up under the weight of their relatives and have very slick bark on denuded trunks. The trick is cutting the mess apart without the pieces unloading suddenly and snapping at you like a bad jungle movie, or sliding down the others on top of the woodsman trapped in the tangle with a running chainsaw. It was scary. Most people use a bulldozer. It was nearly ten years before they were all gone, and new trees are still sprouting every year. One thing about eucalyptus and acacia, they do burn hot.

The broom sprouts by the tens of thousands every year. We also get to fight back the invading thistles, pasture grasses, hairy cat's ear... but there is compensation. The oaks responded gladly, some have grown fifteen feet in but a decade. The ground covers are coming back as an aromatic carpet of roses, poison oak, honeysuckle orchids, yerba buena, jasmine, hedge nettle, native blackberries, numerous wildflowers, and various ferns. There are thousands of variegated irises now and even some scarlet columbine. There are dozens of new lilac bushes in two colors, one new to us, *Ceanothus thyrissiflorus*. There is new monkeyflower, toyon, yerba santa, coyote bush, grease bush, buckeye, manzanita, and black sage, all now growing in and around a forest floor that had been nearly dead or overrun with pests, because a hardwood forest had been thinned. Now after ten years, we are finally planting, replacing poorly structured older bushes and trees with transplanted juveniles that, with space, time, and a few ashes, now have a chance to grow.

So, What's it Like to be an Ax Murderer?

Our three stands of redwood total but three to five acres (depending upon how you measure) along the sides and bottoms of some rather steep gullies. Some of the slopes exceed 200% (63°), over a hundred feet in height. It's about sixty thousand board feet of timber.

After the original logging about 75-100 years ago, the stumps sprouted. In the old days, they didn't cut the trees low to the ground, so the sprouts shot out of the side of the old stumps. They grow away from each other seeking light, leaning out from the stump and then curving upward in a race to the sky. Many are weak, thin, and perilously unbalanced, bending over like a fishing rod under load. There are some that take "S" bends under their own weight, 120' tall, 10" in diameter (dbh).

When the wind blows, these spindly trees sway large distances at the top. They slap into each other. Shearing and collision often breaks off branches on adjacent sides between trees while a lack of light starves those pointed toward the middle of the cluster. The branches they retain are either at the very top or directed away from the center of the original tree in the same direction in which they lean. In one case, there are over 12 trees exceeding 100 feet in height within a 10-foot diameter circle perched over a minor cliff. It's a lot of leverage against a steep slope of loose fluff on hard sandstone.

As the stump rots, the trees have less support on the tension side of their common base. This unbalanced and decaying support system combines with the unbalanced load condition supplied by the branches on the outside of the group. When they fall down they can crunch some nice trees on the way, if they make it to the ground. Some were standing, quite dead, with all their branches. Others were broken, their tops sheared off from the fall of larger trees in the past. A few were hanging in the air, caught in the branches of the living like some sort of arboreal Pieta. These latter, structurally tenuous and unpredictable tangles are charmingly known as "widow makers."

The more successful sprouts were packed so tightly that they were starting to force together in clusters. The right thing to do was to thin them.

With the certainty that there would be people who would be only too happy to advise, calls to various government entities yielded answers all about how much one could legally cut and how fast the trees grow back. They either did not know or would not say what would be the best way to determine the best thing to do to restore forest health. Such an idea seemed too debatable for them to comment. The Registered Professional Foresters indicated that a cut of 35 thousand board feet (MBF) is the minimum cut necessary to break even on the cost of a THP. The size of cut that was appropriate (to me) was maybe 15 to 20 MBF, not including the fir (which was pretty junky). We didn't have a lot of money, so hiring a feller was out. I had already bought the $3,000 worth of tools to get rid of the eucalyptus and thin the broadleaf forest: felling saw with two bars, topping saw spikes and belt, wedges and sledges, block and tackle, miscellaneous chains, ropes, and the like. It had taken five years to work up to this, so I felt ready (sort of), but you are never certain until you get there.

Once you are there, it still takes a long time to decide what to do. Cutting trees is irrevocable. There are an awful lot of factors involved, but some of the decisions are easy:

Step 1: If it was an old stump, cut it to the dirt-line, parallel to the slope.

This wasted saw chains but it did make the area a safer place in which to work. The downside was that many of these old stumps, some only ten to twelve inches across, callused over, rotting, and "dead" for over fifty years, sprouted new shoots! The tree is an incredible survivor.

Step 2: If it was dead and didn't have anything living in it, cut it down.

Cutting these trees was relatively easy. It was getting them down that was a pain. When redwoods are dead and dry, they are light and stiff and often hang up in the dead lower branches of other trees. The process got easier as those hanging matches broke off when felling the others. Most were rotting and the parts that were useless were chopped up and laid across the slope where they were. Since they were dry, they were easy to move.

Step 3: If it was extremely sickly, cut it down.

These weren't so light to move. They had to be carried out in pieces or dragged out over a high-lead block.

Step 4: So, deal with the widow-makers.

These were a real joy to take apart. Some of them were hung up in branches far from support. Some are "tied" onto another tree by poison oak or honey-suckle (thank God it wasn't Ivy). If you are lucky, the butt of the log is on the ground and you can cut them up by taking out chunks from the bottom. Each time you take out a chunk, the butt comes down and hits the dirt closer under the point from which the tree is hanging. Then (again, if you are lucky) it flops back the other way toward the cringing woodsman sporting a hard hat.

What happens if you are not lucky? They flip up into the air, hanging in the arms of their relatives. Then the fun starts. First climb one of their buddies and toss out a rope to grab the beastie or cut and pull on the poison oak and try to shake it out. Sometimes you get to go out on a limb (the one that is loaded with your victim). Here is where that nerd climbing experience as a youth came in. You just part whatever you can safely reach until it comes down. There is risk, and then there is stupidity. It sure would be easier, safer, and cleaner with machinery. But then, if you can't afford that; it's a commercial job and then it's back to the permit and the 35 MBF. Most people don't have an extra $35K lying around as gardening money.

By that time, three to five percent of the wood was down or about one third of the trees by count. Count the rings. One was 90 years old and seven inches in diameter, bark and all. About two thirds of these were rotten up the middle. Some folks say that this was due to a fire right after it was last logged, but there was no charring and the internal grain structure was symmetrical. These trees were simply cut up on the forest floor, and laid across the slope to slow the rainwater down and build some topsoil. Those that were sound were carried out in 10' pieces, maybe to become fence posts. It was steep.

Now the visibility was good enough to study the situation. The plan was to retain the "best" trees. The criteria were size, verticality, slope, straightness, branch structure, root support, and growing space. The plan included a multiphase approach. Some were left for the purpose of protecting good trees from excessive light so that they would not grow too fast or sprout new branches. Others were left to shade the ground until their betters needed the space. One had a triple-leader crotch at the top that had an owl's nest. A few juveniles had promise in terms of location and shape. There was one horrid little 20-foot twig with a nest swinging around on top in the middle of a particularly useful opening that couldn't be hit with anything else during the entire process. The nest came down by itself three years later.

The trick was to remove the less desirable trees in a manner that minimized injury to the keepers. This often involves putting on spikes and a cable-belt, climbing 80 to 100 feet up on one of these weak spindly beasts, and cutting the top off in a way that is safest for the other trees. They say that topping it higher is safer. They say that when they are standing on the ground. You see there is this little matter of Newton's Third Law. When the top starts to fall, its center of mass shifts to one side. The trunk loads up like a big leaf spring (pun intended), whips back, and tosses off the top with the perpetrator waving around like a flag. The Doppler-shifted warble of miscellaneous expletives echoes through the forest. Then you clamber down (shaking) and get out the trusty 30" skip tooth 044 felling saw and drop the trunk where you can get it out and not hurt anything. Often that process involves pulling it over center (it's an extra grand for a hydraulic timberjack), and bless you if you don't get crushed by the falling log and can keep it from sliding back down the hill. Rather than harm a good tree, at times you drop it in such a way that you know it will shatter. For your trouble and personal risk you often get this skinny often kinked log, with lots of knots and often a... rotten core. It really gives you a warm feeling about the climb you just made and gets you all jacked up for swinging around on top of the next one!

Those "next ones" are usually bigger. It takes clearing the junky trees out of the understory to see the others well enough to make choices. There is also more room to drop them without getting them hung up or crunching into anything you want not to injure. These are usually either unbalanced, within five to ten feet of a larger, straighter competing relative, or with severe kinks at higher levels. Some lost their central leader and elected a branch for the job. Some of are infected with rot at the junction of the kink. Some tops are doubled, though less often than with the firs. It really makes you think while you watch the flexure in the top section hinging at that, maybe, rotten kink, especially if you are climbing on one.

What to do about the slash? What slash? These trees had been so crowded, there were very few major branches. Most of it could be chopped up on the forest floor. Five years later you can't see it. Most of the tops fell outside of the stand onto the ridges as the tree were felled uphill, out of the draw. That fraction was dragged into piles for burning. It was harder than it sounds.

The purpose for this work was not to get logs; it was to improve the forest. There was no plan to use the wood. Now that the logs were on the ground, before they were bucked off into lengths, the next job was to come up with a legal set of uses. You can't sell the logs, not even in trade for labor. The State thinks that is illegal. One could get a permit and then sell the logs, but then you are back to the timber tax, the forester, the County officials looking for fine-money, and the horde of consultants to get the permit. Vegetable garden retaining walls appeared to be the only use.

Bring in the local guy with the band-saw mill, and wouldn't you know, the lumber yield off lousy logs is… well, lousy. There isn't too much that is useful and a lot of it is in oddball sizes. The slab cuts taken off the log to square it have been spread around the property across slopes for retaining gopher tailings and organic duff to produce better topsoil. (It really works.) Clear, fine-grained, 3" x 8" redwood; for two-foot retaining walls? What a waste! It could have been furniture or siding. Most of the stuff ended up given away before it rotted. Some of it did. Some of it is baking in the sun. You can't barter, or you are back to the permit. I gave a third of it away.

It's sick. Somebody else logged a forest, and probably with a great deal less care, to make up for material that could have covered the cost of doing an even better job. There were things I did that were less than optimal because there was no way to cover the cost for doing it the best way; i.e., with heavy equipment to pull the logs over and out in the least destructive fashion. There are things that can be done with heavy equipment at lower environmental impact that you just can't do alone.

By the time you do get done with all of this, the cost of the wood nears what you would pay at the lumberyard. Sometimes it is more. Now guess what happens. The sprouts off the cut stumps sprout too! It's not like it wasn't expected. Consultations with numerous authorities all say, "Cut them down and keep them down. Starve the stump until it quits." I don't think they do quit. Redwood isn't a quitter; it's a competitor, and a successful one at that.

Fire could be one of nature's ways of sprout control and tree selection. It might also provide a chance for something else besides redwood to grow by removing some of the duff, exposing soil, raising the pH, adding usable mineral salts and oxides, and scarifying some of the seed bank. Of course we don't really know what nature's way is because nature never cut a tree clean to the ground with a chainsaw. Aboriginal Americans and lightning have been lighting fires over many times the lifetime of a redwood tree. We thus have little idea what the distributions of flora were before then.

Perhaps there might be unsuspected adverse consequences to this kind of forestry? People get all worried that thinning these trees on steep slopes can cause landslides. Some activists worry that, after logging the roots will die back and let the soil mass loose from the slope. It's a theory. It's wrong too. In fact, careful logging of a second growth redwood forest may help to prevent landslides. Here is an example from our property that is *the story behind the stump on the cover* of the book (photos are on pp221–4):

Approximately 250 years ago, a single redwood became large enough on a steep slope that during a rainstorm or earthquake it broke loose from the slope and impaled itself at the bottom of a ravine. It was buried by the landslide that came down with, and probably after it. The log sprouted and grew into two full-sized trees, each about 24"-30" dbh.

About 100 years ago, white guys with steel tools came along and whacked them both. Another landslide buried the stumps and the roots sprouted 31 trees in a 20-foot diameter circle, a third were dead, 16 were over 6" dbh, nine over 20" dbh. There were three to five trees in an arc in the process of joining at the bottom, undercut by a drainage channel through the alluvial substrate. It was an impending wall of wood with half a foundation.

What did I do with the mess? I got some help from my friend, Steve, whose family has been working these trees for fifty years. Steve needed a low-key practice job to help figure out if he had a career left after some serious back surgery. After I whacked out the runts, we set up to fell about a third of the larger trees. I climbed them and set the chokers. Steve pulled them back over center through the clump on a 300-foot-long, 5/8" high-lead cable over a snatch block in a fir that we used as a gin-pole (there was no winching or cat-skidding because all he had to do was back the loader down the ROAD). We dropped them all through a fifteen-foot gap between two trunks 40 and 60 feet away. One of those would have been snagged and broken by the ones we were felling through the gap, so I climbed it to where it was about five inches across (twice), set a rope, while Steve bent it about 25' out of the way.

Once the trees were down, then came the hard part: a week spent digging out that old 5' diameter, double stump. There were two trees perched on its twin tops: one held with but a few cable-like roots winding through rotting wood and the other was perched on top of the solid half of the old stump held by an arc of roots grown together down one side. I moved four feet of dirt with a hand shovel, redirecting the water away from the unsupported alluvium through the middle of the cluster (where all the roots are) and then hacked through three feet of roots with a Pulaski (a type of combo ax and adz). Then we sucked out the stump with a double purchase gun-tackle on said 5/8" cable, and popped out a dozen or more root suckers the same way. I set a choker 40' up a tree with a block on the end and we swung the stump out of the cluster. Then God rolled it downhill into the drainage channel where it sits perfectly to sprout new trees, and capture sediment to fill an old 15-yard pocket eroded out of the alluvium. God makes a pretty good LTO when you really need one, and comes cheaper than heavy equipment.

It's sprouting trees. It's on the cover.

We used the same equipment to yard out the logs. Then what to do with the material? I gave the logs to Steve. Sue me. Neither of us had any intention of financial benefit and it shows. He said that this was like working with his Dad again, and to me, it was an honor. Les Liebenberg was God's gift to redwood in these parts. He died a bitter man for all the damage environ-mentalists are doing. Nobody around here knew and loved these trees, or risked his life to care for them, like Les did.

Where there were 31 trees, nine of them over 24", there are now six large trees, each about 10'–15' apart, with perfectly spaced tops. Unlike many coniferous trees, a redwood trunk puts out new branches in response to light and they will balance.

The next job was cleanup, bucking the slash into pieces, reworking the deer trail, setting small logs as water bars, cutting water bars, laying branches across the road, and scraping up some blackberry nodes to "pave" it. There is also the never-ending task of controlling weeds and sprouts.

It's a lot of work. It might seem like a lot of rather aggressive action taken on the basis of speculation. How did I know about this history? How did I know how these trees ended up where they did and why did I think that the action I was taking had a good chance of preventing a problem?

I dug out that old stump and LEARNED the history while I was doing the job. When we sucked it out, I found the original log, from that original landslide still under the alluvium, dead, but still sound. I did something about it, because I knew that if I didn't, it would burn to death. That is how I know what happened 250 years ago.

The scarp from the original landslide is still visible. The tree that had slid so long ago had left roots that sprouted a half-dozen shoots. Some were fairly big (one 36" dbh) and in clusters of two or three. I removed the larger of the pairs and the wimps of the bunches to reduce the weight against the supporting slope. Then I climbed the remaining trees to prune away the damage from competition.

From what I have seen, the environmentalists have it dead wrong. They demand no logging on steep slopes because the soils would be disturbed, which might cause a little sluffing that they call erosion. This may be true, but the real question is, how much erosion is caused by thinning compared to the alternative? If we don't log those slopes, we'll get trees, large and heavy enough to apply sufficient load to the slope to break loose, just like that tree 250 years ago on my place. If it's winter, that falling tree could start a chain reaction in a saturated alluvium. It's called a landslide. Landslides like that are all over these mountains. They choke with weeds, weep silt for years, and the mud can again become unstable slopes when they saturate while still full of rotting logs. By contrast, a large redwood stump cut to the ground line with a small tree on it makes a living retaining wall.

The biggest risk of sedimentation in streams is if we DON'T thin the stands. If the forest burns too hot in a cataclysmic crown fire, the trees WILL die to a greater degree than if it had been clearcut. It will be no mosaic burn; the disturbed area will be huge. There will be no surface plants to slow the water. There will be no duff to filter the soils. When it rains, the suspended solids will act like abrasive slurry to cut the soil and destabilize slopes. There will be 0% canopy for nearby streams, but then they will likely be so full of mud it won't matter to the fish.

On the other hand, if the cluster that grows from the old stump is thinned, and the weaker trees are removed, those that remain will sprout new branches into the gaps on the side that needs the weight. They will thicken and straighten. The bark will continue to thicken to protect the trees from future fires. They will be more capable of forcing roots around their perimeter.

The County wants to ban anybody doing any such "commercial" logging anywhere within 125 feet of a seasonal watercourse, which includes ALL of our $60,000 worth of redwood trees they won't pay for and won't care for. The Preservation Hypothesis is the rule of the day. "Do nothing and it will get better as long as we don't have a fire for two hundred years or so." Or so they hope. They want to designate all riparian corridors "no entry." If I enter my forest to do any kind of designed experiment, remove any brush, trim any tree, log any rotted stump, cut out any warped and twisted sapling, I will be punished as an environmental criminal? Somebody's twisted opinion of what was done will be permanently entered onto our Record of Title as a crime? Otherwise, we are only allowed to watch it choke, rot, or burn?

📖 Timber and Fuel Management: The Residential Buffer

The West Coast has a climate that is conducive to vegetative growth. The summers are long and dry. Relative humidity is low. It is a combination that insures the potential for periodic fires.

We know that historically some fires were humanly set, although perhaps we may never know how often (summer lightning in this area is rare). The process reduced average vegetative cover, trimmed low branches, provided nutrients, and scarified various seeds for germination. Many plants in these mountains cannot reproduce without it. Frequent fires progress relatively slowly and leave sufficient cover for escaping animals. Frequent broadcast burning is a process that we have, perhaps ignorantly interrupted.

We can't have a fire like that. There is too much fuel.

These mountains are a series of narrow, steep-walled canyons that might as well be chimneys. When the conditions are right: hot, steep, dry, and over-grown, the rising column of combusting gases generates high winds. The condition is called a firestorm. Temperatures reach 1,700°F. The winds blow 60 miles per hour. The flames rise over 300 feet. Burning embers fly over a mile and start new fires of their own. Try fighting a fire like that. CDF can't. They have to let it burn, until either the weather changes or the fire runs out of fuel. We don't dare let one get going. There is too much to lose.

In California, the minimum clearance, between combustibles and a single-family residence for a house to be insured in a rural area is 30 feet. Assume a house in a transitional forest region, typical in Santa Cruz County. Most use electricity to pressurize their water (In a fire, the power is the first thing to go). Not a few have embrittled PVC or polyethylene water pipes on top of the ground. Many stand on 4X4 wooden stilts with wooden lath skirts and are sheathed with redwood shingles over tarpaper, with inadequate roofing and tree droppings in the rain gutters. The trees are huge, often lean, and have heavy branches overhanging the houses.

How much information is needed to estimate the scope and risk of a loss? Is the sheathing material stucco, siding, or shingles? Does it have a deck over-hanging a steep slope? If the house is above a slope of dense conifers or bay trees, triple that 30 feet, at least. If it is nestled in redwoods, how old and how dense are they? How much undergrowth is there? What kinds of bushes there are, how old, and how they are distributed makes a huge difference. How much water is available at what pressure? Are the roads adequate for reasonable access? Do the people know how and where to evacuate? Will the fire crews be able to get in while people are running for their lives?

The price of residential insurance coverage is determined by a rating of the roof material, the age of the building, and how far the house is from the nearest fire station. Think about the above. Should all houses have the same fire control specifications and pay the same insurance, regardless of the external circumstances? If the house meets the 30-foot minimum then, if it burns, the insurers have to pay and pass on the cost to the entire state? Does that self-defeating character sound familiar?

Insurance is a State-regulated system.

If we were to reduce the fuel risk by removing some of the fuel before a burn, we could manage these fires. The problem is that it would cost a lot of time and money and would upset some powerful people. That means it won't get done unless somebody can pay for at least part of it by selling logs.

Most of the urban professionals who inhabit rural forests think that a forest choked with brush and scraggly trees is "natural." Their faith in forest preservation is unchallenged by the tragic personal experience of a firestorm. Many share a cultural history of activism against environmental abuse. Their representatives feed off that angst and are now forcing passage of regulations that may eliminate the very forestry practices that can reduce and control the fuel. Because of the restrictions on logging, there are also fewer people with the opportunity, capital, and trained personnel to fight these fires safely.

The public has demanded rules protecting a socialized commons: "clean air." A rule system can only regulate human sources of atmospheric pollutants. "Natural" air isn't clean. When we have controlled burns with planned ignitions, they cause "air pollution." If it is a wildfire, the media call it "smoke."

Regulating prescribed fire into oblivion may protect CDF and the California Air Resources Board (CARB) from accountability, but it gives us a system that fails its purpose. It is assured to destroy the historic fire balance of the forest and has elevated the risk of fatal conflagration to inevitable.

Environmental activists think they have a better idea of how to manage the inevitable catastrophic fire. Call it "inevitable" and let it burn. It is a policy that has not been subjected to serious scrutiny. When we have conflagrations, there is a real possibility that recovery to pre-suppression condition will be impossible. This is largely because of the threat of exotic weeds and the loss of indigenous species. Conflagrations are a risk to biodiversity through habitat conversion and subsequent species loss. Restoration requires planting and rearing of local natives. One can do irreversible harm to local stocks by going into an area with substitute cultivars. To have a sufficient inventory takes preparation, propagation specialists, and facilities. Sometimes native plants are very tricky to propagate, especially by seed. Animal collection is even more problematic because there are issues of behavior modification. To have replacement native species requires either planning or limited scope.

Would government agencies and environmental activists destroy forest eco-systems over the entire coastal region, put thousands of lives at risk, and waste billions in capital the name of protecting urban air quality and a social preference for shade? Yes. That is what a democratized commons can do.

Every summer in Santa Cruz County, there are many days with temperatures over 90°F. When the wind blows out to sea, the firefighters hold their breath while the RH drops to 15%. There hasn't been a fire anywhere in the area for over fifty years. The fuel load is vastly higher than that which fed the Santa Barbara fire in 1997 or the Oakland Hills fire of 1991, and the infrastructure is far worse. There is only one road in most residential areas, usually but a single lane, often miles long. These roads eventually lead to State Highway 9, which has but two lanes and in many places neither shoulders nor inter-connecting bypasses.

The firefighters don't dare let one get going. It is almost like an addiction. There is no doubt of an eventual day of reckoning. On days with high fire potential, they fly the bombers full of fire-retardant pre-positioned in the air. Infrared sensors have replaced the watchtowers of old. They keep putting out the skirmishes, but they know that someday, the "inevitable" will happen and a small fire will become a disaster. If the conditions are right, if the wind is blowing hard enough, if the relative humidity is low, if it's hot, and if the ignition point is remote, they won't be able to stop it.

It just has to be big enough that it was not their fault. It's not. It's ours.

One burning log or panicked driver blocking the highway and all the roads will be choked, bumper to Beemer, with people trying to escape, perhaps thousands of them. The fire trucks won't get in. The people won't get out.

They'll call it an Act of God.

Motive & Means

The obvious question regarding this proposal is: "Where will we get the MONEY, time, individual energy, and expertise to fix a problem like this?"

We are spending the money now, wittingly or not. The Oakland Fire of 1991 cost $1.7 billion. If one looks at residential insurance as a risk management business instead of regulated bank protection, then we are obviously not managing fuel around homes effectively because insurance is not priced according to risk. Were one to consider the total economic cost of a fire-storm, homes in an overgrown forest are way underinsured. If one includes the ecological costs, such forests are at astronomical risk.

A firestorm is a capital loss no matter who makes money on promises to pay it back. An insurance policy on a $300,000 structure with a $2,000 deductible costs around $900 per year. This calculates to a replacement payback period less a return to the stockholders (assuming no inflation), of perhaps as little as… 75 years without a loss? One might conclude that it is unlikely that the true cost of risk plus a reasonable profit is reflected by insurance premiums. When considering the impact of fire settlements upon future insurance rates statewide it is obvious that one can play that game only so many times.

Suburban residents in Santa Cruz County are demanding that the Board of Supervisors provide them with either timber harvest rules or zoning laws that maintain the forest on someone else's land to their liking. For most of them, their liking is a vastly reduced harvest with "no cut buffers" around riparian and residential areas. What they are demanding is for the rest of the State to bear the cost of an unacceptable risk and subsidize thereby their capital gain in residential real estate while the policy does more harm than good.

The real estate industry would find higher property value in a gardened appearance to the forest over and above what they find so attractive now. They surely do not want to deal with the impact of a catastrophic fire. The only reason these forests are a draw for new homebuyers is that they are still there. At the rate houses are being built, and given the accruing fuel load, these conditions won't last forever. Everybody except the activists seems to understand that.

How disinvested are forest landowners? Where else can you find an industry with billions in assets and no idea within 25% how much that is? Why should some landowners have to cut more trees to pay for permission to do it, while other forests are choking to death and facing eventual annihilation?

Politicians have found environmentalist support to be a direct line to higher office. If they get saddled with a lawsuit the size of Montana for taking the forest the voters will be stuck with a resulting tax bill or fewer services. If the whole thing burns to a crisp, it won't look good for their future. Would they like to have a way for the lawsuit go away and run for higher office upon a popular solution to a longstanding problem?

Equal Opportunity

Maybe we should try another way? Though the principles in this book are scalable to large, complex problems, such things are usually comprised of components that are more tractable. No management scheme should be adopted without tests and trials. This proposal is an experiment to develop means to use free markets to manage competing interests in the forest at the rural-suburban interface. It is a first step in management contracts, risk-based pricing, and best practice timber and fire management.

This plan can deliver a forest that local residents would find aesthetically pleasing, provide a legitimate income to the forest landowner, and safely reduce the fuel load around many of these homes. It would restore a more natural balance of flora and perhaps fire. It invests capital in forest health and can differentiate to local circumstance. It respects individual tastes, and pools risk to temper radical ideas. It might lead to organized, neighborhood-based forest management and habitat restoration activities.

There is an obvious opportunity in the rural suburban forest. If the home-owner really wants to live in an old growth forest, then perhaps they would purchase a management plan from the landowner that will deliver upon that goal and reduce the risk that it won't ever happen. Perhaps that risk-reduction business might finance some of the work?

Were insurance rates reflective of reality there would be incentive for homeowners to thin for an effective distance around structures. It might seem that the preference of the insurer would be bare dirt, but it isn't that simple. There are other risks involved, for example: landslides, falling trees, and floods. Roots hold hillsides together. Vegetative cover reduces droplet impingement erosion and adsorbs a fraction of the runoff. Trees protect aesthetic property value but they might need pruning. Drainage design is an art form. Who is best qualified to make that call, among all these competing ecological needs? Foresters and timber operators are.

The insurance industry could retain foresters specializing in fire ecology and vegetation management to assess the home for its balance of risks as sets the price of coverage. The policy price can be scaled according to the risk score. Given liability for false assessment as balanced against competitive need for sales there would be no incentive for extortion.

The homeowners could then hire the work or perform it themselves under direction and training from a forester (yup, homeowner education). Prop-erties under suburban forest hazard management would then qualify for an insurance pricing scheme based upon the selected landscaping product (even if the product is "no cut"). It could be a range of products, from a mixed parkland forest of majestic oaks and herbaceous groundcovers, to a plan delivering something similar to an old growth redwood stand. There could be a lot in between. There could be various prices for the degree of attention to detail, proximity to the house, value of the stand, and degree of risk. Under InsCert, these plans could recover some of the cost by selling logs without a permit. Just imagine how homeowners might feel knowing that they were participating in the restoration of local habitat instead of making a mistake. Wouldn't it be preferable that the money went into restoring the land, rather than rebuilding after a holocaust?

Now, what happens if some of the land that must be thinned in order to qualify for the insurance benefit is owned by an adjacent timberland owner?

This is where the market in land use contracts comes into the equation.

The adjacent landowner could sell a contract for whatever applicable style of forestry the homeowner prefers. The difference in present value, between the timber resource when managed for maximum capital gain and managed as preferred by the purchaser of the contract, could set the price of the contract. It would cost less if integrated into a larger harvest plan as a sector operation.

The forest landowner or management contractor would collect and integrate scientific data, to be applied to a plan of hazard reduction, mitigation of exotic species, propagation of local natives, or preparation for a controlled burn. The coordination of specialties, required to complete the work under a fiduciary, provides the means to balance competing interests. That management market creates an incentive to get the work done at low cost. Insured accountability provides reason not to take too many risks.

The thinning work can be done and surplus logs sold for renewable fuels, pulp, or lumber, thus offsetting part of the cost. The insurance policy price increase can be used to finance the initial hazard reduction work over an extended term if a maintenance contract is let for the property. If the jobs look too small for the LTO to consider, the residents would have reason to organize in order to bring in economies of scale.

The timber operators want the work, but more importantly, they want steady work. It helps them size their operations and equipment to available jobs. It maintains a steady work force, which improves teamwork and allows for continuous training and higher levels of skill. Would that reduce mistakes?

The local mills want the logs, but even more they want to manage the forest on the stump much the way larger concerns do. This reduces inventory costs for decks of logs outside the mill. It allows a rapid response to price changes.

Foresters would also appreciate continuous management of larger acreage without the need to concern themselves with maximizing production. This might come as a shock to some people, but foresters become foresters BECAUSE THEY LOVE FORESTS. To participate in the management of forests for aesthetic value might be regarded as a privilege. To return lands restore fire cycles, to get rid of exotic pests, to do scientific work and to see the lands they love maintained as productive forest in perpetuity, would befit their personal career goals.

There are arguments that determining risk associated with fuels is a matter of subjective judgement. This will remain true until sufficient experiments are conducted and measurement methods optimized. There is a huge financial incentive to reduce additional risk associated ignorance. There is an array of technical opportunities for this kind of knowledge development work that a rural association of forest landowners could complete and sell.

There is a risk that homeowners with high fuel levels inflict, not only upon themselves, but also upon the entire area. Those who do not pay for risk reduction should bear an increasing fraction of the remaining collective risk as others complete the work. There needs to remain a group motive to assist, educate, motivate, or drive out, the uncooperative individual as a socializing force for neighborhood cooperation. If but one remaining person wants to bear nearly the total financial cost of additional risk to both themselves and the entire neighborhood and also bear the social pressure on the part of their neighbors for the privilege of a half-dead Monterey Pine tree leaning over their shake roof let them pay for it. It's a free country, or it ought to be. The practice of threatening policy cancellation does not work. Price risk instead.

There are also neighborhood capital assets that figure into total risk. Roads should provide a functional means of evacuation to a safe site. Participation in neighborhood evacuation planning should be part of the contract. Once a total neighborhood has achieved a hazard reduction attainment, a second collective insurance discount could be derived.

Perhaps such a realignment of interests would form a more functional political majority. It would be comprised of residents who understood the risk of a fire or trees falling on their houses and preferred a more natural look to the forest, forest landowners who want to thin their forests and make a buck, State fire and regulatory officials tired of failure, insurers tired of losing money, and local banks afraid of ruin, as well as a group of more progressive environmentalists.

This plan reverses the current trend of asking fewer acres to produce more wood. The harvests would be smaller in percentage but from more acreage than before. There would probably be a larger total harvest. The plan raises total revenue for foresters, loggers, and mills and raises tax revenue. Most important: It would be a way to help preserve timberland as a healthier forest, finding its highest value without political distortion. It beats being trapped and burned to death by a random conflagration every time.

Four Fingers and a Sore Thumb

What needs to be done to make it all happen? It will clearly take action on the part of several interests. This section briefly lists suggestions for each.

Insurers and the Certification Enterprise

- Coordinate actuarial research on fire loss with landowners' associations to prioritize research to account ecological risk and provide the data.
- Institute certification programs to inspect properties for fire risk scoring.
- Fight for total deregulation of homeowners' insurance.

- Sponsor research in controlled burn containment methods. Fund startups that introduce products and processes toward that end.

- Maintain servers that have bulletin boards of experiments, data, process documents and procedures, educational links, contractors, resources, and other documentation.

Forest Landowners Associations

- Organize and prepare for certification.

- Organize collection of census and inventory data into usable and communicable formats. Organize tutorials with verification.

- Collect and disseminate process documentation as a library service.

- Form advisory groups, and list contractors to collect applicable scientific documents and post them to a website. Bundle them as management products.

Neighborhood Associations

- Coordinate neighborhood disaster planning activities. Select meeting sites in the event of a disaster, and coordinate drills with agencies.

- Maintain communications. Notify of transfers in ownership. Assist integration of new neighbors. Serve as a focal point for communications with insurers, certification enterprises, government and industry.

Industry

- Associations of certified fire contractors and Licensed Timber Operators (LTO) can compile the results of burning experiments. Individual practitioners can consolidate them into competing plans for sale that balance risks with aesthetics.

- Certified fire replacement nurseries can provide the best available plant collection services and propagation techniques, determine necessary inventories and coordinate revegetation.

- Pest control experts and local nurseries could learn the best means to reduce the cost of control of weeds after a burn and while assisting the return of natives.

Government

As was discussed earlier, one of the main barriers to this plan is the cost of getting a Timber Harvest Plan (THP) and with it, pleasing every other agency with its fingers in the pie. Under this proposal, there is no THP. It is insured, certified best practice management. No permit. Government is in the way.

Government should instead:

- Help inculcate neighborhood government to finance local capital projects. The Community Services District, California Government Code Sections 61,000 – 61,802 is a good example.

- Disseminate and augment plant and animal identification resources, especially exotic species.

- Disseminate pest lifecycle data and processes for pest control.

- Amend air quality regulations to ease controlled burning.

State and Federal law must be amended concerning controlled burns where fire is a natural part of the ecology. When we plan ignitions, we have choices about the atmospheric conditions that minimize the air pollution impact of smoke. If the fuel isn't burned, the carbon will be exhaled as CO_2 from fungi. When we don't have fires, we increase airborne spores that contribute to allergies and asthma. Air quality authorities should amend regulations concerning pellet furnaces for central heating. It is a cheap, renewable way to make fuel reduction more profitable and its combustion less polluting. The Clean Air Act must reconsider "attainment targets" where demonstrably natural polluting processes exist.

- Learn that there is such a thing as a balance of risks.

The National Marine Fisheries Service (NMFS), EPA, and Cal. Dept. of Fish and Game (CDFG) should realize that their plans to protect salmonid populations should balance the risk of siltation released by timber harvest operations against the risks of stream pollution resulting from residential construction and catastrophic firestorms. These people are causing more problems than they solve, as shall be discussed in Chapters 3 and 4.

Photo 3 – Hillside Profile After Logging. *The original tree discussed on p209 likely sat in the pocket below the top stump. The lower stump is over 50" across. Removing it created our "corridor." There is a scarp above. The group in the background has large trees on the outside overhanging a cliff.*

Photo 4 – Looking Over a Cliff at the Stump Cluster Discussed on pp209-10 Before Logging. *(It's a LOT steeper than it looks, the base is about 75 feet down.) The photo was shot at dawn using a 28mm f1.4 Nikkor shift lens, digitally corrected for remaining keyhole distortion and adding contrast to the stump region to expose internal structure of the cluster.*

Photo 5 – Same Spot 18 Months Later. *Look at the ground covers: ferns, maples, blackberries, poison oak, irises... one year. Digital photo.*

Photo 6 – Looking Straight Up *through the cluster after logging. Note the distribution of foliage due to phototropism and collisions. They are now sprouting new branches. The tree we bent out of the way is at the top.*

Chapter 2 – Dangerous Species Act

The Weeds Are Winning

Environmentalists, as a group, under-appreciate the ecological damage due to exotic species. Many have unwittingly abetted the hazard through their manipulation of regulations concerning pest control methods. A market-based system can minimize the risks.

If you don't consider agriculture to be biological pollution, non-native plants have altered more habitat acreage in California than any other cause, including development. Recognizing the scope of damage an exotic plant can do, requires more familiarity with local habitat than is typical of California residents. (Population here has more than tripled in 50 years.) To quote the California Native Plant Society (CNPS):

"To the casual viewer there is seldom anything to see that would indicate an invasion of exotic plants is taking place."

The biggest problem in the Santa Cruz Mountains is currently French Broom, a shrub that is spreading along riparian corridors, roads and developments.

Like most invasive exotics, broom reproduces rapidly. The key to its persistence, and the difficulty in treating it, is the seed, which can remain viable **for 80 years**. Each plant can produce hundreds of seeds in as little as a year after germination. Winter runoff exposes soils and distributes it downhill. The plants germinate in densities of hundreds per square yard. With cycles of fire, stands of broom intensify. The experiment is all too easy to repeat with a simple burn pile. It is a potential ecological disaster.

Meadow species are nature's first response after a fire, and (when healthy) are more genetically diverse than forests. Typically, meadows succeed to shrubs. These are fruit bearing plants such as hazelnut, toyon, manzanita, ceanothus, poison oak, and native blackberry. Migratory birds and primary herbivores that consume these foods suffer when they are displaced.

The usual succession process is for meadow to succeed to chaparral, then broadleaf forest with mixed shrubs and other groundcovers, followed by coniferous forest. Broom accelerates the process of succession beyond the breaking point. It grows fifteen feet tall in but a few years and out-competes the native fire response plant species. It dies, falls over, and rots rapidly trapping decomposing organic duff. Fungi can then attack the roots of broadleaf trees that do not dry as they normally would without the additional shade, air circulation and root cover broom provides. With the additional moisture retention and fungal activity in accumulated duff, coniferous species, notably Douglas fir, which then sprout in very dense numbers. The firs grow to abnormal size for ridge-top locations and can act as lightning rods where periodic fires would normally clear them out. Redwood starts to germinate in the shade ever higher on the slopes, climbing out of the lower draws and gullies. What that represents is the succession to a habitat, not native to those locations in centuries (there are no old redwood stumps to be seen in these areas). Many of the redwood tops scorch when they break through the oak canopy.

The resulting mixed conifer stands are now largely unbroken with few fire-defensible perimeters. Broom burns like a torch. The high winds of a fire-storm can spread seed for miles. The broom often forms a border between the meadowlands and redwood stands. This allows a ground fire to leap into the crown of the forest. The broom then sprouts like a carpet. It is a disaster.

And broom is just one species. Annual Spanish pasture grasses have dis-placed native perennials so completely that the Golden Hills of California serve as testament to the permanence of such conversions. Yellow Star Thistle now infests 22% of California BY ACREAGE and is spreading rapidly, in part, because State-mandated erosion control methods imported seed in hay bales. Purple loosestrife consumes 400,000 acres of wetlands, annually. Each plant can make 2,700,000 seeds. Cape Ivy is choking forested riparian zones along the entire coastal zone. Pampas Grass stretches into Oregon, creeping blue myrtle is in deeply wooded zones, Himalayan blackberry forms mounding thickets both in woods and in open spaces… All of them are on the CNPS list as extremely invasive. Africanized bees and fire ants might make treating them a bit less pleasant, or possibly even lethal. The worst yet to come may be hemlock, spreading thousands of tons of poison.

In every one of these cases, government and activists advocate outrageously labor-intensive methods because they won't use chemicals, no matter how benign the treatment or dire the situation. "Public opinion you know. They would have a fit about the chemicals." Do they DO anything about public opinion? Sure, they make it worse. Most people thus don't know that many of the pests are more toxic and certainly more destructive than the pesticides. The Nature Conservancy knows better:

> "We encourage preserve managers to include a number of tools in their tool-boxes. Sometimes weeds can be best controlled by hand pulling, other times by pulling with mechanical tools. Sometimes a pulled weed rapidly grows back from the rootstock, presenting an even worse problem the next season. Judicious applications of an appropriate herbicide is often the best remedy. Many habitats are best treated by using controlled burns, flooding, or other habitat events which were natural, but which had been previously suppressed. Biocontrols have also been used with success."

"Our philosophy is that if it works, does not compromise the quality of the environment, and is not too expensive in staff/volunteer time or money, it is a good tool."

CNPS agrees,

"Plants can sometimes by removed by hand, especially where invasions are freshly started." "Piecemeal removal simply does not work." "The only answer seems to be chemical, and there are some relatively benign herbicides (RoundUp®, for example) that seem to do the trick. Herbicide should be used with caution, but in many cases there are seldom viable alternatives with the limited labor pools and finances of the conservation organizations."

The introduction of exotic species requires immediate response. CNPS again,

"...the sad fact is that the invasion is sometimes fast; so fast that within a decade the ecosystem of old has completely vanished."

Try to find a good website so that a landowner can identify the variety, type and degree of threat, propagation mode, a range of control methods as appropriate to local conditions, the reported areas of infestation, AND a way to report new infestations and solicit confirmation. There isn't any. There are, however, multiple sites at several universities listing thousands of species of native flora with location maps, siting records with location, date, and method of identification going back 40 years, and with lots of beautiful photos. The CalFlora database is equipped with an intelligent means of assisting with the identification process, but not for the novice.

Couldn't they do it by the same morphological logic that is used in the California Tree Finder? The same type of software would work with insect pests or even pathogenic analysis. Why don't they do it?

No funding. The money for the CalFlora project was provided so that people could identify rare and endangered species and stop development. It says as much on the site. Try to find a comprehensive set of photos so that you can identify weeds. Same answer. The only decent book available costs $75.

OK, but in the case of broom, you know what species it is and that it is a problem. How do you control or eradicate it? Just try to find a website listing of Integrated Pest Management (IPM) methods by species or common name that a landowner can use to identify and control an exotic plant and you'll get the same answer. There is no help, because there is no "funding."

The IPM page in the UC Davis website, has information almost entirely about agricultural or landscape pests; i.e., only those that cost somebody money. Hidden deep within the Davis archives is a series by The Nature Conservancy that approaches objective usefulness, but again they speak as if the only people interested or qualified to do the work are professional conservationists. In short, there is lots of TALK about what the government and the

NGOs are doing. There is lip service given to how they need landowners' cooperation. They just don't DO much CO-operating with landowners. There is a lot of condescending vitriol directed at property owners by environmentalists about how landowners only care about making money and how they negligently import these plants to their gardens, but little help for the landowners to prevent it.

You will find LOTS of IPM sites listing scads of government agencies, universities and adjunct environmental organizations, all talking in dark terms about how serious the problem is, what "ethic" you should follow, which bug they have introduced to do the control, which professors are heroically leading the effort, and how they are losing the battle and so badly underfunded and in need of grant money...

Unfortunately, this is not a simply matter of resources. Think for a moment of the BILLIONS of dollars in legal and promotional money that is spent by environmental organizations and how much of that money is out of fear of pesticides. Little mention, less knowledge, and certainly minimal activity are directed to the problem of exotic species control by environmental organizations. There are other organizations that do a better job but they are spending their efforts on protection.

Herein lies a curious, though all too familiar paradox:

Why do so many environmental activists abet the very conditions that will permanently destroy the habitat they claim they want to save?

The main reason is that their focus is not so much to fight to save ecosystems as it is to control land use. The other is the 60s lore of Agent Orange, DDT, and other industrial toxins that have been very useful to environmental NGOs toward consolidating political power. Their alliance with government agencies to coerce the public toward their other goals precludes them from holding agencies of government accountable for the destructive practices that spread many of these pests.

The local activists have whipped up such a public frenzy about the dangers of herbicides that the County won't spray. The road crews literally chew their flail-mowers right into the ground, ripping up the native seedlings, picking up the broom and thistle seed, and smear it for several hundred yards. They dig out the ditches with graders and side-cast the dirt on the outside bank (a practice for which any timber operator would be cited). Then winter rains wash the seeds downhill in loose, fresh soil.

Imagine fighting exotic plants on your property for seven years. Then you get this idea: "The weeds come from the road, so pull the weeds on the road to stop them before they get here." Imagine you had just spent the better part of a month removing bullthistle along seven miles of County roads. Here comes the County mower, or ditch cleaning grader, chewing up raw dirt (because the weeds are gone and the County employees have to make it look like it was mowed, so they said). Then visualize what it must feel like to find a fresh infestation of star thistle and poisonous hemlock from the year prior, along with a new thistle you had never seen and had no way to identify before it bloomed (Russian). It warms your heart to imagine the kind of ecological improvements we are going to see with government protection.

In that environment, I invested much of ten years of spare time to develop methods of control of French Broom on our property. There were experiments to optimize numerous established practices to reduce overall impact and maximize cost-benefit. There were defined regions for various forms of treatment: pulling, spraying, bulldozing, mulching, burning, whacking, and variations of each. There were formulation experiments to reduce the amount of herbicide to a minimum. There were spray drift control experiments. There were dozens of each of these experiments on disturbed and undisturbed soils, in shade and sun, warm and cold, different nozzle pressures, relative target height, and relative cover over native plants. There were sprout counts under a variety of conditions: burn pile perimeters, gopher mounds, in established groundcovers, and mulch. There were observations of the speed and density with which the evil stuff came back, whether after pulling, whacking or spraying. There were tests of half a dozen types of brush cutter blades and sharpening techniques for first vs. subsequent cuts. There was development of cutting practice, so that one could blow through two acres a day of uncut, heavy brush. There were time and motion experiments to improve applicable control techniques. The goal was to define an overall method that uses all of the available tools to the most efficient advantage under variable conditions while assisting the reestablishment of native plants. The program extended beyond the bounds of our own property, chasing the infestation to its boundaries, utilizing less effective means out of respect for the wishes of neighbors; i.e., no spray. Meanwhile, they planted grapes and brought in star thistle, bullthistle, and cat's ear. Should I sue?

During that ten years of weed control process development, we built a house, I worked a 60+ hour week, carpooled to Silicon Valley, and shared raising two babies up into school age (ask the wife). We home-schooled both kids in addition to private school and one was reading three years above grade when she entered first grade before her fifth birthday (and skipped another grade the same year). I say this to illustrate that it is an efficient weed control method, because it had to be. I don't like excuses about how we are all too busy.

Having done all that research and recognizing the depth and scope of the infestation, one would think it proper to try to contribute the results of all that work to the community. So I wrote it down to share it with my neighbors; but first, since I had done the work alone, I wanted a peer review.

I couldn't get one. There were numerous efforts to interest agency personnel and resource professionals in the article. Unfortunately, the law prohibits anyone who does not have a State-issued license as a pesticide operator from making recommendations regarding the proper storage, transportation, handling, usage, and disposal of pesticides. Although one offered to discuss it verbally over lunch at a neutral location, he wouldn't take the risk of writing comments on methods of herbicide application.

Now, at first, that sounds reasonable. These are hazardous chemicals that nobody should use unsafely. The only way it is legal to use pesticides is exactly the way instructed on the label. The label allows variation in formulation of the sprayed material to deal with various types of plants as well as combinations of that material with other suggested products to improve cost-effective control of the respective pest. From that, one can legally develop minimum effective concentrations, formulary combinations, and application control techniques. Once you have done that, **it is not legal to tell anybody how to use LESS** than the recommended amounts effectively unless you have the license, even if you stay within the parameters recommended on the label.

Less? That's right. Even if one duplicates all the recommended precautions from the product label, and recommends a procedure circumscribed by the label instructions for safe use of a pesticide, that person can be prosecuted for making unauthorized recommendations. It is legal to photocopy the label as a way of informing someone else of the manufacturer's recommendations. It is not legal to transcribe it word for word.

The First Amendment to the Constitution of the United States of America guarantees the right to free speech, especially political speech. Isn't the use of pesticides in The Environment political speech? Isn't that what the Constitution protects? Not this kind of speech. I couldn't get a word out of any of them, other than generally supportive comments about how much careful work I had done. Besides, they were too busy with their projects to spend time on the review. "There isn't any funding for that kind of work."

But, what if the public wants to do it for free? Don't they want to help?

Toxic or Homeopathic?

The chemical industry formulates pesticides toward many goals. They should be highly toxic to target pests while benign to non-target species. The mixing and handling must be easy and "fool-resistant." They must retain shelf-life stability and break down rapidly into safe decomposition products after use. It isn't easy to do, and it is expensive to prove that the goals have been met.

We'll start with some toxicology. The ingestion of any chemical can cause

230

death, given a sufficient dose, even water. Conversely, every chemical is completely safe, depending upon the dose, even plutonium. The danger associated with the use of any chemical isn't the chemical; **it's the dose of that chemical**.

Numerous environmental organizations have made a good living selling the fear of chemical pesticides, most notably the Environmental Defense Fund (EDF). These groups recycle the same "fear of chemicals" product, associating any new threat with historic examples to engender the intended hysteria, the two most archetypal being DDT and Agent Orange.

The two main concerns about chemical pesticides are their presence in food and persistence as decomposition products in water. Almost all herbicides are organic molecules. The half-life of such chemicals in water exposed to sunlight is usually measured in hours and days, not years. Soil bacteria can take longer to break down subsurface pesticide residues, resulting in half-lives of a month or more. The fear of underground water pollution by pesticides is exaggerated, because most pesticides and their decomposition products cling to soil particles near the surface. Many of the tests used to indicate their presence in soils (such as total chlorine assays) are junk science.

The political opposition to chemical pest control is an environmental tragedy. The list of secondary environmental and health consequences are numerous, complex, and significant. Let's look at the implications of current policy.

1. **More toxins, both in food and in the environment, come from plants than from pesticides.**

Plants have worked out clever ways to survive by producing defensive chemicals, which is why so many insects are host-specific. Estimates are that the weight of natural carcinogens humans consume in food is 5,000 to 10,000 times that of pesticides. These are toxic, mutagenic, carcinogenic chemicals, and not just to rats. There aren't many that could pass USDA or EPA toxic screening tests.

Just think: You bought that organic spinach with just a few bug bites because they didn't dare use a pesticide. Now, consider the history of that spinach. It was attacked, harvested, and took a LONG truck ride. It was shuttled through the distribution center, delivered to the store, uncrated, and sat there for a while with the spritzers making it all look better. Then you bought it and took it home to the refrigerator where it might sit for a day or two. Then you take it out and cook it. The whole time, that stressed and dying spinach was biochemically fighting back.

Some 700 plant species, found in California, are poisonous to humans. It is true that many indigenous species are adapted to their presence, but it is also true that many of these plants were successful because that poison is so

231

effective. There is however, no such ambiguity about weeds.

Consider hemlock. This weed (from Eurasia) has been known to destroy watersheds since Biblical times, when it was called "wormwood." The stuff is obviously more toxic than the herbicides that could have been used to control it. Because people were afraid of herbicides, mowers spread the seed along hundreds of miles of roadsides. It's everywhere along the coast north of Santa Cruz, especially in watersheds and draws on Packard Foundation property. These new owners bought the property to "protect the environment" and negligently allowed the hemlock (and thistles) to spread over former farms they let go fallow. The hemlock is displacing rare coastal parkland that is one of the most threatened types of habitat in California. There's no way to use herbicide there! This infestation is producing thousands of tons of poison, yearly. There is legitimate concern about the threat it presents to creeks, animals, and people. Even the pollen is bad.

Just because not all interactions with ecosystems are understood does not mean we should do nothing about an exotic pest until everything is known with statistical certainty. These things should involve reasoned judgements by people trained to reduce total dosage. Why don't we put our efforts into improving education and rewarding integrity? We may never understand everything and never will if experimental development is so badly hampered by rules. We should focus on confining risk and investing in its management while researching total risk reduction.

2. Agricultural yields per acre fall when pesticides are not used.

Pesticide aversion induces more acreage in production with large secondary impacts, such as increased water consumption. This also gives a competitive advantage to foreign producers who use pesticides in unregulated amounts.

Americans end up buying more toxic food, foreign producers end up paying more for less effective pest control methods, using more toxic chemicals or suffering the yield loss. They end up with less to eat and more disease.

If the EDF cared about the third world, then why did they support banning DDT against the pleadings of the World Health Organization when during the entire period of production of DDT, Audubon Society bird counts significantly *increased* nearly universally. Perhaps this one of the reasons why Americans are so often hated in the third world.

3. Preventing the use of pesticides has become a profitable business.

We have legions of public agencies and contractors dedicated to finding and mitigating toxic pesticide residues, processing paperwork, manufacturing regulatory hurdles, and mitigating toxic releases. The trigger level for mitigation is whether the toxic chemical or the residue is "detectable." Detection levels get lower every year, as chemists and equipment makers improve detection technologies. The process creates new markets for often absurdly destructive practices, at obscene costs, to remove amounts of residues so small that they are effectively non-toxic. The adverse impacts of this type of mitigation activity are incorrectly balanced against their purported benefits.

4. We have a civic culture of people who "don't believe in pesticides."

The policy, still advocated by most activist NGOs, is to use pesticides only as a "last resort," similar to the "let it burn" fire management plan advocated by the Sierra Club. Such a bias hinders early treatment that could reduce the amount of pesticide used and the environmental damage caused by the pests.

You have only to remember the sheer tonnage of Malathion and Sevin (used during the Jerry Brown administration to control the medfly in California) because of the delay in the deployment of chemical pesticides. Just imagine whether or not it would be worth five gallons of chlordane to control a Formosan Termite or to have eradicated the Africanized bee in South America before it escaped too far.

Only if invasive exotic species are controlled immediately do we have the best chance to lower overall environmental impact. Many of the pesticides most likely to gain rapid, localized pest control, at the lowest balance of toxicity versus dosage, have been banned.

5. Regulatory barriers inhibit development of less toxic chemicals.

The cost of testing and documentation, necessary to prove that a pesticide is non-toxic, is so high that few large chemical corporations make major efforts to develop them. They reformulate and recertify what they have, the pests develop resistance, and they sell MORE of the same materials with lower research costs and without need for new production facilities.

The disclosures on pesticide labels do more to make chemical companies richer and provide regulators and NGOs with legal advantages than to keep anybody safe. A pesticide "label" is a detailed booklet about 20–30 pages long and costs $20,000,000 to develop. The control system of label and training does little, however, to optimize the use. For example: What should be covered on the label versus with training? Maybe it varies. Perhaps the EDF should tell us what languages they want on the label, or how a manufacturer should test the English of a farmer in Myanmar before a sale by a local distributor? The resulting pesticide application procedures push the liability onto someone with less to lose if they get caught.

The net effect of EPA regulation is that it is less likely that another chemical herbicide as benign as RoundUp® will ever reach the market, or there will never be another insecticide as benign as was DDT (the organo-phosphates we now employ are far more toxic to non-target species). Would it be better to let the parties involved decide how it is best done and hold them responsible for proven breach of contract?

6. Regulatory barriers to new pesticides abet development of pesticide resistance in target species.

Because we have but a very few pesticides that are certified for use, we end up using but a few formulations of chemistries that have been around for many years. The target organisms then develop genetic resistance through selection. This is analogous to virulent and infectious bacteria that have become resistant to many antibiotics.

For example, rats are accommodating increasing dosages of warfarin and other rodenticides such as difenacoum and bromadialone. Higher dosages of these pesticides are necessary to achieve an effective kill rate, causing organ hemorrhages in rat-predators, such as owls. We thus introduce more poison and suffering into the environment and still risk pestilence and disease among both native species and humans, because of regulatory barriers.

7. Pesticide documentation systems don't work.

Government mandated documentation of pesticide use is designed for the purpose of successful prosecution. What kind of a control system is that? This system economically punishes law-abiding practitioners and doesn't motivate them to reduce total risk.

Similar to the label disclosures, are the chain-of-custody requirements for "pesticide free" certification of which the activists are so enamoured. The environmentalists advocate Integrated Pest Management (IPM) methods that often employ various spot pesticide and non-chemical treatments of infestations within a single field. How would one maintain lot integrity down to the last bunch through picking, washing, and packaging of vegetables from multiple countries? The grower would find that more expensive, so he or she might spray the whole field to reduce the cost of the paperwork. Is that what they want? Isn't it just like a batch of attorneys, to invent a system that generates easily falsified paper as a way to keep people safe?

8. Pesticide regulations are so onerous that agricultural industry is motivated to use either genetic modification or biocontrols (introduced exotic species to attack the pests).

Most biocontrols are relatively ineffective for eradication purposes, for the simple reason that a successful predator or parasite seldom destroys its host. Qualifying a biocontrol is time consuming, as one must establish whether it attacks non-target species. Should we rely upon a policy that mandates that we endure progressing infestations and wait for qualification of an expensive bio-control with a high risk of unintended consequences?

Biocontrols can be very risky, and are horrible if they go wrong. Remember when the State of California was going to control the Mediterranean fruit fly with releases of sterile male flies, and got a batch that wasn't? The result was typical of what happens when biocontrols go wrong.

9. Domestic rules induce producers to leave for foreign markets.

When pesticide production and use go overseas, the NGOs try to enforce them through the UN. According to the Sierra Club,

> "The U.S. government should exert its leadership in relevant international organizations, such as the World Bank, United Nations Environment Programme (UNEP), United Nations Development Programme (UNDP), Food and Agriculture Organization (FAO), and World Health Organization (WHO) to influence the procurement, trade, and use of pesticides and to allocate resources for non-chemical, least hazardous pest management procedures and practices."

Would the world be safer with all chemical manufacturing conducted in developing countries (remember Bhopal?)? Where do they think that "the government," of whatever country they are talking about, is going to get the money for pesticide training where many children would love to have enough food and medicine to live long enough to die of pesticides instead of malaria?

It's awful, but it's real.

We can't stop illegal drugs from getting into the U.S. What makes activists think that anybody could inspect all imported vegetables for residues? How many countries will cooperate with us over relative trivialities like smuggled weapons or drugs after holding them hostage with the World Bank over barely detectable chemical residues on exported fruit? Aren't we supposedly trying to get them to grow food instead of coca bushes, hemp, and opium?

How many of the world's poor are to die of malnutrition and infectious disease as a result of U.S. policies that are supposedly in their interest? High infant mortality leads to higher birth rates. Higher population puts more land under cultivation. The dilution of investment into each surviving child contributes to global poverty. Investors do get cheaper raw material, though, because the sellers are desperate.

If NGOs try to enforce these treaties through the UN, how many countries will adhere to their ratification? A lot of them love this kind of law. They know that the U.S. can be forced to obey while they cheat. It's easy to implement pesticide regulations in the U.S. by agency rule subject to a consent decree, or an Executive Order.

This is an easy list to extend, but the point has been made. Is this what we want? Is there a better way?

📖 The Necessary Minimum

The most serious form of pollution today is biological, the only pollution that replicates itself. Exotic species, notably plants and insects (deep ecologists would include people), convert ecosystem function to a greater degree than any other type of passive habitat degradation. Infestations are often impossible to reverse and, in some cases, a destructive thing to attempt.

One thing is certain: **We should be just as concerned about introductions of exotic species as we are about genetically modified plants.**

The goal of this system design is to optimize the balance between maximum control of exotic pest species and minimum dosage of toxic chemicals. This discussion will be broken down as follows: vector transmission, pest identification, treatment, and process development, with the following goal:

Maximum target reduction with minimum total risk.

It is beyond the scope of this book to detail completely how a free market in pest control might work. The purpose of this discussion is to show some examples of the mechanics as a way of demonstrating its potential. The sooner we get started with a free market in ecological risk management, the sooner these systems can develop.

Vector Transmission

Preventing pest transmission is usually the easiest way to prevent the need for pesticide application in the first place. Federal and State governments do relatively little about it in the name of supporting "free trade." This discussion uses the infectious disease model to illustrate control mechanics for exotic species, as well as demonstrate the mechanics of risk pricing.

Let's say that there is an airline transporting people from the tropics where there are known epidemics of tuberculosis (TB) and Ebola. If the patrons of the flight into the U.S. come down with ebola, it is obvious that the airline flight was the carrier transport mechanism. Why is it obvious? Ebola is rare in the U.S., has distinct characteristics, is easily transmissible, infects its host very rapidly, and is often fatal. The passenger manifests would be checked immediately and all flight patrons would be notified and monitored. People would complain that persons so infected should be allowed onto the plane.

If the problem is TB, the symptoms start out looking like a cold and become chronic before anybody goes to the doctor. The diagnosis takes time and the disease is treatable. There is already TB in the US, and the airline could legitimately deny that it was the carrier transport mechanism. It would thus be harder to get anybody to do anything about TB carriers on airplanes than carriers of ebola.

Similarly, it is very difficult to prove who was the vehicle for transporting an exotic plant or bug because infestations start small and take time to develop until they are recognizable. A colony of Africanized bees is easier to treat than a Formosan termite, for example, because their behavior renders them immediately visible. Most often, however, the vector is a seed or larva. Once they hatch, mature, propagate, and become enough of a problem to be diagnosed, the perpetrator may be long gone and the infestation widespread.

If airlines were liable for transporting infectious diseases and exposing their customers, they would likely test for the disease, require proof of non-infectious status at the gate, or charge a lot and then figure out how to make it cheaper. This would provide incentive to develop and distribute effective screening processes that are quick and cheap. We find this obvious because we understand the cost of epidemics and the control methods associated with infectious diseases. The same might be said of exotic species, but if only we understood the cost associated with the infestation.

The problems with affixing responsibility for pest transport are several:

- Duration of the incubation period
- Difficulty of diagnosis of threat
- Scope of the impact
- Relative cost of the infection
- Scope of the control boundary
- Degree of prior infestation of the destination host

There are two optional systems for vector control, one civic one civil:

Civic   Stop every vehicle and vessel at or before the border. Inspect and decontaminate every truck, package, ship container, airline passenger, and boat bilge. Culture all larvae until detected. Hold them up until they are clean.

Yes, it would be expensive. It is the size of the trade subsidy as it exists. It might be cheaper to manufacture domestically.

Civil   Certify, audit, and insure those importers who develop validated systems to prevent the transport and introduction of exotic pests.

Theoretically, no one would want to be an insured and certified transporter unless there is a net benefit: either a cost reduction for adopting the system, or a cost for not doing it. One might assume, therefore, that without the threat of civic regulation of transporting exotic species, it would be difficult for a market to reduce the cost through competition.

That isn't necessarily so. There is every reason to believe that the containment, inspection, and prevention work can be done by private industry. The research and startup costs can be funded out of the financial need to reduce risk. It is a potential business opportunity.

Landowners marketing the value of their ecosystem resources would hold accountable those identified as vector transporters for the damage and the cost of control. What else would you do if you were marketing "weed-free hay" at a higher price and the government road mower brought in star thistle?

It is likely that financial liability for negligently harboring, incubating, and transporting exotic pests would outweigh the cost of prevention. Without measuring that cost, there would be little opportunity to make such a claim.

Gosh, it sounds like a lot of work. Who is going to do that? It just might be a productive use for all those graduates of ecological study programs. Perhaps they would rather start a business performing these services, rather than languish in servitude as bureaucrats. Society has long recognized that nature needs more experts. It is time we invested in a mechanism to help it happen while retaining our freedom and making a buck.

Once there is real focus on the mechanics of pest transport, through the application of the cost of the insurance to cover remediation, research to reduce those costs will happen. It could be a pressure washing process for trucks and construction equipment with pre-emergent to kill seeds. It could be the deployment of detection dogs. It could be machines to decontaminate luggage. It could be antibody detection strips at airports, the purchase of which would obtain a substantial ticket discount. It could be floating fresh-water "dry-docks" off the coast to kill larval shellfish and parasites. It could be broadband communications instead of travel.

Techniques will develop, once we discover the cost of dealing with the alternative. What we cannot continue to do is keep transporting the DNA of every region on the face of the earth and not expect to find habitats destructively altered.

Regardless of whether or not a civil pest control system develops, efforts to prevent transport of exotic species over borders should be greatly expanded. This is one of the great failings of the current fad of trade barrier reduction and a legitimate complaint by environmentalists about the World Trade Organization (WTO). The current policy discounts externalities associated with introduction of foreign pests (including human diseases when the import is labor). It operates as a net subsidy to corporate transportation systems.

Without national sovereignty and enforceable borders, such control systems will ultimately fail, because of corrupting influences. We must stop subsidizing "free trade" with the outrageous cost of managing the damage it does or, worse, failing to do so.

Pest Identification

One person's pest is another's native species. This is where global data networks of intellectual property among landowners can have effect. Not only could an exotic species be identified rapidly, but its behavior within a niche would be available as well, including interactions with local biocontrols. Exotics are usually monocultured. DNA information might help localize the source of infestation, and thereby begin the trace to identify the carrier. Local information is necessary to developing a control strategy, as well to identify the transmission mechanism by which to halt continued reintroduction.

If you detect the power of accountability here, then you understand how this system works. Private environmental management can work with astonishing speed if we invest capital into useful knowledge that prevents introduction, pre-identifies pest sources, and develops both prophylactic and preventative control techniques. It beats flushing the money down a bureaucratic hole of handwringing and ineffective flailing, while watching a habitat get buried in weeds due to "insufficient funding."

Web-based library subscription services for identification of exotic pests in all their forms might make a nice business. People should not only find it easy to identify early pest infestations but also see advantage in reporting them. The result would be to lower the use of costly pesticides and species endangered by loss of habitat. We never seem to notice that pest introduction brings also the risk of the outrageous expense of going to court, listing the species, and fighting it out with activists and government and the lost production that surely follows. Would the cost of a subscription be worth preventing such an event?

Infestations could then be mapped by species. Click its tag name and a spot on a map as a way to report a new infestation. Link to treatment documents for infestation history information. This would be very inexpensive (the advertising to let people know it existed would probably cost more). Without telling people that it is there, what it can do for them, and how to use it, these things will remain arcane. People who have reason to invest in ecological property value would pay for the information systems and would have reason to develop control techniques.

On a more local scale, once an exotic is identified and the site of infestation posted, a control boundary can be established for either quarantine or the limits of applicable treatment. Here again, a cooperative ethic borne out of pooled risk among property owners, not wishing to be infested with a pest, could finance the venue for communication and management of the control boundary through civil liability. The key to such control might be privatized transmission media, including roads.

These arguments again expose the flaws of relying upon civic boundaries for the control of exotic species. The virulence of the pest and the risk associated with infestation will vary by local conditions. How local? What do civic boundaries have to do with the applicability to ecosystem attributes?

If somebody in the road business were responsible for the transmission of exotic species, you can bet that more effective and efficient control measures might develop. They might find a good investment in concentrating transportation across habitats, inhospitable to pest species. It might shock some ecologists that privatization of roads might benefit habitat (if only because the maintenance would be better). Including the cost of externalities in transportation would offset the cost of lower labor costs elsewhere. Why should we trade the cost of treatment or loss of ecosystem health for cheaper products or for subsidized foreign manufacturing?

The key to making the system work, is the knowledge of the property owner of the cost of risk, acquired as a result of accounting treatment operations. Without that data, and a civil system to capitalize upon it, there is no ecosystem management; there is only tyranny, wasted effort, and smuggling.

Treatment

Pesticides could actually reduce the total amount of carcinogen in food by reducing the production of chemical resistance after pest attack. Toxicity of pesticide residues should be evaluated in combination with those naturally produced, for minimum total toxic load, along with the externalities of effects upon the surroundings. That is what is meant by minimizing total risk.

Where is it best to develop processes for pest control? Often, it is from where they originate. The point of origination is where the environmental impact of developing and testing of control mechanics might be most easily and cost-effectively minimized. There would certainly be no risk of escape and it would be a good business for farmers in foreign countries. Landowners could have businesses supporting pest control process development, not just from the standpoint of eradication, but from the perspective of preventing a local pest from escaping a local control boundary. Should such effective control measures be developed, it might bring the economic boon of increased exports. This can occur if, and only if, there is a financial risk associated with such an escape. That risk only exists if domestic landowners have financial recourse for infestations.

Chemical Manufacturing, Process Development, & Regulatory Review

Let's assume a U.S. manufacturer has been producing a successful herbicide for many years. They have billion-dollar chemical plants all over the world. They spend tens of millions on Federal re-certification and then *the EPA changes its mind*? Who pays for that inverse condemnation? Why not just subject the price to a calculated degree of risk?

Are biocontrols better than chemicals? When biocontrol species choose a source of food other than the intended host (rather than starve), it can be a disaster. With the system proposed in this book, the same principles apply to biocontrols as chemicals. That means the risks with both will be compared objectively and honestly by developers, investors, and practitioners.

We should have all the weapons available toward the control of pest species with the goal that overall impact is minimized. There is no substitute for the application of reasoned judgement at all levels of industry, given the variety of threats and conditions. This proposal merely argues that the producer be managed by civil procedure and operational contracts, rather than by arbitrary rules from regulatory agencies. That reasoned judgement might then be more trustworthy. This might return some pesticide production to the US, where it can at least be watched.

Pesticide "bans" can be junked in favor of regulation by price when the risk of damage to habitat is weighed against that of an escaped pest. Under this proposal, Chlordane might be available to eradicate an early invasion of a Formosan termite. It would cost a lot for the material, but it beats letting the bugs get loose and then using thousands of gallons of a less effective material over a wider area. Toxicity to the environment is a matter of dosage just as it is with people. Let the contractor make that decision based upon expert knowledge of risk and efficacy and something to lose if they are wrong.

Individual practitioners will make mistakes, but under this program, there is less motive to cut corners. The scope of damage due to an individual is smaller than a poor decision by a government agency. Government is capable of huge mistakes, like kudzu, a vine introduced to reduce soil erosion that has destroyed 27 million acres of Southeastern forest.

We should eliminate gag rules on disseminating pesticide formulation and application techniques that are circumscribed by label constraints by anyone who can pass an appropriate examination. Put the course and the test on the Internet at the site of the pesticide manufacturer. It could be part of their certified process of verification of buyer competence. Wider dissemination of improved application techniques could broaden the research base on the best applications and uses of the product. It could also serve as a means to identify people operating upon misconceptions before a mistake is made. That would improve both labels and training.

Research on "host-specific pest" biocontrol methods should be consigned to private funding with appropriate financial liability for mistakes, similar to anything else in this proposal. Since when has government been responsible for its introduced species? Government can just raise taxes or let the problem grow until it can justify funding to solve the very problems it has created.

Dose Management

Rather than trying to ban the stuff, pest control practitioners could research minimum total toxicity methods. Under this program, they would have a motive to minimize total toxicity and price the risk of an accident.

The technical names for this principle relate to the "no observable effect level" (NOEL) or the Zero Effect Level (ZEL) of any toxin. (We'll figure out which one to use when the acronym war is over.) Abatement or mitigation of residues at a statistically significant level below a ZEL should not be performed. Research to establish ZEL on proven toxins should be conducted more aggressively than the studies of the limits of toxicity (the LD_{50}).

If we qualify more pesticides, even if they are more toxic, the freedom to use a variety of these compounds in sequence would greatly delay (or could possibly reverse) the development of chemical tolerance in target species. Overall dosage levels would remain effective at lower levels and reduce toxins in the environment.

We should include freshness and natural toxins when discussing food safety, especially for people with a congenital history of cancer. Fruits and vegetables might be date-coded for time of harvest and delivery history. Ideally, pesticides should be evaluated in terms of total toxic load in goods for sale when combined with natural toxins generated by food when attacked. This is a very lofty goal toward metering a correct application by Minimum Total Toxic Load (MTTL) (See? Anyone can make an acronym!).

We should constrain use of Maximum Tolerated Dose (MTD) testing of chemicals toxicity studies. Such data are nearly worthless from a risk management perspective. Instead, we should develop low-dose response models to estimate zero effect levels (ZEL).

Similarly, we should also eliminate the use of "detectable levels" to specify safe groundwater, soils, etc. A measurable value of zero is logically impossible because there is always error and tolerance. "Detectable level" is a criterion that is getting so absurd that it has become a political pork barrel for detection equipment suppliers, remediation contractors, and those looking for new victims to sue. There is no lack of productive work to do, what we lack is a financial motive.

No government, including ours, could successfully police the sheer volume of produce entering the U.S. for compliance to such a system as is proposed by environmentalists. The private sector produces and markets food. A redundant system within a supply chain has a better chance of verifying contracts and remedies than does civic verification. They would hold each other accountable for passing on, or accepting the residues regarding risk to the worker or the consumer.

I f the pesticide degrades it might be safe to handle a load inside a container at the dock, although at the time, it might be relatively unsafe to eat. Post treatments, including rinsing and neutralization processes or distribution time might take care of the chemical residue by chemical decay processes. The benefits are lower cost, fresher food to the consumer, jobs for the foreign workers, and lower environmental impact. On the other hand, if the chemical resistance inherent to certain vegetables develops rapidly, the value of a farm in close proximity to the consumer would rise.

Public Education

The hysteria over chemicals has to stop. The increase of toxic exposure to all species on the planet resulting from the fear of pesticides is inexcusable. The changes in the operation of ecosystems that we accept out of blind fear and self-righteous caution is no excuse either. The sheer acreage and lost habitat, committed to feeding sick people inefficiently, should be enough to stop this madness. Compared to what methods that optimize the use of pesticides can deliver, the pesticide-averse political management system has reduced crop yields, increased hazardous materials exposure, and VASTLY increased the release of both natural and anthropogenic toxins in the environment.

Worse is the damage that exotic pests can do.

This is the voice of hard experience. If you are dealing with tens of thousands of plants, that EACH produce 100,000 airborne seeds and you have two weekends with which to deal with them between the time it is identified and the time it seeds, and can't burn or use heavy equipment, YOU WILL SPRAY OR YOU WILL LOSE. If you don't spray you will have lost the health of the local ecology, maybe forever. It doesn't matter whether you like it or not. It doesn't matter how much you care, or how much the chemicals may scare you. At least droplets don't spread seeds and a few selective methods are available. Meanwhile, support development of a genetically specific, stable, and effective biocontrol and work to educate and hold accountable those who introduced, transmitted, or prevented the effective treatment of the pests.

It's all we realistically can do.

*Photo 7 – **Dozens of Broom Sprouts** from one gopher mound. If you don't see this and stop it... you get what's below in three years. Hairy Cat's Ear (Hypochaeris radicata) is on the lower right. The treatments are different.*

*Photo 8 – **Broom Bushes, Now 6-9 Feet Tall.** These weeds are courtesy of the County of Santa Cruz roadside mowing programme. They don't want to upset the urban voters, who are afraid of herbicides, so they spread the stuff everywhere. Thank you EDF, Sierra Club, Pesticide Watch, NRDC...*

244

Chapter 3 - Endanger Specious Acts

Fraud Under the Endangered Species Act

Unethical uses of the Endangered Species Act are destructive to coho salmon (Oncorgyncus kisutch). Free markets can provide a better balance among both rare plants and animals and human interests.

The creative force of biology is the process that differentiates competitors through randomized trials. Its advantage is to create and select competing genotypes, best suited to changing circumstances. Without mutation, hybridization, selection, and extinction, species could not adapt to change.

The response to selection processes varies from population explosion of successful alleles, assimilation into a competing stock, or total extinction. Between these extremes are varieties of competitors possessing attributes that may become advantageous if the circumstances change. New, and perhaps superior varieties can develop through hybridization. In that sense, the philosophical model of societal diversity owes much of its origins to the concept of biological diversity. It is a policy intended to enhance the ability to adapt to variation in external conditions and express superior attributes.

Given that observation, it might seem at first that maintenance of diverse distinctions is appropriate to conditions under constant change. Under the Convention on Biological Diversity the policy of the EPA has been to protect all alleles in the name of genetic diversity within a species. Unfortunately, preserving diversity then becomes a rigid orthodoxy that accentuates preservation of static measures of difference.

The emphasis upon preserving differences minimizes future adaptability, it is antithetical to competition, and is in antipathy to biodiversity. Managing by preserving genetic differences precludes taking full advantage of hybridized benefits. The combinations resulting from hybridization are mathematically infinite and, in fact, can induce new mutations. Preserving a genetic status quo halts full expression of a superior competitor possessing wholly new individual attributes. The Endangered Species Act does not recognize (and will not allow) the geometric increase of variation obtained when disparate alleles combine. It prevents competition that culls the inferior. The policy is, in those respects, destructive to species diversity and potentially inbreeds every allele. The promise of biodiversity under civic management could thus be destructive to the benefits it claims to represent. It is a maladaptive policy.

If an inferior variety is slowly culled, the response under current policy is to preserve the failing inferior. The causative attribution is universally human harm to habitat, or "incidental take." In the name of often unproven and subjective findings of endangered status, the agencies enact measures to prevent "possible" habitat degradation on the assumption that to prevent one type of harm doesn't have its own harmful consequences. The gambit has gone so far as to act to preserve non-native species! It is as if a family of polar bears escaped a zoo and the agency demanded that the landowners supply imported icebergs and keep them from melting, or go to jail.

Agencies are taking protective actions that not only have no benefit, but are at the expense of successful natives. In the name of preserving habitat for one species in decline for reasons having NOTHING to do with somebody's care, the demand is that landowners be punished for possible transgression of a mitigation or protection policy, even when it is highly destructive.

A Fish Out of Water

This is a discussion of the plight of coho salmon and how environmental laws have become cynical tools of policy-makers. Coho has been declared locally Endangered. It is not native to the County. The fish is being used to control land, to destructive effect. The real causes of its decline are being ignored.

The coho salmon is almost gone from the streams of the Santa Cruz Mountains. Meanwhile, the steelhead run is improving or holding steady. Is this indication of a serious loss of habitat, the old canary-in-the-mine-shaft environmentalists are fond of clamoring about, or is it indicative of something else?

The commercial fishery is in trouble. So what is government doing? Besides using it to justify a virtual shutdown of forestry, the National Oceanic and Atmospheric Administration (NOAA) National Marine Fisheries Service (NMFS) is spending $19.4 million dollars to build a brand new science center. They'll "study the problem" committing an operating budget of about $2 million per year, to start.

From the NOAA press release in 1998,

"What better way to open the National Ocean Conference than to break ground for a world-class marine lab," said Representative Sam Farr (D-Calif.). "This fisheries service lab is one of more than 20 venerable institutions that call the Monterey Bay area home. Their presence here underlines the importance of the oceans to the economic and environmental well being of our community and the world.

"The 53,400 square foot Santa Cruz laboratory will be located adjacent to the University of California Long Marine Laboratory, and the University's Marine Discovery Center that is currently under construction. The new facility will join a growing number of marine science facilities in the Monterey Bay area providing the opportunity for additional partnerships with state, federal, academia and private research entities.

Chapter 3 - Endanger Specious Acts

"'I am most pleased to greet a new neighboring research facility located adjacent to UCSC's Long Marine Laboratory—and I am delighted to welcome a new partner in marine research. The Monterey Bay Region is creating a unique consortium of leading ocean sciences organizations, and the new NMFS facility, with its distinguished scientists, is a major addition to this effort, ' said UC Santa Cruz Chancellor M.R.C. Greenwood, who also is current president of the American Association for the Advancement of Science (AAAS)."

It's really a pretty building, on very expensive property overlooking the ocean. It must be important. It is, but not for the reasons that you would think, or the ones they advertise.

They even name the 'bene fisheries' of this political feeding frenzy: the fishermen, the environmentalists, the University, and the civil servants. Funny, they don't mention the big winners in the deal though: developers! They don't vote in big numbers; they vote in big dollars instead. But, this isn't about land, money, and power; it's about fish… isn't it?

Fishing is a way of life that goes back thousands of years. It is a life of man and the sea weathering the spray, oilskin slickers, the smell of bait, and the cry of gulls. (I lived on a boat in various estuaries for ten years. Such people and that lifestyle are dear to me.) You, the taxpayer, are spending more government money to protect fisheries every year, than the entire economic value of the catch. That is a lot of money for saving fishermen. Why is the situation so dire? Did they over-fish the stocks?

Historically yes, but even if the fish are in serious decline, it is not scarcity of salmon that is putting fishermen out of business; it's a surplus. As you have probably noticed at the grocery store, fish farms in Chile, Alaska Norway, Canada, and Scandinavia (where the water is cold), are making tons of cheap fish: about a $1.50 per pound, wholesale. Salmon and trout are going to be as cheap as chicken. Since 1990, wild salmon have constituted less than 5% of total salmon production. We don't need the native salmon run for food.

If the fishermen are going bust anyway, why are they building the lab? It's not designed primarily for salmon research, even if that is the story they are using today. They are just relocating a lab (in Tiburon, on $5 million/acre property) that was built to study pelagic fish: rock cod and the like. That doesn't give them any reason not to use the occasion for the pitch!

Back to the press release:

"This new laboratory includes a seawater system to provide our scientists the tools to study crucial salmon and rockfish biology and population dynamics along with other important environmental research," said Rolland Schmitten, director of the National Marine Fisheries Service "Once completed in early 2000, the new lab will employ more than 40 fisheries scientists and staff."

"NMFS proposed designating riparian areas 300 feet on each side of the stream channel as critical habitat. Adverse effects in the riparian zone can impede recovery of listed fish, so the logic is that it is vital that a riparian zone of some width be included in critical habitat. NMFS chose 300 feet as a reasonable benchmark, recognizing that this is adopted solely as a definition of the area in which Federal agencies are to evaluate the potential risk of proposed actions on designated critical habitat.

"The designation of critical habitat to include 300 feet on either side of a waterway does not create a "buffer." It does not create new or additional obligations for non-federal parties. It highlights for all where listed salmon live and areas in which to be particularly mindful. It serves to identify the area within which a Federal agency should focus particular attention on potential habitat impacts of intended actions, and would be particularly important information in those relatively few cases where critical habitat may include areas beyond the current range of a species. A critical habitat designation can also focus expenditures for restoration activities whether by Federal or non-federal entities."

Our prescient bureaucrat, Mr. Schmitten can tell you what the policy is going to be before the science is done. Designation of a 300-foot buffer as Critical Habitat, is the same number that has been used by local anti-timber activists in Mr. Farr's district, for years. It is the height of the tallest redwoods found hundreds of miles away. They want trees like that too.

While Mr. Schmitten is reveling in the groundbreaking celebration of a new laboratory on his budget, he is reassuring the public that "riparian buffers" on the land does not mean more control of land... uh, then why did he bring it up? He says the designation only applies to the possibly deleterious actions of Federal agencies. Oh, OK... So, uh, where is the other shoe?

"A designation of critical habitat does not create a wildlife refuge or wilderness area, nor does it close the area to human activity. It applies only to Federal agencies which propose to fund, authorize, or carry out activities that may adversely modify areas within designated critical habitat. Although critical habitats may be designated on private or State lands, activities on these lands are not restricted by the law unless a Federal permit or other Federal involvement is required, or the activity would cause direct harm to listed wildlife."

Now, wait a minute... Critical Habitat means that NMFS can use the Endangered Species Act to control anything that might be harmful? Who decides what might be "harmful"? Nothing to worry about?

The first legal application of the designation in the County of Santa Cruz, has been to attempt to ban all timber activity and road building within riparian zones, even those that don't flow all year. The activists, while they admit that timber operations in a riparian zone is not intrinsically or usually harmful to fish, want all logging to be banned there, only because it might be, citing some jobs that supposedly were, such as Gamecock Canyon (which wasn't).

The Federal government isn't saying that they want to prevent anything, just that they want to process the paperwork before anybody has permission. Are you Schmitten with the idea that they might be going too Farr?

The scientists already know why anadromous salmonids are in distress. It is primarily the ocean survival rate. It may be cyclical with ocean temperatures reducing food stocks, but the decline is also related to predation, including over-fishing. The political target is supposedly low riparian carrying capacity due to logging. The scientists know what the real problem is with the emigration rate of smolts (juvenile fish) and so do the politicians. It's water flow, or more properly, a lack of it. They can talk all they want about forestry, silt, and woody debris, but without an adequate flow of water, there won't be fish. The activists don't talk much about it and the County says even less. In California, water means development and higher property value.

NMFS (pronounced "nymphs") declared the Central Coast a "critical habitat" for coho salmon. The designation is being used as part of the justification for the currently proposed zoning laws that will virtually shut down timber operations in the County. There is one minor problem: It isn't justified.

NMFS and the CDFG are relying upon false evidence to protect coho salmon, **an introduced species**. The fish is in decline because the local habitat was never suited to establishing permanent colonies and because the agencies have virtually halted artificially augmenting their reproduction in hatcheries. They are advocating policies that are eventually destructive to both coho salmon and native steelhead habitat, and they know it.

The rest of the section will focus upon proving these allegations.

Coho salmon are a photoperiodic fish. Their biological clock tells them to immigrate to the coastal streams while the days are decreasing in length, before the winter solstice (except for one run in Gray's Harbor, WA). The fish may make it into the creeks at a later date, but the fraction of viable eggs drops off rapidly after the first of the year. It's proven.

Industrial aquaculture controls egg release dates, by turning lights on and off or by covering and uncovering the tanks, to better utilize their spawning tanks. The practice is performed in fish-farming operations, worldwide. The fish farm people have to know about these things or they go out of business.

One reason the fish has such a difficult time spawning in this area is that a sandbar develops across the river-mouth over the summer. The river does not flow directly into the ocean until after the ground saturates with rain and the river flow is high enough to break through the bar, usually in January, often too late for immigrating coho. If the river doesn't open, they hang out at the mouth until they are eaten or die trying to find an alternative creek. Because of the early termination of spawn viability and the rigid life cycle of the fish, it may be that, in years when the bar doesn't open early, classes from marginal streams get desperate and seek alternatives. Tagging studies on Waddell Creek estimated that an average of 10% of the spawning class immigrates up creeks other than its birth stream, in any given year. The percentage of "strays" is lower in years with adequate flow and higher in drier years. Tagged salmon from Waddell Creek in Santa Cruz County have been recovered in creeks as far as 600 miles to the north.

The steep gradient and shorter length of the creek beds along the Central Coast can induce winter flash floods that wash out the nests of salmon eggs (redds). Summer drought can dry up the water flows and trap escaping smolts in a drying pool. Both flash flood and drought are more common in the southern range of the fish and are conditions that can destroy a class of salmon. It doesn't take much of a change in successful spawning for coho salmon stocks to drop off.

The math works like this: An adult female salmon lays approximately 2,500 to 3,600 eggs. Out of that total, 50% hatch. Of that number, 5% make it to sea. We are now down to between 62 and 90 fish. Of that population, 0.5% to 3% return to spawn. This calculates to a range of probabilities from a 30% chance that one fish makes it back, to the possibility that three fish will return to spawn. It is a somewhat delicate equilibrium.

It is likely that there never were any coho along the Central Coast, other than occasional strays entering the local streams to establish transient colonies until there were hatcheries. There is physical confirmation of this assertion.

Local aboriginal tribes possessed the necessary seines, drift nets, and trident spears to extract spawning salmon in the smaller creeks efficiently, though they usually did so after the spawn. (Beside the logical reason that they want the fish to breed, the lower lipid content of the meat after spawning made the meat less subject to spoilage after drying.) If there were any such fish, then surely their bones would be found in the tribal garbage dumps (middens).

There couldn't have been many. Salmon bones have never appeared in the local archeological record. In one 1995 study, 77,000 fish bone samples were identified in shell middens along the Central Coast between just over the San Mateo County line and San Luis Obispo. Over 80 fish species were identified at 51 sites. And the result:

> "The lack of salmon at any of our sites is consistent with their absence from Central Coast drainages and contrasts markedly with the reported importance of salmon to Native Americans on the northern California coast."

Two hundred four samples of steelhead were found in the Monterey Bay sites near the Pajaro River. It is significant that steelhead were found, but that salmon were not. The two fish have similar chemical composition to their bones. If steelhead bones were identified, it cannot be argued that the salmon bones had decomposed. No steelhead bones were found in the digs near the San Lorenzo River (archaeologists that are still looking). In other studies of the San Francisco Bay area, the archaeological record concerning whether the bones that were found were coho or chinook is ambiguous. It is possible that they were either. The oral histories of visual observations were largely by people with no expertise in the distinctions between coho and steelhead.

There is no hard evidence of a pre-Columbian population of coho salmon on the Central Coast of California. If coho had ever colonized these streams in "abundance," as is commonly asserted, the bones would have been in the middens. Coho is at least a marginal species in Santa Cruz, and no inference regarding habitat "impairment" can be drawn from their failure to thrive.

Coho salmon may have made transient attempts to colonize the streams of the Central Coast, but probably never established permanent runs south of the Eel River, hundreds of miles to the north of Monterey Bay. Yes, the NMFS, Fish and Wildlife Service (FWS), EPA, CDFG officials, the activists, and their consultant friends have been told. When you ask them about it, you get a mere assertion to the contrary. When a paycheck and power are mixed with the need to save the world, it is easy to rely upon a "deeply subjective experience" when that is all that they need to take control of land. Bring your VISA card. You will spend a lot, and maybe help the steelhead (which may not really need the help, but is where they will go when they find out the game is off with the coho), but you will not get permanent colonies of coho.

What is likely closer to the true story is that **coho salmon is a planted fish**.

People have been in the Santa Cruz Mountains a long time. They started out in migrant camps and settled into a few choice spots where there was food and spring water to drink. There were not so many of these people that they had a significant impact on local ecosystem function. The biggest thing they did was light off the occasional fire to burn out the brush, keep off the ticks, and get a little advance warning of grizzly bears and mountain lions.

Then the Spanish showed up in 1769 selecting the current site of the City of Santa Cruz because of plentiful spring water. Even then, the river was too polluted with animal waste to serve as drinking water, so the Spanish used the river as a sewer per the custom of the day. Once they had dispatched the grizzlies, it was fat city for the sea lions at the mouth of the river. The human population was growing fast. Between people, the seals, and the use of the river as a sewer, if there ever were any native salmon, they were probably gone, not long after the beginning of the 19th Century.

By the late 1860s, the San Lorenzo River was biologically dead. Its primary uses were waste transport and mechanical power. The sawmills and tanneries had dumped so much sawdust, acid, and rotting flesh into the river that the water turned maroon. There was so much waste wood in the river that water wheels literally jammed. If there are any native salmonids (including trout) left in the County, they were from minor creeks up the coast.

American ingenuity knew how to deal with these little problems: Breed them! Just release the eggs into the river and the fish come back to spawn. At the time, there was a robust coastal shipping business. People had seen oodles of salmon further north along the Pacific Coast and the transportation process was well understood. California salmon eggs and fry were packed in barrels of ice, transported, and planted in creeks as far away as the East Coast, as early as 1880. Transporting fertilized salmon was an expensive and low-yielding way to raise fish. The homing process requires several generations to stabilize. Fish hatcheries were developed in the name of supporting the economic value of coastal fisheries. It was paid for by private fisherman's associations and later by government fishing licenses. Between 1870 and 1960 in California, there were 170 hatcheries that virtually destroyed most native salmonid populations.

Hatchery fish are reportedly stupid, lacking in specific developmental and behavioral traits. There is little proof, however, that hatchery fish behavior does not resemble that of "native" fish after a few generations of in-stream breeding. (This is a point of contention among fisheries biologists.) In recent years, fish hatcheries have been under attack by environmentalists for raising genetically inferior salmon and diminishing the salmon run elsewhere, by flooding the gene pool with "hatchery bozos" with weak immune systems, etc. American and Canadian studies from Alaska to Oregon have found no difference in ocean survival rates between hatchery and stream-bred salmon, although there are differences in smolt survival rates. In-stream bred salmon also exhibit a marked propensity to reject out-of stream fish for mating, but this is not universally successful. Salmon genetically adapt to a new stream in but a few generations, lending doubt to the argument that loss of a single, local class constitutes a crisis.

Between the environmentalists and political budgetary pressure, the only State hatchery left in the San Lorenzo Valley (on Newell Creek), was shut down, regardless of the science. By the 1960s, one of the few remaining private hatcheries left was doing an OK business raising rainbow trout in Scotts Valley along Bean Creek. Whirling disease (an exotic pest) wiped out that trout farmer's business by 1970.

After a number of years, the Monterey Bay Salmon and Trout Project, a volunteer group interested in preserving the stocks of local salmonids, asked to take over the pens and raise some fish. After a brief period with not a few trials (including a toxic spill from a semiconductor equipment manufacturer), they moved their operation to Scott Creek on Big Creek Lumber property. To this day, they do state-of-the-art fish hatching, on a small scale, selecting only untagged fish to maintain a genetically diverse population. Could these people do more with that $2 million dollars per year the NMFS is spending to operate that lab in Santa Cruz? The hatchery keeps a lot of party boats in business, and that brings in tourist money. Scott Creek has the only decent salmon run left in the area (although over half of the returning fish have these curious marks on them), which perhaps explains why the Monterey Salmon and Trout Project may be shut down. (Their license has been up for renewal by NMFS for over three years.)

If the salmon were not suited to local streams, is it surprising that as the hatcheries were closed there was a corresponding fall-off in the population?

Coho salmon are not physiologically suited to local rivers. That conclusion is supported by archaeological evidence. It is supported by the experimental evidence of hatchery shutdowns in the San Lorenzo, versus the remaining run from the hatchery in Scott Creek. It is demonstrated by the continued improvement in the condition of riparian habitat for anadromous steelhead trout (to be discussed in Part V). It is thus incorrect to conclude, when hatcheries cease augmenting coho reproduction, that a drop in coho population is evidence of impaired watersheds.

Did the local environmental groups see opportunity in developing the perception of a crisis? It has been a gold mine. Various bureaucrats "nominated" watersheds along the entire Central Coast as "impaired" on grounds related to salmon. Now remember, watersheds extend all the way up to the ridgeline of the mountains, over twenty miles from the coast. A nomination of impairment stakes a claim on the use of every square inch of the drainage.

Besides mere power, $70,000,000 was dedicated to stream projects alone (none of it was allocated to the study the decline in ocean survival rates). "Fish experts" appeared out of the universities, chumming consulting and public speaking businesses to sound the alarm and garner public support for various projects. Tolerating some of these events requires either complete delusion or prescription medication. Go see one. They have cool slide shows, video equipment, fancy lighting, blank-faced sycophants, lots of promotional literature, and, of course, the inevitable petition. These people know what they are doing. Although they do have a point about the impact of historic practices in riparian habitat, it's not what you might think, as you will see next chapter.

The conclusion that coho salmon were endangered in Santa Cruz County was founded upon historically dubious assumptions. The designation of the population as an Evolutionarily Significant Unit, by which to list them as Endangered under the Endangered Species Act, was even worse. (The term ESU means that they were genetically distinct, isolated, and significant to species survival.) The local fish are genetically nearly identical with those further north. They are not genetically distinct. They straggle far outside the range boundaries. They are thus not isolated. The local numbers never were significant to the survival of the total species. The listing of "Southern coho" as an Endangered ESU was therefore based solely upon false testimony given before the State of California Fish & Game Commission by the Forester of the County of Santa Cruz. There was no corroborating evidence, there were no attached physical copies of his citations to peer-reviewed publications, there was contrary testimony and documentation that did cite peer-reviewed sources. The Commission granted the designation anyway. To designate impaired watersheds merely because of dropping coho population, contrary to the evidence in peer-reviewed publications, is an outrage.

Even if there ever had been salmon in the San Lorenzo River, one reason neither they nor steelhead will successfully immigrate to the ocean in large numbers still remains: large numbers of people consume large quantities of water. The City of Santa Cruz is permitted to use 12.3cfs (cubic feet per second) of what would otherwise be river flow. The summer water flow rate out the San Lorenzo River is now down to around 3cfs, less than a fifth of what might otherwise be available.

As far as the health of a river and its species are concerned, water flow is critical to ecological health. Higher water flow rate reduces average water temperature, deters the growth of algae, and improves oxygenation. Greater flow depth produces more flow rate variation that drops food for smolts. Deeper pools protect the smolt from predators. Deeper water dilutes background pollutants and can reduce bottom turbulence that disturbs benthic nitrates and phosphates when they can do the most damage. Higher water flow rates reduce salinization of the estuarine habitat. Fish need water.

Activists and the government can gain control of forest acreage by directing the public to vent their frustrations on forest landowners, instead of looking in a mirror. You will always hear about logging in the same news report as discussions of salmon, but you will seldom hear about urban or agricultural water usage, much less production of wine grapes. Conversely, careful timber harvesting increases critical summer water flow by reducing vegetative consumption. It also provides funding, equipment, and expertise toward stream improvement projects that can benefit fish habitat.

"Protecting" forests will please voters foolish enough to think that NMFS will give them what they want. NMFS wants salmon to be a socialized commons with which extend their control over rivers and forests. The designation of the San Lorenzo River basin as an "impaired watershed" establishes coercive leverage over every property in the watershed. It gives NMFS the power to control billions in assets. It places the entire area in severe fire danger, with thousands of lives at risk, ostensibly to save what is at least a marginal, if not introduced fish.

No one argues that the streams should be healthy, but to list coho salmon as Endangered and posit the cause to be impaired watersheds, on the evidence that its population distribution should approximate an augmented condition, is asinine. To do so, without addressing the substantive changes we CAN make in water use, is foolish. To alter land management, in such a manner as virtually to guarantee the kind of conflagration that will destroy salmonid habitat for years, is psychotic.

The rulemaking actions advocated by NMFS will do nothing for coho and will eventually decimate native steelhead spawning habitat instead. About that NMFS does nothing; indeed, the policies exercised under their authority for decades have exacerbated salmonid decline.

Yes, there are much bigger causes of salmonid decline than the condition of riparian habitat. The smolts that leave for the ocean are not making it back to the river. Do NMFS and CDFG know that? Yes. Do they know precisely why? No, but at least two major candidates are under their direct control. Are they doing anything about that? No. What they have done by listing the fish and coddling political constituencies has made the situation worse.

No one knows the precise reasons for declining salmonid ocean survival rates, or so goes the official line. As with most problems, there are clearly a number of contributing factors. Besides mere over-fishing, there has been speculation attributed to competitive consumption of food stocks needed by escaping smolt, but this is not well-documented or sufficient to explain the problem. There has been a kidney disease in the fish that was blamed on hatcheries, but there is only one of those left and it is excellent. Others speculate that there was a die-off in the food pyramid correlating with the warm side of the Pacific Decadal Oscillation of ocean temperature inversions.

There certainly has been one big change in recent years.

A Seal of Approval

One of the causes of coho decline is pinniped predation. This story illustrates that, no matter how we try to isolate our impact upon natural systems, we are responsible for ecosystem population management, whether we like to deal with it, or not.

Seals are intelligent. They know a good deal when they see one. These days, they've got it really good.

It wasn't always the case. Back in the days of indiscriminate whaling and fishing, seals and sea lions (generically "pinnipeds," in this discussion they will be referred to as "seals") were hunted to the point of extinction. They were shot for meat, their fur, and to make lamp oil. Fishermen thought them competitors for fish, so they shot them too. We know better than that now, don't we? At that same time, when the forests were being logged without restriction, when streams were jammed with silt and logs, and when raw sewage was being pumped into Monterey Bay, the salmon runs were larger than they are now. Nobody seems to know why.

People love to eat salmon. They love it the world over. For years, American boats have hook-fished in coastal waters to avoid depleting domestic stocks. Meanwhile, huge Russian and Japanese trawlers took as many as they could net. The Department of State negotiated a multilateral treaty, the Convention for the Conservation of Anadromous Stocks in the North Pacific Ocean. Now that the stocks are depleted, Americans haggle with the Canadians over salmon from the coast of British Colombia. There is a lot of bitterness about this in Canada, about which the Department of State does just as little.

People love to catch salmon. Some pay good money for the privilege of waking up at 3:00 in the morning, riding out to sea in a stomach-churning boat in the gusty, foggy, just-above-freezing dawn, smelling the waft of dead fish guts. For hours on end, they wallow in troughs, drinking and occasionally heaving, dodging the malevolent rain of dung from sea gulls. They do it all for the thrill of feeling the death struggle of a fish from the dumb end of a pole. This is as effective a proof of human insanity as there ever has been (my wife loves to fish). The fishermen tolerate all this for that moment, at the end of the fight, after one last tug, to see that shining gleam in the murky water, to see their fish, to see that... bleeding head on the end of a line?

It's bad for business.

Congress passed the Marine Mammal Protection Act (MMPA) to save the seals from indiscriminate slaughter. Since the banning of seal hunting, the harbor seals and sea lions have made a comeback, growing in population at a compounded rate of over 5% per year. Though there are now over 300,000 of them, it is still not what the government ecologists have guessed is what they call an Optimum Sustainable Population (OSP) level, yet.

The current population is acknowledged by the National Marine Fisheries Service (NMFS) to be higher than it has been "for centuries," so, what does "Optimum Sustainable" mean? It means that it is as many as can survive while completely consuming the food supply. Uh, what does that mean for the salmon? Just whose idea of "optimal" is this?

People complained that they ate too much salmon, so Congress told NMFS to do a study. The entire report goes on and on about harbor seals and sea lions. Curiously, it says very little specifically about northern fur seals. Why not? There are over a million of those, compared to the 300,000 pinnipeds in the study. Don't they eat salmon too? Well, yes, but northern fur seals are not protected under the Act, so there was no legal action to take and there was thus no funding for studying them. Weren't we supposed to be studying pinniped predation because salmon are nearing the point of extinction?

How do they reconcile this paradox of an OSP? Biological population models are dynamic. Predator and prey oscillate in abundance and decline. There is no such thing as an Optimum Sustainable Population in nature.

Some people would like to know how many they plan to have. They eat a lot.

The current estimated minimum consumption of biomass by these seals is about a quarter of a million metric tons (they don't say in the report what the estimated maximum might be). Of that amount, approximately 30-50% (depending upon whom you ask) is their favorite fish (which is the same as yours): endangered salmon and threatened steelhead. NFMS reports that they don't know precisely how much endangered salmon they do eat. That will take more study.

Do you remember hearing that fishermen were wrong to believe that seals had a significant impact on fish population? It was probably true, then. Fifty-five percent of the returning salmon have pinniped bite marks on them, now.

Why don't they change the OSP? Is it simple conservatism in the face of higher authority, such as the UN Convention on the Conservation of Migratory Species of Wild Animals, or is it bigger than that?

Seals are amazing animals and downright beautiful to watch swim. They have really pretty eyes, so they do look good on a calendar. Tourists like to see them and feed them. The seals like that, too. The case is similar to that of Yosemite Valley garbage bears in that they become dependent upon people. A good many like to hang out along the waterfront, and can get demanding about being fed. They have almost bitten off the hands of small children holding shiny toys, thinking that they held a fish.

The Marine Mammal Protection Act mandates that no control action may be taken until the OSP level has been attained. Not only that, it prevents lethal takings for the purposes of direct observation of what they eat. (Just imagine pumping the stomachs on a statistically significant sample of live sea lions with scientific confidence that they are fully evacuated while on the deck of a rolling boat! These people must be committed.)

The protocol of escalating non-lethal control measures they can employ has not been determined much less submitted to the lawyers for review. The way the law is written, before State Fish and Game officials are authorized to kill an offending seal, they have to prove to NMFS that that particular individual is a bad actor. Can you just see it? The OJ trial for a seal. Bureaucrats are sure good at tying their own hands, but then, seals are a socialized commons.

The proposed lethal control is to be done only by government hunters. While to many people, shooting the seals would be an act of barbarism, to others it would be a pleasure for which they would gladly pay. In some cases, it would be kinder to the seals than what is happening now. Read the report. The scientists are begging to do the job to save the fish and the seals.

The salmon stocks have been run down to the point of endangerment. The environmentalists have spent millions of dollars of other people's donated and confiscated money, restoring river channels to assist the coho salmon and steelhead trout into the river to spawn. They did it without much in the way of fulfillment. The fish don't make it that far.

It's pretty cool to be a seal in Santa Cruz. When they get hungry, they just flop off the dock and stroke lazily over to the mouth of the San Lorenzo River. They float and bloat at the river mouth, and then cruise back to the marina to complete the digestive process, crowding people who pay hefty berth rents right off the docks. They are noisy and, uh, messy. The environmentalists passed laws to fine people who pumped their used beer overboard, years ago, but they don't seem to have a problem with the processed salmon from seals. The reek of rotting urine can drift for over a mile.

The sheer volume of feces they produce in these warmer southern waters is polluting the water to the point that, in some places, the fish and oysters won't survive. Along the beach, south of Santa Cruz, the stench of rotting urine is overpowering. The beaches are occasionally closed because of high counts of coliform bacteria, but the source is never mentioned. (People will probably assume that the source is human.) From the air, the nitrogen plume is visible for miles. It is a lot of untreated sewage, but as you will find out, that might be a good thing. The locals don't seem to mind because, of course, it's natural sewage.

Santa Cruz is a tolerant University town with a "progressive" bent. It is a place with a larger-than-usual population of the perpetually twentyish with a lower-than-usual threshold of probity. It has some of the best waves around, with surrounding restaurants, artsy shops, and an ample supply of nubility upon which to expend free testosterone. Young males travel hundreds of miles every weekend to, uh, surf. Local business depends upon it.

Just imagine: You've picked up this date after a couple of drinks in a bar. Gonna go down to see that sailboat that cost you 60 grand for just such a purpose. You're walking down the dock, looking at the pretty boats, giggling and wobbling, telling tall tales about the romance of sailing. Your foot slips, the fetid smell of fully digested salmon wafts into your throbbing nostrils. You look up at your boat and there he is; the offending beast, sleeping on the headfloat, four hundred pounds of bull sea lion. It's his boat now. Your cry of frustration leaps from your throat. The bull, undeterred, swings his head around, and gazes at you sleepily with those soft brown eyes. He belches.

Brazened, you charge at him again, yelling and waving your arms. He looks at you placidly, imperceptibly gathers himself, and responds in kind with a bellowing rush. The violently wobbling float starts to sink under the weight, the sensation of cold water wraps around your ankles and awakens you from your sudden stun. Hustling off in your squishing Nikes with the tattered remains of your wounded pride you begin to ponder, 'Don't they have any natural enemies?'

Surfers are a rather independent and eclectic bunch. Many fancy themselves rebellious. They have an understandable love for the forces of nature that bounteously supplies them with all those tubular waves. Many consider themselves environmentalists and fight for political issues supporting clean water, like stopping silt from those damn loggers. They really like the seals, especially because they like to surf too. They can identify with them in their shiny black wetsuits. We could call them 'pinnipedophiles' but somebody might take offense, or maybe get weird ideas. In general though, they don't care so much about salmon (or seals for that matter) as to want a mass return of Great White Sharks.

The sharks of course, don't know a wetsuited surfer from their favorite meal. Evolutionary necessity hasn't allocated sufficient neurons to care (though the taste of wetsuit probably spoils things a bit). The fishermen, finding harder to get salmon, and with no restrictions on sharks, have found that people will eat sharks too. It's cheap fish. The oils in the cartilage "fight cancer." The skin makes exotic leather. OK, so sharks.

The surfers are happy, but now the sharks are so scarce and the seals so over-populated, that the sick and weak float in on the tide. More seals die from the contagion because sharks aren't there to consume the sick. Volunteers care for them until they die because government doesn't have the funding to do it. Seals are a socialized commons. Maybe a 30-06 isn't so inhumane? Is it less traumatic than "natural controls," speaking of which...

Grizzlies are intelligent and can be cute (if you are far enough away) but somehow seem unlikely to ignore a semi-clad sunbather, without which there won't be many surfers. The bears once did a good job of interrupting the seals in their shoreline sunbathing. The seals, being a little slow on the land, once stuck to offshore rocks as much as possible. Just think of it: Between the sharks and the bears, we could even transform surfing into an "extreme sport." It could be popular!

So what do we do to save the fish? Have surfers pay for shark nets and ocean habitat mitigation? Fence waterfront restaurants so that bears don't saunter in? Sell tags to party boat fishermen for a limited seal hunt? Before NMFS assents to that, a line of animal rights activists will offer their bodies to stop the 'wanton slaughter.' They will demand seal birth control, or relocation, or any other means to sate their consciences, regardless of the cost. Who wants the patent for a rifle-fired dose of Norplant®? How many seal-gynecologists are the Universities training? Ironic isn't it?

It is easier to protect something than it is to take action, because you can't be blamed if it all goes wrong. Rather than do anything drastic, NMFS will just blame loggers and go into real estate by placing the entire Pacific Coast under protection. They will stop the logging that so "devastates" the salmon run and pretend that the forest won't burn. The marine mammal activists love the seals, but don't want the accountability for managing them, much less having to pay for the service.

So what did the government do? Did they pay landowners for the number of successful emigrating smolts they spawned? No, they amended the MMPA and authorized people to use exclusively non-lethal methods to chase seals away. Seals are too smart for that. They can figure out if you really mean to kill them or not. It didn't work at the Ballard Locks on the Columbia River. No, the fishermen get to watch while the seals destroy equipment worth tens of thousands of dollars and the taxpayers pay for part of it with subsidies.

The environmentalists know better than to demand the return of Great Whites and Grizzly Bears near the beach. Too many people like the it. Shark promos would have to come after some expensive advance PR about the need for breeding grounds for ocean species, but perhaps they can find something more appealing and cheaper.

The Snowy Plover (a shoreline water bird) has been listed under the ESA as a Threatened. Recreational use has been assigned part of the blame. The beach is next.

📖 Shoot the Hero

The Endangered Species Act (ESA) has done more to destroy the value of private resource land than any other piece of environmental legislation. It started out protecting animals that were being hunted to extinction. Whether it was passenger pigeons, raptors, or prairie dogs, the main reason for their decline was that people were trying to kill them. Often it was government that was the prime offender, by offering a bounty for the killing.

Biological surveys suggested that one of the contributing factors in the decline of species was destruction of habitat. It was argued that in order to save the species their habitat must be preserved. Preservation was the usual prescription, whether that included preserving conditions that had contributed to the decline in population, or not.

Consider such a forest landowner that has, for generations, cared for a forest by the best standards of the day, learning to do a better harvest each time one was conducted, and complying with the law, as necessary. The land near the property is being developed rapidly and, BECAUSE that family has done such a good job caring for it and preserving open space, the government wants to take it to protect some fish or other species that may be doing fine.

Should the owner resist, the listing of an endangered species can leave the property valueless. It can destroy the ability to raise the capital or provide the cash flow to mitigate the underlying problem for the species. If the mitigation doesn't work, the owner may be held responsible for the results anyway. The "standards" are subject to rapid change and subjective interpretation. If the mitigation isn't performed, in a manner preferred by the enforcing agent, the owner can face an expensive defense against outrageous penalties, even if the specified mitigation is demonstrably counterproductive. These fines can be assessed without due process, even if the owner is not culpable for the his- toric decline. Sometimes, use of the land is taken simply because it MIGHT be a place deemed suitable for reintroduction. From the perspective of the landowner, endangered species have transformed into dangerous species.

What landowner would take "the long view" of habitat management, when faced with an escalating risk that the option to recoup the investment in a land use may be removed forever by exercise of political whim?

If a landowner discovers an endangered plant on the property, the rational response to this policy would be to identify and destroy the species before the authorities find it. If the authorities do find it and protect the habitat, they can end up mandating retention of the very processes inducing the degradation.

The activists have demanded that government take control of riparian corridors to protect fish even if there is no evidence of stream degradation. The public representatives declare the forest "too valuable" to the interests that bought the houses, wanted the freeways, and are unwilling to compen- sate the landowner for that value. Meanwhile, the State still issues fishing licenses for salmon when the ocean survival rate has been established as the cause of decline! Together, they guarantee that a firestorm will destroy houses, forest, and fishery. It is a democratized commons, created because there is a majority constituency that got theirs, wants new products from the land, and doesn't want to pay for them.

The suburban areas are already developed. The owners of all those other parcels, derived ALL the benefit of the conversion at no cost to protect the displaced species. The purchasers of those houses paid NOTHING for protecting endangered species. The owner of that last remaining parcel must bear nearly the entire cost to protect that species and is disallowed any reward for their investment, in order to please those same homeowners. We punish the landowner for patience, or even the desire, to operate a resource business adjacent to an urban area even when the land use isn't the cause of a loss of habitat. Such an owner is, in effect punished for NOT having already destroyed that habitat. When they go broke and try to sell, we accuse them of profiteering and go running off to demand "purchase" of their land at a suppressed price under eminent domain for greenbelts to halt urban sprawl!

The urban public is insane with insatiable greed.

Shouldn't we be thanking these people for finding a way to hold the land intact for all this time? Given that they have been so patient and foresighted, should we not be rewarding that?

📖 Buried Treasure

This idiotic process of punishing those we should celebrate is happening all across the country. It really isn't worth trotting out an endless list of horror stories about suckerfish, spotted owls, fairy shrimp, furbish lousewort, snail darters, kangaroo rats, and the like, to prove the point. We already know about government stewardship of the land, so what is the choice really about?

What might we do to get people to look for rare and endangered species and foster their development and renewal, while maintaining a dynamic balance among competitors? This proposal is about what might be done to have landowners protecting them as if they were indeed, buried treasure.

We could take a lesson from what destroyed so many endangered species. Years ago, if we wanted to get rid of a "pest," the government offered a bounty. It was effective. Bounties are the principal reason why so many of these animals were nearly destroyed. Could we just do the opposite?

Could we pay people to increase the numbers of endangered species at a rate inverse to the difference between current and sustainable levels? Do they want spotted owls? Do they want steelhead? Do they want jealous protection of the endangered species? Do they want good census data? Do they want it done under the guiding hand of the one person who knows the property best? Then they can PAY for it without having to buy the property or lose all its productivity. Those landowners will invent better spawning pools. They will seek new varieties of bugs. They will learn all about how to optimize the quality of habitat.

Would it cost less to pay people to increase the numbers than to pay for all the lawsuits and lost production?

How would we qualify the price? How expensive is the land? How valuable is the alternative use? What is the cost of the work to be done? What is the risk of species loss? It would be great if we knew. Through the insured certification process we would slowly find out. It would be no surprise if government ended up paying less to property owners than the price of the lawsuits alone. Such payment would only have to be enough to motivate the desired result and would yield income taxes in return. It is also likely that a market in risk offsets will replace civic incentives. If it is a good investment, there will be a source of capital to support it. Imagine a commodities market in endangered species credits. Such credits could eventually function in a privately funded market as risk offsets among species management enterprises. It would be mitigation with quantified economic value.

Pay the public, instead? The activists would be apoplectic with fear and rage, 'The situation is too delicate! The public doesn't understand! They could make a mistake!' As if the government never has? At least they won't all try the same thing and would lose money if they were wrong. It would also make the bureaucrats a little more circumspect about declaring a "subspecies" endangered, in the first place. A lot of these declarations of subspecies status are simply for the purpose of confiscating land for variations that are not subspecies at all.

The real reason the activists would howl is that they would be losing what they regard their key weapon in THEIR fight to "save the environment." Why the fight? Do they have to do the saving? Whose environment is it, anyway? Did they buy it? Is this about career, ego, or results? Since when did "weapons" save anything? Isn't there such a thing as collateral damage?

Who would verify the work and the census data? The certifying body that audits best practice land management and the insurers that finance the risk already would require independent verification under this proposal. They could hire the former political activists to do the verification work. Because it would be a competitive market based upon objective data, it would be less corrupt than what is happening now.

The EPA policy goes so far as to demand habitat preservation to protect endangered species when the situation may require the exact converse in order to save it. It is becoming increasingly common for amateur biologists, such as lepidopterists (butterfly collectors), to keep populations of unique insects secret from the EPA in order to protect the species from civic preservation. If they know that the reason the butterflies are in decline is that supporting native vegetation is being displaced by weeds, they instruct local property owners how to raise the necessary plants and the importance of weed control. Sometimes the best thing one can do to bring up native plants is to turn over a vacant lot with a bulldozer!

With the power of creativity that insured certification unleashes, we might even end up with a futures market in risks related to resource assets. There might be speculative value to be found in the knowledge derived from ecosystem interactions, cyclic weather phenomena, and new mitigation technology. The net result would be that capital would flow to the most valuable resources under the greatest degree objectively-measured threat, or with the greatest leverage toward improving ecosystem function. The investment would be more cost-effectively focused toward reducing the scope of the problem and its associated risks.

Does this really seem to be such an outrageous idea? Consider that with the power and the falling cost of computing and broadband communication, such specialized markets for other goods are only a matter of time. Why not ecosystem assets?

How do we differentiate in value between a wetland on the edge of an urban bay and a corridor among high desert communities? Do they want differentiated experiments? Would those civil servants want to go into the business? Would they prefer a system where trained ecologists would have economic advantages in property markets because of their ability to identify and manage ecosystem assets? Do the people who are currently busy fighting landowners and pushing paper in the National Marine Fisheries Service want to join the living and start a company? Would it help to have scientifically trained people bidding for the assets with which to learn to extend the state of the art of improving ecosystem function?

Will the government make that happen? If we shut down the productive assets of the nation, then how would the work be financed? If you think this idea is half-baked, look at what we are doing now.

Chapter 4 – Watershed Events

Watershed Management & the Civil Alternative

A broad discussion of watershed management, erosion, and flood control, along with the beginning of a longer discussion of nonpoint pollution that will be concluded in Part V.

Watersheds collect runoff and percolate it into the ground for domestic and industrial use, flood control, riparian habitat, and scenery. Watersheds collect and feed nutrients to coastal algae that process 70% of the world's oxygen. Riparian estuaries are the breeding ground for ocean ecosystem function.

Out of how many of these uses does a watershed derive economic benefit?

The way it is done now, under the United Nations-inspired Santa Cruz County Local Agenda 21, participating NGOs suggest that the various government agencies assemble and negotiate rule packages with only a façade of public input. The UN is claiming control of the world's oceans as commons. It is a logical extension to control the use of watersheds to "protect" them. If you think it is difficult to get a permit out of the County now, imagine if four are involved, with the real authority in the background. How it works and who relents will be largely a matter of money and connections, but not necessarily a balance of economic or ecological considerations. Let's start by examining the evolution water pollution control regulations for clues.

Just Add Water

The San Lorenzo River Valley is a gorge of loose shale and sandstone with a granite bottom. Over millennia, the looser soils mixed with rotting trees, slid off the walls down "debris chutes," and settled on the narrow valley floor as sediments trapped by rocks and logs that were some-how snagged on their trip to the ocean. The soils are rich and loose. The hills provide shade from afternoon sun and trap the coastal fog. A layer of granite on the bottom retains water all summer just below the surface. Redwoods like it there.

Were it not for the winter rains, most of California would be a desert. The first white settlers in the area were farmers and ranchers. To make anything of the land, they needed water. Before the days of electric pumps, farmers used the availability of gravity-fed water to render the land valuable for farming. The Santa Cruz Mountains leak water all summer. They cleared the lowlands of trees and stumps, plowed what remained of the topsoil, shot all the grizzly bears, and planted potatoes, vineyards, and orchards.

After but a few decades, improved transportation and well pumps brought competing sources of food from the Santa Clara Valley to city markets at lower cost. Most of the farmers in the Santa Cruz Mountains abandoned their land, which then started a tortured sort of recovery. Meanwhile, the Bay Area underwent an industrial boom.

The rate of population growth in California created a condition in which the bulk of voters had not been here so long as to be truly familiar with the local ecology. Local habitat is so diverse as to assure that voters know even less about areas outside their immediate area.

This unfortunately ubiquitous ignorance has often included the local and State politicians, who have wallowed in the property taxes, sales taxes, and happy campaign donors that come with increasing development. Continuing demand for houses raises the price of land and, therefore, property taxes. Farmers then have had to either go into real estate or move further afield. Developers bought the former farmland. Banks loaned the money, for construction loans and mortgages, and people moved in for jobs and weather. When traffic gets worse, the people vote for more roads. More roads were built to more farmland, and the whole thing started over. More people needed more food, so agribusiness put more land into production. When water got scarce, they built more dams and canals to get more water. The process has gone on for decades, all over the State. It's been getting crowded.

Making big money in real estate is a matter of manipulating supply and demand. Housing is a highly inelastic market on the supply side. A person does not need more than one residence at a time, but must have at least one. Therefore, to make capital gains in the real estate business, over and above inflation, requires rising population. (If you ever needed to add another reason for the immigration policies we have, this is certainly one of them.) To create a supply out of worthless land, all you have to do is add water. The real estate history of California is all about adding water and public infrastructure to dirt. Both roads and water are civic monopolies, but they historically required public approval to spend the capital. Making big money in California real estate therefore, REQIURES political manipulation.

After the end of World War II, the County of Santa Cruz, wasted no time positioning itself as a vacation spot. Developers sold oodles of "vacation plots" that the County was very happy to see subdivided into itty-bitty pieces. Government was flooding the market with raw materials from public lands and there was little enforcement of building codes on "vacation cabins," so just about anybody built just about anything that would stand. For the "other end," they dug a hole in the ground and put in a redwood box or a Sears & Roebuck steel drum with a few clay pipes. It was all they needed for "seasonal occupancy" of that cabin in the trees on the banks of the river.

By the end of the 1970s, inflation-adjusted housing prices had tripled. Those without the cash necessary to enter the market in Silicon Valley and willing to brave Highway 17 still needed permanent housing. They paid handsomely for old vacation cabins in the redwoods of the San Lorenzo Valley. It was "over the hill" so it was cheaper. Others built newer homes along the old logging roads that snake up the steep hillsides. That old seasonal vacation cabin on the other end of the pipe was, by then a full-time residence. There were kids with diapers, garbage disposals, dishwashers, and laundries, which together, placed larger demands upon those ancient septic systems. Gravity doesn't forgive or forget, any more than the digestive process. Hillside drain fields can seep effluent to the surface. Nitrate pollution levels in the San Lorenzo River started to climb.

Nitrate is a family of chemical compounds critical to supporting plant life. All aquatic life depends upon some amount of nitrate in the water. It is a necessary foundation for the riparian nutrition pyramid. It feeds algae and plants that feed insects that feed fish and eventually returns into the water as the product of animal feces and decomposed vegetation. The solids from these products form a layer on the bottom of the stream, called detritus. Detritus is loaded with nitrates.

The primary concern over nitrates (or phosphates) is a biochemical process called eutrophication: the result of adding of large amounts of nutrients (over 100ppm nitrate) and organic matter into a slow moving water body. Should the resulting algae bloom be excessive, its decomposition consumes so much dissolved oxygen that many aquatic species can suffocate. Eutrophication can be overcome in one of two ways, reduced nutrient, or higher water flow.

During the 1980s, Silicon Valley was booming, with both computer production and defense spending, but because of Proposition 13, there was no longer any way to drive out the farmers and retirees with rising property taxes. There were additional ways to create the pressure to sell through environmental regulation, labor laws, and competition through indirect import subsidies. More roads were built, more farmland still disappeared, more houses were built, and housing prices still went ballistic.

That little redwood box had been there for 40 years. Even redwood eventually rots and steel, of course, rusts. Clay pipes crack. Once permeable soils are fully infiltrated. Roots are everywhere. That box is now full of it.

There are a lot of those boxes. Most of the houses connected to them are on the bottom of the San Lorenzo Valley. There is silt on top, full of roots, which holds water but doesn't let it flow, and granite underneath, which keeps the water from percolating downward. On the valley walls, the slopes are steep shale, sandstone, decomposed granite, and occasional pockets of clay and sand for variety. The groundwater forces to the surface through fissures, as springs. It is a geologic mess, not amenable to septic systems.

Every winter the slopes permeate and the water table rises at the bottom and septic systems back up all over the valley.

The State of California Department of Toxic Substances Control has designed successive septic systems standards, each of which was to meet all foreseeable circumstances. The County drafted stringent local codes for installation, with tough enforcement provisions in order to reduce nitrate concentrations in the San Lorenzo River. Just in case it didn't work, the landowner needed to allocate sufficient area for a backup drain field, a 100% expansion area. It was big.

In the San Lorenzo Valley, most of the homes are older and not a few of the parcels are not so big. They don't have room for a drain field that meets the current standards. According to a local Department of Environmental Health, perhaps 95% of the systems in the valley can't meet them. Doesn't that seem intrinsically unreasonable? From a legal standpoint, it is a big problem. According to the County, perhaps 5-10% of the homes are on lots that can't be upgraded to meet the new standards. (Try to get that estimate in writing.)

The crucial region was the San Lorenzo Valley, but they didn't stop there. The County drafted rules, per their new fad in "Watershed Management," meaning that any plan for pollution control should encompass the entire watershed. It seems logical because water does go downhill, until you realize that the diversity to be found within a tributary structure of a river sometimes renders the concept ridiculous (unless you are an acquisitive bureaucrat). In this case, the watershed included areas with residential development, miles away from the San Lorenzo Valley. These areas have primarily newer, more expensive houses on acreage parcels with entirely different geology. The County Board of Supervisors passed a new "fee" to be put on the property taxes of every house in the watershed for annual "inspections." They hired "inspectors" through a jobs program, bought a fleet of pretty, white pickup trucks, cell phones, pagers, and the like. Unfortunately, there was insufficient funding for extensive training, for the number of people that they needed to cover such a large area.

Still, a large number of those new, upgraded, and State-engineered septic systems were failing after but a few years. Was the product guaranteed if it was installed and operated as directed? Did the State or County pay to fix it? What happened if a citizen owned a home, had a problem, or already lived on a property that couldn't comply with the new specification? Did they help?

The "help" they got from the County was that new staff of inspectors. These poor people, with only cursory training, have to force their way onto private property, usually when the owner is not at home, and then find and inspect the septic system to determine if it is "compliant." If there is a gate, if they see a large and unfriendly dog running loose (they are working on that too), or if they are in a hurry, they have been known to do that $200 inspection from the top of the driveway. They are known to have looked for other things that might not be compliant, such as a rental cottage or an unpermitted addition requiring a visit from the County assessor. California has a "Right to Privacy" written into its Constitution. Perhaps that "Right to Privacy" only exists for select purposes.

If, upon inspection, there is a problem with a residential septic system, the County puts a notification on the Record of Title of a system failure, even if it has been fixed. If it is on the title, it stays there… forever. If a notification of non-compliance goes onto the title, the mortgage holders catch cold. There are cases where this process has dropped the value of a home from nearly $300,000 to less than $100,000, overnight. Try to borrow money to fix the problem, now. There are cases that have been active for over 7 years without resolution, with tens of thousands of dollars having been spent on legal bills and engineering studies. The house is non-compliant. It's on the deed.

The courts have interpreted disclosure and liability laws to protect consumers from hidden problems when a property is sold. Every potential problem has to be disclosed. If you don't know about a problem, you have to hire expensive experts until you do. What started out as a termite report has escalated to escrow documents over an inch and a half thick.

The County wants no part of the liability and neither does the State of California. They want to make sure that there is no way that the next buyer doesn't know about any faults on the property. They also want the tax money and the fees for any required upgrades.

Most logical homeowners would pump out the box every seven to ten years, before the system backs up. Once the tank is empty, it is a good time to look at it and fix any problems before they get serious. Not any more! Fixing a problem is no longer maintenance or repair of a functioning system: it is a "system failure" and is now documented as such. If the pump truck shows up and the operator suspects that there is a problem, out comes the pad of notices to the County. Once they start writing, you are dead meat; it goes to the County. Once the County gets the paper, out come the inspectors, again. Now that there is a report, they can't be too careful.

People so fear the County septic inspectors that they would rather let raw sewage flow out onto the ground, than call the pump truck.

What happens if you don't call the truck? The tank fills, the sediments clog the drain field and an otherwise perfectly good system fails.

Fear has an adverse environmental impact.

There are other consequences of these rules, besides effectively condemning houses that fail inspection. Let's say you get a new job offer and you have to move. To move you need to relocate. To relocate you need to sell your house. It is too bad it's April. They can't get you a septic inspection until winter, because the water table isn't high enough to know if the system is working under worst case conditions. It is a consultant's dream, unless they have a conscience. Let's see, if a septic engineer made a deal with a bank, they could buy the houses for a song, and…

The County didn't want responsibility for any of it, lest they be sued. Since the homeowner can't sue the State for the law, or sue the County for complying, their only recourse is to try to sue the septic contractors and consultants. Thus, the only people in the area with sufficient knowledge of local conditions to solve the problem are stuck using a system whose design is out of their control. Each time a decision has to be made a licensed professional must make it to the latest Septic System Specification. Slopes and boundaries must be determined by a civil engineer or land surveyor, soil type requires a geologist, diffusion rates and system design need a Registered Environmental Health Specialist. After you have spent all that money, all decisions as to whether these proposals are acceptable have to go to a single, County Environmental Health Supervisor who has never built such a system in her life. If there is any change in your plans, even if it has nothing directly to do with a septic system, you have to resubmit. If you have an existing permit under a superceded specification, you have to resubmit. Plan review alone, may cost you $2,000 in fees, each time around. You had better hope they get it done quickly. Smile when you ask for a status report.

What if they don't approve it? You can try to get a "Non-Standard System" approved. That goes on the title too. There are Black Water holding tanks that get sucked and trucked. Mound systems filter what is essentially a pile of sand. Enhanced Treatment Units electro-mechanically augment bio-degradation of solids by successively encouraging aerobic and anaerobic bacteria. They work, but they do cost more to install and operate and are not intrinsically safe. The average cost of these new systems is exceeding $30,000 including paperwork.

This is largely a working class community. These are not rich people. They felt uniformly threatened.

To their angst, one can add the frustration of the septic system contractors. How would you like to bid a job, with no idea, how the law will be interpreted by a County official who has little training and no experience in septic system construction when their decisions can put you in the position of getting sued?

The contractors effectively went on strike. Everything except new construction came to a halt. Repairs to existing systems, that were contingencies of residential sales, halted too. The real estate people were furious. The tax collector didn't like it, either. When a house is reassessed upon a transfer, the tax revenue on the property can quadruple. The septic systems backed up.

How did this all get started?

The people had voted down a sewer because they had the parsimony to object to the $40,000 per household cost.

The sad thing is that the sewer would have had greater adverse environmental impact upon the fish in the river than an honest effort to fix the septic problem. Sewers have their problems in an area with unstable and erosive soils, earthquakes, and crumbling roads. It is not uncommon for a sewer pipe to break under such circumstances. The septic systems are more reliable than a sewer. Sewers also rob water flow from the river.

Was it really about water pollution?

No. Nitrates in the amounts found in the watershed are probably beneficial to the fish. Even in the drought years of 1977-78, according to the State, there was, and is, no eutrophication in the San Lorenzo River… but, if there is no eutrophication now, why do they need more stringent septic system building codes? Oh, but there might be, maybe, someday.

Are they planning something?

The problem related to nitrate, that has persisted and may require action, is the taste of the water for urban consumers. What would that cost to treat?

In 1995, the City of Santa Cruz paid $66,000 for odor treatment. The cost was less than $0.50 per person, per year. The rural inspections, alone, cost each rural resident $186 per year. The low-nitrate rural septic system upgrade is over $2,000 PER YEAR. The mean cost for the various suggested means of removing rural nitrogen is over $2,000 PER POUND, PER YEAR.

Meanwhile, the City of Santa Cruz pumps most of its water from local springs. The rest is captured from Newell Creek and pumped out of the San Lorenzo River, then stored in the Loch Lomond Dam. It is then piped down the hill, treated, used, and piped to the sewage treatment plant adjacent to the ocean miles away. The water flow from Loch Lomond bypasses the river.

Low flow rate in the river, in part due to the bypass for urban consumption, increases water residence time and reduces average depth of flow in the river. This allows the water to warm in the sun and incubate the bacteria that feed on dead algae that grow on nitrates. Low flow rates can reduce aeration and oxygenation. Lower flow rates increase the fluid shear along the bottom, which increases mixing and releases benthic nitrates. Lower water volume retains less oxygen. Low flow rate increases the risk of eutrophication.

NMFS had declared the watershed "critical habitat" for coho salmon. The

California Department of Fish and Game had shut down the hatcheries to protect "native stocks" from "genetically inferior" hatchery fish. They looked at the declining coho census, the fact that nitrate levels exceeded their attainment specifications (to be discussed in Part V), and declared the San Lorenzo an "impaired watershed." Meanwhile, nobody has any concept of what an acceptable spatial and temporal range of nitrate profiles might be.

Fish need fresh water flow to get in and out of the river mouth. Fresh water floats on top of the seawater. Estuarine productivity (and therefore marine breeding and feeding activity) is especially high at the interface of the two layers. There is also strong historic correlation between anthropogenic nitrate addition and overall marine productivity. One need only witness the decline in tide pool productivity over the last 50 years to notice (since sewage treatment plants along the Pacific Coast became the norm).

Were these treatment plants really such a good idea? Did they study the full impact of sewage treatment plants before they were mandated? Should we perhaps run them differently or was there a better and cheaper way to do it? Are civic treatment plants accountable for marine productivity? Could a market funded by healthy marine productivity figure it out better?

There is one thing that the State and County do know and they don't do anything about it. Fish need water. One would think that someone responsible for caring for a fish, however illegitimately listed as Endangered, would have some interest in that water flow. In the fall, the water flow of the San Lorenzo drops to less than 3cfs (about 20 gallons per second). The City of Santa Cruz is allotted 12.2cfs of the net flow rate out of the San Lorenzo River. The County could double the late season flow in the San Lorenzo River by merely asking the City of Santa Cruz to reduce its consumption by 25%. There are literally hundreds of pipes and pumps sucking water for residential gardens, extended like straws from the riverbank into the river. (Some are legal; many are not.) The County and could add more water by halting illegal extractions.

Is the threat of eutrophication in the San Lorenzo River due to suburban nitrates from septic systems, or is it the demand for domestic water from an urban population? That is the problem with political management.

Sewers involve taxes, big bond issues, union construction jobs, and lots of administration. Sewers are also very effective at controlling who gets to build and who gets to stay. Rural sewers and expensive septic systems are a way of driving middle-income people out of the countryside if they can't afford the extra $1,200-$3,000 cost per year over 30 years. Would the rural residents rather pay the doubled cost of odor treatment for urban water to $1 per year, instead of being forced from their condemned homes by a $3,000 annual bill?

Where would they go? They would have to move into the city where they would use more urban water from the San Lorenzo, instead of distributed groundwater sources elsewhere. Under the Local Agenda 21 Sustainable Development Measure C Plan (the Decade of the Environment Measure) what did they do there? They hemmed the city in from the outside with greenbelts so that the only way to go is up. What does that do to unit pricing, inside the greenbelt?

Public Notification

"Watershed Management" under Sustainable Development.

Any public agency has a structural disinclination to share information about the system to which they have subjected the public, for several reasons. They do not want the interference in "their" work. They would be uncomfortable if they had to listen to public reaction. They do not understand the evolutionary and contradictory layers of the systems they must administer. They have to do these things to comply with the next level up. It's not their fault. They are just doing their jobs...

This communication pathology cuts both ways, both from government to the public and vice versa. The public, fearing the costs of compliance, often fails to inform the government of their personal projects. We also have a cultural standard that allows ignorance to constitute reduced culpability. Usually, the greatest cause of fear is about that which is already done, and not how existing plans have been circumscribed. So they hide it and won't call for help, even if the need is obvious.

The County of Santa Cruz, has resorted to various forms of coercion to get that information and "their" money. For any permit application there is a "site visit," or a search for prior permit violations. For violations found, there are fines (of up to $2,500 per day) and notifications on the Record of Title.

It is the little guy who gets hit hardest by the fine system. This is one of the contributing complications of the septic system story. People who could barely afford astronomically priced and taxed former vacation cabins, could hardly afford an extensive list of consultants before they fixed the place up. They had other priorities: wiring, plumbing, structural problems, and the need to add on, to accommodate growing families. The last thing on their lists would be septic system maintenance, much less protecting the 4th, 5th, 6th, 7th, and 8th Amendments or the Separation of Powers as are violated by this kind of law. When that redwood box fails, when the contractors won't touch it for less than thirty grand, and when the County inspectors red tag the house, the usual reaction is for people to be upset.

What did the County do? They called a public hearing. Did they tell everybody about it and invite them to a hearing for public comment?

Sure they did.

The notice was an inch long, buried in the back sections of The Valley Press. There was to be a public meeting about Septic Systems, on Wednesday evening at the local high school auditorium. The paper was printed Tuesday night. Most people get it on Wednesday. Just think: You hear about it, call your spouse at work, hire a sitter, and show up by 7:00 PM. Perhaps the County knew that subject matter was going to be unpopular?

There were 500 people. They jammed the room, out the door, and down the street. The funny thing is that the County people were surprised.

After about an hour of tears, anger, and obfuscation, the question arose,

"What do all these septic system rules do to fix the problem? These people are afraid of you. They would rather let raw sewage run out on the dirt and into the river than risk asking their government for help, because they are afraid of losing everything they have ever worked for. The rules are therefore having an adverse environmental impact. We have the best in the business right here telling you that it doesn't work. Why don't we certify them to produce systems to operating performance standards, and if it doesn't work, have an insurance fund to upgrade the system or relocate the homeowner and mitigate the site? It might take a marginal cost of 5% for each system. Let the contractors put together a utility business to manage the systems and guarantee operation to specification. Does the County guarantee performance to specification or conformance to the law under the current regime? Can the County fix it if it doesn't work?"

They were stunned. The contractors were taken aback, too.

At a later meeting, the question came up from one of the contractors, "How can we guarantee a system if the homeowner can't operate it correctly?" Note that they were now wondering HOW to make it work and acknowledging that there was a problem. If septic systems cannot be operated safely by the average negligent homeowner with too much to do, either the control functions must not be very well automated or reliable, or a service business is necessary. A few brainstorming minutes yielded at least two patentable product concepts that might well render a system capable of being guaranteed, which would reduce premature failure significantly. It only takes the willingness to ask how by breaking out of the specification loop.

There was still the question of insurance. They didn't want to charge yet more for the job. Now this is laughable. The County Plan-Check services, and unnecessary requirements for professional consultants cost from $2,000 to 5,000 per job. The County assesses $186 per year on every house in the area for the performance and administration of septic inspections. It is a fortune. The contractor is still responsible for the performance of the system for one year. It seems like there is plenty of money available for systems that would work better and cost less as long as the County bows out of the business. The contractors would love to get that much for maintaining the system, and could purchase the insurance for less.

Can you imagine the reaction of the civil servants? Do you think these people like working late at a hearing in front of a howling public? They would much rather cook up a new rule in a back room, publish it in the book, send a clueless inspector to the job site and demand that the contractor comply. It leaves the contractor to bear the brunt of the anger and suspicion from the shattered homeowner, while the bureaucrat is safely behind a desk with a locked door to the public waiting area. That is what you get when you decide that you are too busy earning money to pay taxes to participate in self-government.

So what did the bureaucrats do? They set up a task force, a TAC (Technical Advisory Committee), a "consensus process" designed exactly as intended under the local Agenda 21 (Part V, Chapter 1). What they came up with was a dream for the licensed specialists who got to look very sad and tell the public that they did their best, one at a time, for a price.

It was a done deal from the beginning. It had nothing to do with the water quality, it was about money, bureaucratic power, and future development.

The County can now send a poorly trained person to your property to do inspections, unannounced. They are equipped with a cell phone and pager so that they can call someone at the County Government Center if they do not understand the situation and get a safe answer from the supervisor, safely hiding in her office. The result can be a Notice of Condemnation. Imagine coming home to that little red tag on your front door. One can see the need for one-each, large and territorial dog, with a thing about people in white pickup trucks.

📖 An Effluent Society

A civil servant's idea of "fair" is a uniform solution, often called a conformance specification. Unfortunately, nature doesn't know what either "fair" or "uniform" is with regard to nitrate or anything else. The funny thing is that non-uniform solutions might be more "fair." This is because each asset costs what is appropriate to each circumstance. A market can do that, where governmental agencies simply can't.

Septic systems are in many ways the ultimate rural sewage treatment method. They recharge the water as close to its source as possible, which is a minimum disturbance to the natural hydrologic cycle. They do not require major arterial pipes that are a hazard in an earthquake or landslide. There is usually no requirement for electrical power or other utilities. It is astounding that the State of California and County of Santa Cruz, could turn administration of septic systems into something so terribly complex.

A management system, designed around InsCert septic contractors, solves the problem, permanently. If the contractor guarantees that the system will perform when operated within design limits, that is better than what government does now. Once the guarantee includes operation and maintenance of the septic system, the miracle of the marketplace starts to blossom.

Septic contractors could put together a utility business to manage the systems and guarantee operation according to unique customer circumstances. The first thing that will probably happen when they take over operation is that they will find that they will have a hard time monitoring operation. If a toilet has a bad valve and starts to run 24 hours a day, it can kill a marginal system in the winter. There is a fix: timed flow switches and solenoid valves in toilets. If a house system cannot be monitored for flow easily, because gray water or irrigation systems are mixed with sewerage and domestic supplies, divorced piping systems may be necessary. These things get cheaper and improve under competitive pressure evolving water management systems for the entire home.

A water management system such as this could maintain a marginal septic system on an old house safely until it was economically justified for removal, without a huge waste of capital or a needless environmental impact. It would be a way to create the tools for a functional water market. Can the County do that? Does it sound worthy of investment?

There is even more profit opportunity in converting systems that have a high potential for future failure before the event; something the County system does not address. The pooled risk approach might work well here too. There is no need to wait until the effluent is running out onto the ground to address a problem. If the systems are 95%+ deficient, as the County has suggested, then that fact may serve to motivate more collective action on a neighborhood basis. Isn't 95% a lot though? Does that mean that they are deficient or does it mean that they have designed a spec that can't be met by those earlier systems that they permitted? Would the County bureaucrats have incentive to redefine the specification, so that everybody has to come to them for an expensive upgrade with outrageous fees? Are there any side effects?

The County asserts that 5% of the existing systems cannot be upgraded to meet specifications. It is an easy fix. Let's assume that the certified contractors do the best they can. What if, after all attempts, the systems can't be fixed economically? This is where insurance steps in. If it doesn't work, an insurance fund can pay to relocate the homeowner and mitigate the site. The insurance premiums might cost an additional 10% of the base cost of each system, but this is wildly less than is being assessed by the County for all the plan checking and oversight being done now. It beats the cost to the community of a personal financial disaster and a public health hazard.

A septic "drain field right" is an example of an unrecognized asset. A lower site on a hill with a field of alluvium unsuitable for building could generate open space revenue as a deposition site for houses on a steeper ridge. This would less likely destabilize slopes, the liquid could reduce the need for irrigation, and the asset value of "view sites," unsuitable for septic systems, could be improved with lower impact and a nice view of an open field. The use of easements can allow neighbors to take advantage of minor economies of scale, for example with neighborhood black water systems and gray water leaching. This could reduce the frequency of many undesirable compromises made when the boundaries governing system design is a set of property lines.

People have sold water rights, access easements, and redrawn boundaries for years, so that is nothing new. In the past it has been an expensive process. There is minimal education of participants to keep reins on the gatekeepers. Government has increased the cost in the name of making development more difficult. Transaction volume is so constrained that specific expertise in these matters has not developed into a common professional trade. Perhaps those real estate agents might want to learn?

A private system will be, in all likelihood, cheaper to operate. It will end the idiotic practice of constructing overkill solutions, placed where they are not needed, or are inadvisable. This will end the legal hassles when the real estate agents come under fire for houses that are sold in summer, only to have their systems fail the next winter because those properties that need it would be under continuous management. This will end the waste of capital when a person buys a piece of otherwise excellent property, only to find out that the property is inappropriate to the latest change in the County spec. It will allow in-fill development, instead of forcing continued sprawl, and allow construction of simpler systems to meet unique circumstances.

When people start asking the producers to guarantee the performance of the systems that they are free to design, install, and operate, these products will improve. Consider, for example, a fireproof black-water hose that eliminates the need for trenching steep slopes and absorbs earthquakes without rupture. The technology won't be invented and these products will never get cheaper unless the public is free to buy them. This is something environmentalists have long understood, but seem to be determined only to mandate by law.

The people in that septic R&D department in Sacramento can work for the people who will make the new products. They actually do have expertise for sale that could be put to better use. There are producers of multi-channel control systems, thermal flow switches, and solenoid poppet valves. Most of the technology is there, and it is just a little more humane to devise a water management system than condemning the house, turning families out on the street, and paying lawyers to carve up the turkey over lunch. It also beats cholera, typhoid, or dengue fever spread in a winter flood by people too afraid to call the pump truck.

Finally, if it costs but a couple of bucks per house to improve the taste of urban water, isn't that cheaper than $2,000 per year for an illegal search, unnecessary upgrade capital, and outrageous operating costs? Meanwhile, in some cases, the added nitrate would possibly BENEFIT riparian function on seasonal basis. Speaking of which...

📖 Stream of Consciousness

Local corporations can integrate competing interests among fisheries, domestic water, urban land use, erosion, silt, and flood control, all using risk-based pricing. This section is conjecture for the purpose of illustration.

Debris Flow

A redwood is long and strong and slow to rot. When one falls into a creek it usually gets stuck trapping debris and sediment behind it, These minor dams slow down winter stormwash and dissipate its energy into a pool. The fish get a place to rest and can easily negotiate the minor waterfall.

Sometimes one log collects another. It can make quite a pile. The logs in ancient jams were over six feet in diameter. Logjams eventually break loose in a winter storm and a thousand-yard blob of mud and logs, travelling twenty miles an hour, has a way of clearing things out of its way. Years ago, these "debris flows" accumulated more on their way downhill, entraining mills, bridges, houses... you get the idea. They swept down the canyons, changing the flow of entire rivers through heavily populated towns. People got tired of losing bridges so they build them tough and strong. The debris flows then complicated matters by hanging up the bridge pilings designed to withstand such things. When they did, the water piled up behind the jam, and a minor disturbance called a "flood" ensued. It did it in Soquel, in 1955, and again in 1964, and again in 1982, costing millions more every time.

In response to the outcry from urban business, and taking advantage of the wisdom of the Army Corps of Engineers, the County "coordinated" an effort to remove logjams. They were "barriers to fish." It was done as an environmental program, often by County workers themselves.

Did they do a ten-year study in a single creek as a pilot program? No. Did they subject their ideas to peer review? No. Did they do as much pre-study and documentation as the average forester filing a THP? No. It was done in every stream in the County and, given the "success" of the program at justifying budgetary expenditures, propagated rapidly across the State.

The *engineering* result of the program was that the water indeed flowed faster down the creeks. Unfortunately, higher water velocity caused faster streambed cutting through beds of sandstone, shale, and alluvium. Faster water cut at stream banks and bottoms and undermined hillsides. Landslides can result, usually starting where the slide-mass is interrupted at the top, for example, at a road. The road gets the blame, not the erosion at the bottom.

The *ecological* result of the program was a new set of "barriers to fish": faster running water increased sediment flow and destroyed pools for salmonids. Without logs to create pools and eddies, there were no places for them to rest. There were fewer cool pools for summer smolts and or resting places for returning adults on their way to spawn. Faster water swept out the spawning redds. Now the County and fish activists want the large woody debris (LWD) back in the creek bed as fish habitat and, of course, blame only the roads and loggers for the degradation of fish habitat.

So NOW you need "large woody debris" for fish (we have a new name for logs now, "LWD"), which will require that logs be dropped into creeks? No, not dropped. They want "recruitment" of LWD. What is that? "Recruitment" is a minor landslide that causes a tree to drop into the creek. Recruitment takes a long time and, meanwhile, things can continue to go downhill. These landslides aren't always so cooperative as to provide durable or well situated LWD. They can weep silt for years, and destabilize slopes above by concentrating the flow against the stream banks. While silt from "Natural" landslides is now permissible, the resulting damage from logjams is not.

The State has books full of "good ideas" about how to simulate a "natural" logjam for fish. When they install the LWD into the creek, they sometimes glue bolts into holes drilled into the rocks and cinch them to smaller log segments, to sneak through the local bridge pilings. It is not easy. The logs must be too small to jam in the creek bed but big enough to stay put; which is contradictory because logs float and eventually rot. Bolting them down doesn't work for long because the rock is crumbly, the anchors fail, and the rest is history. Can you imagine the resulting mess if it jams downstream, the riverbank washes out, and sucks in a restaurant or small hotel?

If the landowners upstream are expected to install LWD or mitigate a slide hazard created by its mandated removal, then perhaps landowners deserve compensation for what was taken out by government in the first place. If a claim of a flood liability is assessed against a natural debris flow, one could blame the bridge it hung up upon... Oh, but was that the COUNTY'S bridge? Was it the County who let the building permits in the floodplain? Who made the levees? The legal wrangle could go on forever, and both problems, the management of the debris and the environmental impact of a city in a riverine floodplain, would persist.

Until we reclaim cities in floodplains, this means that the size of these minor logjams will have to be managed. Who is going to do that? If they don't want to move the city, what will the insurers of urban residents pay to have forest landowners manage the debris and water flow in the creeks? Would it be enough to fund these activities? How much are we paying for flood insurance now? Is it actuarially sufficient? Maybe it depends upon the situation.

La Goons

The current plan advocated by some activists is a "buyback program" to create floodplain. The Federal specification for critical riparian habitat is all the land within 300 feet of the bank full-flow-line, including all original flood plain and estuarine lagoons, as determined by that "professional fluvial geomorphologist." One minor problem: The floodplain and estuarine lagoon cuts right through the middle of the City of Santa Cruz. Have they told the general (voting) public where that 300-foot boundary is and how much fill dirt and construction (including the County Government Center) might have to be removed? We are not talking about cheap real estate.

The city of environmentalists could put its money where its rivermouth is. A plan for slow withdrawal of the cities of Santa Cruz and Soquel from existing riverbanks could allow room for rehabilitation of riparian habitat. A plan could be drawn so that a relocation incentive can function against the cost of streambed management. There would be some awfully expensive bridges. It might take 50 years to complete. Then, where do we put the city?

This illustrates what is wrong with the concept of Sustainable Development. Cities are located primarily for historical reasons. The main factors were proximity to utilities (such as drinking water and river/sewers), farmland, and transportation infrastructure (rivers and harbors). In later years, technical and social infrastructure and government largesse became equally compelling, as with Silicon Valley, Hollywood, or Sacramento, respectively. All of these considerations are altered by changes in technology or demographics. For example, Silicon Valley (once some of the finest farmland in the world) is too small and too expensive for all but the most exotic and experimental manufacturing. The addition of water transportation technology to year-round surface transportation made the Port of Los Angeles/Long Beach superior to San Francisco Bay. By contrast, the UN Agenda 21 locks cities in place with greenbelts and refuses to allow alternative locations to grow.

Santa Cruz originally needed a pier to reach deeper water for importing supplies and exporting logs, food, and hides. That need has been superceded by trucks on Highways 1 and 17. The Spanish settlers' need for the San Lorenzo

River as a sewer has been eliminated by pipes and treatment plants. Does it make sense for human habitation to concentrate at a river mouth when there is a crying need for functional estuaries to serve coastal and ocean habitat?

It depends upon the situation, doesn't it? It depends upon how valuable the city is, versus the value of that possible lagoon. It depends upon how much less impact there would be to have humans concentrate in other locations. How can a political control system make such choices among countervailing forces? How would it manage a dynamic transition?

How can a political control system fund investment in remediation if a city moves? Tax-based investments seldom promise a known return and, even then, the lenders may require secured assets. Instead, the County wants over $1 billion in "funding" to gyp the landowners along the river under eminent domain, and restore floodplain as a public works project. Then what?

Hmmm… a swamp in the middle of a city with a fixed outer boundary, a forced concentration of people shoved into traditionally-maintained public housing, and a ban on pesticides. Toss in the UN 'right to migration' and what do you get? Let's see: encephalitis, dengue fever, malaria, and, what with the rats getting used to warfarin and the owls starting to suffer from it, how about plague! Considering its similarity to feudalism (including the pandemics), why don't they just call it, The Global Agenda 14?

Maybe it isn't funny.

Should the answers be defined politically, or should a marketplace, based upon risk management, dynamically optimize the solutions among improving technologies? Could we find the value in maximizing system productivity instead of relying upon massive civic borrowing and pushing equally massive amounts of dirt, based upon the ambitious plans and capricious dreams of unaccountable bureaucrats and activists?

Add Miring Murk

Is erosion intrinsically bad? Most of the Central Coast Ranges are composed of compressed silt. What would happen if we were successful in stopping erosion in the Santa Cruz Mountains?

It would be a disaster.

Beaches and sandbars are nature's way of managing erosion. You have your choice: You can allow erosion from hillsides to bring in sediments or watch it taken from riverbanks and lose the hillside all at once. Sometimes one causes the other. Without enough sand and gravel the river scours the bottom digging the valley deeper at its weakest point and undermining whole slopes. There are times and places where this is problematic.

The very idea that mountains made of mud and sand should run clean water in the winter is delusional. Erosion and silt-transport are necessary processes in such places. So perhaps the real problem with silt and fish is where, when, and how it is generated and transported.

Nobody knows where the best locations from which gravel and silt might be derived and how sediments might be stored and released at times when it would do minimal damage to riparian species. Might managing that process to minimize the negative side effects be valuable? Is there a way to optimize the balance? It would be awfully complex.

If we didn't transport enough silt, would it be a possible problem for the sand spits guarding coastal lagoons? Would it accelerate coastal erosion or cutting streambeds and banks? How could we weigh such tradeoffs by specific location? Who should do those experiments?

Bud McCrary (of Big Creek Lumber) is busily experimenting with concrete "logs" just for fun. He even stains them brown. If it works, does he deserve a profit for that work? Is his property valuable for research and development of stream management technology? He does have an advantageous location in that there is no city downstream from his land.

In most of urban California, agricultural water is oversubscribed when considered against its combined residential, industrial, and ecological value. (This lifetime Bay Area resident is still incensed that the average Southern California household consumes three to four times the water as his family of four.) The case is more dire for coastal counties with no direct access to water from the Sierra Nevada. Were the same case for the coho salmon made for urban water use as for forestry, the City of Santa Cruz would have to begin draconian seasonal water rationing immediately.

Water should be marketed as determined by its total cost. Water units could be auctioned, not just by volume but by flow rate, date, and time of use, to minimize the need for storage, delivery, and treatment capital. The cash could pay for wastewater reclamation, sophisticated metering, and conservation equipment, such as coordinated appliance timers. Water recycling, and the public education effort that goes with it, are also a possibility. Is the city of environmentalists willing to go through what it takes to abandon the Loch Lomond Dam? What they are talking about the need for added storage. Is it for all the development that they plan?

Perhaps the City could relocate its withdrawal point downstream, to increase average river flow. It might implement water recycling (as is being done in Scott's Valley). If they don't want to do that, will they pay the forest landowner for the extra attention to the land, needed to create higher summer stream flow rates? Do they really care about the fish?

Who would sell alternative collection and storage services? If the quality of runoff or the ability to percolate surface water more efficiently is now more critical because of urban population growth, then the urban customers should offset some of the cost of improvements. Why should they be massive public works projects? Are there advantages to distributed storage?

You bet, as any landowner with a pond knows well. Wild animals love them. Ponds could be used to manage timed silt and nitrate releases and buffer storm damage. They are also a crucial factor in mitigating the impact of disasters requiring no electrical power. Self purging? Inflatable? Seasonal? Micro-power generation? Stair-step face with pools analogous to a series of logjams? It all depends. The degree to which dams are a barrier to salmonids is in many cases a scientific farce, attributed to larger and older structures prior to improvements in the last several decades. Modern fish transport systems (barges and ladders) actually provide higher transmission survival rates than native rivers with natural obstructions such as rapids and water-falls. A pond in a Class 3 (dry in the summer) drainage does not impact fish at all, the way a large dam can and stores locally available water for fighting summer fires (ponds are also animal refuges in a fire). It can even serve as a break for woody debris in seasonal applications. Are they really so bad? Like any tool, it all depends upon where and how dams are used. The above may not be politically correct, but it is likely to be provable. Just try to get a permit to run that experiment and it will be obvious that politics have no place in watershed management, especially because removing dams has become an entitlement program for bureaucrats.

Water services would be more profitable and better managed if an increase in water scarcity, due to competition with ecological demand, rendered a higher unit price for water. The cash might help fund the capital for the careful flow management that would optimize riparian health and reduce summer storage requirements. Would the city of environmentalists and its thirsty University be willing to pay an unsubsidized price for that? The landowner would have reason to measure, characterize, and control the quantity, temperature, and clarity of runoff.

In the Santa Cruz Mountains the concept of a "water table" is near myth. Water is found flowing through a maze of fissures in rock strata. These conditions turn drilling a well into a crapshoot, where an expensive, 500 foot hole can miss its target by a few feet and come up dry. Instead of drilling a domestic well, a landowner could sell water right shares or lease contracts, with the extraction risk spread among users by the company that drills the wells and delivers the water. Their underground mapping and database of local water capabilities could assist with risk-based development siting decisions and reduce the number of unnecessary holes. There could be an open market in shares or leases for options on water rights by location. This would help bring economies of scale to subsurface water extraction, reduce transmission costs, and greatly reduce the risk associated with the purchase of property without a developed water source. Here again, it is the fungible resource and distributed ownership that makes it happen.

Super Position

How do we best manage floods, water storage and release, canopy cover, spawning pools, riparian nitrate releases, water for animals, and erosion? How do we balance all those considerations by individual site?

Consider floods. The existing mechanism for managing flood control is a publicly held assessment or service district. These entities have historically provided flood control services subject to the constraints of competing agency interests. The County of Santa Cruz, has at least four separate departments managing overlapping aspects of drainage management, then there is the California Department of Fish and Game along with, the Coastal Commission, NMFS, the Army Corps of Engineers, the EPA...

The tax-exempt status of public districts (particularly flood control districts), and their ability to levy taxes and float bonds, has often turned them into vehicles of real estate subsidy. The particular county arranges for a ballot measure (usually soon after a flood) protecting land that will suddenly be significantly more valuable. Given the regulatory bureaucracy overseeing such projects, one can easily smell the lack of maintenance, poor public participation, eminent domain takings, corruption, and layered bureaucracy in such measures. It has worked that way for decades and is getting worse.

The superposition of considerations applicable to watershed management does become too complex for an average landowner to manage (although it would be a gas to try). The situation screams for watershed management enterprises selling package deals to landowners.

Here is where the insured certification comes in. We don't need taxes for this, because the property owners along the river can incorporate to manage these activities as a profit-making business or purchase a management contract as a group. The landowners along the creek would have a chance to make a buck and the downtown riverfront owners to save one. The difference is that each property can be valued according to its combination of risk and profitability in the enterprise. Those owners not wishing to do the work would have to pay the liability insurance anyway and would thus wish to sell to those who want to invest. The insurers of downtown properties might well fund this startup. They might also fund some of the research into control measures on similar but undeveloped property. The dynamics of that market is an example of how assets come into being when properties are combined to create a new asset, just as they are for a particular liability. It beats people on mountaintops buying flood insurance, which is what we are doing now. The watershed management corporation might well find it worth funding a spinoff in other functions. Why?

Who would insure them if they don't? Historically, the Federal Emergency Management Agency (FEMA) has been partly utilized as a license for civic irresponsibility because it is used as "free" insurance to restore preconditions after nature proves them unsatisfactory. So, if we should not do that because it subsidizes poor preparation, where are they going to get the capital?

If flood management was profitable, a landowner might choose to defer construction next to a creek, and invest in pools, vegetation management, flow obstructions such as LWD, and other habitat improvements. Those activities, provided by the people who maintain the condition of the streams, are services with economic value. It would help offset over-fishing by the tourist industry to improve spawning beds and smolt habitat. It could help reverse the damage from an ill-conceived fad in government flood control and fisheries management policy. It could offset the NOAA/NMFS protection of overpopulated seals. It could reduce the need to move riverfront development. If the owners of those urban riverfront properties owned stock in that service enterprise, they might profit by the attractive location nearer the river. They might so invest. It is cheaper than moving downtown Santa Cruz. That would mean that real estate interests would have to carry their weight and stop demanding a subsidy by asking the government to take over the streams belonging to someone else or augmenting their insurance with FEMA money. That "someone else" could make an honest buck providing services the city now gets for relatively little.

Subsequent to an analysis of flood risk on a replacement cost basis, revenues from insurance offsets could create a cash flow to fund streambed habitat improvements. People could find a profit in the work fixing government mistakes. The alternatives are to move the downtown business district or quit wasting water.

Unlike a 300' setback specification, one would one not need to move the downtown district along the entire riverbank. Buildings on high ground or hard rock would be at less risk. We might not have to move that outrageously expensive Government Center up on a bluff after all, because its risk so situated would be lower. Under the same logic, not all of the owners of creek beds, upstream would have to manage the debris flows for such a service to exist. It would be more important in locations where significant improvements could be obtained and risks were higher. Under a market system that accounted risk, the higher cash flow in those locations would fund work for that purpose.

Over time, as we learn the objective interactions between rivers, lagoons, coastal productivity, oxygen conversion, nitrates, phosphates, and sediments, investors could find it worth purchasing the urban land to reduce the cost of ecological risk. Locating parts of a city in an inter-tidal basin might not be worth its value as lagoon for a coastal habitat!

Would an insurance company like to make a profit financing the development of technologies for loss prevention? Might banks take an interest in financing a startup in the watershed management business instead of reconstruction after a disaster? Would the foundations currently funding environmental groups, that force land into nonproductive use, prefer to see their wealth generating dividends toward reinvestment in nature?

If we render them tradable, how do we manage all the complexity? One could spend forever managing a portfolio, gathering data, and not finding the time ever to work on it... without computational power, remote sensing, and broadband communications. There are opportunities here for intelligent agents, computers, signal integration, distributed processing, and optimization software that boggle the mind. This is truly an ecosystem management ethic whose time is about to come and an endless opportunity that can grow with us into the future. Plant identification, cataloguing, and comparative analyses by wireless communication, distributed nanocomputers tracking through animal guts, stress sensors in rock, flow fields of sensors detecting sediment field-flow, domestic and wastewater management, real time water pricing; the list is as endless as the imagination and the commitment that drives its invention. Of course these tools are not all developed or reliable now, but when the assets to be measured acquire value, the possibilities engendered by profitability and economies of scale make it possible.

That simple natural law is capable of as much complexity, as is appropriate to the circumstances. Natural law is fully capable of ecosystem management.

If you find all that daunting, just remember, by combining what are, at first, simple laws: Newtonian and Quantum mechanics, physical chemistry, and economics, you get the bewildering complexity of a modern automobile, a commodities market, or a powerful computer for under a $1,000. Simple laws have a way of accommodating the complex in a way that complex regulations simply can't.

Some people apparently think that it is justified to coerce other people at the penalty of jail to expend wealth in the name of their desire to fool around with an arguable theory of watershed protection on a massive scale. They use coercion to apply and enforce subjectively interpreted rules, appropriate or not, all in the name of preventing erosion. Meanwhile, the vast majority of the causes of silt flows (by cubic yardage) are due to natural mechanisms.

People used to own unlimited water rights off the land. The acquisition of control of streambeds by the Federal Government under the Clean Water Act was a Fifth Amendment taking for which landowners were never compensated and government never Constitutionally empowered. Perhaps landowners want those assets back? Perhaps they don't want the liability? It comes down to relative profitability, doesn't it? People would pay more for water if they balanced its worth to their survival, against the cost to the eco-systems from which the water was taken. Perhaps it depends upon the income statement and the balance sheet of such an enterprise.

There are other considerations on the selection of investments that apply to a site and to rivers regarding their important role in coastal ecosystem health. So far, this section has discussed just a few resources: LWD, domestic water, flood, nitrate, and silt control, watering holes, vegetation management, burn management, and endangered species. On the downside are erosion problems, fuel loads, exotic species, and more. The balance sheet and income statement will differ by the yard.

When one goes through this process of constructing a mental balance sheet on a property, it can get so overwhelming that you want to sell, and then you realize that you simply can't. The activists of the world should recognize something before they so unwittingly condescend: a landowner's love of the land. Some of us are just stubborn in that respect. If the Earth First!'s Dave Foreman wants landowners "with an affection for the land" he might recognize their resistance to his Wildlands Project as just that. There are landowners who would be simply thrilled to have it be the way it had been before humans arrived or perhaps even better, if they could simply figure out how to survive on it that way. He might learn that it is the means of his minions, and the destruction of capital, that is the source of much of the environmental destruction he decries. The reason it seems so overwhelming to the landowner is that government has stolen the opportunities in the name of pleasing an urban majority. All the landowner can now see is costs. No wonder they do not invest as much in habitat as some would desire.

That affection Mr. Foreman wants is already here and perhaps the land would be better off without his venomous spew. He and his ilk just need to stop trying to take the value of land away by coercive use of government and let it flourish in the hands of those who love it enough to put up their life savings. They might find that there is multigenerational commitment, integrity, knowledge, and the willingness to risk private capital of simply enormous value to the land itself, as well as customers willing to pay their fair share for its products. It is an asset not to be wasted. The problem is, that few of the assets on the land currently have economic worth and nobody yet knows how to trade shares of ownership in process assets or manage the resulting transactions, write the contracts, sell the policies...

So if that all seems too improbable, too difficult to learn, or too slow to develop, what if we did do it Dave's way?

Mitigating Circumstances

Can government do the same thing more efficiently?

Creek restoration is controversial within the environmental community. The disagreements are not usually noted outside the movement. Purists among the group wish that only local plants and the most non-intrusive propagation methods be used. They claim that it is a cheaper way to do the job. Though they do not acknowledge the time, labor, and poor yields involved, sometimes they are right.

In 1998, there was a $700 million ballot proposition in California for such projects, but they didn't explain in the voters' pamphlet how the money was to be spent! The reality is that it is a LOT more than $700,000,000. Other funding is obtained from developers, gas taxes, and bonds for other public projects; even the Army Corps of Engineers gets involved. To some people it looks like extortion. Maybe it's a good thing?

Somewhere in the sleep-deprived memories of raising two preschoolers in 1995, I used to walk the rest of the way to work after my spouse dropped me off from our carpool. It was a nice walk; about 0.8 miles along a bike path on the banks of Los Gatos Creek in Silicon Valley. My interest piqued with the start of construction of the State Highway 85 overpass that was to go across the creek. As an engineer with construction experience, and an amateur doing habitat restoration, it interested me to watch bridge construction over a creek.

At first I had thought they were just building a bridge and piping the water through a temporary culvert, but as the project grew and the amount of grading grew with it, I couldn't figure out what they were doing. It was huge.

They were moving thousands of yards of dirt in a creek bed hundreds of yards away from the bridge. It had to be a government project; anybody else who did that would go to jail. I asked the contractors on site about it and they told me that it was a mitigation project; i.e. if there is an anticipated impact from a large public project, that impact has to be mitigated somewhere else.

Only dimly aware of such things, I was curious about any large-scale creek restoration. Over the year, I plied the actors with questions. Riparian areas are sensitive ecological issues. I wanted to learn from how they were going to handle it. It was an exciting prospect. Over the ensuing years it became more than a bit disillusioning to watch.

As many trees and bushes were to be planted, on two miles of creek bed, as were removed for the construction of miles of freeway. Somebody got paid to count the bushes in vacant lots. Whether the habitat that receives such mitigation, rightly should have that number of plants growing there, in that concentration, is a secondary consideration. A site for the right number of bushes must be found, or no freeway. Plants that grow to six feet across were to be spaced two feet apart: Ecology designed by lawyers.

Thousands of cubic yards were graded to create an artificial flood plain, with little islands for birds. There was trenching. There were concrete valve boxes and wiring. There was plastic pipe everywhere... in a creek bed? There were little metal and plastic flags for the plants. One-gallon potted plants received little chicken wire baskets with jute sunshades. They had the fanciest culvert covers you have ever seen to prevent sewer rats from encroaching. They mortared in 24-inch basalt boulders along the running path for a "100-year flood" (we have had four in the last twenty) under the SR 85 bridge, with silt fences at the bottom. (You really need that 3 feet of filter fabric stapled to little wooden stakes to hold back those 500-pound boulders in case the rain sneaks under the bridge and washes them loose.) There was a chain-link fence along the running path to protect the sensitive riparian habitat from the public. Could the deer and raccoons get a drink? What were they thinking?

The landscaping contractor complained that he had to engage nine different agencies and God knows how many other groups to do the job. To the best of my recollection, these were: the California Department of Fish and Game, the Town of Los Gatos, the U.S. Fish and Wildlife Service, the San Jose Water Company, CAL EPA, the San Jose Water Pollution Control District, the Santa Clara Regional Parks District, Santa Clara County, and the City of Campbell. This is not to mention the activist organizations involved in the Highway 85 project, which included the Sierra Club in a big way.

They spent so much money with their fancy specifications that they "could not afford" to remove a 10 to 20-foot strip of invasive exotic plants along most of the length of the creek. These were on the other side of the running path, all that was left in the area for over a hundred yards in either direction perpendicular to the creek. Seven California Department of Fish and Game officials were standing around drinking coffee and joking. When I asked them why they weren't removing the weeds, one said, "That side of the running path is a different jurisdiction." They didn't seem to be moved by the fact that the project had already moved the path! I noticed a glorious, 9-foot tall Cytisus scoparius (Scotch Broom, an invasive plant) right behind them in full flower, ready to set seed. It was the only one in the immediate area. I asked if they would help pull it. They looked at me in humored disbelief and went back to their chitchat. I guess they don't do that kind of work for fun.

About nine months later, it rained, not a massive flood, mind you but a decent storm. The water came over the spillways of two dams upstream and made a mess of the whole thing. It rolled up tangled wads of brush, tubing, PVC pipe, filter fabric, little balls of jute, and chicken wire. It wiped out most of the plants and it all headed downstream over a 20-foot concrete waterfall too high for the fish to jump (part of the previous flood control project). An excavator had to hold yet more 24-inch boulders in place to keep the banks from chewing away the portcullis walls.

Next spring the weeds had already crossed onto the politically-correct side of the running path. Did anybody pull them? Did anybody clean up the twisted wreckage? Did anybody mortar in the new 24-inch boulders? Did anybody follow up on the plan and hold the responsible parties accountable? You guess. (There must not have been a maintenance budget.)

No, the whole mess was washed further down the creek during another flood the next year. No wonder the purists don't like restoration projects. Did they need drip irrigation? Did they need all that protection? They could have hired a bunch of school kids to adopt-a-plant for a year or two. They might have learned something.

The chain link fence is still there, some of it still buried in mud. The concrete valve boxes are still buried in mud. The drip irrigation system still doesn't work (please don't fix it). There was another, larger flood two years later and there was more of the same. The runners still run on the path, oblivious to the debacle and not even asking about the fence. They've added a really pretty (and spendy) Corten® steel bridge for the running path. The feral cats are still sneaking past the fence and plucking ducklings. The weeds are still spreading. The ivy is still killing the trees. The greatly diminished percentage of the plants that made it are doing nicely. The County Park Officials in their pickups still ticket the kids who go too fast on their bikes and still hustle the girls on roller blades. The environmentalists are still hassling the water district and demanding year-round flows "for the fish," no matter what happens to the reservoir in the park above it or what the estimated natural flow rate without the reservoir would be. The same activists are trying to get industry to use less water, because the flows to the bay are too high for the desired salinity level (check that against the last one), and the people of the State of California are still paying interest on the bonds.

Sure, Dave.

📖 Are You Sure?

Conclusion to Part IV

Perhaps it is a learning experience. Maybe after another few decades or another hundred years, government will learn how to manage the environment without making a mess of it with that one huge mistake of which it seems so uniquely capable.

Maybe you should think twice about that.

Look back at the record of civic management. Does it give you hope that things are getting better or is it a sense of foreboding of what the future may hold? Look at the miles of star thistle escaping from newly constructed highways and acres of toxic hemlock along watersheds. Look at the 7 million acres of forest incinerated in the year 2000 alone. Air quality regulations get ever more stringent, so government mandates MTBE that creates formic acid in air (a known lung irritant). Consider the scope of MTBE contamination in groundwater and think of the cost of the cleanup. Are you pleased to hear that groundwater cleanup is under the supervision of the SAME air quality authorities that mandated the MTBE? Look at the unabated lockdown of resource lands and the escalating cost of energy. Then look at the national balance of payments deficit. How will we pay for all that environmental cleanup? Would it have anything to do with a projected U.S. population growth to 450 million in 50 years?

Have you noticed that there is a lot of that foreboding going around lately?

Look at the more pedestrian responsibilities of government, and ask yourself how well it is working. Roads are a disaster of mismanagement. Weed abatement doesn't get done. Traffic gets worse and broadband doesn't get built.

These failures are symptomatic of political management systems.

Look at your taxes, the state of public schools, or the future of Social Security, and ask yourself if YOU or your children can afford yet another welfare state for The Environment?

Can nature afford it?

Government has the marked propensity to accrue power to its own hands by claiming a monopoly to solve problems, but rather than fix them it has every reason to expand their scope. If government can't even manage simple things like roads, grade schools, and septic systems effectively, why are we giving it a monopoly to run something as complex as an ecosystem?

It's a bigger risk than you might think.

In order to build a sustainable

global community,

the nations of the world

must renew their commitment

to the United Nations,

fulfill their obligations

under existing international agreements,

and support the implementation

of Earth Charter principles

with an international legally binding instrument

on environment and development

– from The Earth Charter

Part V   The Moral High Ground

How To Take It Back, and What is In the Way

The objectives of Parts III and IV were to impart a new way of looking for opportunities in managing ecosystem resources. As ideas were developed, there were many different components to the alternative system: insurers, scientists, contract lawyers, industry, landowners and their associations. Yet each of these has also an investment in and responsibility for the existing system. What might be done to dislodge that monolith and make the free-market proposal a reality?

We must defeat an enemy, strategically deployed against private property rights. You might be surprised who that is.

When we ask government to infringe upon the property rights of forest land-owners, to enter their land and inspect their creeks upon which we have placed a public claim, we give it the power to send the Septic Police to our door. When we ask government to give us "clean water" in our rivers, they set the nitrate attainment specifications so low that it is neither attainable nor healthy for the riparian life. When we ask government to maintain stocks of fish, they botch hatchery management, start calling the shots on the creeks, and end up making a mess of them. When the river isn't healthy, we ask government to save the fish, giving agencies the precedents they need to take total control of the use of land. When we ask government to curtail growth of residential development, zoning becomes a corrupt patronage system that benefits select politicians, bureaucrats, and developers. When we ask government to solve a problem, we are giving it an asset by which to justify a cash flow. When we extend a political claim on the use of private property, we cede our rights to control our own lives, and the freedom to care for the land. The taker, thus, "gets taken."

"We have met the enemy, and he is us."

There are better ways to accomplish our goals as a society. Civic respect for private property rights and insured certification constitute the underpinnings for an operational strategy to provide the public with a choice of management systems. We still have a choice of which system to use: civic or civil, but the way things are going, not for long.

Most people are unaware that our system of Constitutional governance is undergoing a radical transformation. Having never experienced real tyranny, they have no idea how corrupt it really is. Upon observing the results, one would first have to assume normal bungling and greed. The actual situation is, unfortunately, much worse than that. It is a system of international advocacy groups and bureaucracies that bypass the mechanics of a republic to enrich their benefactors and extend their power.

It won't work for the environment because its structural power, to control the factors of production, corrupts its intent.

The vast bulk of the participants are in no way, purposefully evil. They are instead misguided by inculcated assumptions, infatuated with power, and abused with an unshakeable naïveté that they know what they are doing. Whether or not they have been duped, evil they have done and will continue to propagate if left unchecked. It is the desire to control the use of private property without just compensation that is evil, and with it, its progenitors are justly associated. They just don't understand what they could have had from a free market, and instead, focus upon entrenching their power as if there was no alternative.

Chapter 1 – An Unsustainable Agenda is an examination of the apex of environmental management systems: Global Governance through the United Nations. This is a system of multilateral treaties generated by multinational NGOs. It is, in essence, a corrupt Bureaucracy of lawyers, activists, and regulators, implementing the plans of international financiers operating through tax-exempt foundations. The immediate goal appears to be profit by manipulating asset value of competing and substitute goods with environmental regulations. The longer term is more ominous.

Chapter 2 – Defy Gravity explores a local example that unifies the technical discussion of nonpoint pollution, forestry, and anadromous salmonids in the story of a single property owner who has the opportunity to take back control of his land through exercise of the principles presented in the final chapter, the Strategy of the Commoners.

Chapter 3 – The Strategy of the Commoners introduces the proposed counterstrategy to Global Governance. The Strategy of the Commoners turns the environmental management system against itself using the same laws that have served as a weapon against private property rights. The InsCert system demonstrates that the landowner is a superior agent of the public claim for ecosystem health. Ecosystem management is a service with profit potential that has been confiscated by a structurally incompetent monopoly of NGOs and bureaucracies. The idea develops using an analysis of the Endangered Species Act.

The book closes with an exhortation to the reader out of respect for our common heritage of individual liberty. As Garret Hardin said,

"The alternative of the commons is too horrifying to contemplate."

Chapter 1 – An Unsustainable Agenda

Sustainable Development and the Agenda 21

This chapter is not necessary to the rest of the book, but it is necessary to understanding the origins of the antithesis. It documents that the County of Santa Cruz, California, a highly touted archetype of civic environmental management, is instituting policies and precedents according to strategies originating out of the United Nations and evolving toward a vertically-integrated Global Governance under the UN.

Under a TAC

Timber harvesting has been one of the two most contentious political issues in the County of Santa Cruz for as long as anyone can remember (the other being development). The process of instituting new regulations has come in waves, each in response to activist charges of malpractice among timber operators. In recent years, the major complaint has not been about legal harvesting, but about how the rules are insufficient to prevent violations. Local activists asserted that, since rules could not stop unethical practices, the solution was to prevent all timber operations in riparian corridors. There were two ways to accomplish that goal: The State Board of Forestry could amend the Forest Practice Rules for the Southern Sub-district (including both San Mateo and Santa Cruz) or the County would institute a zoning ordinance.

Zoning is a principle tool by which local government has extended its power to control the use of private property. Zoning has been used to close private schools and food programs, ban home prayer meetings from within city limits, dictate who can sleep in which room, regulate the design of offices within homes, or what color must be used to paint a house. What started as supposedly rational means to conduct city planning is degenerating into a tool to control the conduct of society at large.

The use of zoning law to regulate timber operations started in 1992 when the County of San Mateo established 1,000-foot residential "buffer zones" off-setting the visual and acoustic externalities of timber operations. Big Creek Lumber Company challenged the right of the County to regulate timber operations as a State jurisdiction. The California Supreme Court refused to hear the case pursuant to a ruling by the Ninth Circuit Court of Appeals. The Ninth Circuit Court ruled that the County of San Mateo had the power to regulate the location of commercial activity on land within its boundaries.

This was an example of how an unfortunate environmental decision can be rendered by the manner in which a legal case is presented. It is one of the reasons demonstrating why the courts are the wrong tool for ecosystem management and why losing a legal case correctly is so very important.

The commercial nature of timber harvesting is not as if somebody wants to throw up a building and make widgets. The trees are already there. If they are not managed, the forest will be a fire hazard, both to itself and to surrounding real property, no matter what the Ninth Circuit Court of Appeal thinks. It is a growing forest in need of maintenance, not a choice about widgets.

Within months of the San Mateo victory, the County of Santa Cruz initiated a similar zoning effort. In addition to residential setbacks, the Santa Cruz law included buffer zones along riparian corridors, ostensibly to protect them from nonpoint sources of silt, supposedly inherent to timber operations. To assure that protection was adequate, they described the allowed property use within the boundaries of said corridors with the curious words: "no entry."

When the timber industry in the County got wind of the proposed ordinance they immediately requested a series of meetings with the Planning Department. The intent was to discuss the issues surrounding complaints about local timber practice and see if any solutions could be implemented by amending the existing Forest Practices Rules.

A County Board of Supervisors is required by law to give citizens a hearing before adopting legislation. When the public outcry over new regulations begins to look like a lawsuit, the local politicians formed a study group. The Timber Technical Advisory Committee or Timber-TAC was the first such task force after the adoption of the UN Local Agenda 21 in Santa Cruz County. It was chaired by a representative from the County Planning Department (who now works as a consultant to the Sierra Club) and was seated with equal numbers from the activist community and the timber industry.

The goal of the UN-style "stakeholder" process is to get a record of public participation without halting progress toward the intended outcome. Once the TAC is formed, the bureaucrats can confine the real discussion to those on the TAC behind closed doors. The agency personnel then report their recommendations to the County Board of Supervisors as the consensus output of the TAC, having dutifully accepted and considered public input.

Just try to get a copy of the minutes.

The first meeting started with an announcement by the meeting "coordinator" that its purpose was to design the new zoning ordinance and that there would be no other outcome. The foresters demanded consideration of amendments to the Forest Practice Rules. The foresters warned that, if the County moved to enact a new zoning law, they would file a lawsuit. The Coordinator agreed to submit a rule package to the State under the condition that, unless it was both acceptable to the County in total and adopted by the State Board of

Forestry (BOF), a new zoning ordinance was "inevitable."

At the second meeting, the foresters proposed rule changes representing their best effort to fix those problems they perceived as real. After months of poring over individual line items, the activists presented a list of their own recommendations for changes in the Forest Practice Rules, roughly mirroring those in the proposed zoning law.

The negotiations were arduous, in part because the activists were unfamiliar with timber operations. Realize that many Registered Professional Foresters have about as many years of training in forest ecology as lawyers do in law. There is a lot to know. These foresters on the TAC had won awards from environmental organizations for excellence in forest management.

The foresters protested that the rules were impracticable, unmeasurable, and possibly counterproductive to the purported goal of riparian health. The activists came to the negotiations with their plans already set, as represented by their previous threat. After nearly eight months of biweekly meetings, the coordinator announced that they had "run out of time," with no resolution.

What did the Planning Department do? They took the text from their original submission, added whatever the foresters recommended that they thought they could use, and sent it to the Board of Supervisors. The Supervisors took the output to the Board of Forestry threatening that, if the BOF did not adopt the package in toto, the restrictions would be enacted into zoning law.

The BOF adopted 11 rules, of which less than half were supported by the foresters. Ten of the twenty-one total proposed rules were rejected.

The Supervisors made good on their threat by immediately adopting the zoning ordinance. County Staff cited the TAC submission as a "consensus" at the reading of the Staff Report; in other words, the foresters who had spent eight months resisting the adoption of the rules and the zoning law were being told that they had agreed! To this day, the planners call it "consensus." The activists offer their participation on the Timber-TAC as evidence of their technical expertise. It was indeed model legislation, especially considering how it was adopted.

Big Creek and the Central Coast Forest Association sued the County, citing failure to comply with the California Environmental Quality Act (CEQA), preemption of BOF jurisdiction, and a taking under the Fifth Amendment. So far, they are winning in court.

Environmentally Impacted

The political reason that environmental law exists is that people avoid due consideration of the full consequences of their plans. The California Environmental Quality Act (CEQA, pronounced "see-qua") is a piece of legislation designed to coerce such consideration. It structurally favors environmental advocates over commercial and industrial interests at every early decision point. It requires technical review and a process of appeal at every opportunity. It has mushy language that allows for all sorts of interpretations based upon an assumption of harm. If an environmental rationale can be offered for why a project is adverse to environmental health, that project must be investigated and an expensive Environmental Impact Report (EIR) drafted and reviewed. The EIR must provide a preponderance of evidence that concerns are minimal or the effects have offsetting benefits. Without that proof, the project is stopped cold, unless government wants to do it anyway.

The reality of CEQA is that bureaucrats and consultants are to be paid buckets of money to study the situation until either the bureaucrats can't say no, or politicians say otherwise. Under CEQA, one can always cut a deal with politicians, as long as they are willing to agree in writing.

People with large amounts of money already invested get upset when they find out that some niggling detail has brought their project to its knees. They sue, and sometimes they win. Sometimes the politicians cave in early. The activists cry foul. They sue, and sometimes they win. Many such cases were amended into CEQA as subsections. By the time a well-meaning piece of legislation spends a few decades gathering these judicial adornments, it ends up riddled with loopholes, loophole patches, and sections tying together other sections into specific interpretations. There are now over 40 pages of overlapping and contradictory exceptions. The case law fills volumes.

CEQA is a mess. What started as 20 pages of a clear, but arduously rigorous and arbitrary set of review processes (with a glaring loophole), is now over 150 pages of situational ambiguity that takes an attorney to interpret.

Politicians would find laws such as CEQA to be as odious as has private enterprise, so they simply exempted themselves from the process from the beginning. The Federal Government is exempt from CEQA, as is the California State Legislature. Now this is curious, because government is legally a corporate person that does not necessarily represent the public interest. Indeed, from the perspective of the Constitution, the powers of government were limited because it is assumed to operate with interests adverse to those of citizens. Enumerated powers of both the Federal Government and the several States are Constitutionally superceded by the unalienable rights of citizens for that reason. Can a State exempt truly itself from laws regulating the use of private property?

CEQA requires a Preliminary Review on all projects to determine whether an Environmental Impact Report (EIR) will be required. The system is biased toward preparation of a full report, as early in the review process as possible.

Concerning our zoning ordinance , this situation left the County Planning Department with a conundrum. They were under orders to deliver new regulations. The claim of "no impact" from logging restrictions in an EIR might not hold up under technical challenge. The review for an EIR could delay implementation of the law for years. That would have displeased their bosses, who had promises to keep to the activists. To prevent that challenge, the best strategy was to merely assert that what they proposed was a good thing, and use every available procedural tool to ram it through before anybody could challenge it. **The apparent goal was to keep any technical argument refuting their assertions off the public record.**

One could consider it a tacit admission of adverse intent.

The first step in the review is to determine if the project is exempt from CEQA. The only two criteria, by which the County could have claimed an exemption, are if there is no Significant Effect or if zoning law is on a list of projects exempt from CEQA (it is not). If there is a Significant Effect, CEQA applies and the County cannot claim exemption, congruent with 15061.b.3:

15061. Review for Exemption, Subsection (b) discussing possible exemptions:
(3) The activity is covered by the general rule that CEQA applies only to projects which have the potential for causing a significant effect on the environment. Where it can be seen with certainty that there is no possibility that the activity in question may have a significant effect on the environment, the activity is not subject to CEQA.

If the prohibition of timber operations through zoning has no effect, then why didn't the County claim the exemption? The State Board of Forestry has already ruled that single timber harvests of three acres or less have insignificant impact. Jurisdiction under these exemptions was referred to the County. The Santa Cruz County Board of Supervisors passed an Emergency Moratorium on exemptions, pursuant to adoption of changes in its Chapter 16.52 of the County Code. There was no EIR for that, either. They claimed it was an Emergency under CEQA 21060.3:

"Emergency includes such occurrences as fire, flood, earthquake, or other soil or geologic movements, as well as such occurrences as riot, accident, or sabotage."

The County apparently believes that cumulative effects of three-acre timber harvests are of such significance as to constitute an emergency equivalent to a war or natural disaster. Regulation of that process must (in the opinion of the County) also have a significant effect even if it is considered beneficial.

After the Preliminary Review for Exemption, one begins the Initial Study. Without going into detail (the text is two pages), Section 15063(b) unambiguously states that if a project has a Significant Effect on the environment, WHETHER ADVERSE OR BENEFICIAL, the lead agency (the County) MUST perform an EIR or cite its equivalent.

Did the County avoid the claiming the exemption because they would have had to declare a significant beneficial effect?

The test of Significant Effect is where CEQA fails as a control system. It depends upon subjective interpretation of circumstance whether a project has a significant effect or not. Sections 15064, 15065, and 15382 (which was added to "clarify" the rest of it and will, itself, balloon someday) has bloated into eleven pages of law, booklets of advice, and books of case law. All are evidence of a system that cannot provide a simple, understandable, just, efficient, and ecologically rigorous review process.

Banning timber harvesting has both primary (direct) and secondary (indirect) consequences for the forest. It is argued here that the most significant effect of the law is mandating harvest restrictions on trees that grow in unnaturally close proximity, forcing the continuing accrual of an unnatural fuel load.

Primary effects on the record are:

- Arboreal pest infestations, diseases, and structural problems due to overcrowding,
- Possible landslides due to stand weight against steep slopes,
- Shade and duff-related smothering of native plants,
- Increased spread of arboreal pathogens and pests,
- Microbial consumption of the native seed bank, and
- Loss of meadow habitat.

The project has secondary consequences subsequent to a conflagration:

- Combustion of and redistribution of common and endangered species,
- Accelerated spread of invasive exotic species and subsequent loss of endangered species, local genotypes, and subspecies,
- Loss of cover and vegetation accelerating winter runoff that can destabilize slopes resulting in landslides and washed out roads,
- Loss of canopy cover over creeks like no logging project ever could,
- Vastly accelerated siltation damage to fisheries, and
- Resource depletion and manufacturing to support reconstruction.

The economic results of the law will have ecological consequences as well. As was demonstrated in Part II, this kind of asset confiscation removes asset value from timberland. Lacking economic value as timber, the land use ends up converted to residential development, viticulture, etc. With houses come roads, higher traffic, drainage diversions, runoff concentration, and poor percolation (not to mention the necessary vineyard). This conclusion invokes adverse impacts of rural residential development, as asserted in innumerable Environmental Impact Reports, nationwide. The presence of housing in the forest also severely restricts, if not precludes, the use of prescribed fire.

Development is instead, a land use attractive to County politicians. It generates tax money, a new supply of unfamiliar voters, and the continued happiness of campaign donors and activist groups.

The records of eight months of tape-recorded Timber TAC (or T–TAC) meetings detailed both primary and secondary adverse effects. There were letters on the record addressing such concerns, not only from individuals, but also from representatives and officers of public conservation agencies and NGOs. These included the Santa Cruz County Resource Conservation District, and the California Native Plant Society. **The Board acted upon recommendation of County Staff that reported the output of the TAC as a consensus supporting the zoning project, where none had existed.**

Did the opinions of "stakeholders" make any difference?

The County's own actions and statements on the public record prove that a fair argument had been presented that the project will have a significant adverse effect on the environment. They failed to perform the EIR under the threat of a lawsuit. This is in large part because the County staff, as a group, suffers under a common delusion discounting the risks associated with a Type II Error of inaction. This belies the fact that the current processes of degradation are driven by human inaction in response to human-inflicted changes. More objective parties usually call such errors "gross negligence."

They weren't out of the woods yet. There was still weaseling to do regarding sets of effects, so important that CEQA confers the special distinction of a Mandatory Finding of Significance:

15065 Findings of Mandatory Significance

(a)   The project has the potential to substantially degrade the quality of the environment, substantially reduce the habitat of a fish or wildlife population to drop to below self-sustaining levels, threaten to eliminate a plant or animal community, reduce the number or restrict the range of a rare or endangered plant or animal, or eliminate important examples of the major periods of California history or prehistory.

There is no wiggle room here. A conflagration is the worst thing that could happen for fish populations. The watershed has been declared impaired by the State Department of Fish and Game. The coho has been declared endangered and the steelhead as threatened (even if the claims are bogus). There is no option but to declare the impact significant and prepare an EIR.

(b)   The project has the potential to achieve short term environmental goals to the disadvantage of long-term environmental goals.

You can reduce intrusion through restrictions on cutting trees, but if the fuel accumulates for too long... Same conclusion.

(c)   The project has possible environmental effects which are individually limited but cumulatively considerable. ~~As used in the subsection, "cumulatively considerable"~~ "Cumulatively considerable" means that the incremental effects of an individual project are considerable when viewed in connection with the effects of past projects, the effects of other current projects, and the effects of probable future projects <u>as defined in Section 15130</u>.

If the project aids the conversion to development (which the County has admitted in public testimony), again they must prepare an EIR.

(d)   The environmental effects of a project will cause substantial adverse effects on human beings, either directly or indirectly.

Do burned bodies of dead children count as "substantial adverse effects on human beings"? It may sound unnecessarily inflammatory, until you recall that it WILL happen unless somebody does something about the fuel.

So with all that law staring them in the face, what did the County do?

The Planning Department filed an Initial Study consisting of little more than a checklist asserting that there would be no impact at all, either beneficial or deleterious. As part of the Initial Study, there is this final little step requiring State oversight:

(g)   Consultation. As soon as a Lead Agency has determined that an Initial Study will be required for the project, the Lead Agency shall consult informally with all Responsible Agencies and all Trustee Agencies responsible for resources affected by the project to obtain the recommendations of those agencies as to whether an EIR or a Negative Declaration should be prepared.

The legal test of requiring an EIR turns upon whether the Lead Agency (in this case the County of Santa Cruz) had been notified of such significant effects by experts in the field. If there is a reasoned argument on the public record of a potential Significant Effect, adverse or beneficial, the County must perform an EIR. Thus the effort of the County bureaucracy was to discredit elements of public input, avoid comment, and squelch technical discussion and then call it a consensus of the Technical Advisory Committee (TAC). They just as carefully avoided any input from the State as well.

The County knew that the California State Board of Forestry was disinclined to approve the rule package equivalent to the zoning law. They prepared both applications (rules and zoning) simultaneously with the plan to implement the zoning ordinance if the rule package was rejected. The County signed a Notice of Determination of their intent to file a Negative Declaration that there would be no environmental impact on Thursday, July 16, 1998. The State's allotted period for comment was 30 days. In that time they are to determine if a Negative Declaration is appropriate or an EIR is required for a complex zoning ordinance governing detailed forest practices and limits on harvest locations. The closing date was August 19.

It took five days for the "Neg-Dec" to arrive and be logged in at the State Clearinghouse in the Governor's Office of Planning and Research. It sat in a queue at the in Sacramento until August 13 before it was processed and sent to 14 recipients. The Sacramento office of CDF routed it back to the CDF station in Santa Cruz where personnel were buried in day-to-day problems. Nobody "had time" to even look at it, much less give it due consideration.

This is what you get in the way of environmental review from a State agency. Unless there is an organized NGO following the application, the chances of thorough review are nil.

The County is also required to notify the public for comment. They placed a tiny notice for ONE DAY in the back sections of the Classified ads. Nobody saw it. A County Planner was laughing about it at a Board of Forestry meeting. The assertion of "no environmental impact" in the Negative Declaration went unchallenged. Thus, to go for "local control" as an alternative in the name of closer oversight is to have no oversight at all.

Is this acceptable performance in an environmental management system when the health of 150,000 acres of forest is at stake and with it the lives of innocent people? Is it acceptable that the County can proceed without a study, simply because the paperwork takes too long, or because a minor State functionary goes on vacation, is buried in paperwork, or wants to avoid controversy? Have you ever heard a business assert that about an environmental review? **Do you get accountability in environmental management from government?**

The environment is too complex to be managed by a political control system. It is safer to prevent action and deny accountability for an error of inaction.

Would it really have made any material difference if they had done the EIR?

No. CEQA Section 15043, Authority to Approve Projects Despite Significant Effects, **empowers any public agency to do whatever it wants, merely by issuing a Statement of Overriding Considerations.** The County can go ahead and abet development and incur a firestorm if they want to. They would just have to say so, and pay for it if they are wrong. Even then, they must perform an EIR and admit why they are going ahead with the project.

From Section 15043:
(c) If an agency makes a statement of overriding considerations, the statement should be included in the record of the project approval and should be mentioned in the notice of determination. This statement does not substitute for, and shall be in addition to, findings required pursuant to Section 15091.

15091. Findings (Subsection (a) 1 & 2 were omitted as inapplicable).

(a) No public agency shall approve or carry out a project for which an EIR has been certified which identifies one or more significant environmental effects of the project unless the public agency makes one or more written findings for each of those significant effects, accompanied by a brief explanation of the rationale for each finding. The possible findings are:

   (3) Specific economic, **legal, social, technological, or other considerations, including provision of employment opportunities for highly trained workers** (emphasis added), make infeasible the mitigation measures or project alternatives identified in the final EIR.

(b) The findings required by subsection (a) shall be supported by substantial evidence in the record.

(c) The finding in subsection (a)(2) shall not be made if the agency making the finding has concurrent jurisdiction with another agency to deal with identified feasible mitigation measures or alternatives. The finding in subsection (a)(3) shall describe the specific reasons for rejecting identified mitigation measures and project alternatives.

(d) When making the findings required in subsection (a)(1), the agency shall also adopt a program for reporting on or monitoring the changes which it has either required in the project or made a condition of approval to avoid or substantially lessen significant environmental effects. **These measures must be fully enforceable through permit conditions, agreements, or other measures** (emphasis added, again).

The Board of Supervisors would have been required to tell the public that elected it to reduce development, that HOUSING "highly trained workers" and pleasing them politically and aesthetically was more important than the health of forests. They would have to admit that catastrophic fire would be a possible result. They would be accountable for those results.

They would have to prove why careful thinning and prescribed fire would not work. They would have to prove that there is adequate reason not to have CDF manage the forest. They would have to devise means of managing the fuel around the houses while simultaneously conducting controlled burns. Therewith lies liability that might make forest housing untenable under a preservation management ethic. That would cost the County tax money.

Why won't the County of Santa Cruz prepare an Environmental Impact Report? This either displays total ignorance of the environment or a callous disregard for the law. Which one is it?

The Chairman of the Board of County Supervisors wondered aloud why they are being sued for not doing a proper environmental review and has asserted that, because they are preventing something from being done, there could be no environmental impact. What he doesn't want is to have to go on the public record with the Planning Department's technical assumptions in writing, then to be subjected to technical scrutiny and legal test. Such a challenge would remove the underpinnings of their "leave it alone" philosophy. It would expose the enormous farce behind much of the environmental movement for what it is, political pandering for money and power in the name of an unsubstantiated and demonstrably flawed body of faith.

This argument does not advocate return to unrestrained and rapacious timber operations as if it was the only alternative to the County plan. The point is this: When people are forced to confront reality they begin to seek alternatives. If the County had been forced to do an EIR, they would have had to face the real consequences of a "feel good" plan as advanced by the activists. Nobody would have had any easy answers. Few people seek real innovations unless they are looking outside an insoluble problem for alternatives, which is the reason CEQA exists in the first place.

The legal and political control system fails to prevent problems associated with timber operations while inflicting serious financial harm to the best of forest landowners and professionals. The belief that more of the same, with yet more onerous restraints, will prevent these problems is a fantasy.

That many have seen the misbegotten fruit of unethical timber practice is not argued. That many activists have personally suffered financial and personal spiritual loss because of such work is tragic. That some have been duped into believing that a few years worth of recovery after a timber harvest constitutes ecological genocide is intolerable.

The only thing that does not need an EIR, with a peer review is environmental law. What is the logic behind the claim, that its mere intent or the heritage of its political progenitors obviates the need for detailed technical review as if the Law of Unintended Consequences did not exist? Industry can't do that, no matter how many lives might be saved by the product.

This product will kill people, and a forest habitat with it. Is there any alternative? Not for long.

Group Sin Thesis

Recall that the Timber Technical Advisory Committee (T–TAC), convened to make recommendations regarding changes to the Forest Practice Rules under the threat of a new Zoning Law governing timber operations. The T–TAC was a means to give the appearance of public input into the consultation process. The Planning Department Staff reported the committee recommendations as a "consensus" where there had been little agreement at all. Even the Board laughed, just before they adopted it in its entirety.

There was a similar group, the Septic – TAC, initiated to recommend ordinances for septic systems. It too, met behind closed doors, operated under the control of County Staff, and reported consensus recommendations benefiting a select group of developers and consultants.

The Technical Advisory Committee (TAC) is a byproduct of the conversion of what was our government, into a true Bureaucracy. It's operation is so alien that, if a civil servant were to tell you how it works, you might walk away feeling good, but totally without comprehension. It is the public's job to figure out the game, before the *coup de grâce* becomes a *fait accompli*.

The consensus decision making process goes under various other names, including "collaborative," "stakeholder," and "facilitated." It is a variant on a decision model first developed at the Rand Corporation in 1963, as the *Delphi Technique*. It was originally designed as a way to arrive at group decisions, among people with strong and divergent opinions, rendered necessarily subjective due to incomplete information and a limited time-frame; i.e., immediately after a nuclear attack.

Expedient objective decisions involving complex, multivariate criteria, with high associated risk have always been difficult. To get a group of intellec-tuals to agree quickly can be fruitless, unless there is an undisputed leader within, or supervising, the group. Leaders who are capable of sufficient expertise to claim unchallenged leadership, are extremely rare. The search for decision models, capable of integrating disparate interests and expertise, is a legitimate exercise in corporate management. In that respect, the Delphi Technique is no different from any other decision management model.

The Delphi Technique was originally designed to integrate subjective individual evaluations objectively. A disinterested "facilitator" collects an anonymous ballot from each participant with two numeric scores for each decision component: first, the importance of particular criteria, and second, the degree of confidence in a particular course of action. The facilitator then arithmetically compiles the scores and reports the results to the team. It is the report of that composite score that is intended to elicit concessions from the minority or engender further discussion.

The key to the integrity of the method is the manifest disinterest on the part of the facilitator and group acknowledgement of each member's individual integrity. Unless the participants have confidence in the process, they will not report their opinions honestly. Unless they respect each other's integrity, they will not concede on a point of disagreement. Concession will be difficult to obtain if there is any taint of prejudice on the part of the facilitator or bluster by one of the participants, which is why so many corporations remand this role to an outside consultant. The consultant is responsible only for conduc-ting a productive committee meeting and not for the outcome.

Assigning choices to a committee thus isolates both management and com-mittee members from accountability. Lack of individual accountability distorts the individual assessment of risk as an input to the group decision. On the other hand, if they committee members are accountable, they may not share valuable speculative ideas. The study committee system is therefore, likely to produce flawed decisions no matter what the decision model. There is no substitute for true leadership.

Accountability is unavoidable in business. If things are really fouled up the corporation will go bankrupt, be sold, and new management installed. Management is ultimately accountable to stockholders. There is however, a difference between stockholders and stakeholders. The degree of personal "stake" in an outcome is subjective. The amount of voting stock and its price performance are inherently objective and voting power is weighted according to ownership of the risk. When a group decision method is distorted by political manipulation and the job security of civil service, accountability on the part of manipulators, elected officials, and committee members disappears.

It is the encroachment of government into what should rightly be civil matters that engenders the need for the unaccountable and technically incompetent to make so many choices. Lacking a technical understanding of the decision criteria, politicians go about looking for a way out.

A committee, manned by a majority of civil servants and advocacy groups, operates at a conflict of interest to the public. To defer a political decision to a consensus process, dominated by advocacy groups and bureaucrats and deliberately excluding those who would oppose them, is a complete corruption of the intent of the "consensus" process itself. There can be no real consensus under such circumstances and no way for the voting public to know what really happened or who is accountable. There is no check upon its propensity to metastasize because there is no controlling document that has the legitimacy of popular agreement. "Consensus" decision-making is a symptom of a much more serious structural problem in the composition of the civic enterprise. It has changed its fealty from one of Constitutional authority to one of authority itself.

It is Bureaucracy in its purest sense.

It is no surprise to see a decision making system peculiar to multinational corporations make its public appearance through that major global benefactor of corporate foundation largesse: the United Nations. The UN has adopted an objective decision making algorithm, the Delphi Technique, and corrupted it into a subjective, pre-determined output machine by tampering with the role of the facilitator. A system that was intended to be flexible and appears collaborative, is now a means to betray the trust of the participants and overcome opposition. It is no longer capable as an adaptive algorithm. What started as a fad in corporate decision-making has been twisted into a template for instituting a structurally unaccountable form of governance.

Perhaps that conclusion fails to portray sufficiently, the depth of duplicity behind such a process of governance. Perhaps you thought "consensus" meant unanimous agreement. Well, you clearly do not understand either "consensus" or the "collaborative" process as archetypes of the relief from cognitive dissonance that is the product of the Hegelian Dialectic. Perhaps you should ask your children, who are being taught in precisely this manner in the public schools through Outcome-Based Education; a programme that originated at the UN.

"Consensus" now means, 'You didn't object.' Of course, that idea is a subjective interpretation of the concept of "objection," as well. Those who vociferously disagree are removed as "uncooperative" or simply aren't "invited" to participate in the first place unless they agree with the facilitator. In that case, they can assume the role of a protected minority, free to use any tactic or behavior to cower the opposition. Thus, a more appropriate definition of the term "consensus" is that, if the "facilitator" of the discussion is able to report it as a "consensus" or a "collaborative process," then it is one.

Civic consensus-based decision making systems are fundamentally flawed because any in-house coordinator, "facilitator," or activist representative of an advocacy group is necessarily an interested party to the decision. The situation is even worse if the facilitator is an individual who assumes the position with a covert agenda. Under either interested or duplicitous "leadership," the integrity of the group dynamic collapses. It is an opportunity for those who are positioned to take advantage of the situation, a group with no understanding of or concern for risk: the civil servants themselves.

A Hidden Agenda

The Local Agenda 21 in Santa Cruz County

> **Author's Note:** I was unfamiliar with both the Agenda 21 process and the UN when I started participating in the Local Agenda 21. This "consensus process" motivated me to start inquiry that led to writing this book.

In the late winter of 1994, the ACTION – Santa Cruz County (Agenda 21 Teamwork In Operation Now – in Santa Cruz County) announced the Social Environmental Economic Development Summit (SEED Summit). "Everybody" was invited. There were about 125 people present, most belonging to various activist groups. The uninitiated and unaffiliated met with a process already well underway.

At the start of the meeting, the leaders of ACTION–SCC explained that,

> "...the global Agenda 21 document, a blueprint for Sustainable Development... was agreed to by all the 177 nations participating in the UN Conference on the Environment and Development (Earth Summit) in June of 1992."

Chapter 1 – An Unsustainable Agenda

How could 177 *nations* unanimously agree to any document without "everybody" hearing about it unless it was totally innocuous? Well, it was "selected representatives" who had agreed. OK, so, who was ours, how did he or she get the job, and why didn't we hear anything about it?

ACTION – SCC knew all about it. They had been working on "their" Agenda 21 plan for nearly two years. Their goal was to detail Sustainable Development in Santa Cruz for the next seven generations.

Do our grandchildren have any say if it doesn't work?

The topics, issues, and suggested legislative demands for the Local Agenda 21 in Santa Cruz had already been written into a preliminary set of documents requiring "public input." The SEED Summit was to convene Roundtable Discussion Groups, each to prepare a document meeting a predefined format: "I. Current Status, II. Desired State, III. Goals for the Year 2000, IV. What Has Been Done, V. Suggested Actions for Making Progress, and VI. Useful Resources and References." The Roundtable groups were to meet, gather necessary data, and reach "consensus" among all "interested parties" and "community leaders." (Sorry about all the quotation marks, but it really was that bad.)

The SEED leaders introduced pre-assigned "facilitators" for each Roundtable. Nobody questioned their qualifications or how they had been selected. The Ecosystem Management & Biodiversity Roundtable had two representatives from Earth First!, one of them designated as the facilitator. A friend of mine (a volunteer for a local Resource Conservation District and advocate of high-quality forestry) sat down with them, committed to see if anything could be made out of what already seemed to be a grim situation, along with a couple of workers from a research forest owned by California Polytechnic University at San Luis Obispo.

Then came a total surprise: The usual suburban bedroom community anti-logging activists, who would normally have joined the group, announced that they "could not work with these people" and left. There was stunned silence (and honest relief). Nobody familiar with local politics had ever seen them cut and run, especially before a fight.

My friend called me and asked me to join what was left. I had written a few flaming letters about County Ordinances citing ecological issues regarding control of exotic plants and fuels management. Callow as I was, I agreed, protesting that I had no prior experience of public participation, much less writing control documents for ecosystem management, but then as I found out, neither did anybody else.

On the surface, our Earth First! facilitator appeared to be a pleasant enough fellow. He patiently explained that "all the problems in timber were due to "corporate greed" and that "environmental justice" (whatever that was, he never said) was needed for peace and Sustainable Development. He presented documents detailing the evils of the Federal Reserve and the corporate banking aristocracy. He wanted mountain roads eliminated so that the forest could drain correctly. Then he passed out his latest "fact sheet" about the marbled murrelet in the Butano Forest and left without doing any work. After later reading some of his notes, I understood. The man was incapable of coherent writing. After the first couple of meetings, I never saw him again.

Those who showed up met almost weekly, for nearly a year in a local coffee shop. There were never more than six people and usually it was but three or four (myself included). My first concern was the regular and conspicuous absence of our Facilitator from Earth First! (I never met the other Earth First! representative.) I never met any of the "community leaders," nor was I ever told who they were. Other than the "contributors to date" in the newspaper insert, there was never a list of names or phone numbers and there were no assigned responsibilities.

The scientist (or two) who did come (perhaps twice each) expressed concern about the pattern of development, the loss of meadows and lagoons, the threats of exotic species, and loss of truly threatened habitats such as the parklands near sand dunes and estuaries. One local ecologist, highly respected in the California Native Plant Society, had identified the degree of threat to each of 16 local habitats, some of which had no legal protection. Redwood forest was at the bottom of his list, as the LEAST threatened habitat in the County. Foresters disagreed with that conclusion regarding fire risk and I had my concerns about weeds, but most agreed with the rest of his conclusions as a basis for discussion.

You couldn't tell any of this to our facilitator or the few other activists who would show up. To them, this was about redwood trees, and who should control timber harvesting. They talked about illegal clearcuts justifying their stances without producing documentation. They talked about eliminating roads and returning inhabited lands "to Nature," but never about who should pay for it, or how to decide which roads and parcels needed mitigation. They talked, but they never produced any substantial writing.

It was a discouraging process to witness. The people who would have to pay for and do the restoration work were treated as if they were targets. Those attendees who had investigated the activist claims were never able to locate the illegal clearcuts about which they were complaining.

A few professionals and business people made occasional appearances, but still there was little hard input unless it was in their personal interest. In frustration, I thought (and perhaps, by this time somewhat vindictively) that if the activists had no intent to do any work, that this was an opportunity to write a sensible plan focusing upon collection of data, public education, and individual accountability for stewardship. (At the time I still believed in civic resource management.) With a consensus process, we would have the opportunity to confront irresponsible claims and hold out until proven otherwise. "Who knows," I thought, "perhaps the UN has designed a system that can deal with specious charges and support those who doggedly seek the truth until all have to acknowledge objective data." So I wrote a draft, integrating the few submissions with my own thoughts and handed copies to the others, fully prepared for debate and resolution. I only received two comments.

One would normally expect strongly held opinions. Santa Cruz County is an ecologically and politically complex place upon which to "consense." I knew that we did not legitimately represent all interests. Without full representation, how could we get the data from which to make recommendations? I knew we didn't have it and it bothered me (one of my reasons for having included so much hard data about Santa Cruz in this book).

I phoned the regional Agenda 21 Coordinator to put together a real meeting because I was uncomfortable about the lack of hard data. She responded with how she was overwhelmed with it all and just couldn't do it. What she did emphasize was the deadline, which is OK. It was an unrealistic target date for completion, but only if the intent was to be respected. It is not possible to collect sufficient data for anybody to convince every individual in a polarized group to join in a consensus. (Such data do not exist.) Nevertheless, as a project engineer, I understood that you do what you can with the time provided, and submit the output on time. I assembled the input, got what divergent comments I could obtain, put it together, and turned it in, on time.

Concerned that it was to be hacked to pieces, I called the Coordinator occasionally to ask her what had happened. She told me that there had been no progress, and that other Roundtables were occupying all her time. Eventually I just gave up. As far as I knew, it was just sitting in a file collecting dust, at least I hoped so. By this time, the entire process had given me the jitters. I knew that the activists couldn't possibly just leave it alone.

Suddenly, almost two years later, the other Roundtable participants and I each got a phone call from the Coordinator about a week before "the final submission deadline" (a date known to no one but her). She faxed me the "final submission" (our Facilitator had skipped town). The content was somewhat recognizable, but they had cut the font size from 12 point to 8, adding nearly half again the word count. It was a mish-mash of contradictory paragraphs, inserted into the original document.

The lady in charge of the "consensus" process, the Coordinator, had taken the plan back to her friends, the same local suburban activists who had refused to participate in the Roundtable Discussion Groups. They had rewritten the plan in secret.

These were the "Community Leaders." The goal was apparently to take our input, edit it to their advantage, and call it a consensus in which we had "participated." The Coordinator needed the document for Rio+5 and had come back to get a co-opted blessing over the telephone.

There was still no meeting or open discussion. There was no way for me to talk to these "community leaders" nor to find out who they were. All communication went through the "coordinator." The negotiations were by facsimile transmissions, with various inserts that kept changing with each revision. My friend and I held out tenaciously, line by line.

It didn't matter. This was a consensus process. We were "overruled." The coordinator always had the final say as to whose voice should hold sway on every topic and whose side had won the "vote." I never saw nor was I told the tally of such a "vote." No one could explain why the coordinator was to have veto control over the document, or why it was acceptable that a consensus should be determined by mere plurality.

No one could explain how those "community leaders" had been selected. The coordinator indicated that they had such a power by virtue of their status, but could not supply qualifying criteria. There had never been a single public discussion among a representative group of interested parties. The apparent reason the activists had walked out of the original meeting and never showed up for another was that they never really needed to discuss the issues in good faith. They knew that they had the power to fix it later.

Of the thirty-three people listed on the document as Contributors, I had only seen a total of nine at any meeting and four that had attended more than a few. Of the rest, I can account for only thee having ever attended a meeting at which I was not present, other than the original SEED confab, at which the suburban activists had walked out. How do you have a "majority" of "Contributors" decide a "consensus," when that majority never attended a single working meeting?

In principle, a consensus process sounds fine. The process of debate tests beliefs in the search for truth. If the consensus process works as intended, anyone in the discussion who has unalterable objections to a proposition may halt adoption until the issue is resolved or somebody comes up with a new alternative. The system is supposed to be especially considerate of minority opinion. We were certainly both a minority and opposed to the document, but were "overruled" anyway. Perhaps ACTION–SCC meant that minorities could only stop the consensus process when they happen to agree with the outcome intended by the Coordinator.

The majority of the meeting participants refused to support it. I should have gone to the "ceremony" and written my refusal to agree on the document, signed it, and then demanded a copy. Then I should have politely protested the process as a fraud in front of reporters. My friend reports that no one who did show up was asked if they had agreed to anything. She was too polite to stand up and scream. Maybe this account will help redress my tactical error. At least we have the written evidence: faxes, notes, and telephone records.

Why was this document so important that they should so corrupt the very process they were trying to sell as such a success?

The purpose of the consensus process is to lend legitimacy to what the people in power intend to do anyway. The County Board of Supervisors adopted the Agenda 21 plan into the General Plan, sight unseen. The implications of such a system, for such principles as Due Process of Law and Representative Government are truly frightening. It is a process that codifies mob rule democracy, NGO legal advocacy, favorable treatment of select interest groups, and unchecked bureaucracy into every facet of your life.

Act Locally

"What is this about the United Nations Agenda 21?" you might ask. "If this was such a big deal, wouldn't everybody have already heard all about it?"

The Global Agenda 21 is a component of Global Governance, brought to you by that democratic claque representing largely totalitarian states: the United Nations. If you have heard of Sustainable Development, Sustainable Communities, a Sustainable America, or Smart Growth, they are all the same thing and they all originate in the same place.

"Sustainable Development." It sounds like a good thing, doesn't it? We don't want unsustainable development, but who decides what is or isn't?

The Agenda 21 is a very different way of getting things done. It is not a set of principles or a specification for what to do, but is instead a framework or algorithm for how bureaucrats are to manage the environment, worldwide.

Although the document appears highly structured, the implementation ends up as a chaotic system because there is no structural accountability at all. There is no mechanism by which competing ecological interests are weighed and a final objective decision made. There is no way to subject the decision to legal test; indeed there is no check on the system at all. Instead, there are so many options and paths by which whims can evolve into laws that there is no way to predict or redirect the regulatory process to constructive goals. It is as if it existed for only one purpose: Find any means possible to get around the Constitution of the United States.

Sustainable Development ignores representative government via tortured interpretations of existing laws and treaties. The system uses lawyers and bureaucrats in NGOs and the UN to force their strategic actions directly to your local government through the courts (the reason why this book used a local case in Santa Cruz County).

Instead of subordinating government to a clearly explained set of principles, United Nations' Global Governance confers rights to citizens that they can just as easily withdraw or ignore. Although UN documents sound as if they respect all sorts of human rights, they all contain provisions allowing those in charge to withdraw those rights or reinterpret their meaning at will.

The UN Agenda 21 was not published in official form in the U.S. until February, 1996 by the President's Council on Sustainable Development, which President Clinton created by Executive Order 12852, on June 29, 1993. It is difficult to obtain an official copy because it is usually out of print and was not conspicuously published on the UN website until June, 2000. Of the initiatives in the U.S., only three explicitly admit connection to the Agenda 21, and only one includes, "Agenda 21" in its title: The County of Santa Cruz. Did it just go away, or is it the definitive "living document"?

If you think it went away, or that it's insignificant, just do a web search on "Agenda 21," and stand back. At this writing there were over 375,000 literal matches online, including China, Germany, Azerbaijan, Georgia, Sweden, Argentina... It is so huge and so amorphous, that it is hard to grasp.

There are ways to get a line on these things. For example, here in Santa Cruz County, the local Agenda 21 organization, ACTION–SCC, links to the World Forum through the International Council for Local Environmental Initiatives (ICLEI). Interestingly, the U.S. headquarters for ICLEI are in Berkeley, CA, and nearly one fifth of all the Local Agenda 21 governments within the United States are in the San Francisco Bay Area.

The operation of the system is situational because the goal of control matters more than the means or purported ends. If local members of a UN accredited NGO (such as the Sierra Club) don't particularly like what people are doing with their property, they can petition their friends in the local bureaucracy for new regulations. If they need higher authority and the law to be cited exits, both parties, activists and bureaucrats, can approach their designees on the President's Council on Sustainable Development (PCSD) for new regulations or interpretations of existing law (PCSD expired in 1999 but its implemen-ting network remains). If PCSD or the agencies lack the legal tools, both NGOs and civil servants have delegates on the NGO Forum. This body is what is to become the UN "Council of Civil Society," lately dubbed "The People's Assembly" (has a nice Maoist ring, doesn't it?). The NGO Forum may appear to be a private organization, but it receives substantial funding from the UN. Forum delegates can request that the IUCN remind a Federal

Agency that, as a participating member, it has agreed to adhere to IUCN policies that include enforcing terms of multilateral treaties, ratified or not.

If a new multilateral agreement is necessary, the IUCN can form a Working Group of delegates from its staff and/or membership to draft a multilateral treaty under one or more of its five permanent Standing Commissions. When the treaty is ready, the UN often designates the IUCN Working Group as a Preparatory Committee (PrepCom) that adds delegates of sovereign nations and member NGOs. By that time, the treaty is effectively a done deal. An NGO or member agency must agree to abide the principles of the IUCN in order to participate in either Working Group or the PrepCom. The PrepCom then approves the draft for ratification and sets the number of nations necessary for the treaty to go into effect.

Once the PrepCom completes its job, it morphs into a permanent Secretariat (again composed of primarily of the same IUCN staff) that administers the treaty. All ratifying nations are Parties to the treaty. A Conference of the Parties (COP) consists of the political appointees of ratifying nations that nominally govern the treaty. That is how "177 nations unanimously agreed" to the Agenda 21 Document at the COP at the Rio Summit in 1992.

It was a consensus, too.

As things are now, treaties only apply to countries that ratify them. That is to change very soon. The International Criminal Court is the first multilateral treaty that declares itself binding upon ALL nations with only 60 ratifying Parties. The ICC along with a UN standing army would have the power to enforce a treaty against the will of a sovereign nation that had not ratified the treaty. The result would be Global Government.

The IUCN is the key player in creating the environmental treaties that are the principle tools for effecting UN Global Governance. This organization of several hundred permanent employees headquartered in Gland, Switzerland wields considerable power as the principal consultative body to the UN on environmental affairs. Besides organizing and staffing the PrepComs to draft treaties, the IUCN prioritizes UN environmental spending. The UN Global Environment Facility provided nearly $800 million dollars to the IUCN (1998) along with other NGOs such as Greenpeace, the World Wildlife Fund, the World Resources Institute, and The Nature Conservancy who in turn fund projects at the local level. It is closed loop control.

The Agenda 21 uses environmental regulations to institute bureaucratic control at the local level. To impart an inkling of the scope of this monster, we will start by simply listing the Chapter headings:

Social and Economic Dimensions, International Cooperation to Accelerate Sustainable Development in Developing Countries and Related Domestic Policies,

Combating Poverty, Changing Consumption Patterns, Demographic Dynamics and Sustainability, Protecting and Promoting Human Health, Promoting Sustainable Human Settlement Development, Integrating Environment and Development in Decision-Making, Protection of the Atmosphere, Integrated Approach to the Planning and Management of Land Resources, Combating Deforestation, Desertification and Drought, Managing Fragile Ecosystems: Sustainable Mountain Development, Promoting Sustainable Agriculture and Rural Development, Conservation of Biological Diversity, Environmentally Sound Management of Biotechnology, Protection of the Oceans, All Kinds of Seas, including Enclosed and Semi-Enclosed Seas, and Coastal Areas and the Protection, Rational Use and Development of Their Living Resources, Protection of the Quality and Supply of Freshwater Resources: Application of Integrated Approaches to the Development, Management and Use of Water Resources, Environmentally Sound Management of Toxic Chemicals, Including Prevention of Illegal International Traffic in Toxic and Dangerous Products, Environmentally Sound Management of Hazardous Wastes, Including Prevention of Illegal International Traffic in Hazardous Wastes, Environmentally Sound Management of Solid Wastes and Sewage-Related Issues, Safe and Environmentally Sound Management of Radioactive Wastes, Strengthening the Role of Major Groups: Global Action for Women Towards Sustainable and Equitable Development, Children and Youth in Sustainable Development, Recognizing and Strengthening the Role of Indigenous People and their Communities, Strengthening the Role of Non-Governmental Organizations: Partners for Sustainable Development, Local Authorities Initiatives in support of Agenda 21, Strengthening the Role of Workers and their Trade Unions, Strengthening the Role of Business and Industry, Scientific Technological Communities, Strengthening the Role of Farmers, Financial Resources and Mechanisms Introduction, Transfer of Environmentally Sound Technology, Cooperation and Capacity-Building, Science for Sustainable Development, Promoting Education, Public Awareness, and Training, National Mechanisms International Cooperation for Capacity-Building in Developing Countries, International Institutional Arrangements, International Legal Instruments and Mechanisms, Information for Decision-Making, …

Did you ever read the Gulag Archipelago? If you did, how long was it before you realized that it was not just one case of massive injustice that was the point of the book, but the sheer enormity of it?

The Agenda 21 or Sustainable Development makes a farce of representative democracy. It has no place in a constitutional republic, but you are getting it anyway, unless you do something about it very soon.

"Changing Consumption Patterns" is about changing yours. "Programs for Women" and "Demographic Dynamics and Sustainability" are ways to take control of reproduction through healthcare. They want the children first, with their School-to-Work programs and Outcome-Based Education programmes. They want to control unions to control votes. They will use the claims of "indigenous peoples" as a lever for taking land, even though nobody knows who that really is much less the legitimate extent of their claims.

The civil servants will love Sustainable Development because they get to regulate what is or isn't "sustainable" to suit their purposes. They'll have mass-transit and bicycles. They'll have low-income housing, rent control, overcrowded schools, and the social problems that come with them. They'll mix those used-to-be middle class kids with children of immigrant workers raised on a steady media and public school diet of class warfare. They'll produce an ample supply of customers for the criminal justice system and those Psych Majors at the University.

This is Agenda 21. The UN intends to control your life, through incremental mandates **instituted by your local government bureaucracy**. You will never see it. You will never vote on it. No matter which path they use, the agencies can pen the new regulations under "threat" of lawsuit and down the pipe it comes: enforceable administrative rules without legislation.

This book has chronicled but a few of the early manifestations of the Agenda 21 in Santa Cruz County (logging, septic, and the listing of coho). Each time there has been a public protest or threat of a lawsuit, the agency formed a TAC to accept public "input." Each time the TAC convened, it was either advisory in nature (Timber-TAC under the control of the Planning Department or coho under CDFG) or manned by a majority of civil servants (Septic-TAC). Consensus, as defined by any normal human being, did not exist. It is fortunate that in California such public meetings are subject to the much-abused Brown Act, which requires that minutes of the meetings be available. T–TAC meetings were taped instead, just try to get a transcript. You would pay thousands of dollars to get one.

Congress? The Constitution? Public takings of private property? You just don't understand. These problems are about transformation products in Global Commons. Those trees on your property make oxygen for the rest of the planet and consume CO_2 for the poor in China. Shell wants to trade the carbon credits that should have been yours to sell. You middleclass consumers, on the other hand, are producers of that noxious poison, and you use more of those Global Commons than your share. Have you no compassion?

Think Globally

"Does all the foregoing mean that Wild Earth and The Wildlands Project advocate the end of industrialized civilization?

Most assuredly. Everything civilized must go..."

-John Davis, Wild Earth magazine

One may think that Mr. Davis is nuts, and is thus, inconsequential. Anybody concerned about his ilk would be a conspiracy nut, or so goes the line from the corporate media. His beliefs, are being indoctrinated at the universities, and infused into every level of government. They are not inconsequential.

Dave Foreman co-founded Earth First! He is on the Board of Directors of the Sierra Club. Mr. Foreman calls himself an "eco-warrior" and has published designs for devices intended to maim or kill people who do what he thinks is harmful to the environment. Mr. Foreman is a Chairman of the Wildlands Project. The Audubon Society and The Nature Conservancy paid Dr. Reed F. Noss to devise the plan, originally published in Wild Earth. He writes,

> "I suggest that at least half of the land area of the 48 conterminous states should be encompassed in core reserves and inner corridor zones (essentially extensions of core reserves) within the next few decades.... Nonetheless, half of a region in wilderness is a reasonable guess of what it will take to restore viable populations of large carnivores and natural disturbance regimes, assuming that most of the other 50 percent is managed intelligently as buffer zone. Eventually, a wilderness network would dominate a region...with human habitations being the islands."

The list of provisions in the zoning law in the County of Santa Cruz included riparian "corridors" to be designated: "no entry." It's probably a coincidence, attributed by some paranoid author, given that the term is repeated in literally dozens of federal agency and activist documents holding "core reserves" as no entry and proposing to restrict eco-tourism to "buffer zones."

There are precedents for this sort of plan, and they aren't pretty. In 1918, the Soviet Communist Party issued a decree, *On Land,* designating all forests, waters, and minerals subject to "rational use" with protected lands reserved for scientific study only. There is a rich history of totalitarian governments, communist, fascist, and feudal, using similar excuses of protecting nature as a way of controlling subject populations.

Do these people know what they are doing? John Davis, Editor of Wild Earth, and a Director of The Wildlands Project, says people would not be required to relocate if they would,

> "...refrain from any use of motors, guns, or cows. The problem here is not so much people as it is their damnable technologies."

There were cattle in North America long before there were bison or wolves (and not for long after they arrived). How could people, who come up with plans like this, know in their hands and bodies what it takes care for land? IT TAKES WORK to control invasive species, thin a forest, propagate native plants, or correct old drainage problems. It takes years to learn the patterns of light and weather. It takes walking that land every day to catch a weed before it gets out of hand. It takes the time and observational skills to know when the gophers are beneficial, and when they are about to cause a real problem. Sometimes, fixing an old problem takes a lot of money. The time, energy, and capital necessary to optimize ecosystem function and fund it can only come from the productive capacity that is a blessing of the advanced economy that would be destroyed by bureaucratic socialism.

The UN Convention on Biological Diversity was developed by the IUCN, and first proposed as a treaty to the United Nations in 1981. The Global Biodiversity Assessment, an 1140-page document for the United Nations Environment Program (UNEP) is the published set of guidelines implementing the Convention. The Assessment explicitly identifies the Wildlands Project as central to the preservation of biodiversity as required by the Convention. The U.S. Senate refused to consider the Treaty in 1994.

Member agencies in the IUCN are required to affirm that "their objects and activities have no conflict of interest with those of the IUCN." Submitting a membership application "implies endorsement of the principles of the World Conservation Strategy, and the World Charter for Nature."

The following Federal resource agencies are members of the IUCN:

- The U.S. State Department, Bureau of Oceans, International Environmental & Scientific Affairs (OIES),
- The Environmental Protection Agency (EPA),
- The Department of Commerce, National Oceanic and Atmospheric Administration (NOAA),
- The National Marine Fisheries Service (NMFS),
- The U.S. Department of Agriculture (USDA), and
- The U.S. Department of Interior, Fish and Wildlife Service, National Park Service.

Since when did voluntary membership in an international NGO constitute a superceding authority to Constitutional law? How is it that these agencies could agree to terms that violate that law? Who would want such a thing? Is it really for the common good? It should be illegal.

The UN Habitat Conference report concludes:

> "Public ownership of land is justified in favor of the common good, rather than to protect the interests of the already privileged."

Isn't it the privileged who are behind all this? No, it's the VERY privileged.

Maurice Strong is a Canadian billionaire, a Board member of Petro-Canada and Dome Petroleum, and President of Ontario Hydro. He is Director of the IUCN, Chairman of the Earth Council, Trustee of the Aspen Institute, Director of the World Future Society, Director of Finance for the Lindisfarne Association, founder of Planetary Citizens, member of the Club of Rome,

Chairman of the World Resources Institute, and Co-Chairman and founder of the Council of the World Economic Forum and Senior Adviser to the President of the World Bank. He is President of the World Federation of United Nations Associations, Senior Advisor to the UN Secretary General and for the Rockefeller and Rothschild Trusts.

Maurice Strong is the man who is the chief architect of Global Governance, and co-authored the Earth Charter with Mikhail Gorbachev (not exactly what you would call the equivalent of a Constitutional Convention, is it?). Gorby, must have acquired his environmental credentials during his career in the KGB. It is well known what a job he did on the ecosystems of the former Soviet Union. He has his very own "accredited" environmental NGO, the International Green Cross, and says, "Nature is my God."

Mr. Strong was Secretary General of the 1972 Earth Summit in Stockholm and the 1992 Earth Summit in Rio de Janeiro. Mr. Gorbachev addressed the assembly to cheers. What do they know about taking care of dirt?

In addition, Mr. Strong's credentials include membership in the UN-funded Commission on Global Governance. It's 1995 report entitled *Our Global Neighborhood* contained a number of ominous proposals including:

- UN control over global commons: air, oceans, space, the electromagnetic spectrum, …
- The establishment of a global tax system on all currency transfers,
- Expansion of the powers of the World Bank,
- Removal of the veto power in the Security Council,
- Creation of an Economic Security Council to rule the world's economy,
- Expansion of the International Criminal Court to adjudicate it, AND
- A standing UN Army to enforce it.

All rights conferred to "Citizens of the World" under UN Treaty are granted by the UN. What if they change their minds? It is written right into the UN Charter that all rights as conferred are subject to change.

Let's see... The UN foists rules driving production overseas. Imported oil and imported food means lots of currency transfers and the UN taxes those, but this isn't about money; this is about the environment, right?

No. It's about money. Environmental set-asides are capable of manipulating supplies of critical commodities. They increase the value of producing lands and substitute goods in the hands of multinational oligopolies. Regulations depress the price of acquisition by forcing competitors into a distressed sale.

One wouldn't think that titans of altruism were interested exclusively in charity. Oil company foundations fund a coterie of environmentalists to end nuclear power, breach hydroelectric dams, tie up access to reserves of oil, gas, geothermal, coal, solar, wind power, and rely entirely upon a constrained supply of which fossil fuels to supply our high-technology economy? There are so many of such manipulations that no one strategy can describe them all. The scale is breathtaking.

The same corrupt political and legal control system, advocated by so many environmentalists as some kind of solution to "the problem," is the same system we were using in the days of unfettered rape of the land. It's STILL the rich guys in charge. The only difference is that they have tamed an army of NGO lawyers and bureaucrats to do their bidding.

Most of the people doing the dirty work for these financiers call themselves "Citizens of the World." They don't care what it takes to save The Environment as long as it is under their direction. They have egos to feed, mortgages to pay, and a weak understanding of the history of their benefactors. A paycheck makes it easier for them to explain away the ecological damage that betrays the actual priorities of Global Governance: money and power.

Bureaucrats and NGO functionaries have absolved themselves of accountability for the results of their actions with the urgency of their individual and cultural rhetoric, choosing instead to focus upon a final solution. They have already decided that the world will be better off without 80% of its people. They call it "carrying capacity."

The Global Biodiversity Assessment, concludes that:

> "...an agricultural world, in which most human beings are peasants, should be able to support 5 to 7 billion people...a reasonable estimate for an industrialized world society at the present North American material standard of living would be one billion. At the more frugal European standard of living, 2-3 billion would be possible."

The current global population is approximately 6 billion. The trend of growth rate is declining and may turn negative this century. Estimates of carrying capacity range from 1 to 40 billion people, depending upon whom you ask, but perhaps the statement is more revealing than it would at first seem.

That's how many people it will support, the way they intend to run it.

Most activists are ignorant of where a process like this leads, and have no clue that their supposedly altruistic benefactors may be more interested in sequestering or accessing mineral wealth than in healthy habitat. Once the Constitution is gone, they are easily replaced.

When the United Nations adopts the Earth Charter, they will legally consider everyone a "Citizen of the World," superceding national citizenship. Your rights would then be "harmonized" to those conferred by the UN and just as easily taken. The International Criminal Court can then prosecute anyone, anywhere, with no jury, under multiple jeopardy, and with no habeas corpus.

At the opening session of the Rio Conference (Earth Summit II) in 1992, Mr. Strong said that industrialized countries have:

> "developed and benefited from the unsustainable patterns of production and consumption which have produced our present dilemma. It is clear that current lifestyles and consumption patterns of the affluent middle class -- involving high meat intake, consumption of large amounts of frozen and convenience foods, use of fossil fuels, appliances, home and work-place air-conditioning, and suburban housing -- are not sustainable. A shift is necessary toward lifestyles less geared to environmentally damaging consumption patterns."

A shift is necessary for the middle class, the very group capable of making the technologies Mr. Strong can't envision, that might well prevent the environmental crises he supposedly stresses about from ever developing. This from a guy who came up through an oil company and ran an electricity monopoly and was caught trying to drain and sell the Ogalala Aquifer?

Do Ends Justify Means?

Aristotle, in the Nichomachean Ethics, elaborated on the question of ends and means with an answer so clear and simple, it is a wonder that "ends justification" was ever mentioned again. He wrote (this is condensed out of a couple of paragraphs), 'No person selects an end unless it is a means to something else. There are no "Ends." There are only means.'

Take a hard look at the behavior of environmental radicals in that light. How are they acquiring control? Is it with the strength and commitment of ideas and capital, or is it by buying influence, brainwashing children, funding lawsuits, and garbing police in bulletproof vests? Is the goal of their benefactors environmental health or controlling wealth? Are they truly motivated out of love, or is it hatred and contempt? Are their actions to build and to heal, or do they act to destroy? Have forests flourished under their hands, or are they buried under mud, infested with pests, and covered with weeds? Are they preserving nature for future generations, or are they advocating suicide?

Activists assert that landowners are too ignorant of ecosystems to manage them actively, so they would turn over the land to… the government? ..to the United Nations?? …to the DMV??? Do they know how to fix it? Where will they get the money? Do they know how not to waste it? Somehow, it doesn't seem that "repeating over and over" will make that any better an idea.

Environmental management by Global Governance is a policy dictated by subjective science, paid for by its proponents in the interest of power. It is an empire under a hierarchy of self-deception. Imagine the results that come from people who think that way. Will it really be some kind of eco-paradise or a nightmare of people who just follow orders? Might the likely outcome be the unwitting vengeance of self-destruction?

The state of the planet they would have as a goal is unknown to science. To mandate universal inaction is a destructive management plan, incapable of developing adaptive knowledge. Few of those in charge have spent any part of their lives doing the work. They would rob all private property, take all means of production, and justify the idea of billions of deaths to "preserve" the environment, but won't talk about how. They intend a model of government responsible for over 100 million deaths in the last century.

There may be no instantaneous way to end this Malthusian insanity, but it can be accomplished one step at a time. There is little point in trying to force ideas down people's throats. It is better to teach people that we already know better than to use coercion, confiscation, and destruction of public wealth, and expect something good to come out of it. We can lead by example, and respect the innate self-interest, intelligence, and observational skills of our brethren enough to make "repeating it over and over" a complete waste of time. Instead using human energy to stifle human energy we could motivate educated people to maximize total profit fostering the health of the planet.

Hence this book and its alternatives: Laws, not Rules. Principles, not Regulations. Competitive Enterprises, not Bureaucracy. Stockholders, not Stakeholders. Voters and Representatives, not Decision-Makers. A Constitutional Republic, under the primacy of the unalienable rights of Citizens making a profit on improving the function of their land, and not a manipulated mob democracy under selected "rights" as conferred by the State.

It's possible. Wouldn't you rather do everything you could, to make it work before we witlessly subject our children to such an irreversible fate?

[t]he moment that idea

is admitted into society

that property is not as sacred

as the Laws of God,

and that there is not a force of law

and public justice to protect it,

anarchy and tyranny commence.

– John Adams

📖 Chapter 2 – Defy Gravity

Propagating Environmental Regulations

Regulation flows downhill in a cascade, as reliable as gravity. Administrative mandates, supposedly sourced by the Federal bureaucracy, ooze down the pipe for interpretation at the State level, and thence, inundate local agencies for enforcement. That rulemaking rarely sees a legislator, is the reason that the production flow of regulatory government is so alien to the public.

It is in the "rulemaking" process that the environmental NGOs have it all over private parties. United Nations "accredited" NGOs, such as the World Wildlife Fund (WWF) or the IUCN, have sympathetic members in every Federal resource agency. They have libraries full of research. They have experienced lawyers on staff, familiar with the issues and a network of technical experts. They can help the agencies and member NGOs (such as the Sierra Club) bypass the legislative process with lawsuits in Federal Court, regardless of public opinion. It is a political and regulatory juggernaut.

Those property owners who can't afford to comply with the regulations or the resulting fines are squeezed out. NGO buyers, such as The Nature Conservancy, either sell it to government (usually at a profit) or roll it over into development for reinvestment, and everybody is happy: the foundation donors, the NGOs, the campaign donors, the politicians, the regulators, and their horde of enforcers all the way through to the County tax collector.

Federal legislation appropriately lacks specificity regarding implementation at the State and local level. The drafters of such rule strategies, both in the NGOs and in the Executive Branch have little empathy for the complexity of enacting regulatory policy through the web of entitlement and turf in government agencies. They don't care that it takes time to establish the boundary conditions of where the rules apply, whose administrative bailiwick it is, or how that boundary is established. The originators merely expect lower levels of the government hierarchy get the intended precedents established in time for the next move. Because the process gets more rushed as it works its way down, the rule production system is almost guaranteed to make bad law, directed more toward extending the powers of administrative bureaucracy than it is to deliver its purported intent. Proof? Too harsh? Just wait, we're not done with the hypothesis.

High-level executives in target industries are usually smart people. Once government gets its hands upon the factors of production, it isn't long before industry leaders recognize a patronage system for what it is. Those with sufficient political pull are obviously tempted to sell out their competitors and manipulate the deal. They can salve their guilt with the excuse that, when a system is capable of either handing them an oligopoly or destroying them, they had better take advantage of it to survive. Of course, being one of the winners in the marketplace doesn't hurt so much either. Once they learn the game and start to take control of it, the temptation to dominate the market with public money becomes addicting.

The corporate winners can then use their profits to start a tax-exempt foundation with which to fund political advocacy without the annoyance of campaign contribution limits. They use the funding to lobby politicians and direct groups of NGO activists to gather data supporting specific action.

The regulatory system thus ends up as a troika of NGOs, industry oligopoly, and government regulators. The strategies take several forms. To provide an intuitive framework with which to understand some of the behavioral under-currents, we will use those famous fables from Uncle Remus, respectfully and faithfully recovered from Afro-American Oral History by that noted (and unjustly maligned) anthropologist, Joel Chandler Harris. We will refer to this example as "The Briar Patch Effect." The principles are as follows:

1. There are economies of scale associated with regulatory compliance, as with any other cost of production. Capable compliance to rules becomes a barrier to entry and a means to target existing competitors.

2. Rules can be tailored to the advantage of those possessing property with favored attributes. Competitors can be targeted by similar means.

3. Selective enforcement, through bribes, friendships, and political connections, is a problem as old as government itself.

4. Regulatory constraint of supply can raise the capital value of remaining assets in production through monopoly profits. Advocacy can be a very a good investment.

Our example will be nonpoint pollution regulations in the San Lorenzo River watershed of the County of Santa Cruz, California. Our friend, Brer Rabbit is the community of developers, consultants, and large contractors. This group of political contributors consists of both the builders of baronies and the slumlords-to-be inside the Sustained Development, Agenda 14, uh... Agenda 21/Measure C Greenbelt, around the City of Santa Cruz. It also includes the recent purchasers of discreet and carefully selected "in-fill" parcels. If they run out of the latter, the power of eminent domain in the hands of a redevelopment or regulatory agency assures a ready supply of more.

Our "Brer Fox" is the "consensus" of bureaucrats in the County of Santa Cruz Department of Environmental Health, the Planning Department, the State Regional Water Quality Control Board, CALEPA, Federal EPA, NMFS, the California Coastal Commission, and, on top of it all, the Natural Resources Defense Council (NRDC).

The Briar Patch is the seemingly endless, conflicting, arbitrary, ambiguous, in many cases archaic and certainly voluminous stack of rules, regulations, and administrative procedures concerning Section 303(d) of the Clean Water Act. Nobody likes the briar patch, except the rabbit.

Clean Water. It sounds like a good idea. Doesn't it?

A Little History

Contrary to popular opinion, in the really old days before Europeans arrived, river water was not clean. The acid/base balance and other mineral salts in the water depend upon soil pH, the type of rock, the amount and distribution of average rainfall, and the number of years since a fire. Nitrate concentrations depended largely upon the number and type of animals and vegetation. Suspended or dissolved constituents of river water from dispersed sources or passing through diffuse transmission media are called **nonpoint pollution**. If there had been a herd of elk nearby, you wouldn't have wanted to drink it.

In the sort-of-old days, before water pollution controls, cities and factories simply stuck a pipe out over the river. Though no single pipe was "the cause" of "the problem," water quality typically worsened as rivers progressed downstream. It was a consequence of cumulative introductions of pollutants overwhelming the ability of the riparian system to consume the contaminants. It became a national issue.

An outlet of a sewer pipe (or smokestack from an industrial plant) is known as a **point source** of pollution. The end of the pipe is an easy place to take measurements by which to quantify the total added mass and composition of pollutants. One can then assign culpability to those responsible for illegal discharges: Just sample the outfall and cite the owners of the pipe.

Given a fixed discharge rate of pollutants, water quality worsens when the river flow rate is low and concentrations of pollutants are less dilute. In the not so deep past, it was fairly common for an industrial plant to hold its effluent and wait for a rainstorm to make a discharge. The "thought" was that the "solution to pollution is dilution."

There were problems with that dump-it-when-it-rains procedure. Part of the discharge infused riverbanks and floodplain downstream during high flow conditions and then leached back into the river or into groundwater later. If there were nearby sources of similar pollutants, it would then be impossible to hold the owner of a particular source accountable for the pollution.

The 1972 Clean Water Act included Section 303(d), mandating Total Maximum Daily Load (TMDL) values. The law specified a that a maximum mass discharge rate per 24 hours be set for each pollutant for each permitee at which river water quality standards could be met under "worst case conditions." If the discharge rate from the pipe into the river exceeded the specified limit, then there could (supposedly) be no mistake in assigning culpability to the source owner. All one had to do to prove it was install continuous monitoring equipment.

Although the 303(d) legislation could be applied to any source of water pollution, TMDL, as a technical concept, was designed to address problems specific to point sources. There is no legally or technically functional way to apply TMDL to nonpoint sources because their discharge rate cannot be controlled on a daily basis. (There is no such thing as a valve with which to control the flow and composition of polluted groundwater into a river.) This lack of assignable causes or control points is especially vexing.

Congress authorized section 305 of the Clean Water Act to "study the problem" with the hope that technical means could be found to attribute nonpoint pollution to specific sources in a legally conclusive manner. Since Congress is populated with lawyers and lawyers are really smart people, they believed the administrative promise that the experts would be done in two years. EPA has been studying it for 30 years since and there is no end in sight.

It's not an easy problem.

Nitrate is necessary for all ecosystem functions. It is only a pollutant when there is "too much" of it. The problem with the idea of "too much" is that we don't even know, at any given time, what the "right" amount is, which is obviously subject to the intended use of the water. One would think that the way to learn would be to measure it. Unfortunately, that isn't easy either.

Nitrate is produced continuously by animals, bacteria, and fungi and is absorbed by photosynthesis. Natural background concentrations are cyclical on both annual and multi-year bases. It can accumulate for years and be released by climactic events. Even if we could make a representative and accurate measurement of total nitrate, it is nearly impossible to know the anthropogenic fraction of nitrate in a sample. The source could be human or animal urine, decaying grass clippings or rotting trees. Nitrates arrive on a farm as fertilizer or feed and might leave as food, meat, compost, or timber. Thus to arrive at a mandated specification for a rate of discharge, verified by a reliable and accurate test method, is nearly impossible because it is so hard to measure the sources in relation to their effects.

If we did know how much anthropogenic nitrate is added to a system overall, that does not mean that we know whose nitrates are causing the pollution. The sources can be spread over an enormous area and have numerous contributors. A herd of animals can mess things up just by walking over a hill at aperiodic intervals. Once the nitrates are in groundwater, it takes many test holes to estimate a direction of flow. There is little realistic or accurate way to assign individual accountability for a nonpoint source problem in a river. Everybody involved knows it.

If you think that discussion was tedious, realize that measuring nitrate concentration is only half of calculating nitrate loading by which to derive a TMDL. You also have to make an equally precise estimate of the flow rate of the target water body. This measurement is most critical when the flow rates are low during summer perhaps including what is flowing through the gravel along the bottom... It isn't easy without building a permanent concrete weir.

All of the forgoing was initiated out of the intent to measure and attain nitrate levels desirable to regulators for the purpose of enforcement. These technical machinations and legal conniptions don't do much to help people responsibly manage sources of anthropogenic nitrate, do they?

Despite all the efforts expended so far, nobody knows how much nitrate is desirable much less what the system can tolerate as a single-day maximum transient load as relates to a baseline average. What really matters is the integrated profile circumscribing a combination of spatial and temporal peaks that vary by local conditions. Said in English, what matters is how much is added, where, when, how fast, and how it interacts with local conditions some of which are cyclical over decades. The riparian nitrate process is too complex for an enforcement-based system. TMDL, as a concept, has NO APPLICABILITY to management of nonpoint nitrate contributions.

So, What's the Point?

After dealing with the obvious problems of urban sewers and chemical plants, regulators and activists still considered nitrate concentrations in many rivers to be "too high," and most of it came from nonpoint sources. The EPA looked for sources of nonpoint nitrates and easily found them: runoff from fertilized farms, high concentrations of animals (such as feedlots and chicken ranches), and human waste from cesspools and failed septic systems. These were obviously anthropogenic sources of nitrate production, but they weren't point sources of nitrate pollution because they had no single location from which the effluent is discharged into the river.

In 1987, Congress passed new law intended to bypass the thorny culpability problems and unproductive legal difficulties associated with specification, compliance, and punishment of nonpoint source pollution. It was a voluntary grant and incentive program to help people control and reduce the introduction of nitrate: Section 319 of the Clean Water Act. The States set about working with horse ranches, farms, and the like to reduce these large sources of nonpoint nitrates. The only problem with voluntary programs is that they are, well, voluntary. Who has a problem with that?

The assumption is that, if human activity adds nitrate to a riparian system over and above what is "Natural" then it must be a bad thing. Nature complicates that idea because there is no way to know what pre-historic nitrate concentrations were. Humans have a difficult time getting accurate estimates on an everyday basis, even now.

When we measure nitrate in a river, what we are observing is a snapshot in time of a dynamic process in but one part of a continuous reactor processing nitrogen in the riparian habitat. Sampling nitrogen concentration is fraught with error. River flows are usually turbulent unless the water is slow and deep. Mixing efficiency can vary significantly, especially during summer. There are often pockets and pools of stagnant water. Upstream disturbances such as fish thrashing near the bottom (charmingly referred to as, 'bioturbating') can disturb the detritus layer of rotting organic matter on the bottom of a creek and release clouds of nitrates. Depending upon the size and nature of the flow profile, samples of background nitrates can vary within minutes from a compliant state to one that wildly exceeds control limits. The way to reduce the magnitude of error is to increase the number of samples. To get an accurate picture of the actual nitrate cycle within a stream takes hundreds of measurements over many years.

When the Clean Water Act was adopted in 1972, nitrate measurements in the San Lorenzo River had been recorded only semiannually for twenty years. The measured values had remained at or below 1ppm (part per million). Peak values had been much higher (Please see Chart 15, next page). Soon after construction of the University, water consumption rose with increasing urban population and infrastructure demands. By the early 1990s, average summer nitrate concentrations had approximately doubled to 2.25ppm with spikes up to nearly 8ppm. The average 2.25ppm value was only 5% of the maximum allowed for drinking water, but the people of the City of Santa Cruz started complaining about the taste. The State ordered the County to do something or new development would be severely curtailed, something unacceptable to County politicians and bureaucrats on an insatiable diet of property taxes.

The likely cause was a combination of increased rural nitrate production from population growth (horse corrals, golf courses, rotting septic tanks, and failing drain-fields) and reduced outgoing water flow due to urban consumption. There are two ways to reduce nitrate concentrations but only one of them allows more development. One can either cut rural nitrate production, or curtail urban water demand and treat it for taste. Guess which one wins?

At the behest of the State of California, the County of Santa Cruz produced the San Lorenzo River Basin Plan in 1979. While the State of California was willing to see the County meet 2.25ppm total nitrate, our conscientious public servants and environmentalists wanted really clean water "for everybody" and set the nitrate attainment less than one eighth of the State specification,

0.25ppm. The problem was that they couldn't measure it. The reporting instruments of the day were only capable of a detection limit of 0.2ppm with an error nearly as high. (Please see Chart 15.) As late as 1977, multiple test samples (10 or more) taken the same day at the Big Trees station on two separate occasions gyrated from 1.8– 5.8ppm and from 2.7 to 7.1ppm. The variation among nitrate measurements exceeded the target for attainment!

Even more incredible: Early season rainfall measurements report approximately 0.7ppm of dissolved nitrate. That's right, rainwater flunked the 0.25ppm attainment spec by a factor of three times.

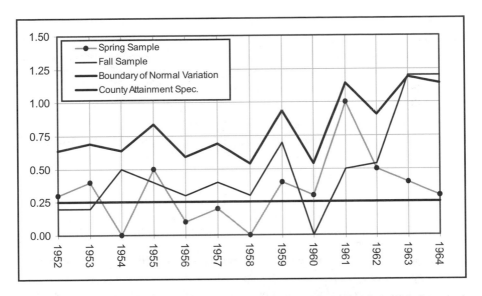

Chart 15 – Nitrate Sample Values Taken at Big Trees Station #31 (in ppm). *Note that the specification limit is lower than the baseline average. Given that rainwater is occasionally 0.7ppm, the arithmetic average plus 2 standard deviation values labeled "Boundary of Normal Variation" would have been a better control limit.*

So why did they set the spec so low? Can the San Lorenzo River deliver 0.25ppm dissolved nitrate? Yes, it can and occasionally does, almost as easily as it fails. Riparian ecosystems cycle nitrates just as they do water and carbon. The vegetation along the banks consumes nitrates as fertilizer on a seasonal basis. The algae that feed the bugs that feed the fish feed on nitrates. The higher-order consumers excrete it back into the system.

The data used to set the nitrate specification in 1979 were from the early 1950s, before the major post-war increase in permanent residency within Santa Cruz County. There were but two samples per year taken at that time and one should rightly doubt the measurement accuracy of the day. Peak values usually occur during late summer and in the wash of early fall rains. The true baseline average may well have been higher than 0.25ppm, even in the 50s. Without accounting for sampling or instrument error, the average measured nitrate concentration, at the very station from which the specification was derived before significant development, was still higher than the attainment specification. Worse, the data from the same 1979 Watershed Plan indicate that the average nitrate values coming into the San Lorenzo from tributaries were more than double the attainment specification. The Waterman Gap Station reported nitrate measurements that naturally varied up to 1.8ppm in 1963, well before any development in that area.

Average background nitrate values vary by location, stage of succession, soil type, and maturity of the forest. As the forest matures, the increase in fungal activity and the decrease in arboreal growth rates may produce higher levels of background nitrates in streams. The forest in the San Lorenzo Valley was not logged so long ago that fungal activity would yield substantial nitrate compared to old growth. It is not so simple a situation that we can say that we know what the "proper" level of nitrate should be at any one point along the river at any given time of year, much less pick a single number for the entire system over multiple years. There is reason to suspect that the desired specification limits are too low to support many desirable aquatic species.

Why then, did the County want nitrate numbers to be so low? Was it just earnest good intentions? An unattainable specification did produce a burgeoning and powerful bureaucracy with a constituency of consultants.

The idea of such a low goal was to set an attainment value that could only be met with a sewer system and treatment plant. A sewer is a perfect way with which to coerce a community and control who must go and who gets to stay while pleasing the construction unions who get to build it. The proposed cost of each sewer hookup was a mere $40,000 per household.

What emerges from these disturbing facts is an archetypal example of why it is dangerous to put the power to set attainment specifications in the hands of an enforcing authority (which was the reason for the Separation of Powers). It also demonstrates why to do so is so dysfunctional as a control variable for the management of a riparian ecosystem. The temptation to use the data as a source of power can override the concern for riparian health. Such a focus is easily explained away by the belief that lower is better, rather than seeking to learn what is optimal.

The sewer wouldn't have fixed the nitrate problem. The San Lorenzo Valley is an awful place to try to build a sewer system. The houses are spread out over considerable distances through heavily rooted forests, way out at the end of a tortuous network of crumbling logging roads. The place is a construction nightmare of converted weekend cabins, with undocumented pipes and wires going all over the place. The valley walls are very steep; rising nearly 800 feet in less than a third of a mile. If there had been a blockage in the piping system, it would have had to be capable of withstanding considerable hydrostatic pressure and shock if such a blockage suddenly released. (People put all sorts of weird stuff down toilets in Santa Cruz County, and sometimes in a big hurry.) Then there are earthquakes. One could reasonably expect broken pipes on a regular basis. Just the act of installing the sewer pipes would have caused many such failures due to severed water mains and tree roots. The resulting nitrate and coliform bacteria pollution from sewer accidents might well have been higher and more destructive than without it.

There was public outcry. The developers led the fight and the voters said NO! There wasn't much the County could do about it, because the nitrate in the San Lorenzo Watershed came from nonpoint sources: cesspools, detritus, and septic systems. The goal was unattainable, even with the sewer.

As the 90s progressed, nitrate measurements became more accurate and more frequent. The information database was growing into an even more confusing picture. Background nitrate levels of water coming into the river valley from the (still) undeveloped Waterman Gap area have seen occasional spikes up to 3ppm, twelve times the allowable limit. Why? Does this indicate a change in background levels, an improvement in measurement, or something else?

No one knows. The forest is maturing with more rotting vegetation, but there might be an another cause, having nothing to do with normal human activity. French Broom is a legume. So is acacia, another pest plant, common in the area. The root nodules of legumes process nitrogen from air into nitrates. Both grow fast don't live long, releasing that nitrate as they rot. There are thousands of tons of rotting legumes displacing native, nitrogen-consuming vegetation. Broom is especially thick in drainage ditches. The County spreads it with their mowing and ditch-cleaning equipment, and illegally side-casts the ditch-cleanings over the outside edges of roads. Neither the State nor the County had considered broom as an anthropogenic source of nonpoint nitrate in any pollution model. The yearly spikes in nitrate values from Waterman Gap are in the least likely month for nitrate from decomposition products or low water flow: March. Is it pollen? Nobody knows.

Well, however difficult "impossible" may be, the County was under orders from the State to do whatever was necessary to control its nonpoint sources and to attain its unattainable 0.25ppm attainment spec, per its State-approved Watershed Management Plan. Given that the main source of human nitrates was septic systems in the San Lorenzo Valley, the most obvious step was to make certain existing systems were up to current specifications and operating correctly. If they weren't, they had to be fixed. No guarantees.

The Board of Supervisors courageously responded by passing the new $186 per household annual inspection property tax… er FEE, to pay for pretty white pickup trucks, pagers, cell phones, and marginally literate inspectors to violate everybody's private property rights by entering any time they wished (the "Septic Police"). Even though the southern forks of the river had not been listed for nitrate impairment, the plan included the entire San Lorenzo. When they started the inspections and notices of non-compliance on Records of Title at the slightest transgression, the cry went up throughout the land. When the contractors ran into the new regulatory buzz saw associated with the new septic system specifications, they effectively went on strike.

The Supervisors were taken aback. They needed to retrench. Strangely, they hadn't told the citizens that the voluntary 319 grant money was already available to help them out, until there were public protests. Once there was a crisis they went looking for money, found the grants, and got to look compassionate by handing it out!

The Board called for public meetings and the results we have discussed in Part IV. They decided to form a committee to "study the problem" and make "consensus" recommendations to the Board. It was the Septic Technical Advisory Committee (Septic–TAC). It sounds ominous for Santa Cruz, but this doesn't affect you, right? Wrongo!

A Pointless Exercise

Two regulatory actions were initiated in the late 1990s, to "force" the EPA to enforce nonpoint nitrate TMDL. One was a debris flow of Natural Resources Defense Council (NRDC) lawsuits against the EPA in 1997. The other, in 1998, was an administrative order from the office of Vice-President Al Gore: the Clean Water Action Plan (CWAP, one of the most tempting acronyms in history). Both of these initiatives demanded that the EPA ignore section 305 and start enforcing the 303(d) TMDL provisions, with or without a way to measure nonpoint nitrates. Water bodies would no longer be listed by pollution measurements. Instead, the decision to declare "nitrate impairment" would now be based upon the "professional judgement" of any nominating bureaucrat. Such a listing can induce millions of dollars in remedial action.

The EPA agreed to settle the NRDC lawsuits by consent decree, each with a deadline for compliance. Does the NRDC really have a legitimate claim to represent the public to dictate the use of private property? How did a Federal Judge arrive at an interpretation of the law that exceeded the limits of Section 303(d) and contravened the purpose of Sections 305 and 319? The severe problems with nitrate levels were obvious. Many of the easier solutions were in the process of implementation. So just what is it that the NRDC wanted the EPA to accomplish?

The NRDC and the EPA wanted to enforce the TMDL on nonpoint sources because the only control mechanics available for enforcement of a nonpoint pollution standard are through civic control of the use of land. They couldn't care less that TMDL, as a concept, was technically inapplicable to nonpoint sources.

The EPA turned to the State and, well, we all know what goes downhill. If the State did not comply, the Feds threatened to take over administration of the watersheds and place harsh restrictions on development. If the County did not comply, the State threatened to take over administration of the watersheds and place harsh restrictions on development.

Thirteen States sued the EPA for unlawfully entering the consent decree. Other states, with more activist bureaucracies addicted to Federal grant money joined into the "collaborative" effort with the EPA, including the State of California. To comply with the consent decree, the State needed a precedent from two complicit local jurisdictions to open the legal door to further nonpoint TMDL regulatory actions, statewide. One of those two was the Department of Environmental Health of the County of Santa Cruz.

So, what do the State of California and the County of Santa Cruz propose to do in the San Lorenzo Valley to institute a nonpoint nitrate TMDL? They are using the "opportunity" presented by the NRDC lawsuit and the resulting EPA mandate to "relieve" the County of its unattainable attainment value of 0.25ppm. They are generously substituting a more lenient sounding, but even more logically preposterous and subjectively pernicious TMDL specification, for total nitrate concentration, regardless of background levels.

Nonpoint pollution can't be measured in terms of "daily load." The estimate of the target loading from an array of septic systems all over the slopes of a valley with variable geology is derived from an oversimplified (and admittedly inaccurate) USGS computer model. EPA will allow the adoption of a new spec that is not much better than a guess, as long as the people accept the inclusion of the words "nonpoint TMDL" in the new rules.

As an example of real creativity, the County intends to continue to measure downstream nitrate concentrations and river flow rate on a weekly basis. Then they will back-calculate the Total Maximum Daily Load as a weekly sample average. A weekly sample average TMDL is an oxymoron. It might be a reasonable thing to do, but it just doesn't have anything to do with the Section 303(d) definition of a TMDL, or the terms of the NRDC/EPA consent decree, but then, it is impossible to rigorously comply with a TMDL for nonpoint nitrate pollution anyway.

Undeterred by reality, State and County officials met, with the ostensible goal of not being held in contempt of the consent decree by the NRDC. The County agreed to reduce average level of nitrates by 30%, by demanding that everybody in the County reduce their nitrate output by 50%, this after several years of near insurrection in the Valley over existing rules. They have a target attainment date of… 2045. Is it really that tough?

According to County estimates, they can get a 10% reduction with a single project, the Boulder Creek Country Club. They'll get another 9% by merely waiting for the nitrate plume from Scotts Valley to dissipate, now that that city has a new sewage treatment plant. If they throw in some high tech septic systems in the Newell Creek area where the soils near the river are coarse sand, they would another major chunk, estimated at another 10%. That is nearly 30% right off the top.

The State has instituted a brand new septic system design: one that everybody in the Valley has to buy if the Septic Police, or the guy in the pump truck, say they "need" an upgrade. The system still has no guarantee and there is no responsible party to manage it. The County of Santa Cruz now wants every household that installs or upgrades a septic system, to purchase a product that costs upwards $30,000 to install and requires electrical power to operate. The design does have the one more important feature though: a sample inspection port. A septic system is now a point source. The Septic Police will test it for you. The State doesn't even call it monitoring or inspection any more; it is "Surveillance" now, including helicopters.

Nobody wants raw sewage running down the streets. Is the problem that bad?

In their year 2000 plan, the County relied exclusively upon statements from the 1979 San Lorenzo River Basin Plan in order to maintain justification for a status of "Threatened Impairment." The only criteria in the 1979 Plan that justified the finding of impairment, was the taste of urban water. Recall that that suburban residents will have to pay the $1,000 to $2,000 per year for new septic systems because of the river that has been designated as an "impaired watershed" because of the taste. Meanwhile, it would cost each urban water user $1 per year to treat the water for taste.

Why don't they treat the water for taste, do the easy 30% reduction first, and see if it's good enough? Is it really necessary for the residents to fork over $2,000 after-tax dollars every year to save the environment?

It is completely unnecessary. According to the County data in the State report detailing the TMDL targets, the average nitrate concentration in the most recent five years on their graph was approximately 2.3ppm. That means once we have implemented this plan over the next 45 years we should see an average nitrate value of 1.6ppm. Strangely, the average value for the period after 1995 does not appear in the State report adopted in the year 2000, even though the current data are plotted on a graph therein AND there is an apparent declining trend on the tail end of the graph. Is there a reason?

The average nitrate concentration at the Big Trees Station in Felton has been 1.6ppm since 1997. The current test data indicate that the river water quality has already met the 30% reduction requirement. If they want the remaining reductions to meet the 50% reduction target, they can get the rest of it by doing the Country Club project and waiting five years for the Scotts Valley nitrate plume to dissipate.

Huzzah! We're done! That is, unless they are thinking about building a lot more urban residential units, using a lot more water, and keeping the bureaucrats in charge until they retire. The real problems with the numbers remain: Natural levels of nitrate, coming into the inhabited areas, as documented in the report that proposes the new spec, still occasionally reach 3ppm. The measured average background nitrate levels are now to exceed the proposed downstream TMDL target values by a mere factor of two. Such a deal.

Are the nitrate levels a problem for fish? No. Is it a problem for tourists and outdoor enthusiasts? No. Are the rocks slimy with algae? There are a few pockets in the lower river during a dry summer, but even during the drought of 1979 there was no eutrophication, although there were fish drying in mud puddles. Is the nitrate situation getting worse? No. Measured values indicate a decline in nitrate concentrations. Can we treat the water for odor? It's cheap, and given that the State's report says that there were no complaints about odor when the nitrate levels in the water were the same as they are now, even odor treatment may be completely unnecessary.

The plan is unnecessary, hugely costly, discriminatory, possibly destructive to fish, and illegally justified in the first place. So why are we doing it?

On the Environmental Impact Checklist for the Declaration of Negative Impact, required for all State Projects under the California Environmental Quality Act, the State bureaucrats declared that it will be OK to continue with needed future **growth in population** without any mention of water consumption, housing, or automobile traffic. Then the staff director from the State signs it, certifying under penalty of perjury that the forgoing is all true and correct... to the best of his knowledge.

From the State Water Quality Control Board Staff Report:

> "This alternative (Postponing the adoption of TMDL – ed.) is not recommended because this Regional Branch is committed to completing this TMDL by May 2000. The U.S. Environmental Protection Agency mandated each Regional Board to complete two TMDLs by May 2000. Postponement will increase the likelihood of litigation for failure to complete the TMDL in a timely manner."

Maybe some cynical author could say it in clearer terms: 'We are going to do it because the NRDC wants us to do it in order to get their nonpoint TMDL precedents established "on time." We can get funding for the project, get this 0.25ppm monkey off our backs, and keep running our profitable bureaucracy until 2045, well after we all retire on full pensions. Meanwhile, development will continue to go on and on and all the bosses will be happy. We'll keep failing that worst-case spec because we can say whatever we want to call it "threatened impairment," and keep busy putting the screws to an ignorant and powerless public, making them buy our outrageously expensive, unwarranted systems, and pay huge fees to our Planning Department. They should stop making so much pollution or move back into town and pay the hefty rents. The people are too stupid to do anything about it. Don't blame us, we are only doing what we were told.'

The new septic system design also provides one other important benefit. It requires a smaller drain field. Gosh, after twenty-five years (and over 200 pages) of holding the bag, those 20 undersized parcels inside of town that were "worth-less" could be suddenly worth LOTS. Interestingly, while the February 7 TMDL report required one-acre minimums in the San Lorenzo Valley in order to protect the environment, by February 9 that requirement had mysteriously disappeared. And what a coincidence that the lead the County representative on the Septic Technical Advisory Committee (Septic–TAC) had discreetly recommended rezoning reduced acreage minimums to 6,000 square feet in 16 select locations in the San Lorenzo Valley (as a way to reduce sprawl, of course). It flew through the Planning Department...

It's a consensus!

No, it was the payoff, and don't you know but it was an election year!

Brer Rabbit now has his very own 501(c3) charitable NGO dedicated to the restriction of urban sprawl and the establishment of social justice in housing (read subsidized housing and rent control for the Gen-Xers and families of migrant farm-workers). The Squeeze is on.

They are instituting the nonpoint TMDL so that the NRDC doesn't sue, even though it will do little to reduce the most significant cause of summer watershed degradation: urban water consumption. Nobody in the bureaucracy cares that the water coming INTO the river basin from an undisturbed source still fails the new TMDL standards. Were the TMDL spec to be set high enough to accommodate natural variation, it would accomplish nothing in the manner of a coercive regulatory instrument. The plan might be more reasonable with a more rational standard, but the manner in which it is to be managed will never be TMDL-compliant.

Never? Perhaps the 2045 date is an indication of their confidence that the plan will produce a river that meets the attainment standards once they build all those new houses. Nobody, including the NRDC or the EPA, seems to care about that and NOBODY is seriously talking about reducing *urban* water consumption in Santa Cruz. Why not?

The NRDC got the precedent they wanted: compliance to a TMDL from a nonpoint source. All of the actors in the game know that the TMDL rule doesn't work. They just use it as a handy lever to get the improvements "they need." The politicians want a way to open the public wallet and please Brer Rabbit. The bureaucrats want the politicians off their backs. It will keep the State and the Feds involved forever. The NRDC can sue later when the TMDL can't be met daily. When the public screams in shock and betrayal, the civil servants can shrug their shoulders, parsing words about how Brer Fox flung them into the briar patch, too.

Even if the ecosystem already does comply with the law, the situation is just too complicated for a monopoly, specification-based civic control system to deliver upon its purported goal. No, not nitrate concentrations, A HEALTHY RIVER. The coercive regulatory ethic is too destructive of fiscal and human capital to solve real problems (like Cape ivy choking the whole valley). Its managers and constituents have too many interests not to manipulate the system to their liking, and every interest in making certain that the river remains in non-attainment. The full range of control variables (such as urban water consumption) remains ignored, but just wait until they go after that one. They want water meters on rural wells, even though the attached septic system returns the water to the aquifer in situ!

Civic regulation is a management system that can't work, either for people or for the Environment. There are better ways to improve BOTH drinking water quality AND riparian habitat for salmonid species:

- Cut urban water consumption with a real water market, based upon the cost of environmental risks associated with high consumption rates.

- Institute insured, best practice septic installations among the contractors and assist with the organization of a competitive market in private operating and management utilities.

- Reduce the release of nitrates from fires, release more late-season water flow, truck sequestered nitrate out of the forest, and assist nitrate-consuming ground vegetation instead of shading all that rotting duff infested with nitrate-producing French Broom, improve streambed spawning conditions, reduce the conversion of productive forest into water-consuming and nitrate-producing houses requiring more polluting automobiles, ALL by introducing a program of insured, certified timber harvesting in the rural/suburban forest.

Instead, the EPA will replicate the nitrate TMDL through the remaining states like wildfire and off goes the NRDC to expand the scope of their newly established nonpoint TMDL precedent.

What now?

It is fairly obvious that the NRDC lawsuit was not the first that the EPA had heard about enforcing 303(d) TMDL on nonpoint sources. Both litigants are members of the same multilateral organization, the International Union for the Conservation of Nature and Natural Resources (IUCN). In this case, both litigants have a confidential, offshore venue at which to conclude the settlement in advance, and get a free vacation in the deal. The litigants can walk into the Federal Court and tell the judge that they'll settle. The judge looks at the backlog and down comes the gavel. It's a done deal: The litigants can enter into a consent decree with a time limit for implementation upon which they alone agree. They can even have the press releases written in advance.

It's called a sweetheart suit.

There are dozens of Federal Courts in the Western United States. No one could possibly monitor all of these lawsuits sufficiently to find out about the suit, notify the affected property owners, gather data capable of refuting the claims, and organize a response quickly enough to block the consent decree. No one is there with the preparation and aura of credibility to refute the legitimacy of the claims or contest their jurisdictional authority to institute and enforce the nonpoint TMDL.

Now, what was the point of all this? Why should the NRDC and the EPA think the nonpoint nitrate TMDL in the San Lorenzo River Watershed is such a big deal? It's gonna take a little while for this one to sink in.

Mud.

Wherever there is dirt and water, there is mud. Whenever you mix mud and water, you get suspended silt. Mud is a nonpoint source of silt. Silt is found everywhere there is dirt, which is everywhere. If you want to control the use of dirt, just call it a pollutant! It isn't clean water any more, it's dirty. People don't want dirty water. They want clean water. Just ask them.

To determine culpability for a source of silt is even harder than for nitrate. Nonpoint mud is a much harder sell for an initial action in nonpoint pollution enforcement than human feces. Natural causes of silt in the County of Santa Cruz vastly outweigh human contributions. Sources of silt vary by location and degree every year. To assign individual causes is highly subjective…

The State Water Resources Control Board employs five specialists assigned to institute nonpoint TMDL standards in the Central Coast Region. At the time of this writing, one third of the TMDL documents on their web site deal with the San Lorenzo River Watershed. Why are they focusing upon such a small community as the San Lorenzo Valley, in a County with timber practices touted as some of the finest in the world?

Santa Cruz County is a perfect test environment for enforcement of TMDL upon sources of nonpoint silt. It is one of the few places in the world with both nonpoint nitrate problems from urban and agricultural sources and silt problems involving a rural/suburban forest, coho salmon, and timber harvesting. It also has an entrenched activist bureaucracy, a thoroughly proven political machine, and a university activist community with which to supply the "experts" to make it all happen.

Sub-Specious Arguments

Let's continue that murky case about nonpoint silt. Our example will focus on the listing of steelhead trout as Threatened under the ESA in the Central Coast region, as regards Waddell Creek in the County of Santa Cruz. This is a story where all the technical, legal, and philosophical factors discussed in this book come together. This is an instance where the level of integrity in public service and the actions of a set of so-called "charitable trusts" are so despicable as to be beneath rationalization.

Immediately after President Clinton took office, various NGOs initiated attempts to list steelhead along with the coho salmon as Endangered under the ESA. Previous petitions, submitted to either the California Department of Fish and Game (CDFG) or the National Marine Fisheries Service (NMFS), had been denied on two grounds: (1) trout were in sufficient numbers to assure survival; and (2) no genetically distinct population, or Evolutionarily Significant Unit (ESU) had been identified.

The ESU is a designation by which EPA had extended the concept of species to "sub-species," without legislative authorization. For a population to be defined as an ESU, it must meet two measurable requirements: It must be (1) locally isolated, and (2) genetically distinct (the third requirement is so subjective that it always qualifies, that the variant is necessary to species survival). The justification for the idea of listing ESUs is that each species needs genetic variability within its numbers, whether to adapt to external changes or to maintain distinctions appropriate to specific local conditions. It may be a good idea in some cases, but it is easy to abuse and wasn't authorized by the ESA. In the case of anadromous salmonids, the significance of genetic distinctions has been called into question. Studies of fish colonizing new rivers created by glacial retreat in Alaska, indicate that salmonids genetically differentiate rapidly, possibly making such distinctions as exist ephemeral differences. On the other hand, without the concept of a genetically distinct local population, there could be no justification to list either coho or steelhead as Threatened under the ESA because there are millions of them. NMFS effectively set about making certain that requirements for listing the fish were met. They shut down hatcheries, using the claim that they were producing genetically inferior fish. They ignored compelling evidence that the problems with hatcheries were more due to poor management than an inherently destructive process. Then they started funding the genetic studies with which to identify variations that could be labeled as locally distinct.

NMFS allocated funds to study DNA and then (when DNA didn't give them many distinctions) mitochondrial DNA (mtDNA). They published a massive report in August 1996, the *NOAA Technical Memorandum NMFS-NWFSC-27 Status Review of West Coast Steelhead from Washington, Idaho, Oregon, and California*. The NMFS Biological Review Team compiled the genetic data and mapped it by "genetic distance." There were neither data proving the linkage between the genetic distinctions and the fit to the habitat, nor did they demonstrate that the measured differences indicated a distinct native population. This is analogous to saying: 'Although we do not know the genetic reason why some people in Norway have dark hair, if they are in one place then that difference must represent critical genetic diversity particularly suited to that location.'

Does NMFS know how distinct an ESU has to be to qualify as such? No. Do they know which genetic distinctions are important or how the respective genetic variations of specific alleles manifest themselves? No. The way the boundaries were drawn, NMFS had to have ignored the genetic data anyway.

In the document designating Critical Habitat for the Central Coast Steelhead ESU, NMFS separated nearly identical fish emigrating to Monterey Bay into two separate ESUs: Fish from the northern part of Monterey Bay were in an ESU including the North Coast, and San Francisco Bay, while fish from the Southern edge of Monterey Bay were combined with those of Santa Barbara County. The ESU boundaries were also in diametric conflict with the EPA's vaunted watershed management schemes. The San Lorenzo River, which empties into Monterey Bay, is lumped into the same ESU with estuarine habitat inside San Francisco Bay, which has more in common hydrologically with the Sacramento San Joaquin Delta.

Politically, however, the ESU boundaries make total sense. The removal of the designation of Critical Habitat for the San Lorenzo River, emptying into Monterey Bay is now dependent upon the restoration of urban watersheds inside San Francisco Bay.

There was simply no scientifically compelling evidence supporting the designated boundaries of the Central Coast ESU. What was it that bound these together? Administrative turf? Budgetary considerations? Political and legal leverage? It wasn't genetics!

Was the linkage of steelhead populations between the San Lorenzo River and the San Francisco Bay Delta system a uniquely complex situation and not indicative of a pattern of administrative behavior? The Central Coast coho salmon was designated an Endangered ESU, even though there is both historical and analytical proof that it is not a genetically distinct population.

The entire Central Coast was designated as Critical Habitat for coho, even though it is at least a poorly adapted species for that type of habitat, if not altogether non-native. (See Part IV, Chapter 3.)

Once the ESU boundaries had been drawn, they constituted specific legal units against which to levy demand for protection. Immediately after the boundaries had been defined, a coalition of NGOs and front-groups filed a petition demanding that NMFS institute a package of regulations protecting critical habitat for steelhead under the 4(d) Rule of the ESA.

Applying the 4(d) Rule requires regulatory actions necessary to prevent a "take" of a Threatened or Endangered species, whether directly (by killing them) or indirectly (loss or degradation of habitat). Habitat degradation is loosely defined as anything that might be harmful. NMFS had one year from the petition filing date to respond with a plan, or be subject to a lawsuit.

So what did NMFS do? They did ban **killing** the fish, didn't they? No, they did not stop commercial or sport fishing. They did nothing significant about pinniped predation. They did nothing about encroaching development.

So what did they do, instead? They focused on timber practices. Do timber practices degrade habitat? It depends upon how they are done; they can be beneficial to fish. Can rules prevent all harm? No. Ban the logging and you get a negligent mess and eventual catastrophic fire. Regulate it and people cheat or sell. On the other hand, regulating timber practices does provide NMFS the opportunity to control the use of dirt.

The Fox in the Hen House

Over the years preceding the 1996 Status Review, NMFS had accepted population data from various "stakeholders." A stakeholder is another way of saying, 'anybody who can lay claim upon a use of private property besides the owner.' Among the petitions citing population decline was a letter from a member of the "Steelhead Listing Project," Mr. Todd Schuman. Mr. Schuman is a known operative for Earth First! He was a "tree sitter" in the Butano Forest in San Mateo County, on Big Creek Lumber property. Mr. Schuman cited, as evidence of population decline, a census of adult fish by the County Forester and Senior Resource Planner of the Watershed Management Program and the Forest Management Program, Dave Hope.

The letter states that Mr. Hope had provided, "stream-by-stream estimates of returning numbers of wild steelhead trout" from, "numerous ongoing conversations with local fishermen, fisherwomen, and residents of the County who live nearby streams used by steelhead trout." Both Dave and the fisher-humans agreed that the fish had been in decline over the previous ten years and provided detailed numerical estimates. These counts made no distinction between instream bred non-native fish or hatchery fish that colonized since the river died in the 19th Century. Though fisherpeople are a renowned source of quantitative data of unquestionable veracity, don't they only know about the number of fish they catch?

The Endangered Species Act calls for, "the best scientific and commercial data available." For several years, neither the California Department of Fish and Game (CDFG) nor NMFS would accept Mr. Hope's anecdotal surveys as compelling evidence of Threatened status for either coho or steelhead.

There were other sources of fish population data, but they were somehow never cited in the Status Report. The NMFS Portland Station Bureau Chief and BRT facilitator, Mr. Garth Griffin, had been contacted several times by one of the local landowners whose family had lived along Waddell Creek for nearly a hundred years, Mr. Robert O. Briggs.

The family's ranch includes several hundred acres of forestland on the upper part of the Waddell Valley and several fields of organic vegetables in the lower floodplain. The entire Waddell Valley had been clearcut and burned over during the late 1800s and early 1900s. The land was acquired by Theodore Hoover in 1913 and remains in his family's ownership. The land has been restored to an aesthetically attractive, biologically diversified, productive tree farm. Most of the timberland has been selectively harvested three to five times by Big Creek Lumber. Each harvest has improved the stand by removing diseased and overcrowded trees and leaving room and sunlight for the young, healthy specimens. Although this forest is new since 1913, people unfamiliar with forestry, when seeing this land, have trouble believing it is not an untouched, virgin forest.

Bob is a retired scientist, having taught at MIT. He founded and managed a successful oceanographic instrumentation company and published numerous scientific papers in aeronautical research, oceanography, and hydrology. He has continued the Hoover family tradition of research into the Waddell Valley's forestry, biology and hydrology.

It was on Waddell Creek that Shapovalov and Taft had tagged both salmon and steelhead and followed the movements of the fish over a period of ten years (the study was published in 1954). It was a massive effort, in part sponsored by the landowner, and one of the best works of its kind anywhere on the entire Pacific Coast, to this day. The study is still regarded as the authoritative reference work for this area and is cited as such by the NMFS 1996 Status Review. It was the kind of scientific work done when objective, government-sponsored science was welcome on private land. Citizens and civil servant scientists once worked together to improve our total knowledge of nature and the total quality of habitat. Those days are long gone.

Bob has made quite a hobby as a part-time hydrologist and amateur fish biologist. His knowledge is extensive and his standards of documentation are impeccable. Bob will go where the data takes him, even if he doesn't like it, because he is an objective scientist. Bob is an archetype of the kind of stewardship advocated in this book, and you will soon see why.

Mr. Briggs was aware that Mr. Griffin had received, as scientific evidence, a collection of written opinions by local fisheries biologists and a Watershed Planning Analyst responsible for the San Lorenzo Water District. These letters, with data based upon actual counts by technically qualified personnel familiar with local rivers, clearly stated that both beginning and ending population estimates, as cited by both Mr. Schuman's letter and the California Department of Fish and Game, were wildly distorted. At least four independent scientists and local fish advocates (one of whom is a member of the Sierra Club and various local anti-logging groups) had provided letters testifying that **the fish were in no way declining in population**. The letters stated that if anything; average counts had been increasing steadily for over 15 years. This was despite spawning and rearing setbacks due to periods of both flood and drought, and predation of adults by both sport fishing and documented pinniped overpopulation as protected by NMFS. You can't ask for more from a local river system in this area without doing something about predation of adult fish, human or otherwise.

The biologists' census data relied upon actual counts of juvenile trout, subsequent to successful spawning and rearing. These people study fish in local streams. The methods they use are a better indication of instream health and average population than any other non-invasive, single-point assessment. It is the same method used by CDFG on their stream assessments.

Bob contacted some of the BRT members to get their impressions on the input and to see if they needed any more data. At that time, he still had faith in the compelling nature of facts.

What facts? The BRT members had never seen the letters. Mr. Briggs again sent copies of the letters to the BRT through Mr. Griffin. No luck. Bob then sent copies to each of the sitting members of the BRT, to no avail.

When questioned about his survey, Mr. Hope indicated that there had once been "thousands and thousands" of fish, many years ago. The initial date of his study came but a few years after the hatcheries in Scotts Valley and on Newell Creek had closed but his case was worse than that. By 1865, the San Lorenzo River was virtually dead from pollution. Indigenous migrating steelhead did not exist. After the construction of at least three hatcheries to restore the fishery, there had indeed been thousands of fish for over a hundred years. The claim that there even was such a thing as a purely "wild trout" or genetically distinct population in the San Lorenzo River Watershed was suspect, though perhaps there were a few in the Pajaro River and some of the more remote Coastal Creeks that could have colonized the San Lorenzo in later years.

Estimates of carrying capacity, based upon anecdotal observations from the 19th Century are subject to gross errors. During the "bounteous" period to which Mr. Hope referred, virtually all indigenous fish predators, such as grizzly bears and pinnipeds, had been exterminated as pests. Shooting seals was a sport. Shooting grizzly bears was a matter of public safety. Commercial fishing was far less efficient. In addition, during the first half of the 20th Century, sewer pipes into the ocean had been enriching the foundation of the marine food chain along the entire Pacific Coast with kilotons of nitrates and phosphates that can greatly increase salmon productivity. Even if there had been more fish under augmented conditions, the claim of recent steelhead population decline was still suspect. The juvenile steelhead counts were proof that either the claim of decline was false, or spawning and riparian rearing habitat were in such excellent health that fewer returning steelhead were producing more surviving smolts.

It didn't matter. NMFS had mandated that they would only consider counts of *adult* fish as evidence of a fish population census.

NMFS has no problem counting adult fish on the Columbia River where they have numerous hydroelectric dams with fish ladders that work beautifully for such a purpose. Many of the soils are granitic and the water much less turbid than on the San Lorenzo, thus the fish are more visible in the water.

The soils in Santa Cruz County are composed of siltstone, clay, and shale. The peak of the spawning run is during winter rains, when even completely undeveloped watersheds will have creeks boiling with sediment. When the adult fish are running, the rivers are opaque (which is why the fishercitizen data is open to question). For the Shapovalov and Taft study on Waddell Creek, there had been a specially engineered concrete weir to channel the fish. A flood blew it out in 1955 (thus ending any further study). Without such a work of engineering (or a very temporary fence arrangement that can be troublesome for the fish when it jams with floating debris), there is no accurate way to channel adult fish into a restricted, one-way path through which to count them.

The BRT presented its Status Review, relying nearly exclusively upon Mr. Schuman's letter because it was "the best scientific and commercial data available," according to them. It was upon this kind of data that NMFS listed the Central Coast ESU, combining it with urban regions of San Francisco Bay whose fisheries are so destroyed by earthen dams, urban development, and flood control projects (aka urban real estate subsidies) that they may never recover. Federal control would thus be permanent.

Here Comes de Judge!

During the year after the petition was filed, 'nothing happened'; at least nothing visible. Upon completion of the time limit, the coalition of NGO groups that had petitioned to list the fish sued NMFS for its "failure to respond." They demanded an "acceptable" package of regulations to protect the steelhead authorized under the 4(d) Rule of the ESA. NMFS appeared in Federal court, with the appearance of having dragged its heels and settled the suit under a consent decree. The order required that the agency submit a comprehensive "recovery plan," notify the public, allow them a reasonable period to collect data and compose a response, conduct public hearings, analyze the input, reach a consensus, and complete the plan encompassing the entire Pacific Coast, within… 90 days?

Aren't lawyers wonderful! All it takes to solve any technical problem in an expeditious manner is a court order (as if they could force wild salmon to thrive in the ocean). Nobody knows why steelhead are in trouble or can even prove if they really are. Few know what can be done to help the fish or even if we have that ability (other than stopping the commercial catch or shooting seals, which NMFS hasn't done). A technically incompetent Federal jurist is ill equipped to extract the truth out of a mountain of partisan disinformation.

The political appointees and the administrators at NMFS had every reason to put up only token resistance to such a suit. NMFS is a direct beneficiary of losing the lawsuit over the fish. If they settle the suit, NMFS can justify a bigger budget for personnel to inflect or control every public and private decision concerning every watershed, containing, or designated as "potentially capable" of containing, steelhead. This is of course everywhere on the entire Pacific Coast.

This says nothing of the interests of the plaintiffs. Who ARE these people?

Among the big shots is Zeke Grader, Executive Director of the Pacific Coast Federation of Fishermen's Associations, so it's no wonder NMFS does nothing about ocean fishing, is it? Zeke is a lawyer, operating out an office in the old Presidio in San Francisco adjacent to the World Forum where Mr. Gorbachev is ensconced. What is an ocean fishing lobbyist doing in such expensive digs?

Mr. Grader runs the Institute for Fisheries Resources chugging grant money from foundations such as the Pew Charitable Trusts (Sunoco, oil money). Mr. Grader and his compatriots have associations with major fishing organizations, worldwide.

The foot soldiers include the Center for Biological Diversity, another creature of foundation grant money and lawsuit revenue, dedicated to the restoration of "Wild America," particularly the reintroduction of the Mexican Wolf. Then there's the South Yuba River Citizen's League (with offices out of state), an affiliate of River Revival, a project of International Rivers Network, which heralds from that urban hotbed of capitalism: Berkeley, California. They are attempting to remove the dams that store and supply all urban drinking water, and eliminate all cattle grazing in the East Bay Hills. The Alameda Creek Alliance also operates out of Berkeley. These people want to get rid of dams, too. No dams, no gravity fed water, and no hydroelectricity means more dependence upon foreign oil and imported food.

Once there is a court order, NMFS has "no choice" but to invoke the 4(d) Rule, and of course, can't be held responsible for effective results. NMFS maintains that they aren't really attempting to gain control of the use of land, they claim that they were "forced" to take such odious action by a group of NGOs with very deep legal pockets, partially funded out of cash paid from similar, prior settlements. NMFS had insufficient funding to fight the lawsuit… **but they can have all the money in the world to administer the settlement because that funding is no longer discretionary**, Congress must pay for it under the consent decree. When confronted with the coalition lawsuit NMFS just rolls over on cue and calls upstairs for your money. Increased budgets, status, and authority of NMFS administrators render NMFS an interested party in any dispute over land use. Problems are assets.

Who gets attorney's fees in the settlement money? The NGOs do. What suffers? The public lands maintenance budget suffers. Who gets the grant money to do much of the "rehabilitation and restoration" work? The NGOs do. Who gets to report violations when they go on site, nominate rare plant communities for special protection, and harass private property owners by reporting violations? Both the agencies and the NGOs do. Who gets a bigger budget to administer and enforce the rules and regulations? The agencies do. Who gets the fine money with which to dole out more NGO grants, that generate more fines? The agencies do. Who gets to make political hay out of all those violations with which to solicit donations and votes? The NGOs and the politicians do. What suffers from lost fine money? Private land maintenance does. What do the landowners do? They sell it, cheap. Who buys it cheap? The agencies, NGOs, developers, and timber corporations large enough not to care buy it, cheap. Who is accountable for healthy salmonid populations? Who will love and care for it for generations after all that?

Sigh.

Mr. Griffin presided over local hearings to collect final "public input" and reach summary judgement. It was the public's only chance to state everything wrong with the listing, the recovery plan, and more important, the assumptions in the connection between the plan and its probability of success. One must have a written response, complete with literature citations and an estimate of the damages if there is potential adverse effect. That is a lot of information to put together in only 90 days. Bob Briggs had some of that data and knew how to find more.

At the hearing, NMFS allotted about two minutes per person to speak (and ten minutes per NGO representative). Two minutes is all Bob was allowed to speak for a lifetime of stewardship. As far as public testimony is concerned, there are several things one needs to say that are not representative of the legal case submitted in the written documents.

The administrator is not the audience, Mr. Griffin is there to collect the paper and fulfill the requirement for a public hearing. Use the two minutes as the public theater it is: to address reporters, activists, and other property owners with the truth. One must focus that anger on its true cause, the roomful of activists and lawyers who will likely be present. Point out the true purpose of the civic plan, and not only that it won't work, but that NMFS has no intent to make it work. Stress the ecological harm the plan will cause, and express it with righteous anger and disbelief. This is public education, identical in appearance to the sound-bites the Sierra Club gets on the Six O'clock News in every respect but one: It is coming from a real person who has worked the land, speaking from the heart, instead of a spin job by a slick lawyer. Bob has acquired the data over decades because that knowledge is in his tired hands and aching back because he nearly weeps with anger and frustration in that final moment of appalling injustice and stupidity. He KNOWS that what he is saying is the truth, and it will sound like it.

None of the public input really mattered in the short term, of course, NMFS had already caved in to the court order. That the County, CDFG, and NMFS were complicit in the threat to the fish within the watershed, through their streambed modifications and their artificially high Optimum Sustainable Population Level for sea lions, was immaterial.

The finding came down in 28 pages of fine print, a mere 36 hours after the hearing. In that time, our Federal civil servants had gone home to Seattle, analyzed the public input, integrated public recommendations into the Rule package and recovery plan, reached a consensus, compiled the plan, sent it through the approval loop, and published it in the Federal Register.

Wow! Do our bureaucrats really work with such efficiency and commitment that they can incorporate the input from all those local experts in such a short period of time? No. The document had been filed over a month prior to the hearing. They submitted it the next morning after the first cup of coffee.

The entire process: Its unnecessary speed, its flimsy justification, its enormous scope, its egregious lack of respect for technical data, and its laughable credibility, served no other purpose than to serve the interest of converting private forest into a socialized commons.

Secret Agent Man

It doesn't matter that steelhead populations have been increasing for over twenty years. It doesn't matter that the plaintiff fisherhumans are more interested in preventing constraint of their catch than anything else, or that they are allied with competing industrial interests. It doesn't mater if the nonpoint TMDL levels for nitrates will rob the fish of food. It doesn't matter if the primary sources of silt are natural or associated with residential development. It doesn't matter that the forest management scheme that will be advanced as a remedy will result in a catastrophic fire destructive to the fish. It doesn't matter that if the farm in the Waddell Creek area is shut down, it will end up infested with weeds, many of them toxic (notably hemlock and star thistle) and that proof exists of that on Packard Foundation property just down the road. It doesn't matter that one can see the difference in forest practices merely by looking at the dilapidated adjacent lands under State control. NMFS will dictate the regulation of the use of the land to the appropriate State and local authorities, regardless of the consequences. They will do so without ever asking the key question concerning the entire action:

Who is the superior agent, representing the public demand to care for forest and riparian habitat along Waddell Creek: NMFS, CDFG, BOF, CDF, State Parks, the Coastal Commission, USDA, CDA, the EPA, the County of Santa Cruz, or Robert O. Briggs?

Read that again.

Objective comparison, of the condition of the State Park across the Waddell Creek Valley versus Bob's forest above the ranch, answers that question. The condition of the Packard Foundation farmland just down Highway 1 versus Bob's farm along the creek answers that question. Bob is a better representative of the public interest in maintaining the best possible conditions for healthy forests and streams along Waddell Creek. He can do it at a profit, create jobs, and pay taxes, instead of demanding them and he can prove it. He is more knowledgeable than the horde of agencies and activists that are trying to take it. They should stop wasting everybody's time and money and let Bob do his best, simply because it is the best that can be done.

So how does Bob make that public choice unmistakably clear?

First, show that NMFS has no intention to save steelhead. NMFS' purpose for the 4(d) Rule Package is to control the use of land with which to accrue power to the bureaucracy. The actual protection of the threatened species will be a secondary priority of the program. Mechanisms and scenarios are easily identified in advance, by which the plan cannot work and adverse consequences are systemically inevitable.

That is just as it is in this case. Nothing is to be done to halt sport and commercial fishing. Nothing is planned that will control pinniped predation. NMFS demanded a halt to all timber activity along riparian corridors, and plans no action to prevent catastrophic fire. The larger trees will be verboten to touch, even if they increase erosion or induce landslides when they fall. They'll call that "recruitment of large woody debris" even if they aren't in the water. (If a landowner cut the tree, yanked the stump and placed it in the creek, it would be "pollution.") They will do nothing about the hundreds of acres of poisonous hemlock slowly infesting the entire region, propagating along the STATE highway.

How do you prove structural intent to fail on the part of NMFS and its local agents in State and local government?

There will likely be a record of such government behavior in the past with which to discredit the civic environmental management regime. An example is the case of politically supported over-fishing and pinnipeds. Another is the record of State hatchery management versus the Montcrey Bay Salmon and Trout Project. Another is found in the ways that regulation and zoning law have abetted development and the destructive effects of that use are obvious. Then there is the risk of catastrophic fire, followed by landslides and weeds, all of which are ignored in the Status Report as secondary consequences, consideration of which is required by NEPA (the National Environmental Protection Act) and CEQA (the California Environmental Quality Act).

Look elsewhere for more of the same type of behavior, as demonstration that civic propensities are systemic, and what do you find?

In Oregon, our government fish experts in the Oregon DFG are indiscriminately killing thousands of salmon by guillotining, electrocuting, and clubbing them to death with aluminum baseball bats. (It's really grizzly. Where is PETA on that one?) These included not only "hatchery fish," as planned, but also "native" fish, prohibited as "illegal take" under the ESA. They have refused to acknowledge the scientific evidence that the "native fish" are, after a hundred years of hatchery operations in the river, sufficiently cross-bred with "hatchery fish" to make any claim of unique genetic adaptation to a specific habitat a possibly fraudulent distinction. Many, if not most of the observable distinctions among "native fish" and "hatchery fish" are behavioral, habituated in but a few generations in situ, by yet unknown biochemical learning and knowledge transmission mechanisms. Meanwhile, terns and herons on artificial islands, built under direction by the government, consume hundreds of thousands of smolts every year. If the hatchery fish truly lacked the supposedly inbred skills to escape predation, they would not have survived in similar fractions to the native fish. Have the citations. Meanwhile, subsequent to the NMFS action, the only fish in the Columbia River for all those terns and herons to eat will be the few remaining progeny of these supposedly "native" fish. Will we have starving birds and decimated fish populations? Perhaps. Note CDFG's behavior is repeating the policy locally, dragging its heels with the Monterey Bay Salmon and Trout Project hatchery permit. Note that when fish populations cyclically rise they are not delisted.

Problems are assets.

Another possible indicator of unconscious regulatory duplicity is the prioritization of the solution set in the "recovery" plan. The ranking of local regulatory priorities will not reflect the most significant causes of siltation, supposedly associated with fish decline. For example, standards for logging roads will be outrageous, but little will be done about the maintenance practices and condition of County roads. The plans will, instead, emphasize how many acres of VALUABLE land can be placed under bureaucratic control, and give its managers maximum latitude to control which choice locations they will be (which is why it emphasizes forestry and agriculture).

The way the uses of these properties are confiscated is through designation of various forms of special ecological status, always subject to interpretation. These interpretations are left to the same jurisdictions, under the same local officials, as designed the local zoning laws.

Now, if you smell a possible rat, you have read this book well.

Best to find out what they want and where.

Better Put Some ICE on That...

So you go to the trusty computer and start to look on the Internet... and, lo and behold, you find ICE, the Information Center for the Environment, a file server at UC Davis. ICE is a mapping program and database that can display layers of information similar to a crude Computer Aided Design (CAD) system. You zoom in from the State view to the County of Santa Cruz and click the "LAYER CONTROL" button and what do you find? No, it isn't separated into categories of soils, biota, endangered species, fire history, and exotic pest infestations. It is a list of types of jurisdictional turf claimed by various State and Federal agencies. The maps detail projects, programs, jurisdictional boundaries, program proposals, and the political districts of specific politicians (complete with links to their offices).

This isn't about ecology: It should be called, 'what we're doing, what WE want, whose is it, and whom to beg for funding.'

Your interest is in future plans. So you check out some of the layer definitions, looking under the 'what WE want' flavor. One of them leaps out as a sure winner:

"Proposed Significant Natural Areas

California Department of Fish and Game, Natural Heritage Division data layer:

Significant Natural Areas are identified using biological criteria only. They may occur on public or private land and may be under different levels of protection.

- Areas supporting extremely rare species or natural communities;
- Areas supporting associations or concentrations of rare species or communities;
- Areas exhibiting representative examples of common or rare communities;
- Areas of high species-richness or habitat-richness.

The Significant Natural Areas Program analyses data from the Department's Natural Diversity Data Base. The Natural Diversity Data Base is a statewide Geographic Information System (GIS) that contains over 22,000 locational records of over 1200 sensitive natural communities and species. The Natural Diversity Data Base receives biological data from field biologists in public agencies, universities, private consulting firms, private utility companies and other organizations."

It's a set of definitions broad enough for a bureaucrat could drive a tank through, and will, if you get in the way. The last two are really precious; especially "examples of common or rare communities." Is that measured in units of "richness" per acre? What kind of "richness" are they talking about?

Now the only question is, where are they going to start?

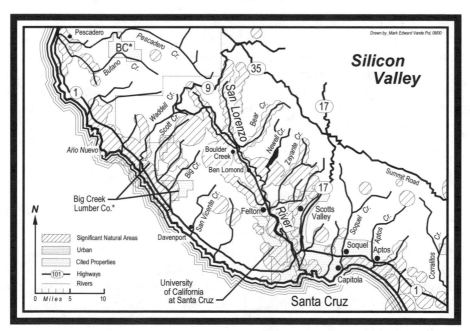

Figure 3 Proposed Significant Natural Areas in the San Lorenzo Watershed. *Data acquired from ICEMaps2 files.*

Click the ICEMap2 checkbox labeled "**Proposed Significant Natural Areas**" Pop the checkbox titled "**EPA River Reach File**" (for "locational" reference) and then click the appropriately-named "SUBMIT" button… and what do you see but nearly the entire map turns blue with wiggly lines, the "rivers." Funny, one thinks of California as a dry place... One also notices little green spots all over the state. Not surprisingly, there are two major concentrations of these little green blotches on the map, so tight they form entire regions. Surprise! They are in the County of Santa Cruz and just south of Humboldt State University. Zoom in to the County and, the vast bulk of those little blotches are along the San Lorenzo River.

Well, at least once the County forms their plan, with the appearance of compliance to the "4(d) Rule Package for salmon recovery" in place, we now know who the victims will be. Interestingly, Gamecock Canyon isn't covered, the Summit Area (where all the yuppies live) isn't so blessed, the Forest of the Nicene Marks State Park isn't there, the Soquel Demonstration State Forest isn't on it, the Butano forest Earth First! declared so precious somehow escaped but for one little circle. Soquel Creek, Aptos Creek, and Scott Creek are clean. Hmmm…

Is the San Lorenzo River so ecologically special? It must be. Zoom the ICE Map out to the whole State, there appear to be more designations in that one watershed than any equivalent area in the whole State!

Yup, all that Cape ivy choking the river valley and climbing the redwoods must be "habitat richness." All those vacation cabins and recreational vehicle campgrounds, a State Highway down the middle, the towns of Felton, Ben Lomond, Boulder Creek, and Brookdale with a mere 25,000 residents, the infestations of Himalayan blackberry, toxic hemlock, periwinkle, broom, gorse, and everybody's escaped yard plants must be "examples of common or rare communities."

This is a Significant Natural Area?

No way. It's gotta be redevelopment, a pretext for forcing the "wrong" people out of the Valley and back into the city, subsequent to letting the "right" back people in. The County wants a way to control it and they will use any legal tool available.

How did those little green circles get onto the map? Was there an independent peer review regarding the precious biotic qualities of those particular parcels? Nope. Once they designate it, though, the homeowner gets to pay for one before they can do anything. $10,000 is not an uncommon price for a biotic review, and then it gets reviewed by the County, for a fee.

Were the landowners told that their property is in a Significant Natural Area? Did the County tell the homeowners when the State or some NGO volunteer "nominated" the parcel for designation, that there would be new compliance requirements? The owners might be happy and proud to know their property is so special. Were they told who made the nomination? They might want to write a thank you letter to the person whose deeply-held, subjective opinion just swiped over a hundred thousand dollars from their land. They might want to personally offer a public testimonial to their local Supervisor, seeing as they voted him in on a platform of environmental protection. Do you think they should feel protected?

Do you think that if the bag-holders of those "worth-less" undersized parcels had refused to sell, they would have been allowed to build without being harassed into bankruptcy because they were in a Significant Natural Area?

The County has had another designation similar to this one for quite some time, the Sensitive Habitat Ordinance. It has a very similar set of ambiguous definitions and proscriptions that include granting the County permanent easements before being allowed to build.

According to the County:

"Violation of the Sensitive Habitat Ordinance or the conditions on a biotic permit may result in the issuance of a Notice of Violation, which describes the actions necessary to correct the problem and **may include restoration of the area to its original condition**. If the required corrective actions are not taken promptly, the Notice of Violation is **recorded on the title to the property** and becomes part of the public record. In addition, the current property owner is subject to a levy of all enforcement costs incurred by the Code Compliance staff in obtaining compliance as well as the possible imposition, through legal action, of **penalties of up to $2,500 a day** while the violation exists (completely unnecessary bold emphasis added)."

If you smell the opportunity for graft or favoritism, you are right on target. They get to decide what a violation is, whether it still exists, and how much of that $2,500 bucks per day the victim should pay.

This is how the County and the bureaucrats control who gets to stay, who gets to build, and where. It is a recipe for graft and extortion. What were the criteria for "nomination"? Is this a Fourteenth Amendment violation of due process? Is this a Fourth Amendment violation of unreasonable search and seizure, or a Fifth Amendment taking of private property?

The designation of impaired status of these watersheds under the guise of a Significant Natural Area, or as possible candidates for "rehabilitation," or as a Sensitive Habitat were left to the verbal opinions of a nominating bureaucrat. Such decisions are based upon sincere and deeply-held subjective impressions of how many fish should be there, how much endangered tarweed might grow in the field, or marbled murrelets might like to nest in the trees. They seldom seem to have hard census data, supporting archaeological records, genetic references, or literature citations attached to the nomination.

It doesn't matter if the taking is unconstitutional. It doesn't matter if the agency lacks jurisdiction. It doesn't matter if the manner in which the regulations were instituted should be prosecuted under racketeering laws. It doesn't matter if the nominating bureaucrat misquotes the literature citations. It doesn't matter if the guy doing the designating is either totally corrupt or a hopeful idiot. It doesn't matter if there are still increasing numbers of steelhead in the creek, despite the County's ignorance and heavy-handedness. It doesn't matter that higher nitrate levels than are optimal for urban drinking water are necessary to support the food supply for fish.

Here is what matters:

Unless property owners can **PROVE** their record of superior habitat management, and demonstrate the crass self-interest and incompetent greed upon the part of colluding civic and NGO antagonists, they will **NEVER** get a lower court to heed the constitutional points of law. The judge won't hear them and will instead settle upon some other fine point of law. Judges get brainwashed, too. The landowners are left to cave in to the pressure or hock everything they own to fund a constitutional appeal.

Why do the State and the NGO activists let Santa Cruz pull stunts like this? How do they get away with confiscating land under the claim of a Sensitive Habitat, and then increase the density of commercial development in the exact same region? It is likely that it is a payoff to those who did so much to get the precedents in place, the people who supported the "right" politicians and volunteered support to the NGOs, the people who make each acre of dirt worth more money for the bankers, the people who kick out the riffraff to churn it into higher tax revenue.

Property owners may think they can ride it out, or that the game will come to an end someday, but the odds are against them.

A Matter of Levitation

It is possible for landowners to halt, and even reverse Gravity Flow using existing environmental laws, but first, they have to understand the strategies against them, own the most relevant data, and construct a case in advance of the action. The rest is a matter of understanding the purpose and mechanics of environmental law and their property rights under the Constitution.

A landowner has to suffer a loss to have a lawsuit. It almost guarantees implementation of the plan, before judicial consideration, as well as minimal resources to resist. Fighting back can bring civic retribution and media vilification. Engaging in resistance, while perhaps justified, can wind up with a bitter ending: a loss of ownership under a crippling burden of compounding fines, over seemingly minute, technical, and arcane violations, probably of little ecological concern. Without data supporting a claim of superior stewardship, refuting the environmental legitimacy of the civic plan, and documenting civic culpability for future decline, the landowner will be without grounds to prove that the regulatory action is a purely political taking. Without proof of the ecological case, it is exceedingly difficult to isolate the Constitutional case. It is essential to have the data.

There is currently little way to estimate the cost of consequential damages to ecosystems caused by these takings, much less make an estimate of direct economic losses. However, if the landowners don't list what the losses will be, they will never be able to put a price tag on it later. They need to know what it costs to control a broom infestation for 70 years. They need to know what it costs to reestablish local native plants. They need to know how long it will take to rehabilitate local topsoil and stabilize slopes with native vegetation. They need to know what it costs to remove toxins from the streams and reestablish local classes of fish after a fire. Without the ecological study and audited records estimating the cost of rehabilitation, they CANNOT make a claim of civic liability. They MUST have validated data.

The NGO perpetrators of this insanity are indemnified from accountability by Presidential Executive Order. It makes winning legal cases more difficult, but it increases the size of the prize to historic proportions. Indemnification of the IUCN, issued under Executive Order 12986 by President Clinton, was totally illegal. The President has no power to exempt a private, extra-national organization from civil liability, nor member agencies therewith.

The same coalition that sued NMFS has already sued the California Board of Forestry under the same auspices. They will attempt to force the State to put a TMDL on nonpoint sources of silt, whether or not that silt is a measurable factor in successful local reproduction of the fish, simply because it might be. The governor will tell the Board to roll over or reappoint them all.

Here we go again. Though the situation is grave, it is time to defy gravity.

Perhaps instead of waiting, Bob could go on the offensive. Maybe there is a local fisherman's association that wants to do a little business. Maybe Bob should pay them for not catching so many adult fish so that he has a few spawners. It certainly sounds a little silly, but the fisherman might take his money. In return for his foolish magnanimity, they might in turn purchase his services for improvements in instream breeding habitat. Maybe they should pay him for managing his forest in such a way as to produce healthy and bounteous smolts. The reduced catch and smoltification improvements might have to be verified by independent observers and the contracts insured of course, but it would create an important distinction. Of course, the net cash difference might not be very significant, but the LEGAL difference is enormous. Bob would have just as much standing in court over the use of fish as does the Pacific Coast Federation of Fishermen's Associations.

Bob could then sue the State of California, the NGOs, and NMFS under the Endangered Species Act for the right to manage the OTHER side of the valley, owned by the State Park that extorted it from his family. For the first time, Bob could open his data file and present it to the court. He could then cite the Endangered Species Act and demand that the State and Federal Governments return control of the right to manage the Waddell Creek watershed because he is the best person to do it. He could negotiate an operating contract to maintain State-owned land. His record of superior stewardship, and that of his family predecessors, has demonstrated over the 87 years that Bob is a better steward of public land than is the government. He should run it. If he doesn't, the condition of that land is a threat both to the health of the river and to his land, as well. His alternative is to fall under yet more rules that might cost him the use of his farm for himself and his heirs. The fight to take it back beats having to prove that each little incremental rule was just another regulatory taking, foisted as protection of The Environment, until he is forced out of business and off his land.

Bob could save an awful lot of money compared to a fire and has a far better chance of winning because he can prove the accuracy of his steelhead numbers with independent census data. He will have an easier time making a claim on their value because he knows how many fish left the property for the sea each year. Heck, he might even make a buck or two selling a few logs. What would it cost to manage its recovery of all that abused property? Bob knows how much work it is and how long it will take. All he needs is a way to verify his data and claims and make them pay for the damage that they have done. Simple, isn't it?

That is why the system, proposed in this book, is so important. You have seen its implications throughout both the free-market solution and the fight to implement it. Cases of this nature require independent, expert opinions to overcome the activist-government-university troika. Property owners have to pay their own cash to fund it. These lawsuits are so expensive that a private party can't afford to bring one unless they have an independent source of income, or suffer damages as a class. Given the civic indemnification, the recoverable damages to individuals are unattractive to a contingency-based action, unless one is willing to go all the way. To win, the property owner needs the personal relationships with the professorate, under which to build that trust. There is no going back in time to get the numbers. Landowners MUST be collecting that data, NOW, or be willing to pay the ultimate price.

Select private landowners provide superior stewardship to government. The key to justifying private environmental management systems is the quality and organization of data proving that fact. Collecting, processing, analyzing, and verifying ecosystem data, as private property, is where the concept of free-market, ecosystem management originates.

Once the landowner has proof of superior competence and an accounting of the economic value of their assets, the civic agency is merely a competing public corporation that used the law to steal the assets upon which to base its monopoly. Government cannot simultaneously protect private property rights and express an interest in its use. As long as government is empowered to express such an interest, it is incapable of providing equal protection under the laws and has forfeited its legitimacy. When government takes private property by force for its own power and security, it betrays the public claim and is an act of theft on behalf of its sponsors.

Who are these sponsors and how might they be redirected? Now that you know the enemy and the tactics, it is time to know the strategy and the goals.

Nobody Home

Historically, there has been somebody who went out onto the land looking for weeds, checking for pathogens, controlling pest infestations, managing predation, thinning forests, and conducting controlled burns. They did it nearly every day, because they made a living there and loved their land.

They had a reason to do it, too, though perhaps not the balance of interests or level of education that some of us would prefer.

What happened? We never paid for those services. Instead, we demanded cheaper food, meat, metals, and wood and never asked about those other products for which we were unwilling to pay and the practitioner could no longer supply. Whoever was unwilling to care for the land set the standard of stewardship. Love could no longer be afforded, and still we wanted more.

We hired an agent with a gun to go out there and enforce a set of Byzantine rules with fines, created out of a system structurally incapable of anything else, and with every reason to make it worse. We donated to groups claiming expertise and hawking feigned altruism to go out there and complain for us about all that harm being done. They sued a colluding government and took the use for themselves and for the benefit of their corporate sponsors. We stood idly by, wondering what to do to save the family farm, the small ranch, or small town America and here we are, fearing the extortionate power of corporate agribusiness, industrial timber, or globalization.

Now we watch what was once our government, out of control. Federal agencies are snatching up half the country and longing for more, conducting illegal raids, charging outrageous fines for insanely minor infractions, demanding tax money to "care" for land that once generated revenue, and bearing no accountability for positive results. They are combusting forests, throwing down barriers to imported pests, plundering farms, bulldozing access roads to homes, and driving ranchers off their land at gunpoint wearing bulletproof vests, and demanding more tax money.

All because there was no mechanism for that resource practitioner to market those "other" services that were once implicit in the price of goods. There was no means to motivate investment to extend the state of the art in habitat management. There was no opportunity for a person to profit by caring for the land and develop the limits of expertise. There was no efficient system to verify the motives of the practitioner. Did we really have to do it this way?

Was there no really other alternative?

📖 Chapter 3 – Strategy of the Commoners

Winning with Their Weapons

"Coercion is a dirty word to most liberals now, but it need not forever be so. As with the four-letter words, its dirtiness can be cleansed away by exposure to the light, by saying it over and over without apology or embarrassment. To many, the word coercion implies arbitrary decisions of distant and irresponsible bureaucrats; but this is not a necessary part of its meaning. The only kind of coercion I recommend is mutual coercion, mutually agreed upon by the majority of the people affected."

THE TRAGEDY OF THE COMMONS, by Garrett Hardin

"The most brilliant propagandist technique will yield no success unless one fundamental principle is borne in mind constantly...it must confine itself to a few points and repeat them over and over."

Joseph Goebbels, Nazi Propaganda Minister

Sorry, Mr. Hardin, but repetition of a bad idea until it is accepted does not make it work. Democracy has historically devolved from chaos into tyranny.

Perhaps Aristotle said it more precisely,

"What is common to the greatest number gets the least amount of care. Men pay most attention to what is their own: they care less for what is common."

No, such things are not new. We are not in a historically unique situation. This has all happened before, and civic tyranny doesn't work any better now than it did then (consider ecosystem management in ancient Greece). The Jacobeans thought France's population level unsustainable...

Turning the Tables

Besides mere technical incompetence, organizational inefficiency, and political decision-making, civic regulation has the potential for serious environmental damage, unconsciously inflicted by people who survive off the existence of perpetual problems in service to distorted priorities.

To a bureaucracy, problems justify a cash flow. Those responsible for managing ecological problems are motivated to expend time and resources to acquire and retain new administrative turf, not to eliminate the need. Any civic investment in a new problem then requires new people and a new administrative body in addition to the old, justifying a new infusion of cash. Problems can be considered the assets of the regulatory enterprise.

The complexity of government rulemaking entrenches a system of opposing lobbyists, either side dependent upon the continuing expansion of civic

361

agency. The only experts in implementation, then, are the direct beneficiaries of regulatory complexity and continued contention. Civil agencies and industry lobbyists are thus inherently likely to develop maladaptive systems.

Political appointees adhere to the fealties that are the source of cash flow. Public agency employees understand how to target legislation to extend influence beyond their numbers. They can also either direct lobbying efforts by indirectly funding NGOs to do it for them. The system consequently grows irreversibly, without effective challenge.

We have allowed administrative government to function as legislator, tax-collector, police, prosecutor, and judge, as funded by the penalties collected. With that much power in control of the factors of all economic production, it is a system motivated to tyranny.

What is needed is a system that is more suited to help people find personal benefit in an increasingly sound form of ecosystem asset management. Upon the appearance of such a competitor, one would expect the beneficiaries of the existing system to attempt to scuttle the whole concept. Let's look at the underlying motivational structures and how they might be redirected. Maybe these people could find more satisfying and productive work to fulfill the intent of their individual career choices.

Competition or Conflict?

The InsCert proposal profits those who can competitively deliver guaranteed products to customers demanding uses of ecosystem assets. It uses stock ownership, pooled risk, and supply chain relationships to account for inter-dependence. Competitive success, as a determinant, flies in the face of the anti-capitalist, anti-competitive rantings to be heard from the environmental movement. Paradoxically, InsCert exactly fits the wish of a Garret Hardin for a Darwinian system with stewardship as an effective determinant. Is it "com-petition" that is really the problem with free markets?

There are other competitive behaviors besides trying to destroy the "other guy"; competition is as often a motive for mutual benefit as it is for struggle. A manufacturer will sometimes invest in the capability of a supplier in com-petition with their own production capability. The motive might be to assure a second source of supply instead of expanding its own production. In nature, competitive species often self-destruct to attract predators that spread their seed. In business as in nature it has long been competitive pressure that is the source of the assurance that individuals can survive.

Many people think that business management tends to regard competitors as adversaries. When one looks at interlocking directorates, webs of subsidiaries and joint ventures, or the behavior of trade associations, a different picture emerges. Competition usually consists of an effort to do better than the other guys, not to put them out of business. To expend effort in an outright attack is generally regarded an expensive waste of time and loss of focus. Competitors are usually regarded with respect as sources of ideas and people, fellow contributors with common interests, or even as investors. It is customary in business to acknowledge competition as a source of higher productivity that motivates marketing and production of better products. Higher total volume reduces the cost of raw material through economies of scale, helping all concerned compete with substitute goods.

CEOs have lost their jobs for having become too embroiled in expensive or unnecessary conflict with competitors. Instead of litigation, the path to prosperity is to maximize the benefits of competition while minimizing the cost of conflict. Private court systems that mediate or arbitrate disputes exist, simply because the civic court system has failed to do the job.

That's not how it works with environmental issues, is it? Most of our critical environmental decisions have come out of courtrooms founded upon an adversarial assumption. Is it the penchant for conflict among environmental groups that has induced such disdain for competition?

The structural problem, with the use of legal processes to decide environmental remedies, is that they are shaped by bipolar outcomes: **Whether by adversarial legal process or two-party political system, bipolar decision-making systems are structurally biased toward conflict.**

Adversarial conflict inexorably proceeds toward a bipolar structure whatever the battleground. Bipolar opposition minimizes possible outcomes because each adversary must maximize its contingent. It drives the bases of argument to reflect differentiating properties and reduces the possibility of acknowledging either common ground or external options. The very facts necessary to achieve a satisfactory synthetic solution may thus be deliberately omitted from the argument.

Legal proceedings are founded upon an assumption of bipolar conflict, not multiparty competition. Lawyers do not make as much money by ending a contest with an agreement or by finding that the whole point of contention was a mistake. There is little likelihood that a pair of adversaries will opt for a solution that reflects the interests of a third party. The adversarial system is a great way for one side of a dispute to gain total victory, but it is a lousy way to share information and consider points of interdependence. It is also destructive to the relationships and communication necessary to discovering common interests. How then would potential litigants discover the optimal plan by which to manage a habitat back to health?

The propensity for the legal system is to make enemies out of people who might otherwise cooperate. Legal struggles between landowners and the government-activist bloc are bitter. The landowners might have been born on their land and descended from generations that fought and died for it. All their lives they have done their best at often, arduous work, under stressful competitive pressures. The "crimes" of which they stand accused appear to them petty compared to what they provide. To lose it all, to what they perceive as arrogant bureaucrats or a bunch of spoiled and destructively ignorant children sponsored by corporate plutocrats and lawyers, is more than many can stand. Rural suicide rates are high.

Environmental activists have deep emotional investments as well. Many come from a generation with overwhelming numbers of distracted or broken families. Their education has been infused with a drumbeat of imminent disaster. Dabbling in nature may have been the sole source of stability and peace in their lives. To see people in pursuit of "mere" profit, inflict harm on defenseless animals and plants is heart wrenching. There are those who justify taking extreme action in defense of that solace.

Does environmentalists' hatred of competition originate from a projection of their own dependent association with attorneys?

The cost of conflict and subordination of ecological objectives to legal strategies preclude objective study of options appropriate to the resolution of disagreement. Both legislative and adjudicative proceedings sponsor supporting expert opinions with consequently divergent bias. Legal training projects the assumption of artful dissemblance in testimony to the listener's personal opinions. Knowing this politicians and lawyers seek "experts in the field" when confronted with conflicting testimony. Points of discussion then graduate to extremes respecting their bipolar origins, diverging from their scientific bases. As legal strategies overtake other objectives within the activist organization, the collection of expensive data increasingly respects its source of sponsorship, the financial grantors for the research. The money source thus skews the data much the way opinion modifies perception. The solution set as intersects the interests of the legal opponent is avoided as a possible point of unnecessary concession and weakened argument.

This process taints the conduct of all science. When government and legal advocacy assume the principal role for distribution of research funds, the propensity for scientists to serve sponsoring interests increases markedly.

Unfortunately, ecological health is not a thing to win or lose in a litigious fight. In many respects, the real barrier to effective ecosystem management is the adversarial assumption itself, because it assumes resolution through bipolar conflict. Perhaps a competitive system among people striving to do their best for ecosystem health might be somewhat less destructive and more apt to engender cooperative behavior.

Re "Education"

Technical decisions are seldom completely deterministic, made instead among countervailing properties that must be weighed. The more complex is the system under consideration, the more likely it is that a large number of technical disciplines apply. Few subjects are more complex, or more inter-disciplinary than human interaction with nature on a real project. **There are no experts** who possess the intellect and experience necessary to weigh ALL practical, technical, and ecological considerations that apply to any situation or circumstance. This fact alone does not bode well for ecosystem management by remote control.

The breadth of expertise on a public university campus should render their consultative product capable of integrating a wide range of technical disciplines toward solving such complex problems. Unfortunately, the political structure of university Environmental Studies Departments precludes that rational expectation. These departments control the process that produces "experts-in-the-field," for environmental testimony in court and before legislative hearings, because they control the system by which credentialed expertise is conferred.

The politicization of the sciences is a testament to the degree that government has assumed so much control over the universities. Investigation of the distribution of Faculty credentials in the Environmental Studies Department of any large university will reveal a large fraction of **social** scientists engaged in projects all over the world. It has rendered research suspect and redirected scientific work toward the socialization of commons. While it may have been bad for science, but has been a bonanza for the "study-the-problem" business where universities and government have a virtual monopoly.

Besides a tax-subsidized monopoly in marketing credentialed expertise, state universities have a virtual lock on the supply of student labor. A professor with a grant to fund a study project can recruit graduate students to do work required for them to earn advanced degrees. Professors who distribute the grant money for graduate study can easily exert undue influence on students with grades and potential faculty appointments at stake. The post docs who aren't offered tenure need jobs and more importantly, they need jobs that provide a return on their investments.

Graduate students need to specialize in order to get advanced degrees, which focuses their expertise upon a narrow topic. Thus, many of our "experts" are people who know an immense amount about very little with less chance that the subject matter will have application to a practical issue. If a problem has multidisciplinary requirements, then a postdoctoral candidate is the wrong kind of expert for real ecological problems. Advance degrees are analytical.

There is no similar credential of expertise for a synthetic academic thinker.

We are not training leaders. Is that why we need consensus decision-making?

When a technical team publishes a study report, it must pass peer review to be considered credible. In its essence, peer review is a wonderful thing. Through objective criticism, one learns what is missing, what is unnecessarily pointed or contentious, where supporting citations or data are needed, etc. The problem with peer review arises when conclusions are presented that are sufficiently controversial to upset the gravy train. It becomes a career-threatening move to break ranks. Such is the case of the coho salmon in Santa Cruz where you will hear a different story from some scientists in private than if they are asked to write it down.

The other constraint in taking controversial positions is that of simple conservatism: the Precautionary Principle of Prospective Punishment. No one wants to be the authority who said, 'Go ahead, there won't be a problem,' only to regret it later. Because it is nearly impossible to affix culpability for a Type II error, it is safer to posture as "protecting the environment" than to risk saying that a particular human enterprise is harmless, or perhaps beneficial.

In order to meet the standards of scholarship, the thesis must properly reflect the evidentiary standards and verbiage of the specialty peerage. The result will be that few outside that group will understand the study well enough to question its conclusions, without technical experts of their own. The real meaning of the data can only be extracted from direct analyses. Research for this book encountered technical papers whose conclusions were diametrically at odds with the supporting data! It is more common than one would think, that the political product of a study, its summary remarks, must be read with circumspection because of the propensity to use that cover to advance the particular agenda of the grantor. The meat is in the hard data.

You don't get funding by proposing to tell grant managers what they don't want to hear or by working for the opposition. NGOs and government issue most grants involving environmental issues. The professors who manage these studies maintain their status by publications. The editors control who publishes. Unless the spin pleases the editor, forget it. Without publications, they have no status as experts and can't raise the grant money to do the studies by which they can market information. Their expertise is directly related to their ability to raise grant funding.

No grants, no credentials. No credentials, no contracts. No contracts, no cheap grad student labor. No labor, no data. No data, no papers. No papers, no spin. No spin, no publishers. No publications, no grants.

What to do?

The structural requirement, for education and research in the InsCert process standard, reclaims university research into a cooperative effort with private industry. It addresses one of the great evils of our education system: the degree to which students and academics are isolated from working society. Students often select fields of study upon the basis of emotional appeal. Then, after using them as cheap grad student labor, we dump them into the world to make it with a late start, without a clue as to how, and desperate to recoup their investment while perhaps starting a family. The higher the degree, the bigger the loans, the later the start, the more desperate the need to recoup that investment.

When insured certification becomes an extant alternative, the bureaucracy and the NGOs living off both public and private grants will cry foul. InsCert will threaten their source of income by turning grant money toward capital investments. The plutocrats might learn that a world rationalized under the intelligence of an elite is a world limited to the intelligence of a few and that there are better ways to make money. Resource landowners might consider it worth the cost and inconvenience of continuing education to learn new ways of making a buck on their land. The public will be unable to demand that government take control of private property without the willingness to pay a FAIR price for the use. It is unconstitutional and immoral to do otherwise, not to mention destructive.

There is enormous investment in the current system. How then are we to break the loop? That is where this proposal offers hope. It is a dual system.

It is proven that there is a fraction of any industry, interest group, or government that will abuse laws as a means of acquiring wealth. The proposal in this work is that the current regulatory system should be focused for the exclusive benefit of persons with no intention of adopting resource enterprise management, either to the standards of InsCert or perhaps something better. If they can't find insurance for their warranties, then they are back to the existing system. Regulatory bureaucracies often assert that their funding is insufficient to hire and train sufficient staff to police the bad actors. This proposal simply acknowledges that request and reduces the size of the population under their scrutiny so that they can do a really good job of making the lives of fewer charges pure hell.

The proposal of this book also encourages any person to join in the ranks of the living and enjoy a system of verified and proven personal responsibility for the process of intellectual inquiry. The insured certification process is no free ride but it might be more fun than dealing with bureaucrats. Might there not be less "collateral damage" to be found in a path of educated integrity?

If insured private certification proves superior to the existing system, those who have no reason to push the limits of best practice, and still are enamored with winning the cat-and-mouse game with regulators, will have a choice.

They can change their ways or go out of business. With fewer victims left to regulate, what will the bureaucrats do?

They will slowly be drawn into productive work. The private management job market will need people with such expertise. What they discover will engender new products and services. We can give these people a place to go with their intent to do good works, where they can actually realize it in verified terms. We must give them a basis to drop their reliance upon conformation and civic "job-security." It will take massive amounts of retraining but in that respect, a profit (or loss) can work wonders.

So too, can the exercise of individual freedom.

The goal of any market-based system would be to integrate economic externalities into conscious selections and then use the market to reduce their costs. The returns are thus greatest where one is looking for the unexpected rather than avoiding it. There may be some costs, which we may not choose to pay because they are unmeasurable to sufficient accuracy by current technology. Although that might seem problematic with the proposed system, isn't that how things are now?

Capitalists, ecologists, and property rights advocates should observe such political resistance, look for its source, and see in it the carrot of opportunity for all concerned. There are jobs, profits, and royalties to be earned identifying and reducing ecological risk.

The research requirements and continuing education for insured certification will bring participation of experienced landowners into the classroom. It will foster more productive relationships among landowners and the academic community. It will help return state universities to the public that pays their bills. It will provide opportunities for early internship and help students meet people who have been working in nature for years before they select a thesis topic. Students will make better career choices if they get a preview of what the work is like. The civil alternative will again become an attractive career, unlike it is now. The civic prospect is not what it seems.

Problems Are Assets

Government programs are self-perpetuating because they do not derive revenue without problems to justify funding. The financial assets of a government agency are the problems, themselves.

It is human nature for people to cling to their problems. Whether it is child or spousal abuse, drugs, thrill seeking, or merely a bad habit, they adhere to the familiar to the end. When those problems are a source of income, or a sense of power or purpose, just try prying them loose. If you want a place to spend infinite cash and watch it all go down the drain while the problem gets worse, you couldn't find a more entangling welfare case than The Environment.

The ostensible reason these problems perpetuate? Over the last forty years we have all heard it, "insufficient funding." We could fix it if only we had the money. The unfortunate corollary is, 'If we don't do it right, then it won't work at all." Does this mean that, if they don't get what they really need, they will quit their jobs because the effort is futile? Of course not.

The masses of classes of environmental graduates are just as indentured by their next review as is the welfare claimant by his or her next check. They have little training to get a job creating new products or services. The acculturated hysteria with which they have been trained is a self-fulfilling prophecy of horrific potential. It is a tragic waste of human intellect and a betrayal of their individual commitment.

There are tens of thousands of these people in the regulation industry. They collect paychecks and watch them disappear just like everybody else. It would be daft to assume that they are, by virtue of either their individual intent, either evil or beneficent. There are, however, many who believe that their ends are so important and, by virtue of their intent, inherently beneficial, that they are willing to subordinate their integrity to a "deeply subjective experience."

Given the laws of hierarchical bureaucracy, finding that the problem is bigger than expected is a way to earn a promotion. This is usually done by association of the problem with direct causes and thence to an ever wider range of indirect causes. The bigger is the scope, the bigger is the budget. We tie their paycheck, the very existence of their job and their personal sense of self-worth, to the perpetuation and expansion of environmental problems.

Their assets ARE the crises that justify administrative cash flow.

The entire worldview of these people is distorted by the compulsive forces by which they are directed and, thence, redirected upon the victims under their jurisdiction. Deep ecologists have combined a misanthropic belief system, a hatred for industry, the armed power of the State, and personal career requirement for a continuing legal justification, with the power to control the factors of production. It is terrifying to contemplate how much damage these people will do in service to such beliefs.

They know not what they do.

Let's say we have a decline in salmon populations, as in the County of Santa Cruz. Now, it apparently doesn't matter that we had just shut down all the hatcheries, that the fisheries biologists say that the fish is at least marginal in this habitat, that archeologists are telling us that the fish was never here in significant numbers in the first place, that pinnipeds are overpopulated, or that ocean temperatures are on a cyclical rise. If the salmon population falls, it's a crisis.

NMFS, PETA, and the Marine Mammal Center are protecting the seals. Don't go there. The city uses an awful lot of water. Nope, too many voters. The anti-logging activists and Fish and Game people are screaming that timber harvests have damaged egg redds in streams. Voters do love trees and cutting them is unpopular. How many forest landowners are there? Do they have a lot of cash to fight back? They sure do have a lot of land that "We" could manage better. It's pretty too; it might be fun to work there...

Ah HA!!! LOGGING! It must be mud in the streams from timber operations. Ban all activity on the part of the landowner that might affect the creek bed, under the Clean Water Act. It is not a significant cause of salmon decline, but we have to do everything we can.

So "we" write rules. To be fair, they are the same for everybody. We write a rule that says, 'No addition of 20% of turbidity to the water due to logging.' OK. They did.

In comes the Department of Fish and Game who can fine the landowner $170 if they so much as walk in a creek bed on their own property. The County starts to order that all "barriers to fish" be removed, such as woody debris in the creek beds, without so much as one multi-year trial in a single creek (it was a crisis). It wasn't just one creek, it was all of them.

OOPS! The higher water velocity wiped out the egg redds, eroded the creek beds, and removed any place where the fish could rest on their trip upstream.

Salmon stocks are still declining. "We" need stronger rules. What to do? OK. NO MUD FROM LOGGING ROADS. Heavy fines for Polluting the Waters of the United States. Uh, how do we know the mud came from the road? Oh. No problem. No mud on logging roads and no logging when there might be mud. That should work.

Does it matter if the mud never gets into the creek? No. Does it matter if the creek can't support fish? No. Does it matter if the road is 100 yards away, across a flat field with grass to filter the dirt? No. Does it matter if the turbidity doesn't have an assignable cause? No. Does it matter that the turbidity is variable across the creek, subject to sampling error and easily falsified? No. Is there an accurate measurement that can't be subjectively altered? No. Does it matter if there is no probable cause that this specific mud caused a problem for the fish? No. Does it matter that this is a violation of Constitutional rights of due process, unreasonable search and seizure, unconstitutionally vague, a Fifth Amendment taking without just compensation, or an assumption of guilt before innocence? No. That mud MIGHT get to the creek, someday, somehow. How big a mud puddle are we talking about? It depends upon the inspector.

We have so many rules like this that we now have a shortage of inspectors. Most often, they don't have a clue and they can't be too careful. It doesn't matter that 95% of the sediment is of natural causes. It doesn't matter that the statistical correlation with levels of suspended sediment and declines in fish populations is weak. It doesn't matter that most problems with logging roads happened on jobs that were done long ago. It doesn't matter if a new logging job could fix the problems with the old roads. It doesn't matter that State-mandated removal of woody debris has undermined slopes and caused land-slides. It doesn't matter that County Roads and development drop more sedi-ment and increase runoff rates more than logging does. It doesn't matter that, if we don't log it, a fire will eventually strip the land of all vegetation and choke that creek with silt. It doesn't matter if the historic correlation of con-flagrations and damage to salmon redds is excellent. It doesn't matter that there was no review on the environmental impact of the law. It doesn't mat-ter that there are no criteria to judge success or failure, we can make you do anything we want, even if it is stupid: 'There might be a mud puddle on the logging road. We just can't be too careful. It's a crisis. Pave it.'

Six inches of base-rock, 12 feet wide, and an oiled surface for a logging road used once every 15 to 20 years? Well, here we are, building roads that are basically badly designed future driveways for new houses. Wanna buy it?

How do we **do** this to ourselves?

The first person that any dishonest person lies to, is oneself. It is an essential step in the self-justification of any unethical act.

Anxiety is a compulsion to defray a potential threat to survival. If people associate an unpleasant event with a cause, the prospective intelligence of humans declares it best to prevent reoccurrence of or avoid blame for the cause. Voters give it to the government to fix it. For government, problems become a source of cash flow, just like any other asset. Maintaining public anxiety and a source of impending threat is the key to marketing that service.

So if problems are assets and the scope of control grows by association, then what happens when agencies compete for problems as they become scarce? After a few rather ugly turf wars, they develop hierarchies and collude. This process is well established in our case of septic systems and nonpoint nitrates and is taking shape now in the battle over fish and forests. The County asserts that the State is "making them do this," but it is actually a careful par-titioning of turf, going back through countless agencies and their sponsoring network of colluding NGOs and tax-exempt foundations.

It's time to make it stop.

Charge for the Guns

To a landowner, government regulation looks like a strategic war, conducted for the benefit of the bureaucracy and the activists, not recognizing the interests of the financial instigators. Their individual resources are sufficiently limited that they have to be certain of a threat before they organize or dig into their wallets for a legal "hired gun."

By that time, it is usually too late. The administrative fortress is in place before most people even hear about its demands. Agencies will have already contracted with purported experts with nothing else to do but publish an array of arcane, single-sided, technical "facts." The consultants will have circled the peer-review wagons. Enforcers in the field will have memorized the code sections to be cited on notices of violation, even if they don't know and can't prove whether what they are looking at directly applicable. The situation is even worse if the agency derives a significant fraction of its revenue from fines levied against its customers, wherein enforcers feel trapped between those whose interests they are protecting and their need for a paycheck. They end up vetting their frustrations by punishing those who make their lives difficult by refusing to "cooperate."

The landowners' only recourse is in the courts, to attempt to overturn what is by then, established administrative law. Should they choose to fight back, the system is so well funded with either taxes or (worse) fine revenue, that to embark upon such an act of defiance can be financial suicide. Even if they win, control of the resource remains with the agency. Meanwhile, a rich and awakened activist community will be ready to help them try again.

The fines for an illegal "take" under the Endangered Species Act are brutal. The owner bears the burden of proof that whatever was done did not do any harm, which, because harm is subjective, is impossible. So when faced with new requirements, landowners complain that compliance is expensive, that the problem is overstated, that the specifications are too vague, or that they aren't the cause of the problem. They immerse themselves in fine points of the rules, struggle with their interpretation, implementation, or enforcement. Perhaps they might even try to build cooperative relations with the regulators, only to find that the demands never end and they end up trapped by the process itself. Meanwhile, the big operators have so much cash and power that the regulators think twice before messing with them.

The regulatory troika among NGOs, industry, and agencies is set up for the big players to win, using expensive regulation (and the power to ignore it) to drive out smaller competitors and enjoy oligopoly profits. In the act of participatory resistance, landowners confer legitimacy to that process. They commit time, money, and energy to a misdirected priority that diminishes their ability to question the legitimacy of the regulatory process itself. We'll call this political flypaper "The Tar Baby Effect."

Both sides can wield that sticky brush.

For the activists and lawyers in the NGOs, control of the environment is a matter of pride and power. For the civil servants, it may start out that way but, in the end, they learn that it's just a job. For the bankers, it's money and ego. For the landowner or a scientist who understands how much work caring for land demands, this is a battle for love and survival.

Have you noticed that one of the reasons rats, cockroaches, and weeds are so successful is that their stake is similar?

The Constitution limited the powers of both State and Federal governments because they operate in inherent conflict of interest with the rights of the people. Action to acquire control of the use of property at variance to its purported purpose demonstrates an interest. Because government derives power from controlling the use of property, it cannot simultaneously act as an impartial agent of the people, maintain the land in health and productivity, and serve its own interests. The key to the Strategy of the Commoners is to demonstrate that interest and set the government and the landowner on their Constitutional bases, citizen and servant, in a market serving the demand for managing ecosystem health.

One of those competitors is breaking the rules.

Instead of going broke entangled in a regulatory Tar Baby, isn't it time that landowners recognized the eventual outcome of the regulatory game and go for the jugular of the civic beast instead trying to cooperate? Should they not question the purpose of the system and its efficacy? This is, after all, about the health of the planet, as the activists are so fond of reminding us, even though their sponsors seem somewhat forgetful once the land is in inventory.

Private property owners are capable of operating in an objective interest as long as the management system is aligned with natural law (one of the beauties of InsCert). Why, then, should we tolerate socialist tyranny and organized crime, fraudulently claiming an interest in habitat management?

Tolerate it no longer. In defense of ecosystem function, in defense of liberty, and in defense of natural law, the property owner must take the Moral High Ground of Environmentalism back from government and activist lawyers. They have failed. The key is to set up businesses to manage the resource, and when these thugs get in the way, cite these very laws against their interested progenitors, until the laws are themselves, unnecessary or totally discredited.

If government wants to preserve trees in order to sequester carbon for oil companies… oops, they'll get the CO_2 back from fungi when the standing trees decompose or when the trees burn. Carbon sequestration rates fall as the trees get bigger. That carbon can be recovered more rapidly and the risk of carbon release is reduced among trees that have been thinned. If they want to halt timber operations… oops, the "inevitable" conflagration will harm fish habitat and clean water by the very criteria used to protect them. Careful thinning and burning will propagate rare understory species that support the bugs that feed the fish. Use the Endangered Species Act. Cite the evidence of damage to watersheds due to conflagration. Use the Clean Water Act to force consideration of fuel reduction and prescribed fire. Use the Endangered Species Act when it comes to the resulting spread of exotic plants and loss of understory species due to overcrowding. The mold from rotting vegetation can induce allergies and trigger asthma. Use the Clean Air Act. The fires will happen anyway and are essential to the health of ecosystems. Smoke from prescribed burning is less likely to be retained under an atmospheric inversion than from natural sources. If the zoning law is supposedly intended to protect forests… sorry, it will abet development as well as constitute a fire hazard. Preserving the economic viability of timber operations is a proven way to slow residential conversion. Use the Endangered Species Act for the protection of anadromous salmonids. If new septic regulations drive people underground, cause deferrals in septic maintenance, and fail to address major problems because people avoid the costs, use the Clean Water Act and the California Environmental Quality Act to demonstrate the secondary consequences of the management plan. Demonstrate the crass self-interest in the attainment specifications. How can government set a TMDL that nature can't achieve and starves the river of nutrients, by citing easily rectifiable complaints about the taste of the water and get away with it for twenty years?

Private landowners do a better job of managing their property than government. They are slowly sinking under the weight of regulatory requirements based upon mere speculation. When the costs of compliance deprive property of value, the landowner sells. The buyer is often operating as a proxy for those with a profit interest in controlling the use of the property. That loop carries the potential for prosecution for racketeering and fraud.

It is important to emphasize that there are many honest, helpful, sincere, and diligent people in these bureaucracies. They really care about their mission, and try to find the best solutions of which they think they are capable. They perceive themselves to be just as stuck in the Tar Baby as any landowner.

However, if civil servants just "follow orders" or blind ideology without considering the balance of risks and the warnings of landowners, at that point they become morally culpable and ethically complicit for the choices that destroy their good intentions. It is an individual, moral choice that betrays the true purpose of civic environmental regulation.

If government is neither a disinterested nor a competent agent for the public demand for ecosystem health, who is?

Private landowners, free to market that insured, certified, and guaranteed management product to the public for a profit, ARE objectively disinterested in producing a return on the investment in the health of that land. They will have invested their own time, money, and education into scientific process development to extend the limits of ecosystem management. They will have a record of stewardship and proof of that record.

Private property owners do a better job of caring for habitat than government. They can do it for less money and make a profit in the process.

All they need is independent verification of the data that demonstrates that superior record to stop the public theft of the economic value of those goods.

Every tool that the government might use as evidence of possible damage to ecosystems can be used against them. Government will charge taxes instead of paying them. It will waste resources instead of improving them. It destroys the wealth that supplies the revenue to fund protection of ecosystem resources. Government programs operate on chronically insufficient funding. Why do they get sole right to dictate the manner of the use of the land? Do they know what they are doing? Do they comply with their own rules?

These laws are tools. Property owners need to learn to use them. What do they need to prove the case?

Validated data. The data that come as a byproduct of the best practice process builds the knowledge that is the way to civil power.

If the Natural Resources Defense Council or the Center for Biological Diversity sues government with the threat of a regulatory Briar Patch, go for the jugular and join their suit as a superior steward with an alternative plan. The civic management system will inevitably make enormous mistakes, if they have not already done so. Offer the alternative as a management contract taking all public goods including tax revenue, into account.

If you need a resource, just remember: the opposition has enormous research tools available that are already networked that describe in gory detail the legal language you will need. The activists have enormous resources on their web sites. If you have a question regarding precedents that you might invoke to protect your land from government and NGOs, send them an email with the request. You are the one protecting the ecosystem from civic ignorance.

Can you be more efficient than the Nature Conservancy? They may have money, but they have to hire much of the work, house people, and travel. They are subject to suit for unfair competition and illegal restraint of trade. If there is competition for their volunteers, what will they pay? Their overhead is structured as a charity with lots of top-heavy legal expertise. They are not structured to focus upon delivery of competitive land management and restoration. Perhaps they may wish to make an honest profit instead of relying upon the government?

The court must allow standing if your business is to improve the conditions for endangered species. Meanwhile, you know that the interests of the NGOs ARE economic. Betray that economic interest that the NGOs are serving a profit interest for their supposedly non-profit benefactors. Find a DA with some cojones to file a RICO complaint. Support a District Attorney and a sheriff who will enforce the Constitution. File a complaint with the IRS. Collect the citations, network the precedents and 'repeat them over and over.'

Get on Their Case

The current environmental management system is a three-legged stool consisting of wealthy foundations, bureaucratic fiefdoms, and activist networks dominated by lawyers.

This strategy has the power to cut out all three legs. It only takes one.

What are the weapons the activist NGOs and bureaucrats use? They use the courts to broaden the Clean Air Act, the Clean Water Act, the Endangered Species Act... They need these weapons (that *is* what they call them).

This example will expose the granddaddy of them all: the Endangered Species Act (ESA). This case shows that civic administration of the ESA:

1. Was authorized unconstitutionally,

2. Fails to protect endangered species,

3. Serves the interests of a financial elite,

4. Disinvests the species into a socialized commons motivated to fail,

5. Obscures the fact that endangered species are the principal asset of a habitat management service and are therefore private property,

6. Destroys a competitive market that can manage species habitat at net benefit to society, and

7. Fails its intent to protect the environment because of its structural inability to balance competing ecological interests.

Up until now, all the landowner gets in a legal victory is a respite until the next round. Now, there is a difference: InsCert creates the potential for a civil alternative that takes back control of the asset. The ESA can be cited as reason to cede control back to the property owner as a superior manager. The Strategy of the Commoners uses existing environmental laws to decouple government agencies and their NGO collaborators from the legal assertion that they are disinterested and objective representatives of the public claim for ecosystem health. Landowners can recount their superior record, expose the record of harm due to civic mismanagement, and reveal the systemic motive for agencies and NGOs to instead serve corrupted interests and maintain endangered species in a state of crisis.

One can interpret anything as having harmful potential.

The ESA has unconstitutional bases in treaty law.

The Endangered Species Act (ESA), Title 16, Chapter 31, Subchapter II Section 1533 of the U.S. Code, assigns responsibility for enacting rules and regulations to the Secretary of the Interior (or the Secretary of Commerce). The text reads,

> "Whenever any species is listed as a threatened species pursuant to subsection (d) of this section, the Secretary shall issue such regulations as he deems necessary and advisable to provide for the conservation of such species."

The delegated powers in this law are so broad that the rule-makers and regulators have the effective power to make law. They define illegal behavior, redefine the burden of proof, set penalties, provide enforcement personnel, and administer punishments, effectively combining all three (supposedly) separate and co-equal branches of government into one. The U.S. Constitution prohibits assignment of legislative authority by the Congress to the Executive Branch under both the Enumerated Powers Principle and the Separation of Powers Principle. Consolidation of legislative power into administrative government is clearly unconstitutional in practice, even if there are tenuous threads of authority that lend them supposed legitimacy. How do they get away with it?

The Endangered Species Act supposedly derives its authority to take private property from multilateral treaties, principally the Convention on Nature Protection and Wild Life Preservation in the Western Hemisphere, that entered into force on May 1, 1942, the Convention on International Trade in Endangered Species of Wild Fauna and Flora (CITES) that entered into force on November 1, 1983 and the Convention on the Conservation of Migratory Species of Wild Animals (CMS) 1 November 1983.

Administration of the ESA is under Admiralty Law, pursuant to amendments to the Trading with the Enemy Act and War Powers Act enacted during the bankruptcy of the corporate United States in 1933. These laws have had enormous effect upon property rights. To discuss them in depth is beyond the scope of this book. Once respect for common law was mortally wounded, all that the executive branch needed to accrue property was justification.

The Convention on Nature Protection must be read to be believed. In his summary report to a distracted Senate, Executive Report No. 5, April 3 1941, Secretary of State Cordell Hull misrepresented its virtually unlimited scope.

From the Preamble (bold emphasis added):

> "The Governments of the American Republics, wishing to protect and preserve in their natural habitat representatives of **all species and genera of their native flora and fauna**, including migratory birds, in sufficient numbers and over areas extensive enough to assure them from becoming extinct **through any agency within man's control**;"

After going on at considerable length about wilderness areas and national parks, they come back with this language in Article V Section 1:

> "The Contracting Governments agree to adopt, or to propose such adoption to their respective appropriate law-making bodies, suitable laws and regulations for the protection and preservation of flora and fauna within their national boundaries **but not included in the national parks, national reserves, nature monuments, or strict wilderness reserves** referred to in Article II hereof."

All species, all land, no limits to the commitment. Mr. Hull made no mention of the scope of Article V in his summary. It was he who, upon Roosevelt's approval, convened the Planning Commission that created the United Nations soon after the adoption of this treaty. It is a document that exceeds the constitutional authority of the government of the United States.

It can't work either. This treaty is contrary to natural law.

Nature is a dynamic, adaptive, and competitive system. Under changing conditions, some species go extinct, indeed, for natural selection to operate, they must. The problem arises because human agency and influence is so pervasive that one can always attribute its loss to being within man's control. When humans ask, "Which ones lose?" the treaty specifies, "None," and demands no limit to the commitment to save them all. This of course destroys the ability to act as agent to save anything, much less objectively evaluate how best to expend our resources to do the best that can be done.

The demand of this treaty is a mutually exclusive logic, based upon an assumption that is a Type II error. It cannot be logically satisfied.

A government that derives power from a genetic status quo is incapable of a solution. This is a system that assumes protection and preservation work. It gives agencies of government unlimited monopoly power to manage all land use as if that would help. It supposes that agencies are experts interested only in fulfilling their mandate. It dedicates unlimited tax resources for protection of an unlimited number of species and their genera. It invokes itself across the entire nation. It assumes that destroying an economy will benefit native species. How would we then fund the research to learn to do better?

This unconstitutional treaty is the root of the proliferation of "sub-species." It is the cited authority for the powers exerted by Federal Agencies through the courts. Proponents for such multilateral treaties claim that they supercede the Constitution, per Article VI, Clause 2:

> "This Constitution, and the Laws of the United States which shall be made in Pursuance thereof; and all Treaties made, or which shall be made, under the Authority of the United States, shall be the supreme Law of the Land; and the Judges in every State shall be bound thereby, any Thing in the Constitution or Laws of any State to the Contrary notwithstanding."

This claim of treaty authorization ignores the facts that treaties are authorized UNDER the Constitution. Therefore, any treaty that violated it would be void, because:

1. The Constitution and the Declaration of Independence acknowledge property rights as unalienable and stated that the purpose of government is to secure those rights.

2. The officers who negotiate and ratify treaties take an oath to abide by the Constitution. They do not have the legal authority to negotiate, ratify, or enforce an illegal document.

Supreme Court decisions have prohibited treaties that violate Constitutional provisions because government lacks the authority to conclude an agreement that violates Constitutional rights.

The Constitution specifies treaties concluded among sovereign nations. It is not possible to conclude a treaty with an unspecified composition of governments capable of *post facto* reservations or changes in scope and application. Post facto changes are effectively changes in the terms of the treaty after ratification. Suits in Federal Court to extend the scope and application of the ESA citing the an extended interpretation of a treaty are in violation of the 11th Amendment that prohibits extending any suit by or for a foreign power, to any of the United States.

The connection between the ESA and its authority in CITES has even less in common with its practical administration or the purpose of the treaty, as ratified by the Senate. The current thread of "logic" is that economic uses of land that alter habitat are equivalent to trading in endangered species. This assertion may be technically attributable to economic theory, however, to believe that this was intended by those who ratified CITES is dubious.

The ESA specifically prohibits any "take" of endangered species as follows in USC 1532:

(19) The term "take" means to harass, harm, pursue, hunt, shoot, wound, kill, trap, capture, or collect, or to attempt to engage in any such conduct.

CITES was sold as a means to protect endangered species by outlawing trade in animal commodities such as ivory. (The theory underlying CITES has been completely discredited in practice. The black market nearly destroyed these animals in Africa. As it turns out, the best way to assure protection in perpetuity is private management, because the owners of the animals have reason to protect them to maintain future cash flow.)

There is no authority to take the use of land in this definition because there is no definition of "take" in the CITES at all. The UN has such a definition in the Convention on the Conservation of Migratory Species of Wild Animals (CMS) Article 1, Chapter 1 that reads:

i) "Taking" means taking, hunting, fishing capturing, harassing, deliberate killing, or attempting to engage in any such conduct;

Note that the CMS definition (including recursive elements) does not include the term "harm." We did this to ourselves, folks. This is a provision of the ESA that could be reformed by Congress as is the scope of powers illegally assigned to the "Secretary" (the rest may require the Supreme Court). There is no basis in treaty law that allows an attribution of "harm" as a basis for taking private property, let alone the potential for harm. If the customary application of the ESA is to control the use of private property in the interest of the enforcing agency instead of species protection, then the ESA is clearly unconstitutional in practice and destructive to its purported intent.

Civic administration of the ESA serves the interests of a financial elite.

The activist community is serving as agent for the prime civil beneficiaries of the Act: those who profit by sequestering competing resources, or reducing the cost of acquisition for conversion in use.

Upon collapse of the Brettonwoods Agreement, the Nixon Administration offered foreign investors the mineral wealth of the Western United States as collateral for U.S. Treasury Bonds. Agencies of the Federal Government are using the ESA, acting to collect and hold that weal as collateral, in violation of Government's most sacred public trust: private property rights.

These priorities, coupled with civic power without accountability, alienate environmental laws from their purpose. Banning offshore oil drilling or nuclear fuel reprocessing serves the interests of Treasury bond-holders in the Middle East. The Grand Staircase-Escalante National Monument sequestered low-sulfur coal deposits enriching Clinton supporter James Riady. Listing salmon as endangered pleased the owners of foreign aquaculture concerns, multinational agricultural interests, exported aluminum production, and increased domestic fossil fuel demand. Hard rock mining has passed increasingly into foreign ownership (reported distinctions in regulatory scrutiny between American citizens and foreign interests are disturbing).

It is a feeding frenzy among the already wealthy.

Civic administration of the ESA expresses a democratic interest in a valuable asset and is an urban subsidy.

Private property owners maintain the land, provide economic goods, and pay taxes that support their communities. The urban assertion is that protection of endangered species is necessary without proof that the owner of the remnant habitat was culpable for species decline. The opposite is more likely true. The species probably experienced the majority of its decline when the urban public converted the use of their land and placed their demands upon natural resources without the concurrent demand to pay for species protection. The rural owner holds all that remains of the asset, and is expected to submit their property to environmental protection for urban benefit without compensation.

Public claims on private property thus place a disproportionate burden on the rural owner for a speculative urban and civic benefit. Those owners of endangered species habitat are those who did NOT destroy the habitat sufficiently to extirpate the species and are expected to bear the sole burden of compensating for prior conversions sponsored by urban interests. This burden of discrimination deprives owners of the equal protection of the laws required by the Fourteenth and Fifteenth Amendments, as enforced through 42 U.S.C. Section 1983. The finding that they are the sole parties responsible for harm because the contested habitat is scarce, is a violation of Fourth Amendment protections of unreasonable seizure without establishing probable cause. It is a violation of the privileges and immunities of State Citizenship.

The reason private investment in ecosystem assets does not exist is that the public enlists a civic agent to take that use at below market value. A democratized commons destroys the product before the fact. The threat of civic monopoly interest in managing species habitat also suppresses the market value of associated assets to the point that the total account goes negative. The principal reason the species management market does not exist is civic price suppression, whether via the costs of regulatory compliance and the threat of confiscation via eminent domain. Both are violations of Fifth Amendment protections against uncompensated takings or deprivations of the use of private property.

Civic and NGO administration of the ESA is motivated to fail.

The idea that mere habitat protection and regulation of commerce constitutes species protection is suspect. With but a few exceptions, Federal protections under the terms and conditions of the ESA have failed. Very few endangered species have been delisted because of Federal protection.

The United States is committed to protect rare and endangered species. That does not mean that the government should own the land and pay the workers to manage the habitat, quite the contrary. As long as government is tempted to acquire and extend its power by projection of endangered status, it will conduct itself in a manner destructive to those flora and fauna in direct violation of that treaty.

There is no accountability in a system that derives more funding if it fails to deliver an effective service. We have already seen that wildlands require management. Federal maintenance of public lands is over $17 billion dollars in arrears. Agencies prefer to expend funds for land acquisition, instead. The State of California maintenance budget for public lands is over $3 billion dollars in arrears. It, too, continues a pattern of land use acquisition. When seven million acres of National Forests were incinerated, the USFS was rewarded with $2 billion dollars for fuels reduction. Given the motivational structure of the agencies, the answer is not simply more money.

In both instances, the cumulative effect of poor maintenance has had adverse effects on the threatened and endangered species that land acquisition was purported to protect. Both State and Federal governments have thus violated the terms of their contract for stewardship of public lands and cost-effective protection of rare and endangered species on a grand scale. They have demonstrated their true intent through their budget priorities.

There are better ways to improve environmental health than civic protection of habitat for endangered species, particularly when the managing agencies have financial and political reasons to fail. A market could work to manage their numbers and improve their health but, unfortunately, the dependent beneficiaries of the ESA stand firmly in the way.

Endangered species are transformation products of private property, the principal assets of private habitat management service enterprises.

Animals and plants result from uses of process assets that transform the state of commons. The bounded right to control of the use of process assets constitutes private property. Any taking of that control is a taking of the use. Any business that manages endangered species therefore must be free to control the use of those assets.

No industry will invest in an asset that has negative market value. No person can trade in an asset that has an indeterminate price. No market can function without civic respect for the rule of law, contract enforcement, and protection of private property rights as unalienable. A market cannot develop, and prices for ecosystem assets cannot be negotiated, while the prospect of civic takings remains. Civic price suppression has been so complete as to negate calculation of the economic value of habitat for endangered species. That does not mean that their potential economic value is nonexistent, quite the contrary. The behavior of civic agencies and the scope of public support for environmental protection demonstrate the pecuniary interests of both civic agents and the urban public.

Civic administration of the ESA expresses agency interest in taking an economically valuable asset and in accruing police power thereby.

The projection of power beyond those specifically enumerated by the Constitution demonstrates an interest on the part of government. Expression of interest denotes a profit motive, whether pecuniary or political. That interest indicates the presence of potential market value in the target asset.

Government is destroying the economic value of managing endangered species as a business, creating conditions for acquisition at minimal cost. It destroys also the ancillary uses of the property that could supply the capital for such a business until it develops. The agency budget rises by virtue of the court order to protect species and administer their recovery. To successfully list a species AND economically harm the owner BOTH benefit select agency interests.

When officers of government operate as interested parties, they are incapable of providing equal protection of the laws. Any confiscation of the use of private property by administrative authority without due process is prohibited under the 14th Amendment.

All citizens are entitled to separate State and Federal processes as a part of the privileges and immunities, equal protection, and due process clauses guaranteed under the Constitution. The United States Supreme Court applied this principle of federalism for the first time in 1992. The Court deemed laws passed by Congress as unconstitutional if Congress renders itself, or the states, politically unaccountable to their constituents, by coercing a State to perform a Federally mandated requirement. The political accountability test has restored the role of the Federal courts to protecting the property rights of citizens against assertions of civic power. The Supreme Court now applies the same Fourteenth Amendment standard against Federal action that it applies against the States.

Civic administration of the ESA is unaccountable, and is therefore destructive to the environment. It threatens worse.

The environment is a competitive system. To assume that after centuries of change in base conditions that it should assume a form similar to before humans or white humans arrived could be hugely destructive, particularly when we do can't know the goal, have no method, and no means to evaluate progress. To assume that humans are so destructive as to require separation from nature and that preservation is the only acceptable solution is worse.

Because of the harm already done, it will require enormous amounts of investment and labor to fix. Many experiments have shown that it can be done. How do we prioritize that work? Who will do it? What technically qualified person would work alone in the woods, bent over weeding under the threat of wolves or grizzly bears? Shouldn't we get the plants fixed first? How many educated people would that take? Aren't we moving too fast?

A civic agent that prospers by coercive acquisition for ulterior purposes having nothing to do with ecology is incapable of objective conclusions. Without honest means to weigh the relative value of species or alleles, or the real threats they face, we cannot learn the importance of their interactions or cannot hedge the relative risks of specific methods. Without a profit motive, no one would want to characterize their adaptive mechanics, improve their response, or avoid doing unnecessary damage. Upon massive change in external conditions, it makes no sense to preserve our ignorance maintaining a genetic status quo under a maladaptive response system.

Executive Order 12986 indemnified the IUCN and their member NGOs and agencies from financial accountability for any damages. Indemnifying oil companies and government from liability for oxygenates gave us MTBE in groundwater and the Sierra Club supported it for years after the danger was understood. Big government and activist NGOs are not agents of either the public interest or environmental health, nor are they capable of satisfying the Equal Protection Clause under the Fourteenth Amendment. Sue them in the name of protecting the environment. They are taking dangerous risks.

Can you just hear the denial to those charges? 'Oh, what we're doing really isn't so bad.' Have you ever heard that before? Are people with no liability for mistakes likely to make them?

The rationale for the ESA was that interactions among species are complex and that, therefore, all species should be protected, because to do so maintains a healthy environment for humans. Without regard to whether this argument was misrepresented, the ESA is developing cumulative secondary effects that, in fact, degrade the global environment and may engender precisely such a catastrophic global environmental disaster. But, not the way that they would suspect.

Regulatory costs force industry offshore. Transportation costs rise and manufacturers pay higher costs for imported materials. Higher import volume brings increasing pest infestations, destroying domestic habitat. Foreign materials are extracted with less environmental protection and the people of those nations suffer the consequences. They don't like that. The balance of payments deficit balloons. Investors and political patrons line their pockets with the results: secure interest payments and military protection of offshore "interests," maintaining corrupt dictatorships of nations with badly degraded local environments. It is a process that threatens global security.

Wars have always been bad for nature and are usually fought over resources. Given that yet another global conflict might include biological weapons, another world war might be catastrophic.

The environment IS about our interaction with natural systems at the control boundary of our influence. It is a discipline of self-control. Consider the incontinent behavior of the activist community and its sponsors and their willingness, no, DESIRE to eradicate 80% of the human community.

The private property owner can do a better job. Take it back.

It's OUR Problem

We have met the enemy and he is us. When we ask government to manage The Environment, we are conceding our property rights and giving up the opportunity to market services caring for it. So what IS the alternative?

Problems are assets. Marketing services caring for the land will require wresting control from democratic and civic claimants. That will require an established alternative: a management system capable of establishing a claim of structurally superior capability to civic management.

For InsCert to exist will require a qualified customer base, a contract lawyer or two, some capital, and a few serious insurers. The components exist; some of the behavior exists. InsCert does not. It is not a company or franchise, though that could happen. It is not a legal specification or set of rules. As of now, InsCert is a it is a way of doing things, a descriptive term for a free market of service products within a motivational structure of checks and balances managed by accounted risk as described in this book.

It's our job to assist (or foment) the conversion to free market environmental management. If you got this far, you have at least that potential and, thus, at least that responsibility.

So where do we start?

Own the Data

This book has defined real property as processes that produce transformation products in commons across a control boundary. That definition proves that socialized control of the use of such assets is a taking. To reclaim ownership under that premise requires a description of the physical properties of the assets and their behavior.

Landowners own the technical facts about their land. Examples are detailed knowledge of soil types, water flow patterns, plants, insects, and infestations of exotic species, even views. It is a lot of work to document and enforce, but not terribly expensive if acquired opportunistically during regular maintenance or just a walk. All it takes is a camera, a notebook or tape recorder, and reference information. It would sure be nice to have a GPS receiver with voice transcription to base software. Much such work dovetails into the record of practice used to qualify for certification and coverage.

Activists and government have generated most of their theories by study of two environmental extremes: the pristine ecosystem and the debacles of industry. The reasons are primarily logistical issues of access and financing. Grant-funded research programs require access to property for collecting samples and taking measurements. Other data are acquired through the permit process. In either case, these data are both easy to get and easy to justify. Parks, rivers, groundwater, oceans, and air are often public resources; the access is free. Collection of industrial waste data is acquired as measurement of transformation products in commons or is required upon initiation of a permit request or a lawsuit.

Private land, particularly resource land such as timberland, is another matter. On that type of property, activists and government have had less access to collect data. This disparity has led to some embarrassing results, as the spotted owl fiasco attests. If property owners had known how many spotted owls they owned before they were listed, would they have saved money? If the Klamath farmers had a 50 year interest in suckerfish would they have saved money?

Landowners need to compile the historical record of problems, their causes, and how they were engendered (a notable source has been various fads in government regulations). They need to document how those problems have manifested per successive civic mandates, including taxation.

Compiling data requires that one must confront organizing it for communication. Ecological causes and effects are complex. It can be startling how tangled and interactive such information can be. There are endless feedback loops, introductions of new variables, and unique events. When these subjects are crossed with the causes and effects of policy and economics, their organization can be a nightmare. The data have to be examined and reexamined, piled, catalogued, filed, piled again, over and over. This is where the real work of understanding ecosystem function and organizing it into useful form occurs.

As data are collected over time, the composite becomes a living record of changing conditions in response to specific measures. It is crucial evidence with which to demonstrate the harm done by government, the benefits of management activities, and the need for specific experiments.

Data acquisition tools are more powerful than ever. Commercial satellites will soon have resolutions down to 10cm. Government has opened that market by unconstitutional Executive Orders with total lack of consideration for who owns the information. Reflected light is a transformation product of the use of property. Data is private property. Claim it now, or lose it forever.

It's a Process

Because the concept of processes as assets is somewhat unfamiliar to some, a few definitions are in order:

- A **process** transforms inputs into outputs over time.
- Process **data** recount the history of inputs and outputs.
- Process **descriptions** detail asset behavior in quantitative terms.
- Process **instructions** document controlled human inputs.

The latter two may sound similar, but are completely different:

1. Process instructions detail how property is used.
2. Process descriptions are of what is owned as property.

One would think that the description would come first, but that isn't how it works. One can't fully characterize dynamic system behavior without perturbing it in a controlled fashion and measuring the response. Process descriptions start with process instructions.

Writing a process instruction is very much like writing a recipe. It takes practice and repetition, even for something as simple as baking a cake. One must account for differences in raw materials, instrumentation errors, and people who don't follow directions carefully. Cake baking is being tweaked to this day as cooking tools and ingredients change. Convection ovens change cake baking just as walking machines might change skidding logs.

When you bake a cake, the inputs are agreed upon, everybody knows what 'preheat to 350°F' means. The process instruction accounts for the degree to which ovens and pans vary by suggesting tests to see if the cake is done.

When writing process instructions for nature, one must accept inputs that are wildly variable, not constant, and totally out of control. (Mother Nature never baked a cake.) Still, natural processes are remarkably reliable. The trick is to figure out how to discover the responses to specific inputs.

Nature offers extreme perturbations free of charge, often called "events." Ecologists love natural disasters (such as fires, floods, and volcanoes) because they are an opportunity to learn from natural adaptations to events that we cannot produce ourselves. Unfortunately, events are, by definition, out of "control" and hard to measure. They leave the practitioner with relatively few means to prepare appropriate instrumentation.

This is why detailed process instructions of experiments, intended to perturb natural systems, are so important. Without reliably knowing what was done, much less what resulted, it is hard to assign causes to effects. Without that connection, a broadly capable process description cannot be derived.

Perturbations by economic processes greatly accelerate that understanding. This is one reason why preservationist policies are so destructive to our knowledge of the dynamic operation of natural systems. While much is learned by simple extended observation, it occurs only within very confined limits after enormously expensive and protracted periods of waiting for stat- istically relevant events that rarely replicate or scale themselves predictably. Components of specific events are easily replicated under scalable and con- trolled conditions. These are opportunities for detailed observations that can teach us much of how to prepare for the real thing, take advantage of them, or (as is the case in conflagrations) eliminate them entirely.

This is what is meant about how tools organize our understanding of nature. We know what "bake at 350°F" means unless our ovens are calibrated in °C. We know about erosion damage, largely because of the mistakes that have been made. Not all the inputs of natural processes have been characterized, certainly not on a basis that integrates collections of inputs into meaningful blocks with controllable knobs and dials, much less means of dealing with error and variation. For many natural processes, calibrated units do not exist.

It is not necessary to have characterized all the systems within a bounded region for a subsystem to have economic worth. People farmed for centuries without a full understanding of soil biology. More intangible products may require a better understanding of the subtleties and interactions among systems. Such instances will require development of process descriptions, particularly when the minimum economically viable scale is very large.

A process description details not only the biochemical and mechanical behavior of process constituents when perturbed, but the limits for every input variable under which the model remains predictive. **The process description is a means to describe what is property; i.e. it is the heart of the transfer functions and characteristic equations** (see Part III Chapter 4). Developing process descriptions (or hazard reviews) identifies long-term threats or opportunities, capable of altering the present value of the particular use. More importantly, the exercise identifies what is NOT yet known and suggests economic justification for performing the necessary research. A process description can identify missing or underdeveloped constituents that would reduce long term losses, thus indicating need for investment in an offsetting or complementary asset. It might identify threats that discount the present value of the current application. They can also estimate the residual life of the asset before the current use must be placed in rotation.

A benefit to this system is that it starts with minimal need to make a universal model. One will end up combining sub-systems into composite models anyway. Sub-system models allow increased variation of specific inputs or minimize certain limiting parameters so that the process does not operate beyond diminishing returns. The model would allow process instructions to be applicable to specific conditions without the limitations inherent to universal specifications. Diverse approaches allow deviation that can assist the process of stumbling upon new models and principles that have so far eluded rule-based systems.

Forgotten among most people's lists of process inputs, is the unique combination of skills, interests, and historical perspectives of the people who care for the land. Individual process designs allow fitting process instructions to skill-sets. This increases yet again diversity of approaches, and improves the chance that competing ideas and skill mixes among workers can improve performance. It is a flexibility that is sadly lacking in rule and credential-driven systems, which rears its ugly head with the horde of required State-licensed consultants, armed with stock solutions.

With all that diversity, it is the need to combine uses into economic units that organizes descriptions of the unique characteristics of one site in terms that are meaningful to others. Commerce organizes such information into useful blocks and resolves differences among individuals. Competition minimizes the propensity to over-complicate the description. This is what is meant by information being somewhat self-organizing in a free market. The nature of inputs and outputs dictates the description of the process, its parameters, and its tolerances in meaningful terms, for unless the reliability of the information has known limits, how would it be tradable?

A full discussion of process descriptions is beyond the scope of this book other than to state what they are and how they are important. Descriptions become apparent and necessary as instructions become more detailed and interactions among factors outside property lines become more important. As property owners combine their process assets into functional economic units, their descriptions organize further into a common language, with hierarchical organizations of complex data into understandable blocks. Sometimes these blocks can be training manuals by which decisions can be responsibly driven to the most appropriate levels, instead of long-winded instructions that nobody reads (been there).

Educate Yourself

Reliable data in a communicable format is the central organizing principle of InsCert. This is the reason for including periodic education in the proposed standard. It is a way to learn the tradeoffs between sample size and error, or the latest developments in instruments and analytical tools. It is a way to stay ahead of a huckster selling management contracts for goods wherewith to take control of the land without buying all of its processes. The threat to do so can awake the owner to the potential for hidden wealth.

Landowners should begin the process of educating themselves to operate environmental management businesses. There is a place to get help in learning, perhaps even online. For once, a landowner may even be treated like a customer and fellow students learn that landowners are respectable human beings. Landowners might learn how best to employ these young people. Professors and students might be more circumspect when confronted with the reality of generations of experience in the classroom. Fields of study could include: process design, documentation, and validation, measurement techniques, statistical analyses, and multivariate experimental design.

Statistically designed experiments are new to many people. There are several varieties, all of which have their unique advantages and weaknesses. There are screening experiments, in which one is performing gross manipulations to determine if a principle applies at all. There are factorial arrays that one uses to make certain nothing is missed among a huge number of trials. Unknown to many people, arrays can characterize multiple variables simultaneously, or expose combinations of variables that only change the output when changed simultaneously (called higher-order interactions). There are also fractional techniques capable of eliminating unnecessary fields.

The awesome power of these techniques is that one can mathematically KNOW the degree to which one has confidence in the results and the possibility of error, given the accuracy of limited assumptions. It is a way of seeing that changes how one sees.

Designed experiments do not require technical expertise, although they can be conceptually daunting, simply because we are not accustomed to manipulating dozens of variables at once while expecting to understand the results. They are not so challenging in execution, as they are an organizational problem. They require excellent record-keeping skills and a computer, not higher mathematics.

Network

Communication integrates data into higher orders of understanding, capable of assuming multiple cross-referenced architectures for targeted purposes. Simplifications of base data are more likely to form accurate models, than are top-down simulations based upon over-simplified assumptions. Higher-order composites are be more rigorous proofs than the typical government computer model, and will be more capable of distinguishing relative interaction between regional problems and unique local circumstances.

So why would the activists and civil servants try to derail all that? It's good for the environment isn't it? It is, after all, certified, validated, and audited data. Isn't theirs?

You already know how lame some of it really is.

The same mechanics by which landowners would document fully private operations could be applied to those operating on federal lands, particularly insofar as specific contracts are concerned. The process may well expose the degree to which the interests expressed through contract have been historic causes of problems or how landowners provided uncompensated that depreciated the value of the producing assets. By these means, they could collect the record of civic mismanagement for objective comparison. It is this kind of documentation that will add breadth and depth to the ecological case demonstrating capricious agency behavior.

Landowners' associations could archive audit records, collate them into composite data, coordinate and publish regional experiments to minimize pooled risk. They might serve as a venue for patent applications and licensing, contract auditors, and discipline members. They could contract with specialists to review experimental proposals and suggest specific measurement protocols. They could market these management tools, and support development of, or provide purchase pools for software to make it easier.

In short, landowners' associations are natural certification companies. The AF&PA certification (Part III, Chapter 2) is an archetype, in that respect (missing are the insurance, audit, and process validation). As management products mature, they move down-market. If the certification companies become popular, packaged management products may become available.

As certification and insurance products mature and propagate, marketing and educational tools will also become more effective and available. The financial justification for insured certification will also become more rigorous. This is essential to identifying the financial opportunities which interest investors in funding a political process to throw off the civic yoke.

Publish or Parish

One is never positive about wishful thinking; which is why we have peer reviews and audits. There are, however, objective measures of product value other than academic approval. It may seem to you that you don't know enough to publish. Neither did I (and by now you might think that I was right). You may think that no one would understand. They will, as long as you go through the pain of figuring out how to say it. If you don't do it, you might as well start praying. You may think that no one cares. You do.

It is through publication and advertising that common interests are collected over great distances. One of the powerful benefits of InsCert as a commercial principle is that it directs communication into targeted markets for honest reasons. This creates potential for combinations of remote property owners to organize and invest in enterprises managing mobile assets requiring non-contiguous resources.

Selling organizes information like nothing else. Making a pitch for a buck has objectivity seldom acknowledged by those who wrinkle their noses at the profession: Both peer and product reviews are forms of independent evaluation. The market carries with it an added means to propagate an idea rapidly: advertising. Like it or not, without advertising there is no product at all, as environmental organizations know very well. They are masters at it. They have prepared the market to want an ecosystem management product. Take advantage of that investment.

Enlist Common Interests

By far the biggest interest that insurance companies currently have in a program like InsCert is in financing risk reduction. We started with fire in the rural/suburban forest, but the motive obviously does not end there.

Validating data within the certification process not only renders it tradable; it converts it into a legal tool. These tools create the points of discussion and negotiation that start a process of balancing competing claims. Data can show how the destruction of resource value abets land conversion, possibly betraying a conflict of interest. Data quantify in detail the scope of economic risk resulting from secondary consequences of tacit civic confiscation. One can then state what the loss would be should the civic plan be a disaster. Having the data makes it possible to tie the government in knots every time they come up with another way to drive down the value of resource land using their own environmental laws.

Models of systemic mechanisms and population census data can be used to invoke the Endangered Species Act against State agencies, the Sierra Club, the EPA, and the local air quality people, for their restrictions on prescribed fire and fuels management versus perpetuation of the risk of catastrophic fire. The cost of environmental risks can be huge. Government abets the risk by hiding it behind FEMA. Insurers could find a good business financing risk reduction. Do they want help getting FEMA out of the insurance business?

The essential requirement for getting started is developing the management systems for support businesses. For example: Insurance companies might want to fund venture capital to enlist firefighters and foresters in developing a rating system for fire-associated risks by which Residential Buffer products can be marketed by local foresters and landowners. Landowners may want independent assessment of animal census data. These obviously vary by location, which cries for the flexibility and dynamism of small businesses. With the information such companies generate and simplify, insurers can start accumulating actuarial information by which to price the insurance according to local conditions. They would also have the motive to lean on state legislatures to get state-wide pooling off their backs.

They, too, might wish to invoke environmental laws.

There is a big competitive opportunity to reduce the risk of prescribed fire in an area with structures. Insurers might fund research that develops limited control technologies and design preventative measures. It might be a plan of plant distributions that meet the local need for habitat, while controlling the pattern of successive future burns. It might be special fixtures for economically salvaging large trees among expensive houses at risk of being crushed. It might be a soap-foam blanket by which to limit a chaparral burn to a mosaic structure or simply limit temperature, flame spread, and retain embers in patch burns. There might be a need for a stilt walker to apply such materials. Such a machine might reduce the spread of weeds.

The insurer is the indispensable player in putting the processes together with the necessary technical developments for the product package to exist. It sounds expensive but consider the alternatives. Chaparral needs to burn periodically, but it is idiotic to let it get out of control. Big trees near houses are beautiful, but they can crush houses and kill people while getting them out makes a mess and wastes material. Risk reduction is good business as long as the practitioners can be trusted. InsCert is key to providing a medium for combining these interests with local knowledge.

Educate Your Leaders

Once the activist base of the environmental community learns how financial interests have used them, would some of them break ranks in support of the best of landowners? Might there be a resulting political realignment? If the local forest residents learned that they could reduce risk to their houses by cooperating with a forester and simultaneously derive a healthier stand in the process, would many of them throw in their lot accordingly? After completion of the work, would the neighborhood be more likely to follow? Is this a basis for a new majority?

Once the courts start to learn, that what we have is not government by committed technical experts operating at the urging of selfless activists in the public interest of protecting endangered species, but is, instead, a destructive tyranny of distracted bureaucrats and hired guns working for corporate foundations and international bankers with a hidden profit interest, a case regarding takings will be easier to make.

Problems are assets. Every product is created to solve a problem, even if it just boredom. The power of ecosystem assets to offset environmental problems is your opportunity; they are your property. Learn to measure and develop their worth. Guard them jealously as precious assets. Open space is your product; view shed is your product, as is biodiversity, as is habitat for endangered species or fire management of accumulated fuels. When government attempts to take them, it is indeed taking something of value.

How much is it worth? To whom should the specifics be marketed?

The only way to know is to measure. We must break the civic monopoly in environmental management with the distinction of insured certification, solving specific problems at which government has systemically failed.

Ask for a Jury Trial

How many times have landowners been denied standing in a court concerning a case involving endangered species? Were they to have a financial interest in endangered species management, would have standing. They may then have more options in the future to recover their losses.

The following is from the case: *CITY OF MONTEREY, PETITIONER v. DEL MONTE DUNES,* decided by the Supreme Court on May 24, 1999:

> This case began with attempts by the respondent, Del Monte Dunes, and its predecessor in interest to develop a parcel of land within the jurisdiction of the petitioner, the city of Monterey. The city, in a series of repeated rejections, denied proposals to develop the property, each time imposing more rigorous demands on the developers. Del Monte Dunes brought suit in the United States District Court for the Northern District of California, under Rev. Stat. §1979, 42 U.S.C. § 1983. After protracted litigation, the case was submitted to the jury on Del Monte Dunes' theory that the city effected a regulatory taking or otherwise injured the property by unlawful acts, without paying compensation or providing an adequate postdeprivation remedy for the loss. The jury found for Del Monte Dunes, and the Court of Appeals affirmed.
>
> The petitioner contends that the regulatory takings claim should not have been decided by the jury and that the Court of Appeals adopted an erroneous standard for regulatory takings liability. We need not decide all of the questions presented by the petitioner, nor need we examine each of the points given by the Court of Appeals in its decision to affirm. The controlling question is whether, given the city's apparent concession that the instructions were a correct statement of the law, the matter was properly submitted to the jury. We conclude that it was, and that the judgment of the Court of Appeals should be affirmed.

Don't ever let a judge do it to you again. This case has yet to make its impact felt. It's up to you to make that happen.

The Knock on the Door

You probably don't have to go looking for an opportunity because the activists or regulators will probably hand you one without knowing it. They will do it by pointing out and trying to control the very assets in need of protection and management services. The key is to be ready to fight back.

Once you win (and you eventually will because they don't have a technical or constitutional leg to stand upon), offer the civil alternative. Although the activist NGOs and bureaucrats will protest, it is lack of faith in their case and their own system that will drive them to resist objective environmental review. They will not subjugate themselves to scientific scrutiny because their faith in their beliefs (and their need for a paycheck) is so strong that they believe that any technical rationale that can challenge that faith must be flawed. Should they lose, they tend to blame the legal resources of industry instead of the technical merit of their case. This is related to the belief that anything they want must be necessarily beneficial, as if their leadership was objectively so interested.

One would have to ask the question: Is it because of a lack of faith in the system or is it more personal than that.

Can you imagine, after courting all that hysteria to raise donations, after all that struggle in the courts, after all those hours of volunteer-time, gleefully (and you should see it) putting their energy into destroying the lives of people who were born and raised on the land they love, what it would be like to find out that it is based upon a false premise? After all those hateful arguments with all those "corporate tree killers," the hours of tortured faces and venom, sign-painting, tree-sitting, and demonstrations; could the activists face the people who had loved their land for over a hundred years, families in pain at the loss of their love and livelihood without any alternative or hope for the future? Are they willing to own creeks full of muck, landslides oozing down the hillsides, and fields full of broom and star thistle among standing towers of combusted trees? After years of pompous breast beating on the moral pulpit, are they going to face the open gazes of small children whose homes and forest playgrounds have been burned to atmospheric dust and tell them that it was all a mistake?

It is for themselves that they cling, not for the trees.

The worst of it is, in order to hold the government and the environmental NGOs and their supporting foundations accountable for a disaster, the forest will probably have to incur perhaps more than one tragedy. At least when the landowners break out the ugly finger of accountability, the public will understand and know why because there will be proof.

Proof:

- That they were warned.
- That the subsequent revision of history was fraudulent.
- That they ignored or contested the evidence.
- That debate was stifled and regulations were railroaded through.
- That both government and the NGOs had acted in the interest of financial gain by select individuals.
- There will be proof of the cost, the perpetrators, and the damages.

One assumes, of course, that there will remain a government under the rule of law through which to affix an assessment. If there isn't, then no amount of proof would matter. What the heck, why not get started?

When the disaster comes, whether it is a firestorm with the attendant death and destruction, massive landslides, rapid infestation of exotic species, fatal contagious epidemics, whatever it is, take "custody" of The Environment. Demand a gradual divestiture and privatization of all non-military public resource land and withdrawal of government authority for specification of conformance. Hold activist organizations and their supporting foundations, criminally and financially accountable for the needless loss of life and destruction of habitat; for knowingly promulgating false and misleading information with negligent culpability in pursuit of financial and political gain. Sue for the privatization of wilderness land to manage it under contract as because you know better what you are doing than they do.

Don't lose faith, you are not losing cases, you are building them. This is a long-term fight. The activists, foundations, and government have enormous resources, personal motivation, lots of practice, a long lead, and the willingness to lie and forget all about their reason for existence, just to get what they want: the power to take private property without just compensation.

For the planet and for all of its living species, it is a fight that the private property owner must win

📖 Our Fathers' Calling

Conclusion to the Book

Enterprise, endeavor, industry... production, hope, pride, and profit...

Sometimes it would seem like these are almost lost words. Some people say them with a sneer of disgust and fear, like there must be something wrong with them. Our forebears spoke them with the quiet simplicity that only comes with having conquered their challenges with their humanity intact.

What they did not know, did hurt them: the broken hearts and broken backs accepted in the price of what only freedom can offer. They may not have expected any more from a life of risk, toil, and filth than a better one for their children, but at least they completed their lives with their spirits intact.

Sometimes it seems we no longer even start with ours. If there is a principal benefit to a constant flow of immigrants, it is their belief in that truth. We, the native born, who have supposedly "elevated" our status beyond the level of bitter struggle, have somehow assumed the dual expectations of prosperity and protection from harm. We seem to have forgotten something, Many, having lived without freedom, need not be reminded.

> "...with a firm Reliance on the Protection of divine Providence, we mutually pledge to each other, our Lives, our Fortunes, and our sacred Honor."

We have forgotten that life is not without risk and personal sacrifice in the defense of liberty. For without that risk, our lives are not our own.

Those of us whom have come to believe that by virtue of our birthright as Americans we have some kind of entitlement to peace and prosperity under a protectorate; that we are due a lifestyle to which we wish to become accustomed, regardless of the price of liberty, have, in submission to a popular chimera, abased the requirement of vigilance, ignored the value of industry, and abdicated our responsibility to regulate our government, our conduct, our selves. We have adopted an optimistic delusion sold by those to whom we are instructed to entrust our choices: those who would profit on the sale.

The price isn't, "Free!" It is freedom.

There was something in that industrial culture that many of us now miss: The certain expectation of the undiluted blessings and daily satisfactions to be found in the practice of what we wholeheartedly believe is productive work, the conduct of personal integrity, and the shared enterprise of individually-held shares. These personal experiences of internal confidence and the power of will were indeed sullied with the knowledge that prices were being paid by others at the expense of our benefit. Out of an overblown sense of guilt, and the consequent belief that no one could be trusted, we gave monopoly control of all factors of production to government, a body intrinsically undeserving of that trust. We thus surrendered to a mere idea, without even considering the full array of the options afforded by a free society under the rule of law. It was a surrender that may yet cost the society itself, and take the planet with it. It was a failure of leadership by those with too much to gain.

What we have before us is an opportunity to add the certainty of having done our best to account for the total effects of our striving to our cultural birthright to improve the lot of our successors. What we can gain is the certainty that responsibilities for our actions have been, or will be assumed, and that the product of our work is of net benefit to all, not at the expense of something or someone else. We can operate with the certainty, that the measure of our success in the marketplace is an objective judge of value.

Though there might be an unwitting cost to others, once it is identified, the vision allotted by conduct with integrity will drive us to measure and calculate its impact. For upon recognition of a cost, there is always opportunity: Profit is found in the reduction and control of risk.

Problems are opportunities. Though we still have a lot to learn, the redirection of human motivation can assure continued insight into the whole consequence of our being.

It is a better way to live and a better way to make a living.

Crocuses in Flanders' Fields

A Personal Epilog

This book was not about the environment. This book was about our relationship with the world: our property, our neighbors, and our government. It was about the truth of our responsibilities and the awful consequences of their abrogation. It is about the release of spiritual power and financial wealth when people begin to value honestly in others that measured fraction that is themselves. Whether it is public schools or public parks, socialism is a massive fraud we have sold to our fears. It is no way to interdependency; it is servitude and dependency.

We have a choice: to succeed or to succumb.

The people of North Korea really believe that things are worse outside their devastated prison. The environmental fascists really believe that global socialism is the only way to save the environment. Their masters really think Global Governance will work, but their priorities will betray their purpose and leave devastation in their wake. As it was in the Reign of Terror, so it could be again under a common belief that one is more capable of representing the interests of the other than they are for themselves.

They just don't know any better.

If the environmental lobby succeeds in killing private property rights, we will never know the depths of their folly, until it is too late. It is a process that is irreversible without the historic price of blood. It is precisely the reason why elitists find the likes of Dave Foreman so useful. As much as these plutocrats may fan their egos with the artful delusion that what they are doing is good and necessary, when it comes to choices they will betray that justification. They have more concern about their need for self-reinforcement by evidence of their primacy than they do about The Environment, respect for unalienable rights, or the blessings of self-government.

It is a hierarchy of self-deception, structured and maintained by power.

It doesn't take a genius to figure out that a system supporting unlimited withdrawal of groundwater, as "water rights," is archaic. It is obvious that, if people pay $1.5 million for a house in a forest, they do not want a denuded hillside next to it. If an industry wants to burn coal, it should have reason to control particulate emissions. It is clear that when people divert water for their own purposes, that they can cause problems for neighbors downhill.

It is, however, worse to go to government to solve the dispute.

Externalities are endemic to all human conduct. They don't get solved without asking how to best resolve individual disputes in a market of civil conduct among sovereign Citizens. Disputes cannot be addressed without the mutual responsibility and respect for others that we should demand out of our political leaders. It is a moral issue, and moral behavior is requisite to its expression. We should expect fewer, more carefully considered laws that describe truths to be settled as a civil matter, instead of asking government to fix it for us by directing compliance under criminal statutes. Government cannot make us moral, quite the contrary.

The idea, that your competitor is your adversary, is that moral failing. The old "golden rule" is as much observation, that one *will* treat others as they see themselves, as it admonition to reflective consideration. It is essential that laws reflect moral values if we expect to foster moral conduct. It certainly makes the job of administration just a tad easier.

If the preceding chapters depressed or angered you, please consider a free market alternative. There are ways of getting this done. Please help get it done. Understand the alternatives. Treat this work as a reference and review the sections on risk-based pricing and contracts for use; go back and read between the lines of the sections on exotic species. Study what might be done with local government. Get to know the few remaining free thinkers at State resource agencies and see if you can set up a program. Contact your State insurance commissioner and industry lobbyists and lean all over them about the management and reduction of risk. If you can, find a lawyer who understands and loves the Constitution. Take the ethic to your community and expose its simple and necessary logic. Make an issue out of it. Improve upon what I have proposed and I will do the same. If you do better than I have (and I am sure that you will), God bless you.

By writing this book I wanted to exhort the landowner to go do the hard work of objective science, to learn from and restore their land, and to measure the costs without getting too discouraged. I struggled to identify the tools to fight those who would destroy, with their fear and arrogance, what they propose to protect. I wanted to show hope to the property owner, a vision of the wealth of opportunities in their land out of which to market all its special attributes. I wanted to show the all-too-often down-trodden scientist in civil service the promise of a new career working with people who love their land, to spend their time actually doing science to help the land they love instead of writing grants to nameless benefactors who place bizarre demands upon the output. I wanted to show the financial elite that they have made a horrible mistake. There are better ways to make money.

The good news is that I probably don't have to do very much exhorting. If you know the land, you are in love. So perhaps it is better that I stop trying to exhort, and instead, sharpen a few ideas and render them a touch more personal before this is over.

In the process of research, I was inescapably led to the *ecological requirement* that the unalienable rights of citizens, especially property rights, *must* supercede the claims and powers of the state. You don't have to be religious to understand the essential mechanics of the God-given unalienable rights of citizens. Without them, there could be no private property or a free market in which to trade and invest in ecosystem assets. The logic is inescapable.

Arriving at these ideas was conducted in relative isolation. Nobody told me to use a free market for ecosystem management. When I started this, I had no idea if anybody else was doing such work. Nobody suggested I use risk-management enterprises to price externalities; it was an obvious conclusion to a more subtle question. Nobody pointed out the need for transactable rights of land use; it was a necessary means to resolve overlapping and dynamic system boundaries. These ideas and observations were simply the result of as honest and logical an inquiry as I could perform.

Once I understood the importance of particular individual valuation, what was left was to resolve the individual claims against externalities within the normal conduct of free enterprise. It was a much more mechanical task than realizing the abstractions, requiring only that I ask the questions, once the abstractions were incorporated. That is still easier said than done.

The challenge was to communicate these abstractions and incorporated them into the reader. That takes other people: smart, tolerant, and objective people. It isn't easy to get their attention, especially when you're nobody famous or eminent, asking for an awful lot of time and patience, and babbling wild ideas incoherently. To those many readers upon whom I inflicted so much frustration, consternation, pestering, and confusion, I beg forgiveness and offer my most sincere thanks. That confusion and consternation unwittingly supplied me with many of the questions, against which to integrate the (by then) too obvious answers. The process teaches humility.

Whether I like it or not this work is probably not done. If you have constructive observations or suggestions please let me know. For my failings to make this clearer (or shorter) I beg this apology: It was a big book already, I was running out of money and it needed to get out to people who are so buried that they need help articulating their perceptions and perhaps some useful tools with which to retake the Moral High Ground.

It is, perhaps paradoxically true, that I cannot own such a thing as an observation, but merely its empowering articulation. For this writing is obviously not only a collection of truths observed. If it had been so, this book would be only a few pages long. It is my hope that I have done a faithful job of offering a well-conceived, logically self-regulating structure that reflects those truths and integrates suggested activities into useful synergies that continuously generate new opportunities and reduce costs. That desire to prevent corruption of such a powerful tool is why I chose to protect it by patent. I hope to see a lot of deserving and talented people get rich. (If you think that I did this much work, and took this much risk just for money, you are certifiably crazy). I do hope it provides me the chance to write yet more. I have enjoyed this process like nothing else in my life. I can only hope that those who see the potentials presented here will not turn the extremely powerful tools into evil. It is certainly possible.

Which brings us all back to intent and motive. Hopefully, I have done something about that, though certainly not nearly enough. In the future, all I can do is ask for God's help, and yours.

Thank you for your time.

Errata

30 Proof Prints were sold or offered to contributors. These are the substantive errors:

Photo 1 in the proof prints was oriented according to reports from the site, but is now presented as it appears in the source photo; i.e., possibly backwards.

Proof prints stated that Fred Keeley "filed an appeal on every major THP." This is not so (but so it seemed to two thirds of the reviewers).

Proof prints stated, "There are several more companies with current applications for accreditation to the FSC, most notably the Certified Forest Products Council (CFPC)." CFPC is an organization that promotes FSC chain of custody programs. It is not a certification program. It is funded by foundations that also fund the FSC.

Endnotes

Endnotes to Part I

Chapter 1 – Stuff, and What You Can Do With the Stuff

1. Hardin, Garrett; The Tragedy of the Commons, Science, 162 (1968): 1243-1248. URL: http://dieoff.com; Charming Web Site.

2. Harris, George Washington; Sicily Burns's Wedding, Native American Humor, Walter Blair (ed.), Harper & Row, 1960, pp368-88. It's really funny!

Chapter 2 – Artificially Preserved

3. Diamond, William J.; Practical Experiment Designs for Engineers and Scientists, 2nd Edition, Nostrand Rheinhold, 1989, pp 20-22.

4. John, Peter W. M.; *Statistical Methods in Engineering and Quality Assurance;* Wiley Series in Probability and Mathematical Statistics, 1990, pp 115, 120.

5. Carnap, Rudolf; *Pseudoproblems in Philosophy*, University of California Press, SBN 520-01417-0; pp305-340; 1967.

6. Bonnicksen, Thomas M.; Department of Forest Science, Texas A&M University; *AMERICA'S ANCIENT FORESTS, From the Ice Age to the Age of Discovery*; John Wiley & Sons, Inc.; 2000.

7. Devall, Bill & George Sessions; *Deep Ecology: Living as if Nature Mattered.* Salt Lake City, Peregrine Smith; 1985.

8. American Policy Center; *Ref to Curriculum Vitae of Bill Devall;* The DeWeese Report, May 1999.

9. Naess, Arne; George Sessions; *Clearcut: The Tragedy of Industrial Forestry*, edited by Bill Devall; Sierra Club Books and Earth Island Press, 1993.

10. Lovelock, James; *Gaia: A New Look at Life on Earth.* Oxford: Oxford University Press; 1979.

11. MacGillivray, Joseph Alexander; *Sir Arthur Evans and the Archaeology of the Minoan Myth;* Hill & Wang Pub; June 2000; pp142, 152, 168; ISBN: 0809030357.

12. James Lovelock's Home Page, URL: http://www.ion.com.au/ourplanet/gaia.html.

13. Drengson, Alan and Yuichi Inoue, Editors. 1995. *The Deep Ecology Movement: An Introductory Anthology*. Berkeley, North Atlantic Publishers.

14. Grey, William; *Anthropocentrism and Deep Ecology*; Australiasian Journal of Philosophy, Vol. 71, No 4. (1993), pp. 463-475.

15. Rifkin, Jeremy, SnuffIt 4, Church of Euthanasia, found at: http://www.enviroweb.org/coe. This site has to be visited to be appreciated. You won't find it on the enviroweb menu.

16. Harding, Stephan; *WHAT IS DEEP ECOLOGY?*; Resurgence 185 http://www.gn.apc.org/resurgence/185/Harding185.htm

17. Dave Foreman, *Confessions of an Eco-Warrior*, (Harmony Books, 1991).

18. McLaughlin, Andrew, *The Heart of Deep Ecology*, from Freedom.org, 1999.

19. Reed F. Noss, *The Wildlands Project*, Wild Earth, Special Issue, 1992, p. 21. URL: http://www.wildlandsproject.org.

20. *IUCN Membership Guidelines*, 1996, p.4.

21. IUCN: *Membership List,* June, 1998, p. 21.

22. Dues: *IUCN Membership Guidelines,* 1996, p. 20.

23. Moore, Patrick; *Green Spirit: trees are the answer; http://www.greenspirit.com*; ISBN 0-9686404-0-0.

24. Fumento, Michael, *Science Under Siege,* William Morrow and Co.., 1993; p.19.

25. Feshbach, Murray; Alfred Friendly Jr.; *Ecocide in the USSR: Health and Nature Under Siege;* Basic Books (A Division of HarperCollins), 1991.

26. East Europe's Dark Dawn; National Geographic, June 1991.

Chapter 3 – What's "The Problem"?

27. Santa Cruz Public Library; *Santa Cruz Weather Statistics;* Record rainfall for Watsonville, 1975-76: 8.49"; Boulder Creek, 1889-90: 124.7".

(Notes 28-36 were acquired from the Save the Redwoods League web site.)

28. Abbott, L.L. 1987. *The effect of fire on subsequent growth of surviving trees in an old-growth redwood forest in Redwood National Park,* California. M.S. thesis, Humboldt State University, Arcata, California, 90 pp.

Fire scarring, basal sprouts, and annual growth rates were examined in 1986 in an old-growth redwood forest to assess the effect of a 1974 surface fire on the subsequent growth of surviving trees. Fire scarring took place predominantly on the uphill side of trees. Basal sprouting was induced by the 1974 fire. Mean tree ring chronologies displayed an increase of ring width following two fires in 1894 and 1974, most likely due to a reduction in competition.

29. Brown, P.M. and T.W. Swetnam; *A cross-dated fire history from coast redwood near Redwood National Park, California.* Canadian Journal of Forest Research 24: 21–31; 1994.

Cross-dating methods (i.e., the use of a master tree-ring history developed from numerous trees to act as a baseline or control for comparison with the fire-scarred tree samples) showed the mean fire interval in the study area to be 7.0 years, between the years of 1714 and 1762. These intervals are shorter than those reported in many previous fire-history studies and the authors suggest that fire frequency in redwood may have been underestimated in many past studies.

Endnotes

30. Finney, M.A. and R.E. Martin. 1989. *Fire history in a Sequoia sempervirens forest at Salt Point State Park, California.* Canadian Journal of Forest Research 19: 1451–1457.

It is difficult to generalize about patterns of fire occurrence throughout the natural range of coast redwood. Part of the reason is due to the different methodologies employed in fire history studies. This study investigated historical fire occurrence in the (coast redwood and bishop pine) forests at Salt Point State Park, California, and compared the results from two techniques used to analyze fire history data. Mean fire intervals estimated from point data (20.5 to 29.0 years) were more than three times greater than mean intervals from composite data (6.1 to 9.3 years.)

31. Finney, M.A. and R.E. Martin. 1992. *Short fire intervals recorded by redwoods at Annadel State Park, CA.* Madroño. CALIFORNIA BOTANICAL SOC., 39(4): 251–262. URL:http://ucjeps.herb.berkeley.edu/Madrono.html.

This paper reports fire history evidence from fire scars recorded on coast redwood trees which grow in isolated groves within oak and mixed evergreen forests. All fire scars are believed to predate European settlement in the early 1800s, and the earliest scars date from the 14th century. During this period, mean fire intervals between 6.2 and 23.0 were found.

32. Greenlee, J.M. and J.H. Langenheim. 1990. *Historic fire regimes and their relation to vegetation patterns in the Monterey Bay Area of California.* American Midland Naturalist 124: 239–253.

Fire history in the Monterey Bay area of California, concentrating on the area forested with coast redwood, was categorized into five fire regimes: prehuman (lightning- ignition), aboriginal, Spanish occupation, Anglo, and recent. Fire occurrence and coverage based on estimates (i.e., modeling fire behavior), natural records (e.g., fire scar dating), or human records (e.g., from newspapers, journals and fire records for Anglo and recent fire regimes) were compared for the five regimes. It is estimated that prehuman fire intervals in the redwood forest of this area were approximately 135 years. The frequency of fires apparently increased in the aboriginal (17–82 years), Spanish (82 years), and Anglo (20–50 years) fire regimes, and has decreased recently (130 years) due to limitation of human-caused fires. It is concluded that the present fire regime is similar in several respects to that which existed prior to the arrival of humans.

33. Finney, M.A. and R.E. Martin. 1993a. *Modeling effects of prescribed fire on young-growth coast redwood trees.* Canadian Journal of Forest Research 23: 1125–1135.

Old-growth coast redwoods are very resistant and resilient to fire; young or small trees are more susceptible to fire damage or mortality. Using controlled fire treatments, models were developed relating fire characteristics, tree characteristics, and tree damage from fire. Tree diameter, surface fuel consumption, flame length, and crown scorch were significant predictors in all models of top killing and basal sprouting.

34. Finney, M.A. and R.E. Martin. 1993b. *Fuel loading, bulk density, and depth of forest floor in coast redwood stands.* Forest Science, Society of American Foresters 39(3): 617–622.

Fire characteristics, such as intensity and coverage, are influence by fuel loading on the forest floor. Measurements of fuel loading can be helpful in predicting the effects of fire on soils and plants. The depth and density of forest floor fuel were measured in two coast redwood sites in northern California. Results suggested that, for practical purposes of estimating fuel loading, a constant bulk density could be assumed.

35. Griffin, J.R. 1978. *The Marble-Cone fire ten months later.* Fremontia, The Journal of the California Native Plant Society. 8: 8–14.

A large fire burned in Los Padres National Forest in Monterey County, California, for three weeks, consuming chaparral, mixed hardwood forests (including Santa Lucia fir), mixed conifer forests (including ponderosa pine and incense-cedar), and some coast redwood groves. The author noted that many of the charred redwoods were sprouting from the base within a month of the fire. He suggests that redwood regrowth will probably be good, although a few redwood groves at higher elevations in the Big Sur drainage may have been killed as no sprouting was observed within a year of the fire.

36. Jacobs, D.F., D.W. Cole, and J.R. McBride. 1985. *Fire history and perpetuation of natural coast redwood ecosystems.* Journal of Forestry, Society of American Foresters. 83(8): 494–497.

Fire scars on stumps were used to determine the presettlement fire history of a coast redwood forest in Marin County, California, near Muir Woods National Monument. The mean interval between fires at one site was 27 years, while at a more inland site the interval was 22 years. The difference in fire intervals is attributed to a summer fog gradient.

37. Nives, S.L. 1989. *Fire behavior on the forest floor in coastal redwood forest, Redwood National Park.* M.S. thesis, Humboldt State Univ., Arcata, CA, 73 pp.

Experimental fires, ignited during the summer and fall of 1986 in stands of redwood located in Redwood National Park, determined the fuel bed characteristics (i.e., fuel depth, load, and moisture) and local weather conditions (i.e., temperature and relative humidity) necessary to sustain a low intensity ground fire. Elevation and topographic position were found to be main factors to determine ease of fire ignition and rates of spread. Fuel depth and load appeared to affect the intensity and duration of the fires and rate of spread.

38. Veirs, S.D., Jr. 1979. *The role of fire in northern coast redwood forest vegetation dynamics.* In Proc. Second Conference on Scientific Research in the National Parks, Nov. 26–30, 1979, San Francisco, CA. Vol. 10: Fire Ecology, National Park Service, Washington, D.C. pp. 190–209.

It is essential to understand the role of natural fires in forests dominated by Sequoia sempervirens to establish appropriate management policies in parks such as the Redwood National Park in California. The role of fire in the northern part of the species' range is studied and found to have a moderate ecological role. Light fires which do not open the canopy tend to maintain redwood dominance, while fires of higher intensity and greater frequency, as tend to occur on the hotter, drier inland sites, favor Douglas-fir over redwood.

39. Lydon, Sandy; Professor of History, Cabrillo College, *Early settlers shunned dirty river water;* Santa Cruz County Sentinel, 3/24/97.

40. 1995-1997 Survey of Graduates, University of California, Santa Cruz; URL: http://planning.ucsc.edu/IRPS/ENROLLMT/GRADS/9597/REPORT.PDF.

Endnotes to Part II

Chapter 1 – Gamecock Canyon

41. Dean, Kathy; Various quotes from her web page on file are from: http://pages.prodigy.net/kathy_dean/index.html. This page is now, defunct.

42. Dean, Kathy; Quotes from The Mountain Network News; URL: http://www.mnn.net/gamecock.htm.

43. State of California Government Code. *Sections 51100 – 51155, Timberland Productivity Act of 1982,* URL: http://www.leginfo.ca.gov/.html/gov_table_of_contents.html.

44. Herbert, Elizabeth; *FAQ -- Frequently Asked Questions, How to combat logging plans, Don't Wait for the Chainsaws* ...URL:http://www.responsible-neighbors.org/crfm.

45. Herbert, Elizabeth; *County Timber Plan Is Laudable,* Sentinel (Santa Cruz), Sunday, 18 Oct., 1998; URL: http://www.netlive.net/tree/sentinel_101898.html.

46. Craig, Joe; *Response to Kathy Dean;* Mountain Network News, Vol XII, No. 4, April, 1999, p6.

47. Hamlin, Mark, President SRA; # # # # #; Mountain Network News, Vol XII, No. 4, April, 1999, p37.

48. Board of Directors, CRFM, *Response to Hamlin;* Mountain Network News, Vol XII, No. 5, May, 1999, p37.

49. Luker, Kelly; *The Timber Wolves;* Metro Santa Cruz, March 20, 1997. URL: http://www.metroactive.com/papers/cruz/03.20.97/logging-9712.html.

50. Luker, Kelly; *Empire Statements, Timber giant Redwood Empire is under continuing attack for questionable logging practices in Gamecock Canyon,* Metro Santa Cruz, April. 16,1996; URL: http://www.metroactive.com/papers/cruz/04.16.98/logging2-9815.html.

51. Hoffman, Russell D.; *Why No Cut? A consideration of the complicated environmental and political Issues regarding the California Redwoods;* 1996. URL: http://www.animatedsoftware.com/misc/stories/redwoods/redwoods.htm.

52. Herbert, Elizabeth; *FIGHT BACK! A citizen's guide to forest preservation in Santa Cruz County*, CRFM; URL: http://www.responsible-neighbors.org/crfm.

53. CRFM, again! URL: http://www.strategize.com/crfm. Strategize is in corporate computing strategy business.

54. Neighbors for Responsible Logging; URL: http://www.responsible-neighbors.org/links.html.

55. Summit Water Protection League URL: http://www.mnn.net/summit.htm. The local newspaper gives them free space?

56. Cal. State Board of Forestry, *Proposed Amendments to Forest Practice Rules*, Santa Cruz Co. Rules, 1998 Proposed Rule Language [Sept. 9, 1998], p14.

57. California State Board of Forestry, *Proposed Changes to Forest Practice Rules*, Santa Cruz County Rules, 1999 Proposed Rule Language [from July 7, 1999] Adopt Section 926.11,15-17, 24-30

58. *DRAFT Review Pursuant to Memorandum of Agreement between the National Marine Fisheries Service (NMFS), Southwest Region and the State of California (State) on North Coast Steelhead Trout, analysis of the California Forest Practice Rules (FPR)*: The NMFS review of the FPRs to the State, and the State response to NMFS analysis. Dated 7/10/98.

59. Knight, Katherine; *The Soquel Demonstration Forest shows why local citizens and California forestry officials are not knocking on wood together;* Metro Santa Cruz, Dec. 12,1996. URL: http://www.metroactive.com/papers/cruz/12.12.96/forests-9650.html.

60. Krumland, Bruce, PhD, RPF #1768; *Comments on the Proposed Amendments to California Forest Practice Rules,* [Santa Cruz County], Oct. 5, 1998, 5pp.

61. *Record of Conversation with David Smelt,* adjacent property owner of Roger Burch; on-site visit dated 5/17/99.

62. Smelt, David; *Periodic Peak Temperature Data from Gamecock Creek,* 1999.

63. *Records of Conversation with Peter Twight, RPF#2555,* 5/15/99, 10/25/99.

64. *The 2090 Agreement, a Memo of Understanding between the California Department of Fish and Game and the California Department of Forestry and Fire Protection dated May 9, 1994;* Section 2090 of the Fish and Game Code.

65. Briggs, Robert O.; *Competition Between the Waddell Creek Forest and Creek for Limited Dry Season Ground-Stored Water,* Davenport Geological Society, Oct. 1997, 22pp.

66. *Key Elements of the CDF Gamecock Canyon File for THP 1-96-275 SCR;* available through CDF Felton Office 831-335-6740.

67. Osipowich, Tom, RPF #1767; Deputy Chief, Forest Practice, CDF, *Letter to Mr. Roger Burch from Caig E. Athony, Deputy Director for Resource Management;* Dated Jan. 226, 1998; 2pp.

68. Briggs, Roger W.; Executive Officer, Cal/EPA *Letter to Mr. Roger Burch,* Dated January 12, 1998;

69. *POST HARVEST INSPECTION OF TIMBER HARVEST PLAN, (THP) 1-96-275 SCR, DECEMBER 15-16, 1997, REDWOOD EMPIRE, GAMECOCK CANYON;* 2pp; HK\H:\WINWORD\FOREST\96275.DOCZZ

70. *CDF Memorandum Detailing List of Major Violations,* December, 1997.

71. From: Department of Forestry and Fire Protection, San Mateo / Santa Cruz Ranger Unit; Memorandum To: Lloyd I Keefer, Region Chief, Coast-Cascade Region; Subject: *Record of Preharvest Inspection dated, 7-10-96 and Preharvest Inspection dated 7-24-96.* Date: July 29, 1996.

Chapter 2 – For Love or Money? An Overview of Redwood Timber Markets

72. US Dept. of Agriculture, Forest Service, *Program for the National Forests,* Miscellaneous Publication No. 794, April 1959, 26pp.

73. Leydet, François; *The Last Redwoods and the Parkland of Redwood Creek,* Sierra Club Books, 1969, pp65-73.

74. MacCleery, Douglas W.; *American Forests, A History of Resiliency and Recovery,* Forest History Society, 1996, ISBN 0-89030-048-8, 58pp.

75. O'Toole, Randal; *Memo to President Clinton: The Forest Service Has Already Been Reinvented --and You Fired the Man Who Oversaw It;* You can find this article from the following URL: http://www.ti.org/index.html.

76. *BAYSIDE TIMBER COMPANY, INC., Plaintiff and Respondent, v. BOARD OF SUPERVISORS OF SAN MATEO COUNTY;* LEXSEE 20 Cal. App. 3d 1; Civ. No. 28244, Court of Appeal of California, First Appellate District, Division One, 20 Cal. App. 3d 1; 1971 Cal. App. LEXIS 1144; 97 Cal. Rptr. 431; 3 ERC (BNA) 1078; 1 ELR 20425; September 16, 1971.

77. Z'berg Nejedly *Forest Practices Act of 1973,* Title 14 California Code of Regulations, Division 1.5, Chapter 4, Subchapter 6, Southern District Rules; URL:http://www.calregs.com/cgi-bin/om_isapi.dll?infobase=CCR&softpage=Browse_Frame_Pg42.

78. Z'berg, Warren, Keene, Collier, *Forest Taxation Relief Act of 1976,* Assembly Bill 1258.

79. Pillsbury, Norman H., RPF; *Timber Inventory, Volume Tables, and Growth Estimates for Santa Cruz County, California*; Oct. 1979, Tables 1, 7-11.

80. Coclasure, P.; Joel Moen; Charles L. Bolsinger; *Timber Resource Statistics for the Central Coast Resource Area of California*, Portland OR: Forest Service, Pacific Northwest Research Station Resource Bulletin PNW-133, 32pp.

81. Waddell, Karen L. and Patricia M.Bassett, *Timber Resource Statistics for the North Coast Resource Area of California*, Portland OR: U.S. Dept. of Agriculture, Forest Service, Pacific Northwest Research Station Resource Bulletin PNW-RB-214, September 1996, 50pp.

82. Waddell, Karen L. and Patricia M.Bassett, *Timber Resource Statistics for the Central Coast Resource Area of California* Portland OR: U.S. Dept. of Agriculture, Forest Service, Pacific Northwest Research Station Resource Bulletin PNW-RB-221, March 1997, 45pp.

83. Butler, Steven M. RPF#2390 & Edward A. Tunheim RPF#79; Edward A. Tunheim Consulting Forester, *City of Santa Cruz Water Department Forest Management Report*, 1994 pp8, 29-31, 44-45, & 83-84.

84. California State Board of Equalization, *California Timber Tax Yield Law*, January 1995, Pamphlet No. 43, 88pp.

85. California Revenue and Taxation Code, Division 2, Part 18.5, Chapter 4, *Timber Reserve Fund Tax*; Sections 38301-38303. (Repealed in 1984)

86. Wilson, Frank and Bob Rossi, California State Board of Equalization, Timber Tax Division, *Fax transmittals of harvest volumes and values,* 12pp, 3/17/99; 3pp, 4/20/99; 2pp, 3/17/99.

87. California State Board of Equalization, Timber Tax Division, *Timber Harvest by County*, URL: http://www.boe.ca.gov/proptaxes/pdf/harvcnty.pdf YTHR2 REPORT YT-36, YTR90-96.xls.

88. Tunheim, Edward A. Consulting Forester, RPF#79, *Price histories 1960-77,* fax transmission, 3/29/99 on file.

89. Lindquist, James & Marshall Palley, *Prediction of Stand Growth of Young Redwoods*, California Agricultural Experiment Station, Bulletin 831, April 1967, pp30,31.

90. Merenlender, Adina M.; Kerry L. Heise; Colin Brooks; *Effects of Subdividing Private Propertyon Biodiversity in California's North Coast Oak Woodlands;* TRANSACTIONS OF THE WESTERN SECTION OF THE WILDLIFE SOCIETY 34:9-20; 1998.

91. County of Santa Cruz, *Comparative Tax Rates Per $100.00 of Assessed Valuation for the Last Ten Fiscal Years; 1965-66 to 1974-75;* pp122-125.

92. Sterling Publishing Co., *The Encyclopedia of Wood,* 1989; ISBN 0-8069-6994-6 Paper, Table 3-3, Chapter 3, 28pp.

93. Santa Cruz Association of Realtors, Inc.; *Multiple Listings Service Books;* This data was hand copied from books and binders of data from 1962-1999.

94. U.S. Bureau of Labor Statistics, *U.S. Consumer Price Index, 1967-1999.* URL: ftp://ftp.bls.gov/pub/special.requests/cpi/cpiai.txt.

95. U.S. Bureau of Labor Statistics, *U.S. Consumer Price Index, 1967-1999U.S. Bureau of Labor Statistics, U.S. CPI for Douglas Fir Lumber, 1926-1999.* Series ID : WPU081 Not Seasonally Adjusted; URL: http://146.142.4.24/cgi-bin/surveymost.

96. County of Santa Cruz, *County of Santa Cruz Statement of Assessed Valuation and Tax Rates 1974-1975*, Annual Financial Report, for the Fiscal Year End of June 30, 1975; Arthur Merrill, Auditor-Controller.

97. County of Santa Cruz, *Comparative Tax Rates Per $100.00 of Assessed Valuation for the 5-Year period 1974-75 to 1978-79*, pp82-87.

Chapter 3 – Developing Hostility

98. Santa Cruz Association of Realtors, Inc.; *Multiple Listings Service Books;* This data was hand copied from books and binders of data from 1962-1999.

99. Chapter 13.41.040, County of Santa Cruz Government Code; *GROWTH MANAGEMENT SYSTEM;* Election Department, County of Santa Cruz; *FULL TEXT OF SANTA CRUZ COUNTY MEASURE"J."*

100. Moore, Wayne L. Jr.; *ARGUMENTS AGAINST MEASURE "J";* Election Department, County of Santa Cruz.

101. Moore, Wayne L. Jr.; *REBUTTAL TO ARGUMENTS FOR MEASURE "J";* Election Department, County of Santa Cruz.

102. Patton, Gary; Phil Baldwin; Ed Borovatz, Supervisors, County of Santa Cruz; *REBUTTAL TO ARGUMENTS AGAINST MEASURE "J";* Election Department, County of Santa Cruz.

103. *LandWatch: Who We Are;* pp1-7; URL:http://www.landwatch.org/pages/whoweare.html.

104. Planning Department, County of Santa Cruz; *MAP "A" EXISTING URBANIZED AREAS.*

105. Planning Department, County of Santa Cruz; *MAP "B" MAXIMUM POSSIBLE 1990 URBAN DEVELOPMENT.*

106. Patton, Gary, et al., Supervisors, County of Santa Cruz; *ENACTMENT OF A GROWTH MANAGEMENT PLAN FOR SANTA CRUZ COUNTY;* 3/16/78.

107. Sanson, Ralph; Dan D. Forbus; Phil Harry; Henry J. Mello; George L. Cress Jr.; Supervisors, County of Santa Cruz; *ORDINANCE NO. 2093 AN ORDINANCE AMENDING CHAPTER 13.08 OF THE SANTA CRUZ COUNTY CODE REGARDING SUBDIVISIONS.* **The ordinance, passed Feb. 25, 1975, placed the cutoff date for preexisting subdivisions at Jan. 21, 1972.**

108. *CALIFORNIA SUBDIVISION MAP ACT;* Section 66410 California Government Code. **The code placed the cutoff date for preexisting subdivisions at March 4, 1972 per 66412.6 (a).** URL: http://www.leginfo.ca.gov/.html/gov_table_of_contents.html.

Endnotes to Part III

Chapter 2 – Getting Off on Good Behavior

109. OP Cit, Hardin, Garrett; *The Tragedy of the Commons,* Science, 162(1968):1243-1248. URL:http://dieoff.com. Still Dreadful.

110. *OP Cit,* Harris, George Washington; *Sicily Burns's Wedding*, Native American Humor, Walter Blair (ed.), Harper & Row; 1960, pp368-88.

111. Alchain, Armen; & William R. Allen; *Exchange and Production: Competition, Coordination, and Control, Second Edition;* Wadsworth, Belmont, CA; 1977.

112. Nicholson, Walter; *Microeconomic Theory: Basic Principles and Extensions, Second Edition;* Dryden Press; 1978; pp568-571.

113. Anderson, Terry L. and Donald R. Leal *Free Market Environmentalism.* Pacific Research Institute for Public Policy. Boulder: Westview Press; 1991.

114. Adler, Jonathan; *Libertarian Solutions: Environmental protection through private property and private action;* Competitive Enterprise Institute in Washington, DC.

115. Society of American Foresters, *SAF Periodicals*, URL: http://www.safnet.org/pubs/periodicals.html.

116. AF&PA American Forest & Paper Association; *SUSTAINABLE FORESTRY PRINCIPLES AND IMPLEMENTATION GUIDELINES*; as approved by AF&PA Board of Directors on October 14, 1994; URL: http://www.batnet.com/woodcom/afpa/afpabp02.html.

117. Forest Stewardship Council A.C;.*FSC Bylaws Reference http://www.fscoax.org* Forest Stewardship Council A.C. *By-Laws. Doc. 1.1.* (Ratified, September 1994; Editorial Revision, October 1996; Revised February 1999).

118. FSC; *FSC Principles and Criteria.* Doc. 1.2; Revised January 1999.

119. FSC; *Roles rights and responsibilities of FSC players. Doc. 2.10.*

120. FSC; *Group Certification: FSC Guidelines for Certification Bodies Doc. 3.6.1*; July 31, 1998.

121. FSC; *FSC Process Guidelines for Developing Regional Certification Standards;* Doc. 4.2; February 1998.

122. FSC; 5.2.2, *FSC Membership List;* FSC Doc. 5.2.2.; July 1999.

123. FSC; *List of Accredited Certification Bodies;* Doc. 5.3.1; July 1999.

124. FSC; *List of Certified Forests*; DOC. 5.3.3; September 30, 1999.

125. AF&PA *Sustainable Forestry Implementation Guidelines;* URL:http://www.afandpa.org/Forestry/guidelines.html.

126. *FOREST CONSERVATION PROGRAM, PROGRAM DESCRIPTION AND OPERATIONS MANUAL, OCTOBER 1995 RELEASE;* Scientific Certification Systems, 1 Kaiser Plaza, Oakland, CA, URL:http://www.scs1.org.

127. Institute for Sustainable Forestry/SmartWood, ISF/SmartWood, 46 Humboldt Street, Willits, CA 95490, Phone: 707-459-5499 Fax: 707-456-185.

128. SmartWood, Goodwin-Baker Building, 61 Millet St., Richmond, VT 05477.

129. Certified Forest Products Council, 14780 SW Osprey Drive, Suite 285, Beaverton, OR 97007; phone (503) 590-6600; fax: (503) 590-6655.

130. Lewis, Robert O.; *Independent Verification and Validation : A Life Cycle Engineering Process for Quality Software (New Dimensions in Engineering);* John Wiley & Sons; ISBN: 0471570117 ; 356pp (October 1992).

Chapter 3 – What's It Worth To You?

131. Canadian Standards Association; PLUS 1139; *Integrated Checklist for Environmental Management Systems and Sustainable Forest Management Systems.* URL: http://www.csa-international.org/english/home/index.htm.

132. Arnold, Ron; *Undue Influence: Wealthy Foundations, Grant Driven Environmental Groups and Zealous Bureaucrats That Control Your Future*;

Paperback - 344 pages (October 1, 1999); Free Enterprise Pr; ISBN: 093957120X.

Chapter 4 – Property Transfer Functions

133. D'Azzo, John J.; *Linear Control Systems Analysis and Design;* Second Edition, McGraw-Hill, 1981, *Figures, 2.12-13 Plant Transfer Functions,* p451.

Chapter 5 – Stuff, and What You Can Do With the Stuff

134. J. Bishop Grewell, *Tiny microbes living in the mud-pots and geysers of Yellowstone National Park have sparked a mammoth controversy,* PERC.org.

135. Caruba, Alan; *Condors Galore;* Conservative News Service, Analysis from the National Anxiety Center, October 11, 1999.

136. National Audubon Society; *Kill the Condors?;* URL: http://www.condor-pass.org/background.html.

137. National Audubon Society; *NATIONAL AUDUBON APPLAUDS ENRON WIND CORP. DECISION TO PURSUE ALTERNATE SITE FOR WIND POWER DEVELOPMENT;* New York, NY; November 3, 1999; URL: http://www.audubon.org/news/release/enron.html.

138. Rural Advancement Foundation, International (RAFI); *Terminator Two Years Later: RAFI Update on Terminator/Traitor Technology* a report prepared for COP5 in Nairobi, May 15-26 2000; URL: http://www.rafi.org/web/docus/pdfs/00may12attach.pdf.

139. Monsanto Statement on Bt Corn: Environmental Safety and a Recent Report on the Monarch Butterfly, PR Newswire May 20, 1999; URL: http://www.biotech-info.net/monsanto_on_btcorn.html.

140. The Biotechnology Knowledge Centre, *Bt Corn And Monarch Butterfly Factsheet;* Reference No.:3287, 28 April 2000; URL http://biotechknowledge.com/showlibsp.php3?uid=3287.

Endnotes to Part IV

Chapter 1 – Landowner On the Loose!!!

141. Russell, Terry and Renny; On The Loose; Sierra Club Books 1967, p7.

142. Thomas, John Hunter; Flora of the Santa Cruz Mountains; Stanford Univ. Press, 1961, p11

143. Lippke Fretwell, Holly; *Forests: Do We Get What We Pay For?;* URL: http://www.perc.org/pl2sum.htm.

144. Peters, David, *Herger-Feinstein Quincy Library Group (QLG) , Record of Decision and Summary,* USDA, Forest Service, Pacific Southwest Region, Lassen, Plumas, & Tahoe National Forests, August, 1999.

145. Peters, David, *Final Environmental Impact Statement, Summary, Herger-Feinstein Quincy Library Group,* USDA, Forest Service, Pacific Southwest Region, Lassen, Plumas, & Tahoe National Forests, August, 1999

146. Botkin, Daniel; *Ecology of Discord;* Oxford Univ Pr, 1992 (Trade); ISBN: 0195074696.

147. O'Toole, Randal; *Tarnished Jewels: The Case for Reforming the Park Service;* URL: http://www.ti.org/index.html. This site is highly recommended for its broad scope of forest issues and well-documented sources.

148. Kaczynski, Dr. Victor J., "No single forest practice — not timber harvesting, nor road building — can compare with the damage wildfires are inflicting on fish and fish habitat." *Wallowa Whitman Nat Forest; Tanner Gulch Fire Thunderbolt Wildfire Recovery Environmental Impact Study;* USDA Forest Service. Spokane, WA, 1995.

149. Barker, Rocky, *Yellowstone fires and their legacy,* Chapter 10 The Legacy of 1988, 1996. URL:http://www.idahonews.com/yellowst/chap10.htm.

150. Sierra Club Conservation Policies; *Fire Management on Public Lands Policy.* URL: http://www.sierraclub.org/policy/conservation/fire.asp.

151. Frost, Evan - *Greater Ecosystem Alliance, Fire & Forest Management: Myth & Reality,* Columbiana: Ecology and Culture in the Pacific Northwest.

152. Campbell, Doug; *The Urban Interface; Wildfire Magazine,* URL:http://www.wildfiremagazine.com/interface.shtml.

153. Waggoner, Ed and Mike Terwilliger *FIRE FIGHTING IN THE I-ZONE: "SAFE TO STAY";* Wildfire Magazine; URL:http://www.wildfiremagazine.com/waggoner.shtml.

154. Babbitt, Bruce; *MAKING PEACE WITH WILDLAND FIRE;* Wildfire Magazine; URL:http://www.wildfiremagazine.com/babbitt.shtml

155. Boswell, Evelyn; Scientists: 1988 *Fires were Good for Yellowstone Park;* Montana State University Communications Services; URL:http://www.montana.edu/wwwpb/univ/firetour.html. (Typical spin job, 'it's all positive, no negative' -ed.)

156. Babbitt, Bruce; *ENGAGING STAKEHOLDERS TO REINVEST IN PRESCRIBED WILDLAND FIRE;* Secretary of the Interior, Tall Timbers Conference, Boise, Idaho; May 9, 1996.URL:http://www.doi.gov/alcove/fire.html.

157. Jacobs, Lynn; *Waste of the West: Public Lands Ranching,* 5/21/99 URL:http://www.apnm.org/waste_of_west/Preface.html.

158. Knight, Dennis, and Linda Wallace; *The Yellowstone Fires: Issues in Landscape Ecology;* BioScience Magazine, Vol. 39, #10, November 1989 edition, p.700-705.

159. Menke, John W.; Review of T. Ingalsbee, *Fire Related critiques of Senate Bill 1028;* Western Fire Ecology Center, 8pp, 1997.

160. Ingalsbee, Timothy, PhD, Director, Western Fire Ecology Center, Western Ancient Forest Campaign; *S. 1028; Outdated Policies that will Increase Fire*

Risk, Endanger Firefighters, and Harm Forest Ecosystems, AND Terhune, George; QLG (Quincy Library Group-ed.) *Response;* 2/6/99; URL:http://www.qlg.org/public_html/miscdoc/Ingalsbe.htm.

161.Keiter, Robert B. and Mark S. Boyce, editors, with a foreward by Luna B. Leopold; *The Greater Yellowstone Ecosystem: Redefining America's Wilderness Heritage,* Yale University Press, New Haven and London, 1991.

162.Finney, M.A. 1991. *Ecological effects of prescribed and simulated fire on the coast redwood (Sequoia sempervirens [D. Don] Endl).* Ph.D. dissertation, University of California, Berkeley, California, 194pp (acquired from the Save the Redwoods League web site as an abstract).

Five papers are presented which describe studies on prescribed burning and fire effects on young- and old-growth coast redwood, simulated effects of fire on redwood trees and seedlings, and methods used for measuring flame characteristics and forest floor loading. In the prescribed burning study, both fireline intensity and surface fuel consumption were found to be related to the amount of young-growth redwood top-killing and basal sprouting responses one year after burning.

163.Clinton, William Jefferson; *Executive Order 12986* dated 1/19/96. URL:http://www.pub.whitehouse.gov/uri-res/I2R?urn:pdi://oma.eop.gov.us/1996/1/19/3.text.2.

164.FLANIGAN, JAMES; *WILL INSURANCE SURVIVE? YES, BUT AT A PRICE;* Wednesday, July 6, 1994.

165.Hirsch, K.G.; M.M. Pinedo; J.M. Greenlee; *Urban-Wildland Interface Fire: The I-Zone Series Overview;* Bibliography; 1996. Natural Resources Canada, Canadian Forest Service, Northwest Region, Northern Forest Centre, Edmonton, Alberta. Inf. Rep. NOR-X-344.

A bibliographic listing of about 2200 urban-wildland interface resource materials that have been compiled by the International Association of Wildland Fire and the Canadian Forest Service, Northern Forestry Centre are listed alphabetically by author. Most items in this collection were produced prior to 1993 and pertain to the United States, Australia, and Canada.

166.Staten, Clark; Executive Director, Emergency Response & Research Institute; *"TWO DAYS of HELL" in Alemeda County, CA,* URL: http://www.emergency.com/oaklfire.htm.

167.Brass, James A.; *Oakland Hills Fire Storm: Remote Sensing and Emergency Management,* NASA/Ames Research Center; URL: http://geo.arc.nasa.gov/esdstaff/jskiles/fliers/all_flier_prose/oaklandfires_brass/o aklandfires_brass.html. Image available at http://geo.arc.nasa.gov/esdstaff/jskiles/fliers/gif_folder/image23/image23a.gif.

168.Coate, Barrie D., ASCA; *WHY ARE TANBARK OAKS DYING?;* Mountain Network News, Vol XII, No. 10, Oct, 1999, p30.

169.Švihra, Pavel; *Western Oak Bark Beetles and Ambrosia Beetles, Killers of Live Oaks;* University of California Cooperative Extension in Marin County, Pest Alert #3, June 1999.

170. Merenlender, Adina M.; Kerry L. Heise; Colin Brooks; *Effects of Subdividing Private Property on Biodiversity in California's North Coast Oak Woodlands;* TRANSACTIONS OF THE WESTERN SECTION OF THE WILDLIFE SOCIETY 34:9-20; 1998.

171. SF Chron 9/30/99 *Bark Beetles and Oak Trees Sapped of their Strength; Bark beetles threaten majestic live oaks;* San Francisco Chronicle, pA21; URL: http://www.sfgate.com/cgi-bin/article.cgi?file=/chronicle/archive/1999/09/30/MN59818.DTL.

172. County of Santa Cruz, *FORMATION AND OPERATION OF COUNTY SERVICE AREAS,* no date, no signature, no originator, no logo, no document code, therefore, a typical County handout.

173. County of Santa Cruz, *ASSESSMENT DISTRICT PROCESSING,* no date, no signature, no originator, no logo, no document code, a typical County handout.

174. County of Santa Cruz, *Assessment Bonds, 1990,* YES, IT HAS A DATE!!! No signature, no logo, no document code, still a typical County handout.

175. Orrick, Harrington & Sutcliffe; *General Memorandum: Proposed Private Activity Bond Regulations and Assessment Bonds and Mello Roos Bonds,* SF2-39475, 1995.

176. State of California, Govt. Code Sections 61,000 to 61,850, *Community Service District;* URL: http://www.leginfo.ca.gov/.html/gov_table_of_contents.html.

Chapter 2 – Dangerous Species Act

177. Mann, Charles C.; Contributing Editor, *Biotech Goes Wild*, Genetic engineering will be essential to feed the world's billions. But could it unleash a race of "superweeds"? No one seems to know. And nobody's in charge of finding out. The Atlantic Monthly and Science; July/August 1999.

178. Tickell, Oliver; *It's a rat trap*, New Scientist, Jan. 23,1999.

179. McDonnell, Tom, Director of Natural Resources, American Sheep Industry Association; *Executive Order 13112 on Invasive Species.* URL:http://www.pub.whitehouse.gov/uri-res/I2R?urn:pdi://oma.eop.gov.us/1999/2/3/14.text.1.

180. Sullivan, Ron; *Time to fight back against horticultural "invasion";* San Francisco Examiner, Sept. 22, 1999. URL:http://www.sfgate.com/cgi-in/article.cgi?file=/examiner/archive/1999/09/22/HABITAT4079.dtl.

181. Howe, Kenneth; *State Plague of Thistles, Nasty weed works its way into coast ranges, Sierra;* San Francisco Chronicle, Tuesday, January 19, 1999. URL:http://www.sfgate.com/cgi-bin/article.cgi?file=/chronicle/archive/1999/01/19/MN12347.DTL.

182. California Native Plant Society; *EXOTIC PEST PLANTS PAGE* URL:http://www.calpoly.edu/~dchippin/exotic.html.

183. Bilger, Burkhard; *Battle for the prairie;* Earthwatch: 6(5):20; 1992.

Endnotes

184. Sierra Club Conservation Policies; *Pest Management Policy;* URL: http://www.sierraclub.org/policy/conservation/pcst.asp. "Bramble, W. C. and Byrnes, W. R.; *Breeding bird population changes following right of way maintenance treatments.* J Arboric. 18(1).p. 29 32, 1992.

185. Brown, Lauren, *Audubon Society Nature Guides: Grasslands;* Knopf, N.Y.; pp19-99, 1985.

186. Westman, W. E., *Managing for biodiversity;* BioScience. 40(1):26, 1990.

187. California Exotic Pest Council; URL: http://www.igc.apc.org/ceppc/index.html.

188. The CalFlora database; URL: http://elib.cs.berkeley.edu/calflora/advanced.html.

189. EPA on total exposure; URL: http://www.msue.msu.edu/ipm/ipmrptv6n1h.htm.

190. University of California Agriculture and Natural Resources; *The Safe and Effective Use of Pesticides, 2nd Edition;* Product Code: 3324 Media: Publication, ISBN: 1-879906-43-0, 2000, 342 pp; URL: http://anrcatalog.ucdavis.edu/merchant.ihtml?id=90&step=2

191. University of California Agriculture and Natural Resources; *IPM IN PRACTICE: PRINCIPLES AND MEHTODS OF INTEGRATED PEST MANAGEMENT; ;* Product Code: 3324 Media: Publication, ISBN: 1-879906-50-3; 2001; 290pp.

192. Integrated Pest Management; URL: www.ipm.ucdavis.edu.

193. Integrated Pest Management; URL: http://refuges.fws.gov.

194. Wilkinson; URL: http://pmep.cce.cornell.edu/facts-slides-self/facts/gen-pubre-carcin-wilkinson.html.

195. DowElanco; *Specimen Label Garlon^{TM} 4,* DowElanco, Indianapolis, IN, Label Code 113-12-012, EPA Date 2/22/94.

196. DowElanco; *Triclopyr Technical Information Guide.*

197. DowElanco; *A Technical Look at Triclopyr.*

198. DowElanco; *Material Safety Data Sheet #001314, Garlon^{TM} 4,Herbicide,* EPA Reg. Number 62719-40, 7/16/92.

199. Young, Raymond A; *Introduction to Forest Science.* John Wiley & Sons NY; 1982; 528pp.

200. *Oral and Dermal Pharmokinetics of Triclopyr in Human Volunteers,* Charmichael, N. G.; Nolan, R. J.; Perkins J. M.; Davies, R.; & Warrington S. J.; Human Toxicology Vol. 8, 1989; pp431-437.

201. Hoshovsky, Marc; *ELEMENT STEWARDSHIP ABSTRACT for Cytisus scoparius and Genista monspessulanus;* URL: http://tncweeds.ucdavis.edu/esadocs/documnts/cytisco.html.

202. Ottoboni, M. Alice; *The Dose Makes the Poison: A Plain-Language Guide to Toxicology,* 2nd Edition Paperback - 256 pages 2 edition (May 1, 1997) John Wiley & Sons; ISBN: 0471288373.

203. Special Assistant to Admiral E.R. Zumwalt, Jr.; *REPORT TO SECRETARY OF THE DEPARTMENT OF VETERANS AFFAIRS ON THE ASSOCIATION*

BETWEEN ADVERSE HEALTH EFFECTS AND EXPOSURE TO AGENT ORANGE; Department of Veterans Affairs, May 5, 1990, available for view at website gulfwarvets.com URL: http://www.gulfwarvets.com/ao.html.

204. Veterans and Agent Orange: Update 1996; Toxicology Summary, Chapter 3 reviews the results of animal studies published during the past three years that investigated the toxicokinetics, mechanism of action, and disease outcomes of TCDD, plus the herbicides themselves. National Academies Press, National Academy of Science; URL http://www.nap.edu/readingroom/books/veterans/toxicology.html.

205. Environmental Defense Fund; *2,4,5-T Cancellation Hearings to Begin;* Vol. V, No. 2 -- March 1974; URL: http://www.edf.org/pubs/EDF-Letter/1974/Mar/j_hearings.html.

206. Edwards, J. Gordon, and Steven Milloy; *100 things you should know about DDT;* URL: http://www.junkscience.com.

Author's Note: This document contains approximately 200 references to peer-reviewed studies documenting that many of the claims made that DDT and/or its decomposition products DDE and DDD were, at least, grossly exaggerated if not patently false. Please compare the technical listings in these references to those of the EDF or Greenpeace. I was unable to find references of comparable quality to refute this data.

Chapter 3 – Endanger Specious Acts

207. Eigen, Manfred; and Ruthild Winkler; *Laws of the Game: How the Principles of Nature Govern Chance;* Trans. Robert Kimber and Rita Kimber; Princeton University Press; ISBN: 0-691-02566-5. This book did more for my perspective toward understanding dynamic population distributions among competing species than any other. It is wonderful.

208. Schramel Taylor, Lee Anne; *DECISION PROVIDES PROTECTION FOR OWLS & OTHER WILDLIFE IN N. SIERRA NEVADA;* AUGUST 20, 1999. URL:http://www.r5.fs.fed.us/hfqlg/.

209. Black, Michael D. Bay Institute of San Francisco and California Studies Association, *California's Last Salmon: Unnatural Policies of Natural Resource Agencies;* Central Coast Watershed Council, Annual Lecture Series, 3/20/99.

210. Lydon, Sandy; Professor of History, Cabrillo College, *Early settlers shunned dirty river water;* Santa Cruz County Sentinel, 3/24/97.

211. Lydon, Sandy; Professor of History, Cabrillo College, *A polluted Soquel Creek wasn't fit to drink;* Santa Cruz County Sentinel, 3/31/97.

212. De Alessi, M.; *Fishing for Solutions, The State of the World's Fisheries,* Figure 5-8, Production Trend for Atlantic Salmon, 1981-1994, Earth Report 2000, Revisiting the True State of the Planet, Competitive Enterprise Institute, p111.

213. Waples, R. S.; *NOAA Technical Memorandum NMFS F/NWC-194, Definition of "Species" Under the Endangered Species Act: Application to Pacific Salmon;* Summary Definition of Evolutionary Significant Unit, March 1991.

Endnotes

214. Buchal, James; *The Great Salmon Hoax;* Iconoclast; 1998; URL http://www.buchal.com/hoax.html.

215. Gobalet, Kenneth W. & Terry L. Jones; *Prehistoric Native American Fisheries of the Central California Coast;* Transactions of the American Fisheries Society, 124: pp817, 819, 821; 1995.

216. Gobalet, Kenneth W; *Fish Remains from Nine Archaeological Sites in Richmond and San Pablo, Contra Costa County California;* California Fish and Game, 76(4): p240, 1990.

217. Follett, W. I.; *FISH REMAINS FROM THE WEST BERKELEY SHELLMOUND (CA-Ala-307), ALAMEDA COUNTY CALIFORNIA;* California Academy of Sciences, San Francisco, pp77, 79.

218. Ricker, John, & Terry Butler; *Community Resources Agency, Watershed Management Section, County of Santa Cruz, SAN LORENZO RIVER WATERSHED MANAGEMENT PLAN, FISHERY HABITAT AND THE AQUATIC ECOSYSTEM TECHNICAL SECTION,* November 1979.

219. MacQuarrie, D.W.; J.R. Markert; W.E. Van Stone; *Photoperiod-Induced Off-Season Spawning of Coho Salmon (Oncorgyncus kisutch), Annals of Biology, Animal Biochemistry, and Biophysiology,* Vol. 18, pp1051-1058, 1978.

220. Flagg, T.A., and C.E. Nash (editors). 1999. *A conceptual framework for conservation hatchery strategies for Pacific salmonids.* U.S. Dep. Commer., NOAA Tech. Memo. NMFS-NWFSC-38, 46 p. U.S. Dept. Commer., NOAA Tech. Memo. NMFS-NWFSC-38, 48 p.

221. Beamish, R.J., Mahnken, C., and C.M. Neville; *Hatchery and wild production of Pacific salmon in relation to large-scale, natural shifts in the productivity of the marine environment.* Ices Journal of Marine Science 54(6):1200-15, 1997.

222. Coronado, Claribel and Ray Hilborn, 1998, *Spatial and temporal factors affecting survival in coho salmon (Oncorgyncus kisutch) in the Pacific Northwest,* Canadian Journal of Fisheries and Aquatic Science. pp. 2067-2077.

223. Kaczynski, V. W.; April, 1998; *Comments on the National Marine Fisheries Service's proposed rule for designated critical habitat for southern Oregon;* Northern California Coast Coho Salmon Unpublished memo prepared for: Oregon Forest Industries Council, Northwest Forestry Association, California Forestry Association.

224. Fergus, Mike, *FEDERAL RESOURCE AGENCY SAYS GROWING WEST COAST SEAL, SEA LION POPULATIONS INCREASINGLY IN CONFLICT WITH HUMANS, SALMON;* NOAA PRESS RELEASE Southwest Region, 2/11/99.

225. Harmon, J. R., K. L. Thomas, K. W. McIntyre, and N. N. Paasch; *Prevalence of marine-mammal tooth and claw abrasions on adult anadromous salmonids returning to the Snake River;* N. Am. J. Fish. Manage. 14:661-663. 1994.

226. U.S. Department of Commerce, NOAA, National Marine Fisheries Service; *Report to Congress, Impacts of California Sea Lions and Pacific Harbor Seals on Salmonids and West Coast Ecosystems,* February 10, 1999.

227. Briggs, Robert O., *Competition Between the Waddell Creek Forest and Creek for Limited Dry Season Ground-Stored Water,* Davenport Geological Society, Oct. 1997, 22pp.

228. Shapovalov, Leo & Allan C. Taft, *The Life Histories of Steelhead, Rainbow Trout, and Silver Salmon,* California Department of Fish and Game, Fish Bulletin 98, 1954, 375p.

229. Kaczynski, Victor W.; *Marine survival of OPIA hatchery coho salmon related to marine temperatures;* Proceedings of the 49th Annual Pacific Northwest Fish Culture Conference. Boise, ID. Pp131-147. 1998.

230. Forests & Salmon, *Forest-Fisheries Management Relationships in Northern California During the 19th & 20th Centuries;* The Forest Foundation, August 1998.

231. Alley, DW; *Recommended Monitoring and Logging Guidelines for the Soquel Demonstration State Forest Related to Aquatic Resources and Flood Control,* Dec. 1992.

232. *INITIAL STATEMENT OF REASONS, Protection for Threatened and Impaired Watersheds,* [July 23, 1999], Title 14 of the California Code of Regulations.

233. Simon, Julian L. and Aaron Wildavsky, *Extinction: Species Loss Revisited,* NWI Resource, Volume 5, Issue 1, Fall, 1994, p. 4f. (Note: An excellent foundation for understanding the conflicting claims about species loss. The authors also wrote "On Species Loss, The Absence of Data and Risks to Humanity," in The Resourceful Earth: A Response to Global 2000.)

234. *DRAFT Review Pursuant to Memorandum of Agreement between the National Marine Fisheries Service (NMFS), Southwest Region and the State of California (State) on North Coast Steelhead Trout,* analysis of the California Forest Practice Rules (FPR): The NMFS review of the FPRs to the State, and the State response to NMFS analysis. Dated 7/10/98.

Chapter 4 – A Watershed, Eventually?

235. National Marine Fisheries Service, *DRAFT Review Pursuant to Memorandum of Agreement between the National Marine Fisheries Service (NMFS), Southwest Region and the State of California (State) on North Coast Steelhead Trout, analysis of the California Forest Practice Rules (FPR):* The NMFS review of the FPRs to the State, and the State response to NMFS analysis. Dated 7/10/98.

236. STATE OF CALIFORNIA, CALIFORNIA REGIONAL WATER QUALITY CONTROL BOARD, CENTRAL COAST REGION, *San Lorenzo River Nitrate Total Maximum Daily Load and Nitrate Objective,* STAFF REPORT FOR REGULAR MEETING OF May 19, 2000, Prepared on February 9, 2000.

237. STATE OF CALIFORNIA, CENTRAL COAST REGIONAL WATER QUALITY CONTROL BOARD, *San Lorenzo River Watershed Total Maximum Daily Load for Nitrate, Santa Cruz, California (Impaired Waters: San Lorenzo River, Carbonera Creek, Shingle Mill Creek, and Lompico Creek),* DRAFT February 7, 2000.

Endnotes

238. Santa Cruz County Sewage Treatment District, 1999, *Annual Report.*

239. Copeland, Claudia, Specialist in Environmental Policy Resources, Science, and Industry Division Congressional Research Service; *Report for Congress 98-150: The Clean Water Action Plan: Background and Early Implementation;* Updated May 3, 1999. Obtained from http://www.cnie.org.

240. FINDINGS FOR THE CALIFORNIA COASTAL NONPOINT PROGRAM, *California Coastal Nonpoint Pollution Program Submittal,* September 1995, authorized under Section 6217(a) of the Coastal Zone Act Reauthorization Amendments of 1990 (CZARA).

241. Clean Water Act of 1972, *Section 303(d) , U.S. Code, Title 33, Chapter 26, Subchapter III, Section 1313,* URL: http://uscode.house.gov/usc.htm.

242. Nixon, Scott W. & Michael E. Q. Pilson; *Nitrogen in Estuarine and Coastal Marine Ecosystems, excerpted from:* Carpenter, Edward J. & Douglas G. Capone; *Nitrogen in the Marine Environment;* Chapter 16; pp565-648; ISBN 0-12-160280-X; Academic Press, 1983.

243. Research on EPA interpretations of TMDL derived from http://www.epa.gov/owow/tmdl.

244. Clean Water Act Amendments of 1987, Section 319, U.S. Code, Title 33, Chapter 26, Subchapter III, Sections: 1288 Areawide Waste Treatment Management, 1311 Effluent Limitations, 1314 Information & Guidelines, 1329 Nonpoint Source Management Programs. URL:http://uscode.house.gov/usc.htm.

245. Septic system history in the San Lorenzo Valley is based upon interviews with long-time contractors and consultants.

Endnotes to Part V

Chapter 1 – An Unsustainable Agenda

246. *Big Creek Lumber Co., Inc. v. County of San Mateo,* 31 Cal. App. 4th 418 (1st Dist. 1995) (holding that county zoning ordinance that regulated where timber operations could occur was not preempted by the FPA).

247. *Notes on formation of TIMBER-TAC* and false testimony re "consensus" were derived from public testimony of: Bob Berlage, Big Creek Lumber; Steven Butler, Ed Tunheim Professional Foresters; Mark Deming, Principle Planner, County of Santa Cruz; Jodi Frediani, Sierra Club; and Jan Beautz and Mardi Wormhoudt, Supervisors, County of Santa Cruz. Testimony at the Board of Supervisors, County of Santa Cruz, dated 14 December 1999.

248. Arnold, Ron and Alan Gottlieb, *Trashing the Economy,* (Bellevue, Washington: Free Enterprise Press, 1993), p. 242.

249. *Op Cit.* to California Board of Forestry, *Coho Considerations,* document for consideration as amendments to the Forest Practice Rules.

250. Lewis, Jack and Raymond M Rice; *Site Conditions Related to Erosion on Private Timberlands in Northern California: Final Report.* Critical Sites Erosion

Study; California Department of Forestry and Fire Protection, Forest Practice Section, 1989 Estimated total of 0.31 cubic yards per year per acre net sediment introduced to streams attributable to logging pp62-65.

251. Rice, Raymond M. and Jack Lewis; *Estimating Erosion Risks Associated with Logging and Forest Roads in Northwestern California;* Water Resources Bulletin (27)5; 1991 p810.

252. Big Creek Lumber Company vs. County of Santa Cruz, *Petition of Writ of Mandate and Declaratory and Other Relief;* Case No. 13486.

253. Big Creek Lumber Company vs. County of Santa Cruz, *Memorandum of Points and Authorities in Support of Preemptory Writ of Mandate and Declaratory and Other Relief;* Case No. 13486.

254. *INITIAL STATEMENT OF REASONS, Protection for Threatened and Impaired Watersheds, 1999,* [July 23, 1999], Title 14 of the CA Code of Regulations.

255. Hill, Norman E., Chief Counsel for the California Department of Forestry and fire Protection, *Appeals of NTMP 1-99-003 SCR and THP 1-99-009 SCR.*

256. Butler, Steven, RPF, *PROPOSED AMENDMENTS TO THE CALIFORNIA FOREST PRACTICE RULES; Draft dated 4/4/98.*

257. References to California Environmental Quality Act (CEQA) came from the Ceres Server. URL: http://ceres.ca.gov/ceqa/. Note, for specific articles from the Act, change the digit in the final file name, i.e. http://ceres.ca.gov/ceqa/guidelines/art5.html where art5 is the text for Article 5 of the CEQA handbook.

258. Cline, Alan; *Prioritization Process Using Delphi Technique;* Carolla Development White Paper; 1997-1998; URL:http://www.carolla.com/wp-delph.htm. A good description of the original Delphi consensus process.

259. Spitzer, Skip; Santa Cruz Action Network (SCAN); *Decision-making by consensus: A Brief Introduction;* URL :http://gate.cruzio.com/~scan.

260. ACTION–Santa Cruz County, *SEED Summit on Sustainability;* Mar. '94, p2.

261. *Ibid.* ACTION–SCC; *Preliminary Reports, Ecosystem Management & Biodiversity,* Team Contact person and contributors to date list, *SEEDing a Sustainable Future;* March 1994, p6.

262. Copies of submissions and draft critiques from Dean Rimmerman of Earth First! and Randall Morgan of the California Native Plant Society.

263. Shaw, Michael; *Santa Cruz Residential Program h;* submission for consideration of local Agenda 21.

264. Santa Cruz County Earth Day Journal, *Sustainable Santa Cruz, Unlimited Possibilities...* Earth Day 1995, April 1995, p8.

265. Vande Pol, Mark Edward & Rudnick, Lisa; *Personal File References to development and notes taken from various Agenda 21 meetings.*

266. Various *facsimile documents* between Jeannie Nordland of ACTION–SCC, Lisa Rudnick, and Mark Vande Pol concerning final adoption of the Santa Cruz Local Agenda 21 Biodiversity and Ecosystem Management Plan.

Endnotes

267. Nordland, Jeanne, *An Agenda 21 Report for Santa Cruz County;* URL:http://www.cruzio.com/~ecocruz/Agenda21/index.html.

268. Nordland, Jeanne, *Agenda 21 Biodiversity and Ecosystem Management Document;* Chairpersons Dean Rimerman & Betsi Sites, Steve Singer, Lisa Rudnick, Mark Vande Pol, Grey, Dennis P. Davie, Howard Liebenberg, Ted Jones, Deidre Kerwin, Kent Reeves, Dawn Pencovic, Robert LaRosa, Kathleen VanVelsor, Vicki Nichols, Frank Barron, Michael Shaw, Randall Morgan, Elizabeth Herbert, Jade Lovell, Julie Hendricks, Celia & Peter Scott, Mary Tsalis, Bonnie Hurd, Rich Casale, Josh Fodor, Fred McPherson, Thom Sutfin, Steve Butler, Dave Hope, Jerry Busch, & Chris Johnson-Lyon. (Compiled & final edit by Jeanne Nordland).
URL:http://www.cruzio.com/~ecocruz/Agenda21/A21Ch02.html.

269. Mauriello, Susan A., J.D., County Administrative Officer, *MEASURE C ANNUAL PROGRESS REPORT; BOARD OF SUPERVISORS, JUNE 8, 1999;* URL: http://www.co.santa-cruz.ca.us/bds/19990608/079.pdf.

"Measure C also established a series of eleven principles and policies to guide local government efforts related to: offshore oil drilling; global warming and renewable energy resources; protection of the ozone layer; forest protection and restoration; **greenbelt protection and preservation**; recycling; toxic and radioactive materials; endangered species and biological diversity; development of a sustainable local economy; future growth and development; and education and outreach."

270. Mauriello, Susan A., JD, County Administrative Officer, *CONSIDER ADOPTION OF ENVIRONMENTAL PRINCIPLES AND POLICIES TO GUIDE COUNTY GOVERNMENT,* November 3,200, attachment to the proposed Ordinance; *ORDINANCE ENACTING CHAPTER 16 OF THE SANTA CRUZ COUNTY CODE RELATING TO ENVIRONMENTAL PRINCIPLES AND POLICIES TO GUIDE COUNTY GOVERNMENT,* URL:http://www.co.santa-cruz.ca.us/bds/20001114/037.pdf.

271. IGC Publishing; *Sustainable Development International;* Welcome to Sustainable Development International, which aims to educate the readership by providing a showcase for strategies and technologies for local-global Agenda 21 implementation. http://www.sustdev.org/about/.

272. Absent, Name Conspicuously, *United Nations Global Agenda 21;* United Nations Publication E.93.1.11, ISBN 92-1-10059-4, URL: http://www.un.org/esa/sustdev/agenda21text.htm.

273. Solzhenitsyn, Aleksandr Isaevich; *The Gulag Archipelago Vol. I;* Thomas P. Whitney (Translator), Reprint Vol 001, May 1997, ISBN: 0813332893 672pp.

274. United Nations Commission on Global Governance, *Our Global Neighborhood, The Report of the Commission on Global Governance;* paperback, $14.95, ISBN 0-19-827997-3, 410 pages. Oxford University Press. Call (919) 677-0977).

275. Commission on Global Governance, *Our Global Neighborhood; Phasing Out the Veto;* URL:http://www.cgg.ch/unreform2.htm#veto.

276.Reed F. Noss, *The Wildlands Project*, Wild Earth, Special Issue, 1992, p. 21. (Note: Wild Earth is published by the Cenozoic Society, editorial address: P.O. Box 492, Canton NY 13617, (315) 379-9940. Dave Foreman and Reed F. Noss are Directors.) URL: http://www.wildlandsproject.org.

277.Convention on Biological Diversity, UNEP/CBD/COP2/5, 21, *Report of the First Meeting of the Subsidiary Body on Scientific, Technical and Technological Advice*, September 1995, p2.

278.Sovereignty International, This site has more resources to investigate the Agenda 21 than any other. URL:http://www.sovereignty.net/p/sd/a21.

279.*Global Biodiversity Assessment,* URL: http://www.biodiv.org ;Cambridge University Press.

280.*OP Cit., IUCN Membership Guidelines,* 1996, p4.

281.*OP Cit., IUCN: Membership List,* June, 1998, p21.

282.*OP Cit., Dues: Membership Guidelines, IUCN,* 1996, p20.

283.Gorbachev, Mikhail; *The Earth Charter speech at the Rio+5 Forum;* URL: http://www.gci.ch/GreenCrossFamily/gorby/newspeeches/speeches/speech18.3.97.html.

284.*Meet Maurice Strong*, ecologic, November/December, 1995, p4.

285.Hage, Wayne; *STORM OVER RANGELANDS, PRIVATE RGHTS IN Federal LANDS;* Free Enterprise Press, 1994, ISBN 0-939571-15-3.

286.*Sustainable America: A New Consensus;* available from the U.S. Government Printing Office, Superintendent of Documents, Mail Stop: SSOP, Washington, DC 20402, ISBN 0-16-0485299-0.

287.Lamb, Henry; *New Treaty In the Making, Covenant on Environment and Development;* (treaty law pursuant to Agenda 21) eco-logic; Jan./Feb., 1998.

288.Lamb, Henry; *NGOs Drive Global Climate Agenda;* 1999.

289.Lamb, Henry; *World Concerns;* Sovereignty Intl., Vol. 1, #2, Dec. 2, 1997.

290.Rummel, R.J.; *Death by Government;* Transaction Pub; ISBN: 1560009276; March 1997; URL: http://www.bigeye.com/rummel.htm.

291.Aristotle, *Nicomachean Ethics, Book III,* translated by Hugh Treddenick, Penguin Books, 1976.

292.Christ, Jesus, House of David; *Matthew 7:20,* The Holy Bible, King James Version, 1611, Thomas Nelson Publishers, Nashville, TN,

293.Ibid. Jesus, *Matthew 7:21.*

Chapter 2 – Defy Gravity

294.Knutson, Gary A., Auditor/Controller, County of Santa Cruz; *Final Budget for the County of Santa Cruz, Fiscal Year, 1999-2000.*

295.Op Cit.; 1995-1997 *Survey of Graduates, UCSC*; URL: http://planning.ucsc.edu/IRPS/ENROLLMT/GRADS/9597/REPORT.PDF.

296. Mayhugh, Candice Jackson; *Liberal LSAT Bias;* Accuracy in Academia Address Delivered at AIA's 1998 Summer Conference at Geo. Washington University.

297. Haga, Dr. William James, Nicholas Acocella, *Haga's Law, Why Nothing Works and No One Can Fix It and the More You Try to Fix It the Worse It Gets;* William Morrow & Co. 1980. Out of pint.

298. Parkinson, Pete, Principle Planner County of Santa Cruz, *Notice of Exemption From the California Environmental Quality Act;* Dated 4/12/94.

299. Harris, Joel Chandler, *HOW BRER RABBIT WAS TOO SHARP FOR MR. FOX, Uncle Remus, His Songs and His Sayings,* Hawthorn Books, Inc., ISBN: 0-8015-8106-0, p18.

300. Op Cit., Harris, *THE WONDERFUL TAR BABY STORY,* p7.

301. *Clean Water Act of 1972,* Section 303(d) , U.S. Code, Title 33, Chapter 26, Subchapter III, Section 1313, URL:http://uscode.house.gov/usc.htm.

302. *Clean Water Act Amendments of 1987, Section 319,* U.S. Code, Title 33, Chapter 26, Subchapter III, Sections: 1288 Areawide Waste Treatment Management, 1311 Effluent Limitations, 1314 Information & Guidelines, 1329 Nonpoint Source Management Programs. URL:http://uscode.house.gov/usc.htm.

303. United States Environmental Protection Agency, *1998 CALIFORNIA 303(d) LIST AND TMDL PRIORITY SCHEDULE,* 12-May-99.pp 36,41, &45.

304. STATE OF CALIFORNIA, CALIFORNIA REGIONAL WATER QUALITY CONTROL BOARD, CENTRAL COAST REGION, *San Lorenzo River Nitrate Total Maximum Daily Load and Nitrate Objective, STAFF REPORT FOR REGULAR MEETING OF May 19, 2000,* February 7, 2000.

305. STATE OF CALIFORNIA, CALIFORNIA REGIONAL WATER QUALITY CONTROL BOARD, CENTRAL COAST REGION, *San Lorenzo River Nitrate Total Maximum Daily Load and Nitrate Objective, STAFF REPORT FOR REGULAR MEETING OF May 19, 2000,* February 9, 2000.

306. *Daily Load for Nitrate Santa Cruz, California* (Impaired Waters: San Lorenzo River, Carbonera Creek, Shingle Mill Creek, and Lompico Creek), Executive Summary, DRAFT Plan for California's Nonpoint Source Pollution Control Program; February 7, 2000, pp ii-v.

307. California Regional Water Quality Control Board, Central Coast Region, San Lorenzo River Nitrate TMDL and Nitrate Objective; *Staff Report for Regular Meeting of May 19, 2000,* 36pp.

308. Planning Department, County of Santa Cruz; *SAN LORENZO RIVER WATERSHED MANAGEMENT PLAN, Appendix C, Water Quality Analyses, historic nitrate values,* pp137-172, 12/18/79.

309. Ricker, John, & Mount, Jeffry; Community Resources Agency, Watershed Management Section, County of Santa Cruz, *SAN LORENZO RIVER WATERSHED MANAGEMENT PLAN, HYDROLOGY TECHNICAL SECTION,* November 1979 (Part IV, Chap. 4, Sec. I).

310. Ricker, John, Planning Department, Co. of Santa Cruz, *SAN LORENZO RIVER WATERSHED MANAGEMENT PLAN, PHYSIOGRAPHY AND EROSION AND SEDIMENT TRANSPORT TECHNICAL SECTIONS,* 11/79.

311. Aston, Robert; Community Resources Agency, Watershed Management Section, County of Santa Cruz, *SAN LORENZO RIVER WATERSHED MANAGEMENT PLAN, WATER QUALITY TECHNICAL SECTION,* October 1979.

312. California Coastal Commission, *FINDINGS FOR THE CALIFORNIA COASTAL NONPOINT PROGRAM, California Coastal Nonpoint Pollution Program Submittal, September 1995,* authorized under Section 6217(a) of the Coastal Zone Act Reauthorization Amendments of 1990 (CZARA).

313. Copeland, Claudia, Specialist in Environmental Policy Resources, Science, and Industry Division Congressional Research Service; *Report for Congress 98-150: The Clean Water Action Plan: Background and Early Implementation;* Updated May 3, 1999. Obtained from http://www.cnie.org.

314. EPA interpretations of TMDL derived from http://www.epa.gov/owow/tmdl.

315. *Convention for the Prevention of Marine Pollution from Land-based Sources* (1974 Paris Convention) http://www.nesarc.org.

316. County of Santa Cruz, *Santa Cruz County Sensitive Habitats Protection Ordinance;* http://www.co.santa-cruz.ca.us/pln/sensitiv.htm.

317. County of Santa Cruz, *Santa Cruz County Riparian Corridor Protection Ordinance;* http://www.co.santa-cruz.ca.us/pln/riparian.htm.

318. Haynes, Al; *Letter to Garth W. Griffen, NMFS;* 1/6/97.

319. Smith, Jerry, PhD; *Letter to Garth W. Griffen, NMFS;* 1/6/97.

320. Alley, Don; *Letter to Garth W. Griffen, NMFS;* 1/6/97.

321. Schuman, Todd, *Steelhead Listing Project, Letter to NMFS Re: ONRC Petition to List Pacific Coastal Steelhead Trout Populations;* 5/5/94.

322. 318. Clark, Jamie Rappaport, Director U.S. Fish and Wildlife Service, UNITED STATES DEPARTMENT OF COMMERCE; *Designated Critical Hapitat: Critical Habitat for 19 Evolutionarily Significant Units of Salmon and Steelhead in Washington, Oregon, Idaho, and California; National Oceanic and Atmospheric Administration, National Marine Fisheries Service, #7764,* Federal Register / Vol. 65, No. 32 / 2/16/2000 / Rules and Regulations.

323. UNITED STATES DEPARTMENT OF COMMERCE, National Oceanic and Atmospheric Administration, *NMFS, PUBLIC HEARING ON THE PROPOSED LISTING OF STEELHEAD TROUT;* 10/17 1996.

324. *NOAA Technical Memorandum NMFS-NWFSC-27 Status Review of West Coast Steelhead from Washington, Idaho, Oregon, and California,* Aug. 1996.

325. Nielsen, Jennifer L., Gan, C. A.; Wright, J. M.; Morris, D. B.; and Thomas, W. K.; *Biogeographic distribution of mitochondrial and nuclear markers for southern steelhead;* Molecular Marine Biology and Biotech. 3(5):281-293.

326. Information Center for the Environment, Click ICEMaps2 at http://ice.ucdavis.edu.

Chapter 3 – The Strategy of the Commoners

327. *Title 12 U.S.C, Section 95b Emergency War Powers:* "The actions, regulations, rules, licenses, orders and proclamations heretofore or hereafter taken, promulgated, made, or issued by the President of the United States or the Secretary of the Treasury since March 4, 1933, pursuant to the authority conferred by subsection (b) of section 5 of the Act of October 6, 1917, as amended (12 U.S.C., 95a), are hereby approved and confirmed." - (March 9, 1933, c. 1, Title 1, 1, 48 Stat. 1).

328. *National Emergency of March 9, 1933* amended the War Powers Act to include the American People as enemies. In Title 1, Section 1 it says: "The actions, regulations, rules, licenses, orders and proclamations heretofore or hereafter taken, promulgated, made, or issued by the President of the United States or the Secretary of the Treasury since March 4, 1933, pursuant to the authority conferred by subdivision (b) of section 5 of the Act of October 6, 1917, as amended, are hereby approved and confirmed."

329. *Ibid. National Emergency of March 9, 1933* "Section 2. Subdivision (b) of section 5 of the Act of October 6, 1917, (40 Stat. L. 411), as amended, is hereby amended to read as follows: emergency declared by the President, the President may, through any agency that he may designate, or otherwise, investigate, regulate, or prohibit, under such rules and regulations as he may prescribe, by means of licenses or otherwise, any transactions in foreign exchange, transfers of credit between or payments by banking institutions as defined by the President, and export, hoarding, melting, or earmarking of gold or silver coin or bullion or currency, BY ANY PERSON WITHIN THE UNITED STATES OR ANY PLACE SUBJECT TO THE JURISDICTION THEREOF."

330. *Barefoot's World,* Resources documenting the accrual of unconstitutional powers to the national government. URL: http://www.barefootsworld.net/.

331. Carter, James Earl, President of the United States, *Executive Order 11990, Protection of Wetlands,* May 24, 1977; 42 FR 26961; URL:http://www.wetlands.com/fed/exo11990.htm.

332. *Convention on International Trade in Endangered Species of Wild Fauna and Flora (CITES);* URL: http://www.cites.org/CITES/eng/index.shtml, or better, http://environment.harvard.edu/guides/intenvpol/indexes/treaties/CITES.html.

333. *Convention on the Conservation of Migratory Species of Wild Animals (CMS);* URL: http://sedac.ciesin.org/pidb/texts/migratory.wild.animals.1979.html.

334. *Convention for the Prevention of Marine Pollution from Land-based Sources* (1974 Paris Convention) http://www.nesarc.org.

335. Title 16 United States Code Sections 1532 Definitions (Endangered Species Act) http://uscode.house.gov/usc.htm.

336. *CONVENTION ON NATURE PROTECTION AND WILD LIFE PRESERVATION IN THE WESTERN HEMISPHERE (1940);* Entered into force: 1 May 1942; 56 Stat. 1354; TS 981; URL: http://sedac.ciesin.org/pidb/texts/wildlife.western.hemisphere.1940.html.

337. U.S. Supreme Court; *CITY OF MONTEREY v. DEL MONTE DUNES;* No. 97—1235. Argued October 7, 1998–Decided May 24, 1999.

338. 16 USC 1533 *Determination of endangered species and threatened species.*

339. 16 USC 1537 *International Cooperation (ESA).*

340. 16 USC 1538 *Prohibited acts (ESA).*

341. Madison, James, et al., *The Constitution of the United States of America;* Cato Institute, ISBN 1-882577-67-1.

342. Marcussen, Lana E.; CIRCA; *JEFF & TINA ESPLIN, et. al., v. WILLIAM J. CLINTON; BRUCE BABBITT, Defendants, COMPLAINT FOR DECLARATORY JUDGMENT AND INJUNCTIVE RELIEF AND DEPRIVATIONS OF Federal CONSTITUTIONAL RIGHTS,* U.S. DISTRICT COURT FOR THE-DISTRICT OF ARIZONA, CIV 00-0248 PCT PGR.

343. U.S. Supreme Court *NEW YORK v. UNITED STATES,* 505 U.S. 144 (1992); Nos. 91-543, 91-558 and 91-563 Argued March 30, 1992, Decided June 19, 1992.

344. Kmiec, Douglas W.; The Court Rediscovers Federalism; Heritage Foundation Policy Review, September-October, 1997.

Index

Index

Index

Index

To Purchase Books From Wildergarten Press

FAX Orders: 1-831-438-5335

Mail Orders: Wildergarten Press, P.O. Box 98, Redwood Estates, CA 95044-0098

Purchaser

Name

Title

Company

Street Address

City _____ State _____ Zip _____

Country _____ Email _____

Ship To
(If different from above)

Name

Title

Company

Street Address

City _____ State _____ Zip _____

Country _____ Email _____

Bill To
(If different from above)

Name

Title

Company

Street Address

City _____ State _____ Zip _____

Country _____ Email _____

Purchase

	Item	Qty.*	Price	Total
1	Natural Process		29.95	
2	Algebra for Small Children (coming in 2002)		19.95	

Shipping Handling & Taxes

US Orders

	Tot Qty*	

Shipping and handling $5 each.
All single-book US Shipments by USPS Priority Mail

| | 5.00 ea* | |

International Orders (Credit Card Only)

Shipping, duties, and handling will be processed at cost.
Foreign buyers will be notified for written acceptance of the total upon request.
Total Negotiated International Shipping, handling, and applicable taxes

California Residents Add 7% Sales Tax ($2.10 ea)

Total Purchase (US $)

Payment Method
(No CODs)

☐ Check
☐ VISA
☐ MC
☐ Discover
☐ AmEx

_____ / _____ / _____   _____ / _____
Credit Card Account Number   **Exp. (mm/yy)**

Signature _____

Returns Fax us or see our web site at www.wildergarten.com for our returns policy

*Bulk Qty To ship orders of 3 books or more, please contact Wildergarten Press.